D1648879

GLOBAL MEDIA ECONOMICS

Global Media Economics

Commercialization, Concentration and Integration of World Media Markets

ALAN B. ALBARRAN
AND
SYLVIA M. CHAN-OLMSTED

IOWA STATE UNIVERSITY PRESS / Ames

THIS BOOK IS DEDICATED IN HONOR OF OUR MOTHERS,
JEAN McALISTER ALBARRAN AND MINNA TOSHIKO CHAN

Alan B. Albarran, PhD, is assistant dean for research and information technology in the Meadows School of the Arts at Southern Methodist University, Dallas, Texas.

Sylvia M. Chan-Olmsted, PhD, is assistant professor in the Department of Telecommunication at the University of Florida, Gainesville.

Iowa State University Press
2121 South State Avenue
Ames, IA 50014

Orders: 1-800-862-6657
Office: 1-515-292-0140
Fax: 1-515-292-3348
Web site: www.isupress.edu

♾ Printed on acid-free paper in the United States of America

First edition, 1998

Library of Congress Cataloging-in-Publication Data

Global media economics : commercialization, concentration and integration of world media markets / [edited by] Alan B. Albarran and Sylvia M. Chan-Olmsted. — 1st ed.
p. cm.
Companion volume to: Media economics : understanding markets, industries and concepts / Alan B. Albarran. 1996.
Includes bibliographical references and index.
ISBN 0-8138-2690-X (alk. paper)
1. Mass media—Economic aspects. I. Albarran, Alan B. II. Chan-Olmsted, Sylvia M. III. Media economics.
P96.E25G57 1998
338.4′730223—dc21 98-14142

Last digit is the print number: 9 8 7 6 5 4 3 2

CONTENTS

CONTRIBUTORS

Alan B. Albarran, PhD, co-editor, is assistant dean for research and information technology in the Meadows School of the Arts at Southern Methodist University, Dallas, Texas. His research interests are in the management and economics of the communication industries. Dr. Albarran also serves as the editor of the *Journal of Media Economics*. He is the author of two books: *Management of Electronic Media* and *Media Economics: Understanding Markets, Industries and Concepts*.

Osabuohien P. Amienyi, PhD, is an associate professor of radio–television at Arkansas State University. His research interests focus on communication and national development, political communication and international media. Between 1982 and 1986, he worked as a media consultant and independent producer in Nigeria.

Penghwa Ang, PhD, JD, is a lecturer in the School of Communication Studies at Nanyang Technological University, Singapore. Dr. Ang is a certified lawyer in Singapore and holds a doctorate in mass media from Michigan State University. His research interests lie in information technology. He has published and presented papers on such topics as telecommunications and economic development, copyright, free speech and censorship.

Menahem Blondheim, PhD, is a lecturer in communications at the Department of Political Science, Bar Ilan University, Israel. He earned his doctorate from Harvard University in 1989, taught at the Hebrew University of Jerusalem, and served as vice president and scientific manager of Jerusalem-based Meimadim Ltd. from 1993 to 1996. His research interests include business and technological aspects in the development of communications in both Israel and the United States.

Sylvia M. Chan-Olmsted, PhD, co-editor, is an assistant professor in the Department of Telecommunication at the University of Florida. She has researched and published numerous articles on the economic analysis of media markets. Her research interests include the economics of multichannel television and news media. Dr. Chan-Olmsted also serves as the "Book Review" editor for the *Journal of Media Economics*.

Charles N. Davis, PhD, is an assistant professor in the Center for Communication Arts at Southern Methodist University, Dallas, Texas. His research agenda includes mass communication law, telecommunications policy and related media issues.

Nadine Toussaint Desmoulins is a professor at Université Paris II, Institut Français de Presse, Paris, France. Her research specialization is in media economics with a particular interest in media concentration.

Pieter Fourie is professor and head of the Department of Communication, University of South Africa, Pretoria.

David H. Goff, PhD, is professor of radio, television, and film at the University of Southern Mississippi, Hattiesburg. His research interests include the regulation and organization of electronic media, past and present. He is engaged in a long-term project on the historic dispute over the licensing of WLBT-TV (Jackson, MS). Other research interests include the adoption and adaptation of new media and new technologies by existing media industries.

Geoffrey Gurd, PhD, is a teacher, consultant and researcher in Ottawa, Ontario, Canada. He has a master's degree in media studies from Concordia University, Montreal and a doctorate in communication from Montreal University. He has taught in Montreal, Pittsburgh, and Ottawa. His eclectic research interests touch on organizational communication theories, government broadcasting, cultural and technology policies, new information technologies and the nature of technology, telemedicine, cyberspace and theories of space, and notions of self and identity at different levels of analysis.

Kazumi Hasegawa is an assistant professor in the School of Communication at the University of North Dakota, Grand Forks. Her research interests are emerging communication technologies in mass media, international/intercultural communication, women and minorities in mass media, cross-cultural/national advertising practices, and consumer behavior. She is a doctoral candidate in mass media/telecommunication, Michigan State University. She received her master's degree in telecommunication and a bachelor of science in journalism/advertising from Southern Illinois University at Carbondale and a bachelor's degree in Arabic studies and language from Osaka University of Foreign Studies, Osaka, Japan.

Patrick Hendriks has been a research associate at the Department of Communications at the University of Amsterdam in The Netherlands. His research interests include media economic issues such as strategic behavior of media companies and government interference in communications markets. Recently he completed a 4-year research project concerning strategic behavior of newspaper publishers in The Netherlands and the United States. Currently he is working at the corporate headquarters of the multinational publisher Wolters Kluwer as a business development specialist.

C. Ann Hollifield, PhD, is an assistant professor in the Department of Telecommunications at the University of Georgia. Her research focuses on the strategic management of telecommunications and media companies, with emphasis on transnational media companies. Her work also includes study of the performance of media and telecommunications systems in the area of business and economic communication. In 1991–92, she spent a year in Germany as a Fellow of the Robert Bosch Foundation, where she worked in the Media Policy Department of the German Ministry of Press and Information and, later, for one of Germany's largest newspaper publishing companies. During the Fellowship she conducted research on the market-entry strategies used by German publishers to enter the then newly opened Eastern European markets.

Rudolph de Jager is an assistant lecturer in the Department of Communication, University of South Africa, Pretoria.

Tuen-Yu Lau, PhD, is an international communication consultant currently based in Indonesia and Singapore. Between 1994 and 1996, he was part of a senior management team based in Jakarta, leading a group of multinational TV professionals to plan, build and operate a new terrestrial TV station in Indonesia. Dr. Lau has taught classes in media management, broadcast and print journalism and new communication technologies at Purdue University. He has published in academic and trade journals in the areas of telecommunication policies, cable and satellite television and new communication technologies. He is on the editorial advisory board of the *Journal of International Communication* and the *Asia Pacific Media Educator*. He holds a doctorate in the mass media from Michigan State University.

Alfonso Nieto is a professor in the Media Management Department at the University of Navarra in Pamplona, Spain.

Robert G. Picard, PhD, is a professor in the Department of Communications at California State University, Fullerton. He is a specialist on the economics and financing of communication firms and has conducted extensive research on Nordic media economics for more than two decades, during which time he authored the book *The Ravens of Odin: The Press in the Nordic Nations* and spent two years as a visiting professor with the Media Economics Research Group at the Turku School of Economics in Finland. Picard is also the author and editor of 10 other books, including *The Newspaper Publishing Industry, Media Economics: Concepts and Issues; Press Concentration and Monopoly: New Perspectives on Newspaper Ownership and Operation; Joint Operating Agreements: The Newspaper Preservation Act and Its Application; The Cable Networks Handbook;* and *The Press and the Decline of Democracy.*

Andrew Sharma, PhD, is an assistant professor in the Department of Communication and Media, State University of New York (SUNY), New Paltz. Before obtaining his doctorate from Syracuse University, he worked in the advertising industry in India. His research interests focus on the impact of advertising messages and social, economic and cultural issues in the media. He has also researched and taught in the areas of television, radio and film production.

Joseph D. Straubhaar, PhD, is professor of communications and director of the Communications Research Center, Department of Communications, Brigham Young University, Provo, Utah. He has a doctorate in international communication from the Fletcher School of Law and Diplomacy, Tufts University. He was a professor in the Department of Telecommunication, Michigan State University for 11 years. He worked as a Foreign Service Officer and research analyst for the U.S. Information Agency. He has published extensively on such topics as television in Brazil, regionalization of television markets in Latin America and Asia, telenovelas, television and politics in Latin America, new video technologies in the Third World, international spread of VCR and cable TV, television flows between countries, and privatization of telephone systems in the Third World.

Yiu-Ming To is an assistant professor in Journalism at Hong Kong Baptist University. Previously, he worked as a journalist for various news media in Hong Kong, specializing in investigative reporting and China reporting. He earned a master of social sciences degree in urban studies and is now pursuing a doctorate in political philosophy and journalism ethics at the University of Hong Kong. His research interests include news media in China, political communication and journalism ethics.

Silvio Waisbord received his licenciatura in sociology at the University of Buenos Aires, Argentina, and his master's degree and doctorate in sociology at the University of California, San Diego. He is an assistant professor in the Department of Communication at Rutgers University, Newark, New Jersey. He is the author of *El Gran Desfile*, a book on election campaigns and media in Argentina. He has also written on politics, journalism and media industries in Latin America. His research has been published in the *Journal of Communication, Critical Studies in Mass Communication, The Communication Review, Political Communication, Gazette* and other publications.

Maria A. Williams-Hawkins, PhD, is an assistant professor in the Department of Telecommunications at Ball State University, Muncie, Indiana. She earned her doctorate at The Ohio State University. Her professional background is in the area of broadcast journalism, and her research interests include news analysis, women and minorities in media professions, international joint ventures, media and technology criticism and Afrocentric studies.

PREFACE

More than thirty years ago, the late Canadian scholar Marshall McLuhan coined the phrase "global village" to represent the growing presence of mass media around the world. Today the global village exists, but perhaps different than what McLuhan theorized. We live in a global marketplace for entertainment and information products, with a number of major media conglomerates striving for market share and dominance across the various sectors that make up the burgeoning communication industries.

What created this global marketplace for media-related goods and services? A number of factors, including company mergers and acquisitions, technological advances, changing regulatory policies and the interdependence of a world economy, have all focused attention on the importance of the mass media industries as economic entities.

Global Media Economics will help to educate readers on the different economic issues and concerns media industries face in various countries and regions of the world. Readers will understand which companies and industries are leaders in their respective areas and will also recognize how different political systems and policies impact the economic processes within a particular country or region.

Global Media Economics is designed as a companion text to *Media Economics: Understanding Markets, Industries and Concepts*, also published by Iowa State University Press, which focuses on media economics at the domestic level within the United States. Coupled with an understanding of domestic media economics, readers will be better prepared to grasp the different macroeconomic and microeconomic considerations and concepts involved in the study of media economics at a global level.

Unlike many other books that have been published on the broad subject of international communications, *Global Media Economics* is a true media book. In short, the chapters discuss all media forms, including electronic and print media, filmed entertainment, digital media, and telecommunications. The contributors were encouraged to describe not only patterns and trends in their individual chapters but also to provide analysis at both the macro and micro levels.

Plan of the Book

Global Media Economics is an edited work, featuring chapters written by a number of distinguished scholars from around the globe with expertise in media economics theory and research. In Chapter 1, co-editors Chan-Olmsted and Albarran present a framework used by the individual contributors in writing their respective chapters. The framework focuses on four areas: (a) the country or region's role in the global media marketplace; (b) identification of the key media industries and companies unique to the country or region; (c) an analysis of each of the media industries with respect to the degree of concentration, barriers to entry, and other criteria; and (d) directions for future research and study. Each author addressed the framework somewhat differently, adding to the flavor of the book.

Following the initial chapter, the chapters are clustered into five specific regions, containing individual chapters devoted to countries within the region. The order of presentation for the respective regions and chapters is as follows: North America (United States, Canada and Mexico), South America (Brazil and Argentina), Europe (United Kingdom, Germany, Spain, Nordic Region, The Netherlands and France), Africa and the Middle East (Nigeria, South Africa and Israel), and Asia and the Pacific Rim (India, China, Japan, Australia, and the Pacific Rim). A final chapter, authored by the co-editors, serves as a capstone to the book, presenting media economic trends and patterns found around the globe and recommendations for further study.

Some readers may be troubled by the exclusion of certain countries or regions of the world. The limitations on the number of chapters presented in the book involved both practical concerns and publication requirements. To edit a book that attempted to include all countries and regions of the world would require several volumes. Our goal in this work was to present at least two chapters representative of each region of the world. Readers may disagree with the areas selected for inclusion, but the editors believe that these chapters adequately represent the region at the time of publication.

Global Media Economics can serve both classroom and reference purposes. The book should have utility as a text for college courses in media economics, international communications and comparative systems.

Alan B. Albarran
Sylvia M. Chan-Olmsted

ACKNOWLEDGMENTS

There are a number of people to whom we owe thanks for assistance in the publication of this work. We are grateful to the fine staff at Iowa State University Press for their encouragement and support. In particular, we would like to thank Director Linda Speth and Acquisitions Editor Judi Brown, as well as our Editor, Lynne Bishop. Likewise, we are grateful to the anonymous reviewers who were enthusiastic about the proposal for this work and encouraged publication of this book.

Our individual chapter contributors represent a diverse range of scholars who accepted their assignments and were very conscientious about answering electronic mail and meeting deadlines. We appreciate each of their contributions to the book. Any errors or omissions in the final product are the responsibility of the co-editors, not the individual contributors.

Both of us are blessed with loving families who enrich our lives and our work. We thank our spouses and our children for their support and patience in completing this project.

Editing a volume with this many chapters is quite a challenge, but it has been a rewarding experience for each of us. We hope that as the reader you will share with us your comments and observations on *Global Media Economics.*

GLOBAL MEDIA ECONOMICS

1

A FRAMEWORK FOR THE STUDY OF GLOBAL MEDIA ECONOMICS

Sylvia M. Chan-Olmsted and Alan B. Albarran

It is an exciting time. We are witnessing the transformation of a world in which the economic, social, cultural and political structures are gradually integrated by the dramatic developments in telecommunications and computer and information technology, as well as the rise of global products and markets. Clear evidence of today's globalization is the extent to which the activities of individual manufacturers and service providers cross national boundaries. As either a defensive or offensive strategic move, corporations are increasingly aggressive in establishing consortia and alliances outside their domestic markets. The media industries are no exception to this trend of globalization. The expansion of media conglomerates such as Time Warner into many European markets and of Australia's News Corporation into the U.S. territory reflects the development of an integrated global media marketplace.

Fundamentally, mass media are economic institutions that produce and distribute communication content and services to members of a society. To understand accurately the workings and effect of media in a society, one must be able to examine the media as industries and to analyze media content and system providers in these industries as entities that need to allocate their resources efficiently to survive.

The purpose of this book is to describe and analyze selected media economic systems in our global community. This book intends to interpret the economic trends from the viewpoint of an increasingly interdependent global economy, one in which many developed countries are forming policies to accommodate the broadening of their mass media base from the traditional print and broadcasting industries to include other multichannel telecommunication systems. The study of media economics, as analyzed in a global context, provides insight for reviewing this globalizing economic trend. Twenty-four scholars from 18 countries have contributed to this book. Chapters 2 through 20 each contains a description and analysis of media economic systems in one of the countries covered. A summary chapter draws conclusions based on the foregoing contributions.

This chapter presents a descriptive and conceptual framework so that readers will have a cohesiveness and familiarity with which to explore the contributions of the individual chapter authors. To accomplish this, we first discuss the principal elements in the study of media economics to provide a base for the analyses of different media systems. Next, we rationalize the importance of such studies by reviewing the forces that have shaped the globalization of the media marketplace. Finally, the analytical framework used by each of the contributors is introduced.

What Is Media Economics?

The study of media economics applies key economic concepts to analyze media industries. Media firms are economic institutions, engaged in the production and dissemination of media content targeted toward consumers (Picard, 1989). By examining a media firm's business activities such as mergers and acquisitions, competition, and production or pricing strategies, one can better understand the function of media and their impact on consumers.

According to Albarran (1996, p. 5), "[m]edia economics is the study of how media industries use scarce resources to produce content that is distributed among consumers in a society to satisfy various wants and needs." Various macroeconomic and microeconomic principles may be useful in this process of study. We will begin with a brief review of these basic economic concepts and how they can be applied to the media industries.

Differences Between Microeconomics and Macroeconomics

The study of media economics involves both macroeconomics, which examines the overall economic system at a national level, and microeconomics, which focuses on individual markets, firms or consumers. More specifically, macroeconomics deals with political economy, aggregate production and consumption, economic growth, employment and inflation, whereas microeconomics deals with specific markets, market structure, conduct and behavior, and the activity of producers and consumers (Albarran, 1996). Putting this in a media context, an examination of media industries from a macroeconomic perspective may entail the analyses of public media policy and its influence on overall media consumption and investment, whereas a microeconomic–oriented study may consider the competitive behavior and market performance of individual media firms. For example, in both Israel and Argentina, the political and national economic environment has had tremendous impact on the development of their media industries. Macroeconomics and microeconomics are closely interrelated, as the activities of individual media entities and consumers are governed by the overall political economy and influenced by the ecumenical economic development of a country. On the other hand, the decisions of media firms and consumers constantly reallocate a country's resources in the production and consumption of media products and services. For example, the growing demand for Internet-related services has prompted changes in telecommunications policies in many countries.

The following section reviews some fundamental macroeconomic and microeconomic principles to help in understanding mass media in an economic context and to establish a conceptual framework for the analysis of media industries in various countries.

Basic Economic Concepts

The Platform of Political Economy

The political system of a country fundamentally shapes the business practices of its media firms. The types of political economies range from a totalitarian system with tight government control to one of mixed capitalist economies in which private companies produce and distribute products to consumers under some regulatory directions. The other extreme is a laissez-faire capitalist system without any government intervention, leading to total economic individualism and freedom. The United States, Canada and most industrialized European countries operate under the mixed capitalist political economy in which both private individuals and government exercise their economic influence in the marketplace. Note that capitalism operates under conditions of competition: rivalry among sellers of similar goods to attract customers, among buyers to secure the goods that they want, among workers to obtain jobs, among employers to obtain workers, and among buyers and sellers of resources to transact their business on the best terms that each can obtain from the other.

The Nature of a Market System

Because many countries covered in this book operate between a mixed capitalist and totalitarian economic system, with various degrees of governmental control and market activities, it is appropriate for us to understand the nature of a market and the role of government in a market. There are two sets of markets: the product markets and the resource markets (Spencer, 1993). In the product markets consumers buy the goods and services that businesses sell, with expenditures that become the receipts of businesses. In the resource markets businesses buy the factors of production that consumers sell with payments, which become the money incomes of consumers. For example, when you study the exchange activities between cable television (TV) subscribers and cable system operators, you are examining a product market. On the other hand, the employment of human, land and capital resources by media corporations occurs in a resource market. Most of the authors in this book examine product markets. Those who discuss resource markets focus on the programming resources. A market is sometimes referred to as an industry; to be more precise, a market consists of both buyers and sellers, whereas an industry consists of only the sellers in a particular market or across several markets (Albarran, 1996). Traditionally, the study of media economics has focused on media "industries." This book is no exception. Note that many mass media systems operate in a dual product market (Picard, 1989). Media firms in these markets provide two separate goods and services: one of media content to audience and the other of access to audience to advertisers.

The inclusion of the government sector increases the complexity of a market system. A government buys resources to produce many nonmarket, or free, social commodities such as national defense and public safety, as well as various market commodities such as public transportation and utility services, for both consumers and businesses. Consumers and businesses, in turn, provide the government with the revenues it needs in the form of taxes and fees to carry on its operations. A government may also own resources, such as land and broadcast frequencies, which it may lease or sell in the resource markets. In addition, governments may participate in the product market (e.g., public broadcasting systems) and in competition with other private businesses in the sale of some commodities. For example, the participation of the Chinese government in its resource and product markets made this country a very unique media economy.

The Laws of Supply and Demand

The interplay of supply and demand in an economy fundamentally influences the answers to the three great economic questions: what to produce, how to produce, and for whom to produce (Spencer, 1993). Supply is a relationship between the price and the quantity of a product that sellers are willing and able to sell at a given time. The law of supply states that this relationship is usually direct. Hence, supply curves slope upward from left to right, meaning that as the price for a product increases, the quantity supplied by sellers increases. Demand is a relationship between the price and the quantity of a product that buyers are willing and able to purchase at a given time. The law of demand states that this relationship is inverse. Therefore, demand curves slope downward from left to right, meaning that as the price for a product decreases, the quantity demanded by consumers increases. The intersection of a market demand curve with a market supply curve determines the equilibrium price and quantity of a product (see Fig. 1-1). Note that a market demand curve is an aggregate of individual consumer demand curves. In dynamic markets, demand and supply curves are always shifting either leftward or rightward, resulting in a new equilibrium price, a new equilibrium quantity, or both. Demand curves may shift because of changes in prices of related goods in consumption, perceived value of a product, preferences, number of buyers and incomes. Supply curves may also be

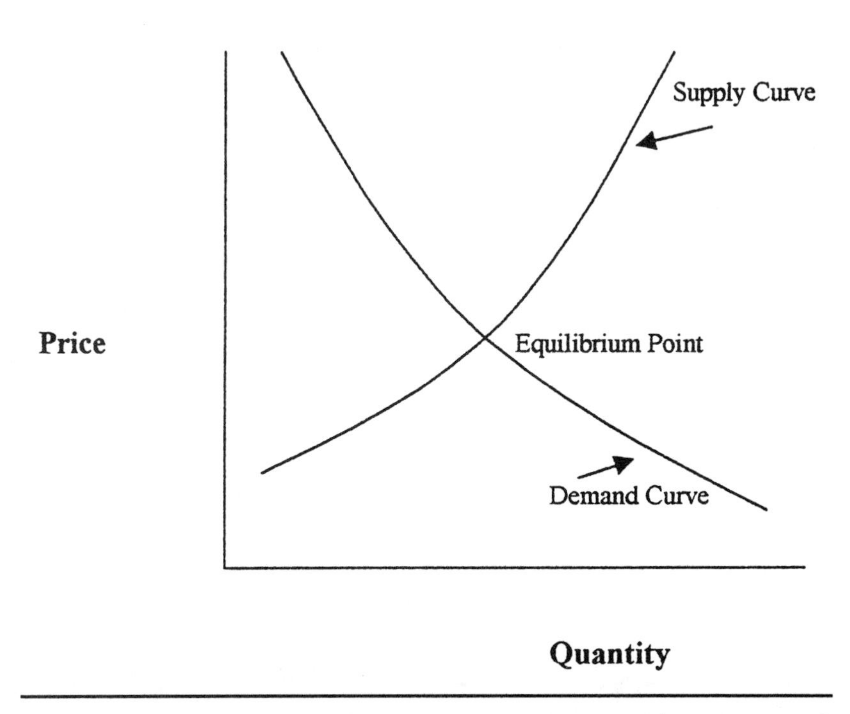

FIGURE 1-1. *Market supply and demand curve and the equilibrium price and quantity.*

influenced by resource costs, prices of related goods in production, and technology (Spencer, 1993). Note that many media markets supply public goods, such as broadcast TV programs, which are offered with very low or even zero incremental or marginal costs to sellers. Thus, the need of a mass audience may influence the nature of supply and demand in these media markets.

Another important concept related to the laws of supply and demand is price elasticity of demand, which is often referred to as the responsiveness of changes in quantity to changes in product prices. When a product demand is elastic, a change in the product's price will often result in a greater change in the quantity demanded. When a product demand is inelastic, a change in the product's price will result in a lesser change in the quantity demanded. When a demand is unit-elastic, percentage change in quantity demanded is equal to percentage change in price. This concept is important to the study of media economics, as it illustrates how the different price levels set by media firms and their impact on business revenues affect consumer demand. In many media markets, cross-elasticity of demand, which measures the responsiveness of changes in quantity demanded to changes in the price of a substitutable product, is also an important tool in economic analysis. For example, it was used in analyzing antitrust cases that examine competitive practices in media markets (Albarran, 1996).

The Theory of the Firm

The competitive structure of a market underlies the operation of supply and demand. The continuum of market structure ranges from perfect competition, monopolistic competition, oligopoly, to monopoly. Perfect competition refers to an industry characterized by a large number of buyers and sellers all engaged in the purchase and sale of a homogeneous commodity, with perfect knowledge of market prices and quantities, no entry barriers, and perfect mobility of resources. Under such a market structure, individual firms have no market power and the market sets the price for the product. Monopolistic competition refers to an industry characterized by a large number of firms of different sizes producing similar but not identical products, with relatively easy entry into the industry. Under this market structure, product differentiation is possible and both the market and the individual firms set prices. Oligopoly refers to an industry characterized by a few mutually interdependent firms, with relatively similar shares, producing either a homogeneous product (a perfect oligopoly) or heterogeneous products (an imperfect oligopoly) (Sherer and Ross, 1990). Under such a market structure, the industry leader often sets the price. The entry barriers are relatively high, but not as significant as those found in a monopoly. Monopoly refers to an industry characterized by a single firm producing a product for which there are no close substitutes. The firm thus constitutes the entire industry, operates under very high entry barriers, and sets the product price to maximize profits.

Media industries operate across this continuum of market structure, with the exception of perfect competition. Depending on the specific geographic and product market definitions, the closest examples of a monopoly market structure in media industries are cable TV systems and daily newspapers in most local markets. Broadcast TV stations and networks operate in an oligopolistic market, whereas magazines, book and radio industries reflect the monopolistic competition market structure (Albarran, 1996).

Industrial Organization Paradigm

Industrial organization is the subfield in economics that studies competitiveness of firms within an industry and the performance consequences. Historically, the principal concern of industrial economics has been with respect to public policy-making and the assessment of market performance of an industry in correspondence to the effective demand a society places on that industry's output. The methodological approach often used by industrial organization researchers focuses on three concepts: (a) industry structure, which refers to the relatively stable features of the industry environment such as seller concentration, product differentiation, barriers to entry, buyer concentration, and barriers to exit; (b) industry conduct, which refers to the patterns of behavior that firms follow in adapting to the market in which they participate. Dimensions of market conduct articulated as being important include pricing, advertising, research and development, and coercion and entry deterrence; and (c) industry performance, which refers to the evaluation of the composite performance of firms competing in an industry. The emphasis of evaluation is often on societal goals such as efficiency, technological progressiveness, full employment, and equitable distribution of output (Caves, 1982; Sherer and Ross, 1990). The three concepts interrelate in a causal manner such that industry structure determines the conduct of firms, whose joint conduct then determines the collective performance of the firms in the marketplace. From a business perspective, basically it indicates that a firm's performance in the marketplace depends critically on the characteristics of the industry environment in which it competes. For example, a media privatization policy implemented by the Argentine government in 1989 reduced the barriers to entry to its broadcasting industry, which changed the configuration of the industry structure and, subsequently, broadcasters' conduct and performance in that country.

Note that firm conduct is not merely a superfluous intermediate concept. The importance of industry structure lies in the way it induces firms to behave, and with the possibility of reverse causalities, conduct links an industry's structure to the quality of its performance. In fact, industry performance can be interpreted as an evaluation, or the logical extension, of the results of firms' behavior. Under this perspective, firm conduct needs to be explicitly taken into account in analyzing the state of competition in an industry because of its potential influence and feedback in both directions. For example, the aggressive global alliances and expansion behavior of many United States-based media conglomerates have definitely impacted the industry and firm performance and national media policies. Figure 1-2 illustrates the flow of this analysis. The industrial organization paradigm provides the context for us to understand the relationship between media firms and their industry environment. It also offers a systematic approach of examining the conduct of media firms and its consequences.

Why Global Media Economics?

Many people have compared the dramatic development in computing technologies and telecommunication systems during the latter half of the 20th century to that of the discovery of fire in the Stone Age. We are indeed living in a new historical era in which the economic, social, cultural and political structures that shaped relations between people during the past two centuries are rapidly transformed by the rise of global products, markets and corporations. The development of mass media, telecommunications, computer and other information technology has made such global integration possible.

During the past decade, we have observed a noticeable trend toward globalization of media markets. This globalization encompasses not only the extension of media ownership into different countries but also the development of comparable alternative distribution systems such as cable TV and direct broadcast satellite systems, which in turn facilitates the rise of more regional and global content distributors.

The trend of globalization can be attributed to five major forces: regional economic development and alliances, movement in the political control of mass media, technological progress, lifestyle parallelism, and the changing role of the U.S. media markets.

Regional Economic Development and Alliances

During the last decade, many Pacific Rim countries have exhibited significant economic growth and become important markets to the U.S. media firms. The development of regional trading blocs, such as the North American Free Trade Agreement, the European Community and the Association of

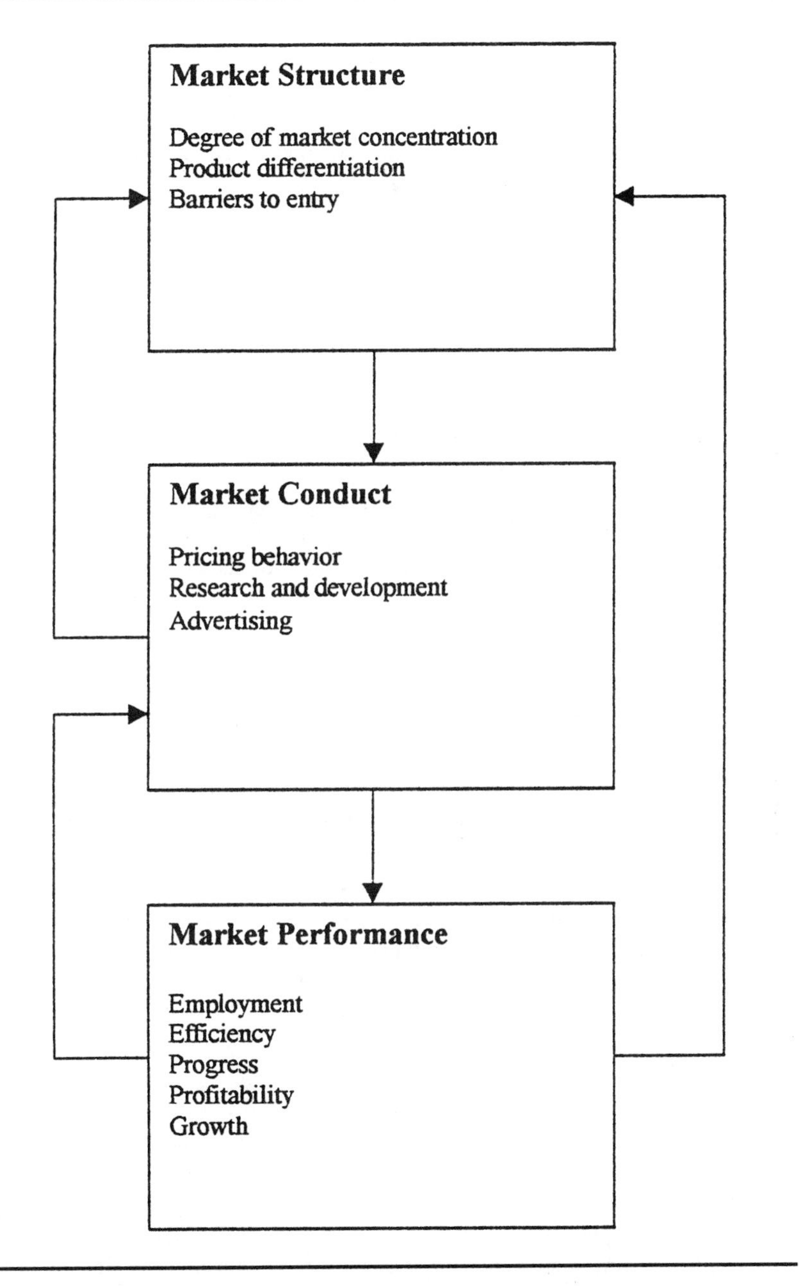

FIGURE 1-2. *Industrial organization analytical framework.*

Southeast Asian Nations Free Trade Area, presents both obstacles and opportunities for American media companies (Bergsten and Noland, 1993). To capitalize on the integration of regional markets and stay competitive, now a U.S. media company must establish operations in some member countries in the regions and exploit the rest of the regions from these bases (Valentine et al., 1991).

Movement in the Political Control of Mass Media

It was postulated that in countries at comparable stages of technological and economic development, the political system and its corresponding public policy would largely explain much of the differences in media systems (Humphreys, 1996). Facilitated by the technological changes, which pose unavoidable challenges to existing policies, many countries have instituted policies in media commercialization and privatization. In fact, the development of distribution systems such as cable, and especially satellite, has diminished the rationale of public-service monopoly and the reality of national autonomy in today's blurry telecommunication boundaries.

Technological Progress

Powerful technological forces are bringing about fundamental change in the media industries around the world. Many traditional media industry structures are now undergoing dramatic alterations with the introduction of integrated telecommunication systems. For example, recently the governments of the United States and Argentina implemented new telecommunications policies to address such technological developments. These combined forces of advances in computers and telecommunications and the prospect of convergence between all content distribution systems have facilitated the speed and scope of media globalization as media conglomerates scramble to build competitive advantages for tomorrow's media marketplace.

Lifestyle Parallelism

Also attributed to the telecommunication advances, the lifestyle differences between individual societies are less pronounced. The traditional market segmentation approach by demographics such as age and location is not as practical with the rise of information-based attitude groups that share similar consumption patterns. For example, New Age media consumers from Chicago and Tokyo may have more in common with each other than the same consumer in Chicago may have with a person from a nearby suburb. This parallelism provides further incentives for globalization of companies and their respective products.

Changing Role of the United States Media Markets

There has been a decreasing dominance of the United States-based media companies in the international marketplace during the last two decades (Carveth et al., 1993). Many high-profile mergers and acquisitions brought about the development of foreign-based global media conglomerates such as News Corporation and Sony, with significant American media properties. The trend of economic regionalization and changes in the degree of political control in many countries also modified the market behavior of many U.S. media firms. For example, after the 1992 formation of the European Community, which imposes programming import restrictions, co-productions and other joint programming ventures became a common occurrence for American programming exporters (Carveth et al., 1993). The importance of the international market is further magnified as the demand for certain media products in the United States, such as broadcasting and cable TV, is saturating.

An understanding of media economics in a global context is essential in today's study of media economics as well as mass media. As demonstrated earlier, the forces in media globalization make it impossible for us to ignore the world environment in which the U.S. media industries operate. Because the consumption of media content is essentially an exchange of scarce resources between producers and consumers, it is just as critical for us to examine the economic activities, whether state controlled or commercialized, of media systems in different countries as it is to observe individual countries' cultural differences as reflected by their media contents. By studying media industries in different countries or regions, we can also understand the analytical distinctiveness in market structure, behavior and performance of different media environments and learn how the descriptive and analytical tools have to be modified to suit the particular political and economic structure of that country or region.

The Framework for Economic Analysis of Media Markets

The general framework that our chapter contributors used for the economic analysis of media markets in their respective country or region focuses on four areas. First, the author may discuss the country's role in the global media marketplace and the major historical developments that shaped today's media markets in his or her respective country or region. More specifically, the unique economic, political, geographic and cultural characteristics, as well as historical events, of the country or region may be presented to establish a context in which media markets are analyzed. Where feasible, this context and the country or region's media industries are related to other specific countries or regions to illustrate its global position. For example, for the chapter on the United States, we discussed the major telecommunications policy implemented in 1996 and the role of the United States as a leading entertainment exporter.

The second and third section of the chapters review the major media industries in a country or region and provide a more in-depth industry analysis of selective media industries in that country or region. Although some authors separated the section of the overview of major media industries and the specific analysis of certain media industries, others integrated these two sections. To be more specific, they examined all major media industries and home companies in their respective countries or regions and simply added more industrial organization analysis of competition, mergers and acquisitions, entry barriers, and regulatory trends for certain media markets.

The last part of the chapters summarizes the significant regulatory changes, technological development, and/or current market characteristics of the major media industries in the country or region. The authors may also discuss the emerging media economic issues in that country or region and their potential impact on the global media marketplace and may identify areas for future research. It is hoped that this review of presentational framework subscribed by our contributors will give you a clear structure of reading and provide some cohesiveness and familiarity with which to explore the work of the individual chapter authors.

We made our selection of countries for this book with a regional approach. A sample of countries located in the region of North America, South America, Western Europe, the Middle East, Africa, and Asia are included in the book. Additionally, our selection decisions were largely influenced by the concept of Triad global economy, the three regions that are of greatest strategic importance in today's international marketplace. The notion of the Triad suggests that the three most important areas of the world for the U.S. businesses are North America, the Pacific Rim, and the European Community. The countries of the Triad combined account for 80 percent of world gross domestic product (GDP) and 75 percent of world imports and exports (Valentine et al., 1991). These regions are the fastest growing economic regions in the world, with a trend toward the development of regional trading blocs. This book places an emphasis on the media markets of the Triad countries and their relative roles in the regional as well as global media marketplace. A number of countries outside of the Triad are also reviewed to provide a more complete picture of our global community. Readers may consult Table 1-1 for general comparative economic and media information of the countries included in this book.

Table 1-1. Comparative Economic, Geographic and Media Information of Selected Countries

	Population (1995)	Area (km²)	GNP/ Capita (in US$)	No. of TV Sets[a]	No. of Radios[a]	Circulation of Daily Newspaper[a]	Major Trading Partner
Argentina	34,587,000	2,780,400	7,290	219	673	138	US
Australia	18,025,000	7,682,300	17,510	489	1,291	258	Japan
Brazil	155,822,000	8,511,965	3,020	209	393	45	US
Canada	29,463,000	9,970,610	20,670	685	1,051	189	US
China	1,206,600,000	9,572,900	490	189	184	23	Japan
Denmark	5,223,000	43,094	26,510	539	1,036	365	Germany
Finland	5,101,000	338,145	16,840	511	1,003	473	Germany
France	58,172,000	543,965	22,760	591	891	237	Germany
Germany	81,912,000	356,733	23,630	560	935	317	France
Hong Kong	6,205,000	1,067	17,860	719	677	291	China
India	935,744,000	3,166,414	290	40	81	N/A	US
Indonesia	195,283,000	1,919,317	730	62	148	20	US
Israel	5,386,000	20,700	13,760	275	478	281	US
Japan	125,362,000	377,835	37,560[b]	681	912	576	US
Mexico	91,145,000	1,958,201	3,750	163	256	113	US
Netherlands	15,487,000	41,863	20,710	494	909	334	Germany
Nigeria	95,434,000	923,768	310	38	196	18	US
Norway	4,360,000	323,878	26,340	428	799	607	UK
Singapore	2,989,000	622	19,310	390	645	364	Malaysia
South Africa	41,465,000	1,219,080	2,930	101	314	33	US
Spain	39,188,000	504,783	14,230	402	312	104	France
Sweden	8,826,000	449,964	24,830	475	879	483	Germany
United Kingdom	58,586,000	244,110	17,920	439	1,429	351	Germany
United States	263,057,000	9,529,063	25,850	817	N/A	228	Canada

[a]These are 1994 data for per 1,000 inhabitants in each country.

[b]All gross national products (GNPs) are 1993 figures except the one for Japan, which is a 1994 figure.

References

Albarran, A. B. (1996). *Media Economics: Understanding Markets, Industries and Concepts.* Ames, IA: Iowa State University Press.

Bergsten, C. F., and Noland, M. (1993). Introduction and overview. In: Bergsten, C. F. and Noland, M. (eds.). *Pacific Dynamism and the International Economic System.* Washington, DC: Institute for International Economics, pp. 3–13.

Carveth, R., Owers, J., and Alexander, A. (1993). The global integration of the media industries. In: Alexander, A., Owers, J., and Carveth, R. (eds.). *Media Economics: Theory and Practice.* Hillsdale, NJ: Lawrence Erlbaum Associates, pp. 331–354.

Caves, R. (1982). *American Industry: Structure, Conduct, Performance.* 5th ed. Englewood Cliffs, NJ: Prentice-Hall, Inc.
Encyclopaedia Britannica (1997). *Britannica On Line*. Available on-line: http://www.eb.com
Humphreys, P. J. (1996). *Mass Media and Media Policy in Western Europe.* Manchester, UK: Manchester University Press.
Picard, R. (1989). *Media Economics.* Beverly Hills, CA: Sage.
Sherer, F. M., and Ross, D. (1990). *Industrial Market Structure and Economic Performance.* 3rd ed. Boston: Houghton Mifflin Company.
Spencer, M. H. (1993). *Contemporary Economics.* 8th ed. New York: Worth Publishers, Inc.
UN/ECE (1997). *Trends in Europe and North America.* Available on-line: http://www.unece.org/stats/trend/
UNESCO (1997). *UNESCO Statistics.* Available on-line: http://unesco.org/general/eng/stats/
Valentine, C., Lew, G., and Poor, R. (1991). *The Ernst and Young Resource Guide to Global Markets 1991.* New York: John Wiley and Sons.

North America

In this book, North America is represented by the three largest economies in the region, the United States of America, Canada and Mexico. Co-editors Alan Albarran and Sylvia Chan-Olmsted discuss the rapid technological change affecting the media industries in the United States. The chapter on Canada, authored by Geoffrey Gurd, discusses how Canadian media industries face intense competition from United States–based media content that easily crosses Canada's national borders. The chapter on Mexico, written by Charles Davis, presents a stark contrast to Canada and the United States. Besieged for years by political problems and devaluation of the peso, the Mexican media industries appear poised for explosive growth in several areas, most notably telecommunications.

2

THE UNITED STATES OF AMERICA

Alan B. Albarran and Sylvia M. Chan-Olmsted

The United States and the Global Media Marketplace

The United States of America is one of the leading economic powers in the world. The U.S. economy continues to grow and expand, as it has since the early 1980s when the country experienced its last significant recession. A combination of macroeconomic factors, including lower interest rates, relatively healthy employment, strong corporate earnings, consumer spending, low inflation, a move toward a leaner and more fiscally responsible government, and the reduction of defense spending after the end of the Cold War have produced record gains across the major money markets and have strengthened the dollar abroad.

A diverse country with a population of approximately 260 million, the United States is a "young" country compared with many European and Asian neighbors. Throughout its history, the United States has evolved from an agrarian society, to an industrialized nation, to today's information-based society. An innovator and leader in communications technology, the United States helped establish standards for radio and television (TV) broadcasting, satellite transmission, and digital media.

What role does the communications industry play in the U.S. economy? To answer this question, various sources were consulted. One source used extensively is from the investment firm Veronis, Suhler & Associates, which specializes in tracking and analyzing the U.S. communications industry. The firm publishes two annual documents, the *Communications Industry Forecast* and the *Communications Industry Report.* The *Forecast* is used as one of the primary data sources for this chapter.

In the *Forecast,* the communications industry consists of 10 segments: TV, radio, subscription video, filmed entertainment, recorded music, newspaper publishing, book publishing, magazine publishing, business information, and interactive digital media. Telecommunication services (local exchange, long distance, cellular, paging, etc.) are listed separately in the *Forecast,* and revenues are not included when discussing communications.

With respect to its importance to the U.S. economy, the communications industry generated $251 billion in 1995, ranking it as the country's ninth largest industry in terms of revenues (Veronis, Suhler & Associates, 1996). From 1990 to 1995, the communications industry grew at a compound annual growth rate of 5.4 percent, compared with the gross domestic product (GDP) of the United States as a whole, which grew at a rate of 4.8 percent. Projections for 1995–2000 by Veronis, Suhler & Associates (1996) indicate that the communications industry will grow at an annual compound rate of 7.0 percent, compared with the country's GDP of 5.5 percent. Clearly, the communications industry will continue to be an important part of the overall U.S. economy.

The United States is one of the leading exporters of information and entertainment products, further strengthening its importance to the global media marketplace (Andersen, 1993; Fein, 1995). In many developed and developing nations of the world, content created in the United States in the form of TV programming, filmed entertainment, audio and video recordings, printed material, and interactive digital media are consumed by millions of people on a daily basis. As later chapters in this book will attest, many United States–based media companies have invested heavily in partnerships and ventures with other global companies to address both the infrastructure (e.g., distribution) and software demands of consumers around the globe.

Sweeping structural changes continue to impact the composition of the U.S. communications industry at both the national and the local level. Many segments of the U.S. communications industry have become concentrated as a result of mergers and acquisitions (Albarran and Dimmick, 1996). In addition to rising within-industry concentration, concentration between industries is also growing, indicative of the strategies of several large conglomerates (e.g., News Corporation, Viacom, Disney) to offer products and services across a range of horizontal markets (see Albarran and Dimmick, 1996).

In 1996, merger and acquisition activity in the broadcast industry alone reached $25 billion. The radio industry was especially active, increasing 315 percent from 1995 to 1996. Cable industry mergers were valued at $23 billion the same year. Mergers were also setting records in telecommunications, led by NYNEX–Bell Atlantic, Southwestern Bell–Pacific Telesis and MCI–World Com.

The growing merger activity is a direct result of the 1996 Telecommunications Act, which eliminated a number of regulatory barriers in terms of ownership limits and cross-industry ownership, especially in the cable and telecommunications industries. Over time, these actions will further consolidate many market segments. Critics deplore the growth of large media conglomerates and their perceived control over information (see Bagdikian, 1992; Schiller, 1981), and proponents claim the larger companies are better able to utilize economies of scope and scale, eventually resulting in lower overall costs to consumers (Litman, 1988; Picard, 1989).

Technological convergence and the move toward a digital environment are reshaping how Americans consume entertainment and information products (Tapscott, 1996). The digitization of content products, whether in the form of film/video, text, or still images, and the means to distribute computerized bits of information will continue to expand into the next century (Negroponte, 1995).

Technological convergence has also impacted the strategic planning of many U.S. companies, leading to an increasing level of binational mergers, partnerships, cooperative agreements, and joint ventures between domestic and global entities (Du Bois, 1996). Like many regions of the world, the media industries in the United States are in a period of sweeping transition and change, with the outcome beyond prediction. What is clear is that the United States will continue to play a major role in the global media marketplace well into the 21st century.

Major Media Industries in the Country or Region

Virtually all of the media industries in the United States are considered healthy in terms of earnings and revenue projections. Of the $251 billion in revenues generated across the entire communications industry in 1995, newspaper publishing accounted for the largest segment at $50.38 billion, whereas interactive digital media represented the smallest segment at $7.6 billion (Veronis, Suhler & Associates, 1996). Before describing specific industries, we first look at four common characteristics shared by many of the U.S. media industries.

CONSUMER DEMAND. Consumer demand for media products in the U.S. is often described as insatiable (Albarran, 1996). Americans spend a great deal of their leisure and nonleisure time consuming media content. The average TV set is on more than 7 hours a day. Almost two thirds of the U.S. households receive multichannel programming via cable or a direct broadcast satellite (DBS) system. The average citizen listens to the radio around 3 hours a day and spends about 22 minutes a day with a newspaper (Albarran, 1996). Daily, millions of Americans rent videos, cruise the Internet, play video games, read magazines and books, and listen to sound recordings. With a large population base, the media industries have plenty of audiences for their content. The majority of the U.S. media industries are supported by advertisers seeking to reach specific audiences.

ROLE OF ADVERTISING. Most media industries in the United States operate in what Picard (1989) identifies as a dual product market. That is, while media companies produce one product, they participate in two separate good and service markets. In the first market, the good (in the form of a newspaper, TV program, magazine or film) is marketed to consumers. The second market involves the selling of advertising. The multimillion dollar advertising industry eagerly purchases time and space in various media channels in order to reach audiences. In 1995, the top 100 advertisers spent $47.3 billion, the largest advertising volume in history (Endicott, 1966). This interdependent relationship is important to the stability of the media industries over time.

REGULATORY ENVIRONMENT. The United States is a capitalist democracy, built on separation of the media from government control. Further, the First Amendment to the U.S. Constitution guarantees freedom of expression without prior restraint. As a result, content regulation of the media is limited. The broadcast and cable industries are overseen by the Federal Communications Commission (FCC), whereas the print media enjoy nearly complete freedom. The Federal Trade Commission regulates advertising, protecting the public from false or deceptive content. Large media mergers and acquisitions are scrutinized for possible antitrust violations by the Department of Justice. Few regulatory barriers, however, inhibit the growth of media companies. For the most part, regulatory agencies at both the federal and state levels have adopted a pro-competitive stance toward the media industries, ensuring that the United States maintains a competitive edge in the global marketplace.

BLURRING MARKETS. Historically, media companies operated in distinct markets as a result of either technological or regulatory restrictions. Today, media companies create content that appears in a number of different forms. For example, many daily newspapers are supplemented by an on-line edition (in 1996, the number of electronic newspapers was estimated at 800; Levins, 1997), with some papers delivering personalized electronic versions of the newspaper to individual subscribers. Radio stations from across the country can be received via the Internet using audio plug-in software.

Perhaps the ultimate manifestation of seamless market boundaries was the creation of MS/NBC, a joint venture between NBC and Microsoft, to provide news and other content to audiences through cable TV as well as through the Internet (Auletta, 1997). In short, media industries no longer think of their products as being specific to a particular channel or distribution system; now they can be consumed in a variety of ways. In the near future, media industries may be more easily classified by functions (information or entertainment content creation, storage, processing, distribution, etc.) rather than by the types of products or services they provide.

The scope of this chapter prevents a complete discussion of all of the media industries operating in the United States. Our focus is on three key segments of the communications industry: newspaper publishing, TV (including subscription services such as cable) and filmed entertainment.

NEWSPAPER PUBLISHING. The number of daily newspapers in the United States has steadily declined for the past several decades, yet the newspaper industry continues to be the largest revenue-producing form of mass media in the United States. Newspapers routinely attract the largest percentage of advertising expenditures when compared with TV, direct mail, and radio, although the margin between newspapers and other media, particularly TV, has shrunk in recent years.

In 1995, the newspaper industry generated a total of $50.38 billion, with the majority earned by daily newspapers through advertising sales ($36 billion) and circulation sales ($9.6 billion). By the year 2000, daily newspapers are expected to earn total revenues of $59.46 billion (Veronis, Suhler & Associates, 1996).

Weekly or suburban newspapers have increased in number and popularity. Desktop publishing has made it much easier to enter the publishing industry at affordable costs. Weekly papers accounted for $4.6 billion in revenues in 1995, mostly from advertising ($4.2 billion). Revenue for weekly newspapers is expected to reach $6.7 billion by 2000 (Veronis, Suhler & Associates, 1996).

The majority of the newspapers in the United States are owned by corporations and are known as "chains." Several companies have been in newspaper publishing for decades, including Gannett, Knight-Ridder, Times Mirror, the New York Times Company, Dow Jones and Company, W. W. Scripps, Cox, and Hearst. The largest newspaper chains, ranked by revenues, are listed in Table 2-1. Approximately 13 percent of all U.S. newspapers are foreign controlled. Thomson is the largest single foreign owner, with more than 100 dailies (Albarran, 1996).

The newspaper industry faces several issues of concern, including sluggish circulation, aging readership, the cost of newsprint, competition from other media, and rapidly changing technology. Newspapers continue to play a prominent role in American society, both as a source of news and information, as well as a commercial entity linking advertisers and consumers.

TELEVISION. The United States has more TV stations and programming networks than any other country in the world. Nielsen Media Research estimates that TV receivers are found in 99 percent of all households and that the average set is on more than 7 hours a day (Nielsen, 1995).

Table 2-1. Top 15 Newspaper Publishers Ranked by Revenue (1995)

Company Name	Newspaper Revenues[a]
Gannet Co. Inc.	$3,226
Knight-Ridder Inc.	2,250
The New York Times Co.	2,161
Advance Publications	2,108
Times Mirror Co.	2,058
Tribune Co.	1,304
Dow Jones & Co. Inc.	1,192
Cox Enterprises Inc.	976
Hearst Newspapers	824
Thomson Newspapers Inc.	770
The Washington Post Co.	729
Walt Disney Company	665
W. W. Scripps	640
Central Newspapers	580
Hollinger International	538

Source: Standard & Poor's (1997).

[a]In millions.

The broadcast TV industry (composed of TV networks and local stations) generated more than $30 billion in revenues in 1995 (Veronis, Suhler & Associates, 1996). Television revenues are expected to reach $41 billion by 2000 (Veronis, Suhler & Associates, 1996). Subscription TV services, which include cable TV, DBS, premium and pay-per-view channels, and emerging wireless services, accounted for an additional $28.9 billion in revenues in 1995, with projections of $43.6 billion by 2000 (Veronis, Suhler & Associates, 1996). If these estimates hold true, subscription TV will outperform broadcast, or "free," TV for the first time in history.

The broadcast TV industry functions at two different levels. At the local level, TV stations (network affiliates, independents and public stations) compete with one another for audiences and advertisers. The number of competitors varies in local markets, depending on the number of TV channels allocated to each city by the FCC. At the national level four major broadcast networks (ABC, CBS, NBC, and Fox) and two smaller networks (UPN and WB) also compete in a dual product marketplace for audiences and advertisers, along with nearly 100 satellite-delivered channels.

The TV industry has experienced many structural changes since 1990 as a result of mergers and acquisitions and lessened governmental regulation. Several networks (ABC, Fox, UPN, and WB) have become aligned with production studios. The integration of both studio production and distribution systems gives the networks greater presence in marketing programming and

Table 2-2. Top 15 Television Owners Ranked by FCC Audience Reach

Group	Rank	% Households Reached
Fox	1	34.8
CBS	2	30.9
Paxson Communications	3	26.8
Tribune Broadcasting	4	25.9
NBC	5	24.6
Disney/ABC	6	24.0
Gannett Broadcasting	7	18.0
Chris Craft/BHC/United	8	17.6
HSN/Silver King	9	16.4
Telemundo Group	10	10.7
A.H. Belo	11	10.5
Paramount Stations Group	12	9.96
Univision Television Group	13	9.9
Cox Broadcasting	14	9.5
Hearst-Argyle Television	15	9.2

Source: Special report. Top TV Groups. *Broadcasting & Cable* (1997).
Note: Station ownership changes rapidly in the United States.

secures the survival of the networks in the competitive media marketplace. Programming regulations that restricted network ownership of syndicated products and limitations on access programming have been eliminated.

Ownership limits have increased, allowing a single group or individual to own any number of TV stations capable of reaching up to 35 percent of the national TV audience. As with newspapers, corporations dominate TV ownership. A listing of major TV owners is found in Table 2-2. The networks are among the largest owners, as they require a stable group of stations to ensure clearance for network programming and promote economies of scale (Litman, 1993). Aside from the networks, major owners include Tribune, A. H. Belo, Gannett, Silver King, and Paxson.

The cable TV industry is dominated by the major multiple system operators (MSOs): Tele-Communications, Inc., Time Warner, US West, and Comcast and is typically ranked by the number of subscribers served. The largest cable MSO providers are listed in Table 2-3. Direct broadcast satellite operators include Direct TV, Primestar, EchoStar, and AlphaStar; by mid-1997 these services cumulatively reached approximately 5 million subscribers.

The U.S. TV industry faces several issues in the future. At the network level, audiences have declined by one-third during the past 20 years owing to competition from cable and DBS, home video, independent stations, subscription services (premium services and pay-per-view) and the Internet.

Table 2-3. Major Cable Operators—1997

Top Cable (Multiple System Operators)	Basic Subscribers	Rank[a]
Tele-Communications, Inc.	14.3	1
Time Warner Cable	12.3	2
U.S. West Media Group	5.25	3
Comcast Corporation	4.3	4
Cox Cable Communications	3.28	5
Cablevision Systems Corp.	2.86	6
Adelphia Communications	1.85	7
Jones Intercable, Inc.	1.48	8
Century Communications	1.23	9
Marcus Cable	1.19	10

Source: Adapted from Special report. Cable. *Broadcasting & Cable* (1997).

[a]Ranked by number of subscribers, in millions.

Competition for viewers will stiffen in the years ahead as new technologies and delivery systems expand options for multichannel viewing. The conversion to a new, digital TV environment mandated by the FCC will be costly, especially for public stations and stations in smaller markets. Still, the economic outlook for the U.S. TV industry remains strong into the 21st century with combined broadcast and subscription revenues expected to reach $85 billion (Veronis, Suhler & Associates, 1996).

THE MOTION PICTURE INDUSTRY. The U.S. motion picture industry reaches audiences through several different means of domestic and international exhibition (Owen and Wildman, 1992), beginning with the box office and continuing through other distribution windows such as home video, premium services, pay-per-view, and syndication sales. Box office and home video make up the two largest revenue streams. In 1995, box office receipts totaled $5.4 billion, and home video reached $15.35 billion (Veronis, Suhler & Associates, 1996). By the year 2000, revenues are expected to reach $6 billion for box office receipts and $19.75 billion for home video (Veronis, Suhler & Associates, 1996).

It costs millions of dollars to produce and market a feature film, and a film is considered a hit when box office sales surpass $100 million. Only seven films reached the $100 million figure in 1995, but in 1996, 13 films achieved the hit ranking, led by *Independence Day, Twister, Mission Impossible,* and *The Rock* (Lippman, 1997).

The motion picture industry does more than simply produce movies. Hollywood studios are heavily involved in the production of TV movies and programming for broadcast and cable outlets (Gomery, 1993). Revenues from the production of TV programming brought the industry an additional $10.5 billion in revenue in 1995, with projections of $15.2 billion by 2000 (Veronis, Suhler & Associates, 1996).

The exportation of filmed entertainment far exceeds the importation of foreign material into this country. Statistics compiled by the Commerce Department's Bureau of Economic Analysis determined that U.S. exports of film and TV entertainment in 1992 was $2.5 billion compared with only $90 million in payments (imports). In terms of filmed entertainment, the United States holds a strong position in global trade.

Major companies in the motion picture industry include domestic entities such as Time Warner (Warner Brothers), Walt Disney (including Buena Vista, Touchstone, Hollywood Pictures, and Miramax) and Viacom (Paramount), along with international companies such as News Corporation (20th Century Fox), Seagrams (Universal) and Sony (Columbia Pictures).

Although the motion picture industry is economically stable, rising cost structures for films and sluggish projections for box office admissions are concerns for the industry. Home video will continue to grow at a much faster pace than box office receipts. International piracy is another area in which the motion picture industry experiences revenue losses. In 1994, international piracy of film and video was estimated at $2 billion (*U.S. Industrial Outlook,* 1994).

Media Industry Analysis

This section examines the newspaper, TV and motion picture industries with respect to selected variables commonly used in economic analysis. These variables include the type of market structure, barriers to entry for new competitors, regulatory impact, and technological impact. A brief description of each of these variables is found in Chapter 1; for more detail readers should consult either Albarran (1996) or Picard (1989).

Newspaper Industry

The newspaper industry functions primarily as a monopoly structure at the local level. Fewer than 30 U.S. cities are served by more than one newspaper (Albarran, 1996). Although suburban or weekly papers have shown strong growth, the high start-up costs to enter the daily newspaper industry form significant barriers to entry. Wirth (1986) has shown that it is easier to enter the market for local broadcasting than to begin a daily newspaper.

The newspaper industry faces little governmental regulation. The 1970 Newspaper Preservation Act remains the most recent regulatory action toward newspapers. The Act was designed to promote diversity of expression in communities where the market could no longer support two competing papers. The Act allows for establishment of joint operating agreements among newspaper firms. In a joint operating agreement, editorial operations remain separate, but other operations are combined. Fewer than 30 cities have existing joint operating agreements, and the number is expected to decline slowly.

Technology has impacted newspapers primarily with respect to production and distribution. Papers can now be produced faster and more efficiently, allowing for later deadlines. One of the key challenges for the U.S. newspaper industry is developing the Internet as a tool to generate new readers and possibly new revenue streams (Levins, 1997). Presently, only about 10 percent of all on-line newspapers are profitable (Outing, 1997).

Television Industry

At both the national and local levels, the TV industry functions as an oligopoly. Products for the most part are similar (e.g., news, situation comedies, movies), although content differentiation provides qualitatively different material. Barriers to entry are high; at the national level, operating a network demands significant capital, a strong base of affiliated stations, programming capable of attracting sufficient market share to interest advertisers, and constant marketing and promotion (Litman, 1993). Locally, starting a new station is nearly impossible, as most existing channels are in use. The fastest way to enter either market is through acquisition, and prices during the 1990s have been very expensive. The cable industry is still a local monopoly for multichannel service, but competition is imminent with the expansion of DBS, wireless, and telephone company delivery.

The most recent regulatory action to impact the U.S. TV industry is the introduction of an individual age-based rating system on both broadcast and cable programming (Getting specific, 1996). The controversial system went into place in January 1997, after months of debate among industry representatives, legislative officials, and consumer groups. Critics contend that the rating system is useless without the addition of content-based ratings that consider the amount of sex, violence and profane language in programming. During the summer of 1997, regulators were pushing the industry toward expanding the system to include content labels.

Still ahead is the transition from an analog transmission system to a digital TV environment. The FCC is requiring all existing TV channels to move to newly assigned digital channels by 2006. This regulatory action will completely change the face of TV for both industry practitioners and consumers. The move to digital TV will require massive expenditures at both the industry and consumer levels.

Motion Picture Industry

With the majority of industry revenues controlled by the six major production studios, the motion picture industry operates as an oligopoly. Independent film companies that enjoy any degree of success are often acquired by other firms. As in other industries, the motion picture industry has moved toward greater consolidation in recent years.

The motion picture industry primarily operates under self-regulation, through its own content rating system established by the Motion Picture Association of America. In terms of technology, the film industry continues to amaze audiences with creative applications of technology, including the creation of the first computer-generated feature film, Disney's *Toy Story.* New distribution technologies, such as the digital video disc, may revolutionize the home viewing experience and lead to a gradual consumer shift away from VHS tapes to the new technology.

Emerging Media Economic Issues in the United States

The United States will continue to maintain a powerful global presence as a leader across the mass media industries. The combined exportation of thousands of hours of TV and film content, as well as the growing presence of U.S. media firms in other countries, will ensure the continuing dominance of the United States communications industry on a global basis. Further development in interactive digital media and the Internet also represents growth opportunities for U.S. media companies.

While the U.S. presence in the global economy will continue to be felt, at the domestic level numerous issues remain to be resolved that will affect the future growth of the mass media industries. This concluding section examines a few of these issues and possible questions for future research.

Who Will Lead the Information Superhighway?

The 1996 Telecommunications Act was heralded as a milestone in the development of communications in the United States. But which industries and companies will take the leadership role in developing the idea of an information superhighway? Initially it appeared that a combination of telephone companies and cable companies would spearhead growth, but both have retrenched within their own markets.

Cable is highly leveraged, with an average of 20 percent of their revenue devoted to debt, compared with a 4 percent average for the telephone companies

(Chan-Olmsted, 1997). Cable MSOs have had difficulty acquiring new investment capital for expansion, and telephone companies have traditionally distributed excess earnings to shareholders. In turn, technology companies such as Microsoft and Netscape have emerged as leaders in developing consumer interest in the Internet, the primary leg of the superhighway.

Not to be left out, TV broadcasters intend to have a role in the development of the information superhighway. Broadcasters still attract the largest audiences and significant advertising. The move toward digital transmission and the potential to offer ancillary services with their new digital channels (e.g., paging, text services, consumer services) positions the broadcast TV industry for a new era of opportunity and growth.

What Will Be the Outcome of Media Industry Consolidation?

At both the domestic and international levels, the rate of merger and acquisition activity has been stunning. In 1995, U.S. mergers totaled a record $375 billion across all industries (Late nights, 1995). Data for 1996 were still being compiled at the time of publication, but it was anticipated that 1996 figures would surpass 1995's, with the possibility of yet another record year in 1997 (Bagli, 1997).

This heavy business activity raises a number of questions. Which U.S. media companies will emerge as the global leaders of the communications industry during the next decade? Will there be major international consortiums grouped around categories such as distribution, media/software content, and telecommunications? Which companies will survive and which companies will fail?

How Will the Individual and Society Be Affected?

The explosion in information and new technologies has raised concerns about the impact on both the individual consumer and society. Among the questions to be addressed include how to provide access for all members of society, how to ensure privacy, and how to meet changing consumer demand. Other areas of concern include intellectual property protection, building the U.S. competitive edge globally, promoting competition while limiting vertical and horizontal integration, and ensuring reasonable interconnection price and quality.

How Will Markets Be Defined in a Digital Environment?

The blurring of market boundaries caused by a shift to a digital environment raises numerous questions about how domestic and global media markets will be defined, measured and analyzed in the years ahead. These topics are of great interest to industry analysts, policy-makers and academicians.

The melding of TV, home computers and the Internet has the potential to create a paradigm shift in the way citizens do everything, from voting to banking, shopping and education. As personal computers and TV receivers become more integrated, the rise of entire digital communities clustering households and individuals with common preferences and interests from around the globe will no doubt impact how media companies refine their products and marketing strategies (Internet communities, 1997).

In conclusion, the U.S. communications industry will continue to experience further transformation and change in the years ahead. Converging technologies, mergers and acquisitions, a strong economy, and relaxed regulatory policies are together reshaping the players, the markets, the industries, and the strategies of U.S. companies as they compete with other nations in the global media marketplace of the 21st century.

References

Albarran, A. B. (1996). *Media Economics: Understanding Markets, Industries, and Concepts.* Ames, IA: Iowa State University Press.

Albarran, A. B., and Dimmick, J. (1996). Concentration and economies of multiformity in the communication industries. *Journal of Media Economics,* 9(4):41–50.

Andersen, K. (1993). No tariff on Tom Cruise. *Time,* July 19, p. 67.

Auletta, K. (1997). *The Highwaymen: Warriors of the Information Superhighway.* New York: Random House.

Bagdikian, B. H. (1992). *The Media Monopoly.* 4th ed. Boston: Beacon Press.

Bagli, C. V. (1997). Conditions are right for a takeover frenzy. *The New York Times,* January 1, p. C3.

Chan-Olmsted, S. (1997). *Mergers, Acquisitions and Convergence: The Strategic Alliances of Broadcasting, Cable Television, and Telephone Services.* Unpublished manuscript.

DuBois, M. (1996). Together but equal. *The Wall Street Journal,* September 26, R20–21.

Endicott, R. C. (1996). Top marketers invest $47.3 billion in '95 ads. *Advertising Age,* September 30, p. S3.

Fein, A. (1995). Yank toons worldly: Major exports going strong. *Variety,* June 19, p. 56.

Getting specific over kids. (1996). *Broadcasting & Cable,* December 16, p. 6.

Gomery, D. (1993). The contemporary American movie business. In: Alexander, A., Owers, J., and Carveth, R. (eds.). *Media Economics: Theory and Practice.* New York: Lawrence Erlbaum Associates, pp. 267–281.

Internet communities. Special report. (1997). *Business Week,* May 5, pp. 64–80.
Late nights in the M&A lab. (1995). *The Economist,* November 11, p. 73.
Levins, H. (1997). In search of: Internet busine$$. *Editor & Publisher,* February 8, pp. 4i–6i.
Lippman, J. (1997). Hollywood reeled in record $5.8 billion last year, boosted by blockbuster films. *The Wall Street Journal,* January 3, B2.
Litman, B. R. (1988). Microeconomic foundations. In: Picard, R. G., McCombs, M., Winter, J. P., and Lacy, S. (eds.). *Press Concentration and Monopoly: New Perspectives on Newspaper Ownership and Operation.* Norwood, NJ: Ablex Publishing Company, pp. 3–34.
Litman, B. R. (1993). Role of TV networks. In: Alexander, A., Owers, J., and Carveth, R. (eds.). *Media Economics: Theory and Practice.* New York: Lawrence Erlbaum Associates, pp. 225–244.
Negroponte, N. (1995). *Being Digital.* New York: Alfred A. Knopf
Nielsen Media Research. *Nielsen Television Information.* (1995). Northbrook, IL: Nielsen Media Research.
Outing, S. (1997). Few newspapers make on-line profits. *Editor & Publisher,* January 18, p. 26.
Owen, B. M., and Wildman, S. (1992). *Video Economics.* Harvard Press.
Picard, R. G. (1989). *Media Economics.* Beverly Hills: Sage.
Schiller, H. I. (1981). *Who Knows: Information in the Age of the Fortune 500.* Norwood, NJ: Random House.
Special report. Cable. (1997). *Broadcasting & Cable,* June 16, pp. 36–40.
Special report. Top TV Groups. (1997). *Broadcasting & Cable,* June 30, pp. 30–41.
Standard & Poor's. *Standard & Poor's Industry Surveys.* (1997). New York: Standard & Poor's.
Tapscott, D. (1996). *The Digital Economy.* New York: McGraw-Hill.
U.S. Industrial Outlook (1994). Washington, DC: U.S. Department of Commerce.
Veronis, Suhler & Associates. (1996). *Communications Industry Forecast.* New York: Veronis, Suhler & Associates.
Wirth, M. O. (1986). Economic barriers to entering media industries in the United States. In: M. McLaughlin (ed.). *Communication Yearbook 9.* Beverly Hills, CA: Sage, pp. 423–442.

3

CANADA

Geoffrey Gurd

The conventional wisdom is that Canada's cultural industries are shaped by the interplay between the symbolic environment and the industry environment (Dorland, 1996b). The symbolic environment includes government organizations responsible for cultural production and regulation, the relevant legislation and regulatory bodies, the collective wisdom of numerous royal commissions, Senate committees, and task forces, as well as the indefinable psychic and cultural consequences of all of these discourses over time (e.g., Canada, 1996a). The industry environment, which is a more recent perspective, pertains to comprehending the economics of particular industries. One should probably add the technological environment because neither of the other environments seems to include it and because new technologies drastically undermine government policies and change the balance of power in the industrial environment. The ongoing interaction between these three environments is framed in this chapter in terms of the information society, the growth of the Internet, the digitalization of all forms of communications, advances in communication and computer technologies, and the pressures to open up Canada's cultural markets for increased global competition.

The tension between these environments in Canada is based on a number of geographic, economic, linguistic and political characteristics that have influenced and continue to affect the cultural industries (Stewart, 1983). Canada is the second largest country in the world, with a highly urbanized population of 30 million people, the majority of whom live within a 100 miles of the Canada–United States border. The United States is Canada's largest trading partner, and both economies are linked regionally through the North American Free Trade Agreement (NAFTA) and internationally through the World Trade Organization's (WTO) agreements. The dependency of the smaller Canadian economy on the U.S. economy is a constant theme in Canadian intellectual history and cultural debates (Melody et al., 1981). Cultural products of the United States are often perceived as a threat to Canada's cultural industries. They serve to undermine the content and circumstances for understanding Canadian national identity and present a major dilemma for Canadian policy-makers.

The linguistic makeup of Canada is such that Quebec is predominately French speaking, whereas the rest of Canada is English speaking.[1] Government policy has supported Canada's dualistic linguistic situation by favoring English and French services. The fact that Quebec is mostly French speaking has protected Quebecers from the impact of English-language media products in contrast to the vulnerability of English-speaking Canadians to English-language products, especially those from the United States. The question of language is central to Canadian politics and is an important issue for government agencies such as the Canadian Radio–Television and Telecommunications Commission (CRTC) to regulate in their role as guardian of the public airwaves.

The political response to these geographic, economic, and linguistic conditions is a concern on the part of different levels of government with protecting and developing mutually beneficial cultural and economic policies. "Canada's position starts with culture, acknowledges the industrial nature of cultural productions in our modern information economy, and ends with cultural goals which may be achieved in part by industrial means" (Lorimer and Duxbury, 1994, p. 277). Support for the cultural industries is enshrined in government legislation, regulatory mechanisms, and financial aid. For example, legislation such as the Broadcasting Act (1991) states that "the Canadian broadcasting system, operating primarily in the English and French languages and comprising public, private and community elements, makes use of radio frequencies that are public property and provides, through its programming, a public service essential to the maintenance and enhancement of national identity and cultural sovereignty."

The current Canadian federal policy is concerned with promoting the cultural industries in light of the growth of the information highway and the convergence of the cable and telecommunication industries, the threat of open markets, and the need to ensure adequate Canadian content and participation (Canada, 1996b; Information Highway Advisory Council, 1995). The convergence policy framework (August 1996) covers interconnection and interoperability of network facilities; support for Canadian cultural products; and competition in facilities, products and services (Babe, 1996). Because the policy is relatively recent, it is difficult to know how it might impact on the economics of either telecommunication or cable companies or content providers.

Total government support of the cultural sector was Can$5.84 billion in 1994–95 (*The Daily* [Statistics Canada], August 12, electronic edition). Almost 50 percent of this was from the federal government. Of that amount, Can$1.5 billion went to broadcasting and the CRTC and another Can$412.6 million went to other cultural industries such as film and video production, book and periodical publishing, and the sound recording industry. This support of the cultural industries is threatened by national and international events. Nationally, the obsession with deficit reduction by the federal government has resulted in severe financial cuts for the Canadian Broadcasting Corporation (CBC), with potentially drastic long-term effects on the public broadcasting system (CBC/SRC, 1996). On the international scene, a recent WTO interim ruling struck down a number of policies that protect the Canadian magazine industry (Eggertson, 1997; Fagan and Eggertson, 1997; O'Neill, 1997). There is a fear that the ruling is the precursor to a comprehensive assault on Canada's cultural industries by proponents of open markets and free trade.

Given this emphasis on open markets, Canada's success in the international marketplace is uneven. The successes are evident in newspapers, cable, commercial television (TV), and audio–visual products. Both Thomson Newspapers and Hollinger International Inc. are major newspaper companies with holdings in the United States, Britain, Australia and Israel, to name a few countries. The Thomson Newspapers holdings are among the largest in North America, with more than 70 daily newspapers and other information products. The major cable companies, Rogers and Vidéotron, own or control important systems in the United States. In broadcasting, CanWest Global has controlling interest in two New Zealand TV networks and a desire to move into the U.S. market. Canada is also the world's second largest exporter of audiovisual products after the United States (Enchin, 1996).

The cultural industries are weak if one examines book publishing, film exhibition and distribution, and music and TV content. A central contradiction is that the infrastructure (e.g., distribution systems) is largely Canadian owned and operated, but the content is skewed in favor of the dominant English-language market of the United States. American publishers supply the majority of textbooks to Canadians and dominate magazine newsstand distribution. Film distribution is controlled by U.S. companies, which results in considerable exposure of U.S. feature films in Canadian theaters. This domination is less apparent in Quebec, where all types of home-grown, French-language cultural products are popular. United States products also dominate the TV industry in terms of both over-the-air broadcasting and specialty channels. In economic terms, the differences in the size of the markets simply means that it is cheaper to buy products from the United States than it is to produce a comparable product in Canada.

Regardless of the strengths or weaknesses of Canadian companies, there are very little data for making cross-national comparisons. There is some hope that the North American Industry Classification System standards for measuring the goods and services sectors of information and communication technologies, adopted in 1997, will permit a more informed comparison of cultural industries (Mozes et al., 1996).

The following description of Canadian cultural industries briefly describes the role of media consumers, advertisers and regulators and focuses on the newspaper, cable, and specialty TV industries. Information on other cultural industries are obtainable from Audley's pioneering work (1983) and Dorland's edited collection (1996a), as well as print and on-line Canadian government sources such as Statistics Canada.

Major Media Industries

The daily newspaper industry was chosen because it is becoming more concentrated and is one of the few areas in which Canadian media companies have extensive non-Canadian holdings. The issues that Audley raised in 1983 concerning corporate concentration, cross-media ownership, and conflicts of interest are still relevant, especially as the Hollinger–Southam companies continue their acquisitions. Not only is the concentration of daily newspaper ownership increasing, but sheer size appears to correspond with healthy corporate profits and acts to shield newspapers from increased competition for readers and advertisers from local and regional newspapers, free weekly entertainment papers, on-line employment services, and the newer 24-hour TV news services such as CBC's Newsworld and RDI, as well as the other traditional media. The response of the industry has been to expand into magazines, books and Internet activities (e.g., Southam New Media Centre and CANOE [Canada online explorer, a joint project of Toronto Sun Publishing Inc. and Rogers Multimedia Inc.]). Clearly, the Internet experiments are a response to the perceived threat of the Internet and electronic publishing to the industry (Gooderham, 1996).

The cable industry in Canada is also generally successful. Revenues for 1995–96 were Can$2.532 billion, expenses were Can$2.352 billion, and pretax profits were Can$434.1 million (Canadian Cable Television Association 1996; Canada, 1995). Cable is still a growth area, although it is constrained by long-term debt and uncertainty about the role that cable systems will play in the new deregulated, competitive information economy. There are 370 owners of 1,987 systems; however, the industry is dominated by four major companies; Rogers Cable TV, Shaw Cablesystems, Vidéotron and Cogeco Cable, who collectively control approximately 75 percent of the total number of subscribers.

The Canadian specialty TV industry was selected because its English-language audience share has doubled to 30 percent since 1989, it represents the direction of narrowcasting in Canada, and the companies involved in the industry reveal the increasingly intertwined corporate relationships and strategic alliances. Furthermore, the growth of the specialty TV industry (e.g., satellite-delivered channels) is fueling a need for additional Canadian programming, as required by the CRTC, to provide opportunities for Canadian film and TV producers.

The Nature of the Media Consumer

The media consumer in Canada is well served in terms of quantity and quality of different services. Canadians have a broad choice of commercial and public radio and TV programming, ranging from Canadian programming in French and English, U.S. programming, as well as international, ethnic/multilingual, educational, children's and other specialty programming. Ten cities have more than one daily newspaper. The *Globe and Mail* is distributed nationally, and Montreal's *La Presse* is distributed to major French-speaking areas outside of Quebec. Cable passes 81 percent of all Canadian homes, resulting in more than eight million residential and commercial subscriptions to basic cable (Canadian Cable Television Association 1996). There are 49 existing and planned pay-TV and specialty channels (movie, music video, sports and all-news channels in both official languages).

Canadian consumers are buying fewer newspapers and magazines, watching a bit more TV (23.2 hours per week), listening less to AM radio and more to FM radio (21 hours of AM and FM radio per week overall) (Filion, 1996). In general, media consumption patterns are stable following the recession of the early 1990s and the introduction of the Federal Goods and Services Tax (GST), which caused people to curtail their spending.

The Role of Advertisers

There are two continuing trends in the advertising industry. First, the share of advertising dollars has continued to increase for TV and decrease for newspapers, while radio has remained stable (Canada, 1994). In 1992 the total advertising revenue for all media was Can$8.295 billion. The second trend is the emphasis on voluntary regulation. For example, the Canadian Advertising Foundation administers the Canadian Code of Advertising Standards, which is the principal instrument of self-regulation. The foundation also administers guidelines for gender portrayals and a broadcast code for advertising to children. As noted later in this chapter, changes to tobacco and alcohol advertising will alter the nature of advertising in print and broadcast media.

The Role of Regulators

There is indirect and direct government regulation and industry self-regulation. There is no government ministry directly responsible for the newspaper industry. Instead, it is indirectly regulated by the federal government through Canadian ownership regulations that prevent foreign companies from owning more than 25 percent of a Canadian newspaper. The broadcasting and telecommunications industries, including cable, pay TV and specialty TV, are regulated by the Department of Canadian Heritage and the CRTC, as well as other ministries such as Industry Canada (ownership) and Revenue Canada (tariffs and taxes). Canadian Heritage develops broadcasting policies and programs in light of social, cultural and economic objectives to support the production and presentation of radio and TV programs and access to these cultural products, and the development of cultural industries. More specifically, the CRTC develops policies and regulations for local programming, Canadian content, program development, network and syndication programming, pay, pay-per-view and specialty services, community channels, and other cable-delivered programming services; pre-clears scripts of advertisements for alcoholic beverages for broadcast on Canadian radio, TV and specialty services; and certifies Canadian productions for broadcast.

The Canadian Broadcast Standards Council, with the approval of the CRTC and the support of the Canadian Association of Broadcasters, promotes the self-regulation of the private broadcasting industry through a number of codes on ethics, violence and sex-role portrayals.

Until recently, one of the distinguishing characteristics of the regulatory framework in Canada was a total ban on tobacco advertising and significant restrictions on alcohol advertising. The Canadian Tobacco Products Control Act (1989) was overturned by the Supreme Court of Canada in 1995. As a result, all tobacco advertising is now legal. Health and Welfare Canada is currently working on replacement legislation. For TV, the Code for Broadcast Advertising of Alcoholic Beverages was also declared invalid in a federal court ruling in 1995. The code previously prohibited broadcast advertising of spirits-based beverages containing more than 7 percent alcohol by volume and restricted advertising of other alcoholic beverages. According to the CRTC, all alcoholic beverages can now be advertised, but they must be reviewed by the CRTC and the appropriate provincial authority where they will be broadcast.

In general, then, it is fair to state that the Canadian public is well served by the variety of media outlets and programming choices and accepts the federal government's role in promoting and protecting the cultural industries. The dark cloud on the horizon involves how the government will respond to the WTO ruling and the court rulings on alcohol and cigarette advertising. The industry environment is clearly beginning to challenge the supremacy of the symbolic environment in the governance of Canada's cultural industries.

Media Industry Analysis

Newspapers

Circulation, which has dropped for the sixth year in a row for the 105 daily newspapers, now stands at almost 5.2 million copies a day (Canadian Newspaper Association, 1996). The largest circulation papers are the *Toronto Star* (519,000), *Globe & Mail* (314,000), *Journal de Montreal* (287,000), *Toronto Sun* (250,000), *La Presse* (211,000), and *Vancouver Sun* (210,00). The 19 tabloid dailies continue to gain ground on broadsheets. The former now account for one of every four newspapers sold in Canada, or 1.3 million copies.

Although individual companies have unique strategies, the trend in the industry is toward fewer newspapers and few owners. The prime example of increased industry concentration is Hollinger's 1996 purchase of a controlling interest in Canada's largest newspaper chain, Southam Inc. Southam remains the largest publisher, with 32 dailies accounting for 31.8 percent of circulation. Hollinger owns 26 dailies and has 9.6 percent of circulation. The Hollinger-Southam combination with a total of 58 Canadian dailies controls 41 percent of the total market. Both companies are controlled by Conrad Black (Wells, 1996). *Financial Post* magazine's annual list of the top 500 Canadian corporations ranked Southam as the sixth largest media company in Canada, with revenues of Can$1.022 billion. There is concern that Black's companies control too many major newspapers and therefore amount to a monopoly of ideas. The federal government's response was to approve the deal despite an appeal of the decision by the Council of Canadians.

The Thomson Corporation is taking a different strategy from that of Hollinger. Thomson Newspapers is the largest publisher of regional and local papers in England. They rank second in Canada in terms of both daily newspapers published and total circulation (Thomson, 1996). In the U.S., Thomson publishes the third largest number of daily newspapers and ranks seventh in total circulation. *Financial Post 500* for 1996 listed The Thomson Corporation as the largest media company in Canada, with revenues of Can$9.916 billion. Thomson, as part of its corporate strategy to refocus their activities on information services and the travel industry, purchased West Publishing in 1996 for Can$3.425 billion and reduced the number of dailies in Canada and the United States from 163 to 80. The company still retains 12.3 percent of total Canadian newspaper circulation and publishes the prestigious *Globe and Mail* newspaper.

Sun Media Corporation, part of Rogers Communication until 1995, has 10 dailies and 11.2 percent of circulation. Among its publications are four tabloid newspapers in Ottawa, Toronto, Calgary and Edmonton. The other major newspaper chain, Quebecor Inc., has four dailies in Quebec and 8.6 percent of total circulation. Quebecor, although comparatively small as a national publisher, is one of the largest printers in North America. The largest circulation newspaper in the country, the *Toronto Star,* is still independently owned and operated by Torstar.

Content for the newspaper industry comes from reporters, the news agencies of Southam and the Canadian Press, and other national and international press agencies such as American Press, Reuters, and Agence Presse. Local and regional news comes from Canadian sources, and international news comes from a variety of sources. The largest content source outside of Canada is the United States.

The newspaper industry faces a number of challenges: attracting young readers, competition from alternative weeklies in most major cities, postal rate increases, fluctuating newsprint prices, the GST and, most importantly, the challenge of new technologies such as CD-ROM, multimedia, online databases, and the Internet. For example, national classified services on the Internet bypass newspaper classifieds. The digitalization of most forms of communication has rendered many of the newspaper industries strategies obsolete. There are, however, little systematic and reliable economic data on these kinds of global changes. For example, national surveys of Internet usage vary considerably.

Cable

The cable industry is undergoing a period of increased concentration and new alliances as it gears up for increased deregulation and competition and the promotion of its two-way communication capabilities for the development of the information highway in Canada. The top four cable operators, Rogers Cable TV (2,264,137 subscribers), Vidéotron (1,653,086 subscribers), Shaw Cablesystems (1,632,301 subscribers), and Cogeco Cable (745,228 subscribers), control more than 77 percent of the total market (Canadian Cable Television Association 1996).

After the recession of 1991, the cable companies went on a consolidation spree. Rogers Cable Systems, the preeminent cable provider in Canada, bought MacLean Hunter for Can$3.1 billion in a hostile takeover bid. At the time, MacLean Hunter owned a vast publishing empire including Canada weekly newsmagazine *MacLean's* and the Sun newspaper chain. The acquisition of MacLean Hunter left Rogers with some debt problems. The company has addressed their high debt load by selling off the Sun newspaper chain to a management group, much of its U.S. holdings, its Calgary TV station, and cable systems serving 300,000 subscribers.

In the province of Quebec, Vidéotron is the largest cable operator and has a critical mass of contiguous cable TV licenses unique in North America, including Montreal and Quebec, the two largest metropolitan areas. Groupe Vidéotron also controls Télé-Métropole Inc., the leading private French-language TV broadcasting company in North America. Télé-Métropole covers most of Quebec through its TVA network comprising six stations and four affiliates. The network flagship station holds the highest ratings in the Montreal market and leads all Canadian TV stations in total viewing hours. All the company's other stations dominate their local markets. Vidéotron is selling its British cable holdings for Can$825 million. This will reduce their debt to three times cash flow, making them one of the least indebted cable companies in North America. The company bought CFCF Inc. in Montreal in 1996. Vidéotron is expected to keep CFCF's 427,000 cable subscribers and sell its broadcasting arm. Hearings are under way at the CRTC to decide on issues on monopoly in the Montreal-area market, as Vidéotron controls both of the commercial TV networks in Quebec, the TVA network, and through its purchase of CFCF, Television Quatre Saison. The company also has 70 video store franchisees and industry expertise in two-way communication through its Vidéoway multimedia system.

Total pre-tax profits of cable TV in 1995 were almost Can$50 million higher than in 1994 (Fig. 3-1); more than 90 percent of the operating systems were profitable in 1995. The average profit-to-revenue ratio of all cable systems was 17.1 percent in 1995 (Canadian Heritage, 1996a). In addition to debt reduction, increased concentration and higher profits, the major companies are exploring interactive services, home monitoring, Internet access, videogames, and related specialty services (Enchin and Surtees, 1996; Gooderham, 1996). For example, the cable companies jointly launched a high-speed Internet access service called Wave. Of course the new service requires the installation of fiber-optic wiring. Upgrading cable lines with fiber-optics is essential for the cable companies if they want to compete successfully with the larger telecommunication companies in connecting people to the information highway and delivering information and communication services.

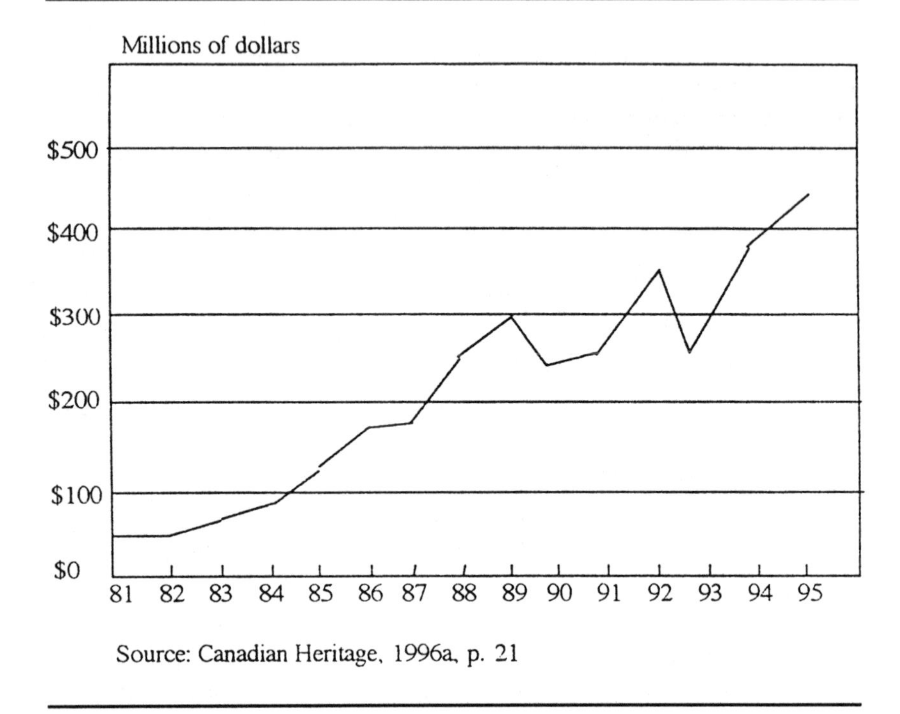

FIGURE 3-1. *Cable television pre-tax profits.*

Pay Television and Specialty Services

In 1995 pay TV had revenues of Can$124.6 million, expenses of Can$110.5 million, and a pre-tax profit of Can$16.4 million, and Can$31.4 million was spent on Canadian programs. Specialty services had revenues of Can$451.8 million, expenses of Can$384.1 million, pre-tax profits of Can$57.6 million, and Can$206.2 million was spent on Canadian programming (Canadian Heritage, 1996b). The four English-language channels approved for immediate broadcast (1997) have stated that they plan to spend Can$137.3 million during the next 7 years on Canadian programming (Saunders, 1996).

The specialty TV industry is not the biggest portion of the broadcasting sector, yet it is the fastest growing and is expected to grow further with the recent announcement of 23 new licenses. The pay and specialty TV audience share for English-language TV among cable households has grown from 13.8 percent in 1989 to 29.7 percent in 1996 (Canadian Cable Television Association, 1996). The top two English-language specialty services, in terms of subscribers, were CBC's Newsworld (7.3 million) and YTV (7.2 million). The top two French-language services were TV5 (6 million) and RDI (5.6 million). The top pay-TV service was the Family Channel (407,093).

Ownership is typically Canadian, with some joint partnerships with U.S. providers. Government rules state that a U.S. specialty service can be bumped from cable systems when the same type of Canadian channels is available. This has led to a dispute regarding country music channels. It was resolved when the Nashville Channel bought into the Canadian equivalent.

The trends toward increased narrowcasting was boosted considerably by the approval of 22 new specialty TV licenses and one pay-TV license in 1996. Table 3-1 summarizes the start date, ownership, broadcast language and service reach of these channels.

The specialty channels were singled out because the different media companies that are involved in existing pay-TV and specialty services and the newly licensed services reveal the different ownership concentrations and cooperative arrangements between cable companies, newspaper chains, broadcast networks, independent producers, foreign companies, and other organizations. Table 3-2 illustrates key companies involved in the new services, along with other existing services. These relationships are symbolic of cross-media ownership and the need to hedge one's bets of where the market is going and which technologies will be accepted by consumers. Evaluating these new services will also be one way to measure the financial and cultural success of the government policies. What is clear so far is that there is no evidence of convergence between the telecommunication and broadcasting companies.

Emerging Media Economic Issues and Their Impact on the Global Media Marketplace

Several key issues will determine the success of Canada's communication policies and industry strategies and the nation's overall competitiveness in the global marketplace. These are the introduction of more new communication technologies, the continuation of the trends toward digitalization of broadcasting, the development of the Internet and increased narrowcasting, and the revamping of government policies to protect the cultural industries.

In many respects, it would appear that technological nationalism is still apparent in attempts to promote new technologies and new services such as direct-to-home satellites, local multipoint communication services (LMCS), and Internet access (Charland, 1986). The reality is, however, that although the will to promote different technologies by the government and its regulatory bodies is clearly evident, the success of many of these new endeavors is still questionable. The most obvious disappointment is the failure of direct-to-home satellite services (Brehl, 1996; Enchin and Rowan, 1996). Thus there is reason to be skeptical about whether many of these new services will find their niche in the marketplace and a sufficient number of customers to ensure their success. This skepticism extends equally to the evolution of the Internet.

Table 3-1. New Speciality Channels in Canada

Startup Date	Ownership	Language/Reach
1997		
La Canal Nouvelles	Télé-Métropole	French/Quebec
La Canal Vie	Radiomutuel	French/national
Comedy Network	Baton (65), Astral (15), Shaw (15), Films Rozon (5)	English/national
CTV N1	CTV Network (100)	English/national
History & Entertainment	Alliance (88), CTV (12)	English/national
Musimax	Musique Plus	French/national
Teletoon	Family Channel (53), YTV (27), Nelvana (10), Cinar (10)	English/French, national
1999[a]		
Canadian Learning TV	CHUM (60), Olympus Mgmt (20)	English/national
Home & Garden TV	Your Channel TV (Atlantis) (80), Scripps Howard (20)	English/national
MuchMoreMusic	CHUM	English/national
Odyssey TV	Five individual owners	Greek/Ontario
Outdoor life	Rogers (30), Baton & Ellis (37), Outdoor Life Network (33)	English/national
Prime TV	Global	English/national
Pulse 24	CHUM (70), Toronto Sun (30)	English/national
ROBTV	Globe & Mail (50), WIC (26), Cancom (24)	English/national
S3 Regional sports	CTV (40), Rogers (20), Molson (20), LMC Int'l (20)	English/national
South Asian Television	Asian Television Network International (100)	Asian/Ontario
Space	CHUM	English/national
Sports/Specials PPV	CTV (60), Molson (20), LMC (20)	English/national
Sportsscope Plus	Clairvest Group (66), First Control (28), Digimation (6)	English/national
Star-TV	City-TV	English/national
Talk-TV	Baton	English/national
Treehouse TV	YTV	English/national

Source: Compiled by the author from various sources.

[a]The 1999 date means that the service is either digital or requires negotiation with cable networks to get carried.

Table 3-2. Cross-Media Ownership of Selected Canadian Companies

Cable ownership	
Rogers Communications	The shopping channel (TSC), Outdoor life, S3 Regional sports
Shaw Communications	YTV, Country Music TV, The Comedy network, Treehouse TV, Teletoon
Newspaper ownership	
Globe and Mail	ROBTV
Toronto Sun Publishing	Pulse 24
Broadcast ownership	
Baton Broadcasting	The Comedy Network, Talk-TV, Outdoor Life
CBC	Newsworld, Show case
CHUM	MuchMusic, Bravo!, Canadian Learning TV, MuchMoreMusic, Space: The imagination channel, Star-TV, Pulse 24, Musimax, Alberta Educational Communications Network (ACCESS),
CanWest Global	Prime TV,
CTV	CTV N1, History and entertainment network, S3 regional sports, Sports/Specials PPV
Moffat Communications	WTN
Radiomutuel	MusiquePlus, Le Canal Vie,
Pelmorex	The weather channel
Télé-Métropole	La Canal Nouvelles
Western International Comm.	Superchannel (west only), Family channel, Home Theatre (west only), Moviemax, ROBTv
Producer ownership	
Alliance Communications	Showcase, History and entertainment network
Astral Communications	The Movie Network (east only), Family Channel, Moviepix, Canal D, Canal Famille, SuperChannel, SuperEcran, Comedy Network, Teletoon
Atlantis Communications	Life Network, YTV, Home & Garden TV, Teletoon (through YTV)
Cinar Films	Teletoon
Nelvana	Teletoon
Others	
NetStar Communications (formerly Labatt's)	TSN, RDS, Discovery Channel, Viewer's choice PPV
Molson	S3Regional Sports, Sports/Speciality PPV
Canadian Satellite Comm.	ROBTv
Clairvest Group	Sportsscope Plus

Sources: Atherton, 1996; company web sites; CRTC information.

New technologies are important beyond simply providing new channels of communication. The V-chip technology and its rating system are an example of how technologies and government policy come together. In 1996, the CRTC delayed by 1 year plans to implement an electronic rating system of violence, language and sex. The delay was allowed to enable the industry to perfect the V-chip technology. Under the new timetable, trials started in January 1997 of the improved V-chip system and its programming classification system. The issue is complicated by the U.S. decision to implement another type of classification system. It is likely that Canada will need to harmonize whatever system it adopts with the U.S. system, although it is still hoped that cable companies will apply the Canadian system to U.S. broadcasts.

The most obvious trends are the continuing digitalization of all media, the growth of the Internet, and continued narrowcasting. The Task Force on the Implementation of Digital Radio states that all AM and FM stations will be converted to digital by 2010 (Bray, 1996). Satellite delivery of digital radio is expected no later than 2004. The installation costs for digital radio is estimated at approximately Can$80,000 per signal (Bray, 1996). The Canadian Associates of Broadcasters Task Force on the Implementation of Digital Television forecasts an optimistic start-up date of mid-1998. The problem is that both radio and TV stations need to invest at a time when profits are low. An equally important barrier is the need for manufacturers to produce digital radios and TVs and for consumers to buy them. Because consumers have been burned by buying the wrong technologies (beta videocassette recorders, digital audiotape recorders) or worry about buying obsolete technologies, there is a healthy skepticism in the marketplace. There seems little doubt, though, that the wholesale transition from analog to digital radio and TV will have important economic impacts on the national market, especially if it occurs as rapidly as the shift from vinyl albums to music compact discs.

As far as the Internet is concerned, Internet radio is taking off as youth-oriented stations and the CBC establish web pages. One advantage of Internet radio is that it will enable precise market research information based on the number of hits, although it is too early for there to be any reliable data. Unfortunately the Internet and its various spin-offs are growing too fast for any organization or government agency to know with any certainty how to proceed. The economic status of the Internet needs to be better understood, and data need to be collected on an annual basis if researchers are to have a better idea of how the Internet is changing other industries.

The introduction of 23 specialty channels during the next 3 years will increase the trend toward narrowcasting, as well as the demand for Canadian programming. What is ironic is that the CBC TV and radio services are undergoing radical cutbacks to their funding while reaffirming their commitment to Canadian programming, especially during prime time. The target budget reductions for 1998 for the entire CBC system are Can$414 million. Reductions in just under half of this amount have been achieved, but at a cost of some 1,700 jobs attributable to retirements, layoffs and the elimination of vacant positions. The leaner CBC will have more repeats, fewer programs, less sports, smaller program budgets, more of a focus on Canadian programs, and a total of 4,000 fewer employees (CBC/SRC, 1996). Depending on whom one talks to, these cuts are devastating and the end of the CBC and public broadcasting or are a necessary reality adjustment for a bloated bureaucracy that is unaccustomed to the downsizing experienced by most other government departments. The result of these two developments is on one hand a promise to spend money on made-in-Canada programming and, on the other hand, a fiscal obligation to reduce spending. It is clearly too early to know whether one event will cancel out the other one, with the result that there will be no net gain for Canadian program providers.

The latest tendency is a strong, but mixed, reaction by governments, private industry and the general public to the WTO ruling that so-called split-run magazines—those with American content and Canadian advertisements—could be sold in Canada. The calls for a review of all cultural protection mechanisms is but the first order of business in what will be a heated debate between forces supporting either the symbolic or industries environment described in this chapter.

Future Research

More research needs to be conducted on the Internet, the new TV specialty channels, cross-media ownership, the newly licensed services such as LMCS, personal communication services, satellite-based, 24-hour, digital pay-audio compact disc music service, services that are licensed but not yet available such as direct-to-home transmission, and the impacts of the convergence policy. The convergence policy is based on the idea that the basic competition is between the cable and telecommunications industries, two lanes to the information highway. This is a decidedly unbalanced competition. The entire cable industry had revenues of Can$2.532 billion in 1995. The telecommunication service industries had revenues of Can$17.4 billion in 1994. Clearly, the telecommunications companies have a revenue advantage over cable companies.

Additional competition between the cable and telecommunication companies will be created when the two national and one regional license holders for LMCS, or what is called the third lane of the information highway, begin their services. Although this new wireless technology, operating at very high radio frequencies, is intended to increase competition and lower costs, the larger question is can this new delivery system generate sufficient revenues to be competitive? Because the convergence policy is still recent, there is plenty of time to research how the telecommunication, cable and new LCMS services will compete with each other.

When it comes to collecting data about some of these areas, it is hoped that the North American Industry Classification System standards will help. Organizations such as Statistics Canada, Industry Canada and Heritage Canada need to be adequately funded and staffed so that they can carry out these functions. Much of the most valuable data for this chapter came from government analysts. It would be a shame to lose their work in the future because of government downsizing.

Finally, Table 3-2, listing the complex ownership relationships behind the new specialty channels, demonstrates a need for more research into cross-media ownership issues. It is often easy to complain about powerful corporate concentrations such as the Conrad Black's domination of the Canadian newspaper business through his control of Hollinger and Southam group; however, there are often inadequate or out-of-date data supporting these kinds of arguments. What tax breaks are given the different media companies as they merge or buy each other out? Are different government departments working at cross purposes in their support and regulation of the same industries? How does the interplay between the cultural, industry and technological environments get translated into programming, jobs, and profits in light of continued calls for open markets and globalization?

Notes

[1] Approximately 76 percent of all Canadians speak English, while the remaining population speaks French. There are, however, other languages spoken in Canada by different cultural groups but English and French are the dominant languages.

References

Atherton, T. (1996). Wanted: Your TV. *The Ottawa Citizen,* September 21, pp. B1–2.

Audley, P. (1983). *Canada's Cultural Industries: Broadcasting, Publishing, Records and Film.* Toronto, ON: James Lorimer.

Babe, R. E. (1996). Convergence and the new technologies. In: Dorland, M. (ed.). *The Cultural Industries in Canada: Problems, Policies and Prospects.* Toronto, ON: James Lorimer, pp. 283–307.

Bray, D. (1996). Radio revs up for the Internet. *Broadcaster*, March, p. 21.

Brehl, R. (1996). What's in the stars for satellite TV? *The Ottawa Citizen,* November 12, p. F2.

Canada. (1991). Broadcasting Act. R. S., C. B-11 amended by C.16 (1st Supp.), C. 10.
Canada (1994). *A Question of Balance: Report of the Task Force on Canadian Magazine Industry.* Ottawa, ON: Ministry of Supply and Services.
Canada (1995). *Canada's Culture, Heritage and Identity: A Statistical Perspective.* Ottawa, ON: Statistics Canada, Education, Culture and Tourism Division.
Canada (1996a). *Making Our Voices Heard: Canadian Broadcasting and Film for the 21st Century.* (Report of the Mandate Review Committee). Ottawa, ON: Minister of Supply and Services.
Canada (1996b). *Building the Information Society: Moving Canada Into the 21st Century.* Ottawa, ON: Minister of Supply and Services.
Canadian Cable Television Association (1996). *Cable TV Facts 1995–1996.* Ottawa, ON: Canadian Cable Television Association.
Canadian Heritage (1996a). *Canadian Cable Television: Industry Overview 1995.* Ottawa, ON: Canadian Heritage, Broadcasting Regulatory Policy.
Canadian Heritage (1996b). *Pay-TV and Specialty Services: Industry Overview 1995.* Ottawa, ON: Canadian Heritage, Broadcasting Regulatory Policy.
Canadian Newspaper Association (1996). Available on-line: http://www.cna-acj.ca/english/Facts.html
CBC/SRC (1996). *Annual Report 1995–96.* Ottawa, ON: Canadian Broadcasting Corporation.
Charland, M. (1986). Technological nationalism. *Canadian Journal of Political and Social Theory* 10(1/2):196–220.
Dorland, M. (ed.) (1996a). *The Cultural Industries in Canada: Problems, Policies and Prospects.* Toronto, ON: James Lorimer.
Dorland, M. (1996b). Cultural industries and the Canadian experience: Reflections on the emergence of a field. In: Dorland, M. (ed.). *The Cultural Industries in Canada: Problems, Policies and Prospects.* Toronto, ON: James Lorimer, pp. 347–365.
Dornan, C. (1996). Newspaper publishing. In: Dorland, M. (ed.). *The Cultural Industries in Canada: Problems, Policies and Prospects.* Toronto, ON: James Lorimer, pp. 60–92.
Eggertson, L. (1997). Culture not safe under NAFTA. *The Globe & Mail,* January 29, A12–13.
Enchin, H. (1996). Coscient charts international course. *The Globe & Mail,* December 24, pp. B1, B4.
Enchin, H., and Rowan, G. (1996). DTH use illegal, Ottawa warns. *The Globe & Mail,* November 14, pp. B1, B8.
Enchin, H., and Surtees, L. (1996). Cable firms launch Internet access service. *The Globe & Mail,* November 13, p. B20.
Fagan, D., and Eggertson, L. (1997). Canada loses magazine case. *The Globe & Mail,* January 17, pp. A1, A7.
Filion, M. (1996). Radio. In: Dorland, M. (ed.). *The Cultural Industries in Canada: Problems, Policies and Prospects.* Toronto, ON: James Lorimer, pp. 118–141.
Gooderham, M. (1996). Newspapers enter the new, wired world. *The Globe & Mail,* July 23, p. C3.

Information Highway Advisory Council. (1995). *Connection, Community, Content: The Challenge of the Information Highway.* (Final report of the Information Highway Advisory Council). Ottawa, ON: Ministry of Supply and Services.

Jeffrey, L. (1996). Private television and cable. In: Dorland, M. (ed.). *The Cultural Industries in Canada: Problems, Policies and Prospects.* Toronto, ON: James Lorimer, pp. 203–256.

Lorimer, R., and Duxbury, N. (1994). Of culture, the economy, cultural production and cultural producers: An orientation. *Canadian Journal of Communication* 19(3/4):259–289.

McFadyen, S., Finn, A., Hoskins, C., and Lorimer, R. (eds.). (1994). Special issue on cultural development in an open economy. *Canadian Journal of Communication* 19(3/4).

Melody, W., Salter, L., and Heyer, P. (eds.). (1981). *Culture, Communication, and Dependency: The Tradition of H. A. Innis.* Norwood, NJ: Ablex.

Mozes, D., Sciadas, G., and McCarrell, H. (1996). *Measuring the Global Information Infrastructure for a Global Information Economy: Concepts and Performance Indicators.* Ottawa, ON: Industry Canada.

O'Neill, J. (1997). Protection of arts open to negotiation. *The Ottawa Citizen,* January 29, pp. A1–2.

Rogers Communications (1996). *Annual Report 1995.* Toronto, ON: Rogers Communications.

Saunders, D. (1996). Licensees promise to spend. *The Globe & Mail,* September 6, pp. A10–11.

Stewart, W. B. (1983). Canadian social system and Canadian broadcasting audiences. In: Singer, B. D. (ed.). *Communications in Canadian Society.* Don Mills, ON: Addison-Wesley, pp. 17–40.

Thomson Corporation (1996). *Annual Report 1995.* Toronto, ON: Thomson Corporation.

Wells, J. (1996). The prince of papers. *Maclean's* 109(November 11):56–61.

4

MEXICO

Charles N. Davis

Despite its economic struggles, the United Mexican States, a federation of 31 states and a federal district comprising Mexico City, remains a formidable competitor for Latin American dominance of the mass media. Mexico holds a pivotal position in the Western Hemisphere because of its economic, geographic and historical centrality in the Americas. It is Latin America's largest economy (Alexander, 1996), borders the United States and the often troubled Central American region, and has by far the largest Spanish-speaking population in the continent. A growing population of 82 million, highlighted by an emerging middle class, will profit from imported technology and a newly privatized telecommunications infrastructure.

Mexico continues to reel from double-digit inflation fallout from the 1995–96 collapse of the peso, coupled with political intrigue, as the ruling Institutional Revolutionary Party (PRI) faces serious challenge for the first time in decades. Mexico's mass media have endured crises before: the peso also collapsed in 1976, 1982 and 1987, but the political situation is far more precarious than in crises past. After nearly 20 years of economic stagnation, the PRI faces real political peril for the first time in decades. Political reform doubtless will usher in economic change, a cycle Mexican media outlets know well.

Mexico's gross domestic product (GDP) grew from U.S.$171 billion in 1984 to U.S.$282 billion in 1996 (Bear Stearns, 1996). Per capita GDP was U.S.$3,872 in 1993, up roughly 3 percent from U.S.$3,333 in 1991. The figure represents about 15 percent of the per capita GDP of the United States. Although low by U.S. standards, Mexico's per capita GDP actually has risen dramatically from its 1987 post–World War II low of U.S.$1,537 (Alexander, 1996).

Unlike many other world economies, Mexico is among a handful of Latin American nations in which the income gap actually increased from 1960 to 1990. Inflation-adjusted wages rose 32.3 percent between 1988 and 1992, but this brought purchasing power back up only to the level that it had occupied before the 1987 collapse of the peso. Meanwhile, the inflation-adjusted minimum wage fell by about 40 percent from 1988 to 1992, and the share of total wealth held by the bottom two-fifths of the population fell to 12 percent in 1992, down from 15 percent in 1988 (Condesa, 1995).

Mexico's economy has suffered from a myriad of arcane and restrictive regulations, corrupt bureaucracies maintained by nepotism and colonialism, and the lack of a developed middle class. This last is the most direct result of colonialism, in which the government monopolized most economic activity, delegating the bulk of the remainder as patronage to a handful of powerful families. Business relationships in Mexico have traditionally been conducted more on a hierarchical patron–client basis than as free contractual arrangements.

This overall pattern was reinforced during the latter part of the 19th century and the first three quarters of the 20th century. By the early 1980s, more than 50 percent of all investment in the Mexican economy was being made by the public sector, and more than half of the GDP represented direct or indirect government spending, with the state reaching further and further into the infrastructure of the economy (Condesa, 1995). Yet Mexico's mass media stand on the verge of widespread expansion for the first time since the introduction of television (TV), thanks in large part to economic reforms brought on by the 1995–96 collapse of the peso.

Most importantly, Mexico enjoys the advantage of Spanish-speaking media. Brazil currently is Latin America's top media producer, but this could change as the number of Spanish-speaking citizens of the region continues to outpace that of Portuguese speakers. Mexico City has used this advantage to become the dominant media center of the region, according to Consulate General Antonio Oscarenza of the President's Office of Media Policy (A. Oscarenza, personal communication, November 19, 1996) and other sources (Drost, 1991).

Mexico must overcome its aristocratic past, however, if its media economy is to continue to grow. Ownership of many mass media outlets has grown so concentrated that new entries are met by a host of monopolistic practices. The market is dominated by Televisa, whose major shareholders now include three media billionaires—Emilio Azcarraga Milmo, Romulo O'Farrill and Miguel Aleman Velasco. Velasco's father, Miguel Aleman Valdes, took a personal role in the development of TV in Mexico as president from 1946 to 1952 (Drost, 1991). Facing a virtual TV monopoly by the 1970s, the Mexican government then tried to undo the damage by creating its own commercial operation, Instituto Mexicano de Television (Imevision), which has failed spectacularly. Indeed, Televisa's only major rivals, Television Azteca, a government network privatized in 1993, and pay-TV operator Multivision, pose no real threat to Televisa.

As Mexico's media institutions move from the crisis management mode, consolidation may wane. Televisa, Organizacion Editorial Mexicana and other large media corporations are shedding noncore businesses, returning to content delivery, and strengthening cash reserves in the wake of the collapse of the peso (Dombey, 1996). Many smaller print and broadcast properties—likely targets of consolidation—have folded as a result of the peso's steady devaluation. Expansion by Mexico's largest media conglomerates will continue, but on a global scale.

Major Media Industries

Telecommunications

Mexico's media markets are dominated by TV, but not to the extent of other smaller Latin American nations. Telecommunications is fairly well developed in the commercial centers of the country but often does not reach into many of the less developed regions (Winsor, 1995). More-advanced communications technology, such as satellite-based TV and integrated services digital network (ISDN) telecommunications, is practically nonexistent. This will change, however, as the Mexican government has eased many of the restrictions on imported technology that slowed the growth of cellular communications and personal computers in the marketplace.

After decades of neglect, Mexico's telecommunications infrastructure finally appears to be on the verge of modernization. In fact, Mexico is rapidly acquiring the largest and most comprehensive and modern telecommunications network in Latin America. In 1995 the government relented to the demands of the Mexican business community and removed the last of the barriers to telecommunications competition (AT&T, 1994). Mexico's telephone market, estimated at $6 billion in 1996, is expected to grow to $15 billion in 10 years because of rapid growth in telecommunications technology. Telefonos de Mexico, long a symbol of the inefficient state-owned businesses that crippled economic development in Mexico, was privatized in 1991 and now faces competition from eight new phone companies, including joint ventures between Mexican firms and AT&T, MCI Communications Corporation and Atlantic Bell Corporation (Rangel, 1996).

The North American Free Trade Agreement (NAFTA), which became effective January 1, 1994, reduces barriers to the Mexican telecommunications equipment market and for the first time allows foreign entries to provide long-distance services and ISDN lines. Mexico's demand for imported telecommunications services is expected to grow by 42 percent by the year 2000 (Aviles, 1996). United States exports of telecommunications equipment and enhanced services, which in 1991 reached $750 million and $22 million, respectively, are expected to grow significantly under NAFTA (Nolan, 1994).

The North American Free Trade Agreement will speed Mexico's telecommunications development through provisions streamlining testing and certification requirements of equipment while eliminating more than 80 percent of the tariffs on U.S. telecommunication exports to Mexico. It also provides that public telecommunications networks be made available on reasonable, nondiscriminatory terms and conditions. Of utmost importance is the movement toward compatibility of network services in Mexico, Canada and the United States. The North American Free Trade Agreement frees telecommunication network providers to operate contracted networks, ensuring exports of expertise as well as equipment (Nolan, 1994).

Competition should lower the cost of installing a telephone (now $240 for homes and $415 for businesses [Winsor, 1995]) and initiate the development of advanced telecommunications applications, including the installation of fiber-optic cable and integrated digital networks (Aviles, 1996). Cellular telecommunications has grown spectacularly: the number of cellular customers in Mexico topped one million in 1996. The vast majority of telecommunications products still are imported, however, creating a vast trade deficit in communications technology (Winsor, 1995). Observers cite Mexico's developing telecommunications market as the next great consumer niche for international investors and predict a rapid rise in consumer acceptance of advanced communications technologies. The resultant growth in ISDN- and satellite-based communications could enable Mexico to bypass other nations in the region (Grossman, 1993).

BROADCASTING. The potential of Mexico's consumer markets is best illustrated by the broadcast industry. In 1995 there were 50 million TV households in Mexico, which translates to a 95 percent penetration rate. Color TV, however, accounted for only 15.9 million TV households (31 percent) in 1994 (Electronic media, 1995). While cable is gaining popularity as the number of cable-ready TV sets in Mexico increases, cable penetration remains low at

11 percent of TV households, for a total of 1.7 million subscribers. Radio remains a very important medium, as many rural households depend on the nation's 900 stations for all of their media consumption. Urban centers are marked by fierce competition between large numbers of competing broadcasters. Mexico City alone has 25 FM and 35 AM radio stations broadcasting in Spanish (Condesa, 1995).

Seven networks control Mexico's broadcast TV stations. There are two government-funded channels (11 and 22), run by Imevision, and two main terrestrial networks, Grupo Televisa and TV Azteca. Another dozen or so independent networks located in Mexico City broadcast in Spanish nationwide, but reception and availability vary widely (Condesa, 1995).

Mexico's broadcast market has undergone tremendous change in the past few years as the government has sold off its state-owned networks to private investors. As in most Latin American countries, ownership of the media is concentrated in the hands of individual entrepreneurs and a handful of powerful conglomerates. The movement of broadcast properties from the state to a small number of Mexican businessmen has made several Mexican broadcasters among the richest people in the world.

Dominating the market is Telesistema Mexicano, reportedly the largest media conglomerate in the Third World. Known to viewers as Televisa, it wields tremendous economic, cultural and political influence in Latin America, reaching some 415 million viewers (Villegas, 1996). Unabashedly pro-PRI, Televisa has former government spokespeople on its board and praises the incumbent administration in its newscasts (Drost, 1991).

Televisa's $1.3 billion conglomerate includes TV stations, cable networks, radio networks, programming for broadcast and cable, record production, video production and distribution, cinemas, and advertising and marketing, and it has recently diversified into real estate, tourism, hotels, night clubs and discotheques. Overall, Televisa controls 80 percent of Mexico's TV market and 70 percent of the newspaper and magazine publishing industry (Dombey, 1996). Televisa sells programming to 90 countries and last year joined forces with Rupert Murdoch's News Corporation, the international arm of U.S. cable company Telecommunications, Inc. and Brazil's Organizacoes Globo to bring direct broadcast service to Latin America (Malkin, 1995).

For Televisa, which also owns a 25 percent stake in Univision, the largest provider of Spanish-language programming in the United States, the News Corporation alliance offers a chance for global delivery of programming and new customers in Latin America. Direct-satellite TV, in fact, may provide Televisa with its first competition in years. In 1995, the first direct TV service in Latin America was launched by Hughes Communication, Multivision,

Venezuelan programmer Cisneros Group, and Brazil programmer Televisa (Malkin, 1995).

A review of Televisa's competition confirms that its only competition likely will come from other Latin American nations. Imevision, formed as a public holding company in 1968, operates two national networks, Red Nacional 7 (Canal 7) and Red Nacional 13 (Canal 13), as well as several regional and specialty channels. Canal 13 was nationalized in 1973 to serve as a balance of sorts to the private sector, but it has suffered from management coups and financial cuts for years (Winsor, 1995).

The difficulties of Canal 13 and public broadcasting in general led to the concentration in broadcast ownership in Mexico. To achieve greater efficiencies and to cut costs, the two leading networks were allowed to merge to form Televisa in 1973. Televisa now runs two national networks (Cadena Canel 2 and Cadena Canal 5), a regional network of six stations (Cadena Canal 4) and a local channel for Mexico City (Canal 9). It also owns the dominant cable companies in Mexico City.

PRINT MEDIA. Thanks in large part to the infrastructural weaknesses of the telecommunications market, Mexico's print media enjoys nearly total control of the advertising market. The 15 daily newspapers printed in Mexico City and more than 320 other regional newspapers combine for a claimed daily circulation of more than 20 million copies (Winsor, 1995). Although large, the number still represents only a fraction of the population; few Mexicans read daily newspapers. In fact, while the circulation figure appears to be the largest in Latin America, publishers are known to exaggerate circulation in order to attract advertising revenue. Actual circulation and readership levels are believed to be significantly lower (Winsor, 1995).

Ownership of Mexico's print media industry is far more diversified than in the broadcast market, but the industry is reeling from the collapse of the peso. The number of newspapers fell by 10 percent in 1995 to pre-1990 levels (Alexander, 1996), and the magazine market remained static despite the launch of several new titles. Advertising is down, newsprint costs have skyrocketed, and readers have reduced spending on nonessential consumer goods, causing the demise of several of the nation's oldest newspapers (Rangel, 1995). The country's largest newspaper group, Organizacion Editorial Mexicana (OEM), owns 90 papers, but total readership of OEM newspapers is equivalent to less than 15 percent of the nation's total circulation.

The largest daily newspapers are all independent, with the exception of the government-owned *El Nacional*. The most prestigious national daily, *Excelsior*, is generally known as one of the world's leading analytical papers. Its breadth of coverage and analytical style leave its rivals struggling to differentiate their products in a market in which less than 2 percent of the population buys more than one newspaper (Drost, 1991). *Excelsior* is occasionally challenged by *Unomasuno*, founded in 1977 by several *Excelsior* journalists. *Excelsior* is known for its aggressive political reporting and investigative series and has increased its circulation in recent years by outworking the competition on scandal after scandal.

In addition to *Excelsior* and *Unomasuno*, the conservative national daily *Novedades* is widely regarded as a leading opinion maker. The oldest of the traditional quality dailies, *El Universal*, serves as an object lesson for its competition: It is struggling to regain market share lost in the 1980s after its editorial board sided repeatedly with the government on fiscal issues. Circulation in 1996 was nearly 10 percent lower than a decade earlier, and although management has publicly announced that it will aggressively cover the presidential administration, many readers have taken a wait-and-see approach (Drost, 1991).

There are five other national dailies: the conservative *El Heraldo de Mexico*, published in Puebla and Mexico City; *El Nacional*, the official newspaper of the federal government, published in 11 cities via satellite transmission; *La Prensa*, a tabloid with the highest circulation of all print material in Mexico except the sports newspaper *Esto*; *Ovaciones*, the sensationalist daily focusing on crime, sex and scandal; and *El Sol de Mexico*, the rather staid flagship of OEM (Condesa, 1995).

A lively regional press has developed outside Mexico City in recent years. *El Norte*, for example, has grown to more than 150,000 in circulation from its base in Monterrey, Mexico's second-largest city. Other regional papers have developed in Guadalajara *(El Informador* and *El Occidental)*, Tijuana *(El Mexicano)* and Ciudad Juarez *(Diario de Juarez)*. The regional newspapers place tremendous pressure on the national dailies, which have had no effective competition in outlying areas for advertising and readers (Condesa, 1995).

The government provides much of the advertising support, in large part to control indirectly editorial freedom and content. Examples abound of governmental interference with journalists, just as many journalists in Mexico openly admit accepting unofficial "subsidies" in exchange for favorable coverage. Periodicals routinely run *gacetillas*—paid articles—that are seldom if ever identified as such (Winsor, 1995).

Overall, the print industry has been hurt severely by newsprint costs and declining advertising rates. Newspaper advertisement sales decreased by more than 30 percent in 1995, and although newspapers have managed to recover some business, newsprint stands at $750 a metric ton, 67 percent higher than in 1995 (Rangel, 1995). Mexican newspapers depend heavily on imported newsprint from the United States, Canada and New Zealand. The rise in newsprint prices is a global trend, but coupled with the collapse of the peso, real newsprint prices account for 60 to 70 percent of a Mexican newspaper's operating budget. As a result, at least eight metropolitan dailies have folded in Mexico since 1995, and media analysts predict more will do so in the next few years. Hundreds of newspaper employees have been laid off since the collapse of the peso (Rangel, 1995).

Media Industry Analysis

Media usage in Mexico is slowly increasing as the nation's telecommunications infrastructure slowly develops. The transformation from a radio-dominated to a TV-dominated media market has been a slow process, but usage patterns in Mexico are beginning to mirror those in the United States and Europe. The 1996 collapse of the peso temporarily slowed the consolidation of the Mexican communications industry, but analysts expect a series of mergers and acquisitions in the next few years as major media competitors seek to diversify their holdings (Villegas, 1996).

For example, in 1995 Televisa purchased a TV station in Tijuana, just across the border from the United States, and has publicly stated its intention to aim its Spanish-language programming at markets in the southwestern United States. Company officials have indicated that they want half their revenues, or about $8.8 billion pesos ($1.2 billion), to be earned outside Mexico (Villegas, 1996).

The makeup of the rest of Mexico's broadcast industry illustrates the move toward concentration of ownership. The radio industry is dominated by some 20 networks, with 92 percent of radio stations belonging to a network. Ten major radio networks control 72 percent of that total; fully half of the radio market is controlled by five networks. Among the main networks are Grupo Acir, owner of 140 stations and producer of three major news programs daily relayed to more than 200 stations, and Telesistema Mexicano, which runs several regional networks and a dozen stations in Mexico City, including the popular La Voz de la America Latina desde Mexico.

Concentration of radio ownership is fueled by concentration in news gathering. Most stations rely on news material prepared at network headquarters by a small team of journalists, and there is very little independent news content.

Television programming likewise is dominated by a small ownership group, led by Televisa. Televisa runs a highly centralized distribution network, locking up the nightly newscast time slots with its "24 Horas." Content varies little by market, and Televisa quickly defeats competing shows with its ability to run a single programming slot nationwide.

Mexico's regulatory structure resembles other free-market media economies but operates within the political realities of a one-party state. Many regulations exist only in the statute books; others are strictly enforced for no apparent reason (Drost, 1991). The arguably monopolistic practices of several media conglomerates have never been investigated, but public pressure is growing for free-market protections for new market entries.

Freedom of the press is guaranteed by the Constitution, but the Mexican government has a long history of interference with journalists. At first glance, however, Mexican press law differs little from the laws of other democratic nations except for those of the United States. Article 6 of the Mexican Constitution declares that "the right of information will be guaranteed by the state" (Constitution of Mexico, 1917). Article 7 forbids prior restraint. The 1917 Press Law, however, instructs courts to balance press rights against the citizenry's rights to protection of privacy, health and morality (Drost, 1991).

The media also are closely regulated by other civil and criminal statutes. Article 36 of the 1960 Law on Radio and Television forbids the transmission of material "offensive to national heroes" and Article 130 of the Constitution prohibits members of the clergy from publishing on national political issues or criticizing national institutions. Criminal libel laws still exist but are not enforced, although civil libel suits occur with regularity, challenged only by the United States (Winsor, 1995).

The most intrusive of the government regulators, the Secretariat of State for the Interior, wields tremendous power. It grants publishing certificates, promulgates vague "norms" for editorial publications, supervises the issuing of broadcast permits, handles relations between the media and the federal government, and issues press passes for governmental coverage. The Secretariat of State for the Interior has a long-standing history of corruption and insider deal-making, and many journalists work underground to avoid its censorship (Winsor, 1995).

The legal framework for Mexican broadcasting is established by the 1960 Law on Radio and Television. Article 4 of the law states that radio and TV are to be maintained in the public interest and that the government's regulatory stance is to facilitate the fulfillment of broadcasting's "social function." Under the law, broadcasters must respect morals, human dignity and the family, foster the development of youth and preserve national values and beliefs (Drost, 1991).

Only Mexican citizens are allowed to apply for broadcast licenses. They are issued for 5-year periods, with renewal generally automatic. The Secretariat of State for Communications and Transport oversees broadcast licensing and regulation and has long been noted for its hands-off approach and for its many connections to the PRI.

Emerging Media Economic Issues

The role of the mass media in Mexico will expand rapidly in the coming years as the nation's economic recovery, coupled with NAFTA's easing of tariffs and technology import regulations, welcomes foreign investment, equipment and expertise. Mexico's economic instability has long frustrated its potential as a major media market. With a population of 82 million, its consumer sector is simply too large for many international media conglomerates to ignore. As disposable income rebounds from the collapse of the peso, real growth in subscriber-based media could be staggering. For example, 98 percent of all households owned TVs and radios in 1995, but only 9.8 percent owned satellite TV service and 11 percent were cable subscribers (Alexander, 1996).

Mexico's media industries are thoroughly consolidated; few independent outlets remain. The dominant media chains—Televisa, Multivision, Organizacion Editorial Mexicana and Grupo Acir—have all shed noncore businesses in recent years to focus on mass media industries. Mexico's largest media conglomerates now have three strategic options: maintain the status quo, merge with one another, or expand their operations by moving outside Mexico.

Already, Televisa has teamed with Rupert Murdoch's News Corporation to bring direct broadcast satellite service to all of Latin America. Univision beams its Spanish-language programming to the United States, Canada and parts of Europe. Multivision has signed direct broadcast satellite agreements with Hughes Communications. Such multinational alliances likely will increase as Mexico's major media conglomerates attempt to control Latin American market share.

The North American Free Trade Agreement encourages transborder mergers by easing each of the North American nations' long-standing restrictions on foreign ownership of mass media outlets. Mexico's print industry, rocked in recent years by soaring newsprint prices, is crowded with struggling participants. Newspapers and magazines continue to suffer from the erosion of the currency, which has made a newspaper purchase (3 pesos, or 50 cents) a major consumer decision for a population earning an average of $3 a day (Rangel, 1996). The potential exists for acquisitions by international investors looking for an entry point into the Mexican market; acquisitions of Mexico's largest and most influential newspapers and magazines are likely given the shakiness of the domestic market.

Central to the revitalization of Mexico's media economy is the modernization of its telecommunications infrastructure. The lucrative long-distance market, open to competition on January 1, 1997, now offers consumers the choice of AT&T Corporation, MCI Communications Corporation, Bell Atlantic Corporation and Southwestern Bell in addition to Telefonos (Smith, 1997). Bell Atlantic's investment in the Mexican cellular company Grupo Iusacell serves as a high-profile example of investment in Mexico: the 1995–96 collapse of the peso cost Bell Atlantic half the cash value of its 42 percent stake in the company, but long-term prospects are bright (Smith, 1997). Other U.S. telecommunications firms will follow as price reductions in the long-distance market create demand for advanced telecommunications products.

There are signs that Mexico's latest economic upheaval may have accelerated key structural changes brought on by NAFTA. More Mexican companies, media companies included, are streamlining, making them more competitive in a global economy. Technology imports have risen dramatically, as corporate managers seek to automate while reducing personnel costs.

For Mexico to realize its potential as a media market, however, the political reforms proposed by the current administration must be realized. Mexico's economy is among the world's most concentrated: as of 1993, economists estimated that an identifiable group of 36 Mexican businessmen controlled more than 50 percent of the nation's GDP (Perot and Choate, 1992). The North American Free Trade Agreement likely will reduce that figure, as international investment will increase in many sectors of the economy. The biggest question for Mexico is whether after years of rising expectations were dashed by the latest collapse of the peso, the country is destined to remain just another emerging market, or whether it still has the potential to become a First World economy.

Mexico's future as a Latin American media center poses several questions for further research. Mexico's legal and regulatory systems must be analyzed in light of the many changes in the competitive landscape. Regulatory changes in the wake of NAFTA merit further study as well, as does scrutiny of the vast cross-ownership of media outlets long allowed by the Mexican regulatory agencies.

Future studies of Mexico's media economy should also address fundamental differences between Mexico and many developed media markets. The impact of Mexico's tradition of oligopoly and monopoly media ownership on foreign competition is unknown, as is consumer demand for many new media technologies. Demand for media products is often reflective of disposable income, and Mexico's demand for new media products must be studied in light of the macroeconomic condition of the nation.

The rapid privatization of Mexico's telecommunications market offers another rich area for scholarship. Mexico's long-suffering domestic telephone market now is crowded with global telecommunications providers eager to modernize and introduce cellular service to consumers who often never have been able to obtain wire telephone service. Studies should explore the effects of such rapid privatization on state-run media economies in an effort to determine the costs and benefits of foreign competition in Mexico's media economy.

References

Alexander, K. (ed.). (1996). *Consumer Mexico 1996.* Chicago: Euromonitor International.

AT&T plays $1 billion venture with Mexico's Alfa. (1994). *The Atlanta Journal & Constitution,* November 10, p. G7.

Aviles, R. (1996). Mexico's circle of misery. *Foreign Affairs,* July/August, pp. 92–96.

Bear Stearns raises Mexico GDP estimate. (1996). *Reuters News Service,* March 29.

Condesa, C. H. (1995). *Medios Publicitarios Mexicanos.* Mexico City: Medios Mexicanos.

Constitution of Mexico (1917). Article 6.

Dombey, D. (1996). Televisa plans big reshape following PanAmSat sale. *Financial Times*, April 18, p. 28.

Downie, A. (1996). A newspaper war in Mexico City. *American Journalism Review*, January, p. 16.

Drost, H. (1991). *The World's News Media.* London: Longman.

Electronic media. (1995). *L.A. Screenings Special Edition/May-June 1995,* June 1, p. 7.

Grossman, C. (1993). The evolution of free trade in the Americas: NAFTA case studies. *American University Journal of International Law & Policy* 11:611–697.

Malkin, E. (1995). The Rupert Murdoch of Mexico? *Business Week,* December 11, p. 61.

Nolan, J. L. (ed.). (1994). *Mexico Business.* San Rafael, California: World Trade Press.

Perot, H. R., and Choate, P. (1992). *Save Your Job, Save Our Country: Why NAFTA Must Be Stopped—Now!.* New York: Vantage.

Rangel, E. (1995). Bad news for Mexico's papers. *The Dallas Morning News,* August 29, p. D1.

Rangel, E. (1996). Mexicans to pick long-distance firms as monopoly ends. *The Dallas Morning News*, November 18, p. D1.

Reding, A. (1988). Mexico at a crossroads: the 1989 election and beyond. *World Policy Journal* 4:616–700.

Smith, G. (1997). A Mexican morass for Bell Atlantic. *Business Week*, January 20, pp. 42–43.

Villegas, C. (1996). Mexico TV sets sights on U.S., Latin markets. *Reuters Financial Service,* BC Cycle, June 5.

Winsor, A. (1995). *The Complete Guide for Doing Business in Mexico.* New York: Business Press.

South America

The region of South America represents a media marketplace that is historically shaped by its political and economic environment. In the chapter on Brazil, Joseph Straubhaar examines the role of the powerful media groups such as TV Globo and Editora Abril and the extent of cross-ownership and its impact on Brazil. The chapter on Argentina, authored by Silvio Waisbord, analyzes the decline of the once popular newspaper industry and discusses the horizontal ownership pattern, which is somewhat different from the U.S. model.

5

BRAZIL

JOSEPH STRAUBHAAR

The Road to Media Concentration and Cross-Ownership

Brazil is one of the largest economies in the world, usually ranked from eighth to tenth largest. The relative weight of Brazil's media economy is perhaps even larger. Brazil's major television (TV) network, TV Globo, has often been ranked as the fourth or fifth largest commercial network in the world (Straubhaar, 1991).

Brazil has tended to be a rapidly growing and rapidly industrializing economy. It slowed down considerably as a result of foreign debt, internal debt, balance of payments changes, and inflation in the 1980s. The gross national product (GNP) in 1994 was U.S.$3,370 per capita, which represented an annual growth of only 0.3 percent between 1980 and 1993 (World Bank, 1995). Brazil has regained a 4–5 percent growth rate after 1994. Brazil has also considerably reduced its ratio of debt service to export earnings, from 63.1 percent in 1980 to 24.4 percent in 1993 (World Bank, 1995). Brazil makes and exports cars, motorcycles, light to medium aircraft, weapons, agricultural machinery, steel products, electronic goods, and media products, particularly TV programs, music, movies and comics (Editora Abril, 1995). Brazil primarily exports both physical and cultural goods to the rest of Latin America; however, Brazilian music has made some inroads in the United States and Europe. Brazilian TV, particularly prime time serials or *telenovelas,* has been exported much more widely to a global market of more than 110 countries (Marques de Melo, 1988), including southern and eastern Europe. The relative share of manufacturing in Brazil's GNP, however, has not grown since 1980. In 1993, agriculture accounted for 11 percent of GNP; industry, 37 percent (manufacturing per se was 20 percent); and services, 52 percent (World Bank, 1995).

Brazil is a major importer of media products, particularly music and feature films. Current estimates are that around 50 percent of the music played on radio stations is imported and that more than 90 percent of the feature films shown in theaters or available on video are imported. During the 1960s, most TV programs were also imported (Straubhaar, 1984). Brazil has been moving to replace many imported media or cultural goods with national productions. During the military governments (1964–85), this was seen as an issue of national security. In the early 1970s, the military communications minister, General Euclydes Quandt de Oliveira, urged TV producers to import less to cut down on violence in imported programs and to reinforce a stronger sense of national identity (Straubhaar, 1981).

Table 5-1 shows the decline in importation of TV programs, particularly in prime time, from 1963 to 1991. The table reflects the proportions of programming in prime time and in the total broadcast day that were produced in Brazil, imported from the United States, or imported from elsewhere within the Latin American region. Overall, U.S. programming declined, particularly in prime time, from 1962 to 1972, rising in 1982 and declining again in 1992. Imports from within the Latin American region appeared for the first time in 1992. Overall, however, Brazilian programming tends to occupy three quarters of prime time and two thirds of the total broadcast day, reflecting a very strong national industry and a clear audience preference for local or national production. Brazil also imports about half of the music that is played on Brazilian radio stations. The other half is produced in Brazil and is made up of a very diverse set of genres.

Table 5-1. Percentage of National, U.S. and Regional Programming in Prime Time and the Total Broadcast Day in São Paulo

	1963		1972		1982		1991	
	Prime (%)	Total (%)	Prime (%)	Total (%)	Prime (%)	Total (%)	Prime (%)	Total (%)
Brazilian	70	69	86	55	64	63	75	64
United States	30	31	14	44	36	37	19	30
Regional	0	0	0	0	0	0	6	4

Source: Straubhaar (1984, 1991).
Prime indicates prime time; total indicates the total broadcast days.

Although Brazil has had a prominent film industry in times past, most of its films are imported. They come primarily from the United States, although a number are imported from Europe, particularly to the southeast and south of Brazil, where European roots are still strong and where French and Italian cultural products are preferred by many to those from the United States. The Brazilian film industry was supported for years by a state financier and distributor, Embrafilme. Since the time Embrafilme was shut down in the late 1980s, very few Brazilian films have been produced or distributed, but the industry began undergoing a minor revival in the mid-1990s (Johnson and Stamm, 1996).

Major Media Industries

The most significant Brazilian media industries are probably TV, newspapers, and music or radio, although magazines are also important to the more affluent and literate parts of the population. In all four, commercial industries supply most of the material consumed by audiences. The Brazilian government historically has not invested directly in the ownership of media. Because private capital took the initiative to create and build up media companies in most parts of Brazil, the government tended to reserve its capital for other sectors in which private investment was judged inadequate.

Television

Brazil has been characterized in its own media as the "country of television" because the TV audience is so large. In a survey by the newspaper *Folha de São Paulo* in São Paulo in 1983, 24 percent said they watched TV because it is "the cheapest form of entertainment" and 17 percent because they "lacked other leisure options" (Sarti, 1981). In 1996, there were an estimated 32,600,000 TV sets (20.7 per 100 inhabitants) and 60,000,000 radio sets for Brazil's population of 157,912,000 (Paoletti, 1996).

Brazilians watch a lot of TV. Average household daily viewing is generally more than 5 hours. A study of young people in São Paulo found that sixth graders tend to watch 5 hours a day, and tenth graders, 3 hours. Sixth graders also listened to 2.1 hours of radio, and tenth graders, 2.4, indicating that radio is relatively more important for adolescents than for younger children. Younger children also watch TV more with their parents. Regarding TV, young people preferred comedies, movies, rock music, *telenovelas* and action/adventure programs. Regarding radio, they preferred rock and international music, although girls also preferred more Brazilian pop (Greenberg et al., 1992).

TV Globo has dominated TV audiences. This is especially true on weekdays: A May 1990 São Paulo survey showed that TV Globo had 70 percent; TV Manchete, 12 percent; SBT, 7 percent; and others, 5 percent. The weekend audience is slightly different. TV Globo had 53 percent on Saturdays, whereas SBT (emphasizing variety shows) and TV Bandeirantes (emphasizing sports and talk) each had 9 percent, and Manchete, 8 percent. On Sundays, TV Globo had 43 percent; SBT, 26 percent (revealing a higher Sunday audience for variety shows); TV Bandeirantes, 9 percent; and Manchete, 4 percent (Venturini, 1990).

TV Globo's hold is being challenged, however. In the same survey, two non-Globo programs achieved a higher spontaneous recall than any Globo program: the SBT variety show "Programa Sílvio Santos" (53 percent recall) and the TV Manchete *telenovela* "Pantanal" (51 percent), compared with the TV Globo news program "Jornal Nacional" (37 percent) (Venturini, 1990).

Newspapers and Magazines

Both historically and currently, Brazilian newspapers have been very regionalized. Even the major chain that dominated many Brazilian cities until the 1970s, the *Diários Associados,* was very decentralized and regionalized. Each major Brazilian city tended to have one or two major daily newspapers and several minor ones. The major newspapers in Rio *(O Globo* and *Jornal do Brasil)* and São Paulo *(Folha de São Paulo, Gazeta Mercantil* and *O Estado de São Paulo)* have some limited circulation to other parts of the country, but almost all readers are local.

There has been a severe shakeout in newspapers in Brazil, similar to that in the United States, so many newspapers have folded or been consolidated into larger operations. A number of regionally dominant newspaper groups used to offer several papers in the same city, such as morning, afternoon, elite and popular newspapers. Many of these multiple paper groups have been consolidated while smaller operations struggle or go under.

In contrast to newspapers, magazines in Brazil emerged in the 1940s as the major national medium before TV's take-off period of growth in the 1970s. They remain a major national medium for news and culture. After TV, newsmagazines are the most widely shared news and information source available to Brazilians. The main newsmagazine, *Veja,* has a circulation of almost 800,000 and a readership of several times that, as copies tend to be passed around.

As in the United States, magazines are also the starting point for an increasing segmentation of the audience by social class and interest. Magazines are widely read among the upper and middle classes but are too

Table 5-2. Magazine Circulation in Brazil, 1994

Publishing House	Magazine	Circulation	Genre
Editora Abril	*Veja*	789,600	News
	Claudia	401,200	Feminine
	Manequin	384,300	Feminine
	Superinteressante	309,000	General interest
	Playboy	240,200	Masculine
	Capricho	229,300	Feminine
	Exame (business)	144,700	Newsmagazine
Globo	*Marie Claire*	181,100	Feminine
	Criativo	179,000	Feminine
	Globo Ciéncia	151,800	General interest
	Globo Rural	150,000	General interest
Bloch	*Ele e Ela*	81,200	Masculine
	Manchete	81,800	Newsmagazines
Trés	*Isto É*	233,500	Newsmagazines
Caras	*Caras*	164,100	Entertainment

Source: Editora Abril (1995, p. 708).

expensive for many in the lower middle class, working class and poor, who are also likely to have limited literacy. In 1996, *Veja* cost almost $4 at the newsstand in a country where the modal income is between $150 and $200 a month.

As Table 5-2 shows, ownership in the Brazilian magazine industry is highly concentrated. Editora Abril dominates most of the top circulation magazine genres, noted earlier in this chapter. The once dominant position of photo magazine *Manchete* and of the Bloch group has slid considerably, as have photography oriented newsmagazines, such as *Life,* in the United States. The other primary magazine group is now Globo, which is dominant in TV.

Radio

Unlike many other Latin American nations, network radio has not been important in Brazil since the early days of Radio Nacional, which was used by Getúlio Vargas in the 1930s as an instrument of political mobilization. Since then, radio has become a very localized medium. Hundreds of local stations have emerged. The number of medium wave or AM stations increased from 440 in 1956 to 1,557 in 1990, and FM stations went from zero to 1,215 (in fact, FM stations virtually doubled even from 617 in 1988) (Borin, 1991). Most of these stations are independent; however, in major cities, the network-affiliated stations, such as Rádio Globo and Rádio Bandeirantes, tend to be the most popular.

Media Industry Analysis

Media Ownership and Concentration

While some media areas are dominated nationally by one or two major producers, particularly TV Globo in TV and Editora Abril in magazines, newspapers and radio tend to be more localized and competitive. Cross-ownership is weakly regulated, at best, and two to three major ownership groups have extensive ownership and market power in several media. The largest group is the Globo Group of the Marinho family, which owns the major TV network (TV Globo), one of two main cable and satellite TV groups (NET), one of the four main newspapers *(O Globo)*, and several of the main radio stations and magazines. The second largest group is the Abril Group of the Civita family, which publishes seven of the 10 largest magazines, the MTV partnership in Brazil, and one of the two main cable and satellite TV groups (TVA). Other major ownership groups include the Mesquita family, which publishes the newspapers *O Estado de São Paulo* and *Jornal da Tarde*; the Frias family, which publishes the largest Brazilian newspaper, *Folha de São Paulo*; the Bloch family, which owns the Manchete TV network and the magazine *Manchete*; Silvio Santos, who owns the second largest TV network, SBT; and the Jornal do Brasil group, which owns the Rio newspaper of the same name and several radio stations.

Barriers to entry in the print media are primarily economic but significant. The same family media groups have dominated print for decades. Although competition has raised some groups and lowered others, there have been few recent newcomers. In electronic media, there have been powerful political barriers to entry as well, as licenses have been awarded in a very politicized manner, with several powerful print media groups shut out of broadcasting for political reasons. The electronic media, however, have been somewhat more open to newcomers not previously connected with existing groups, as long as they had the political connections required to get broadcast licenses. Although the Brazilian government has not tended to own and operate media, except in telecommunications, it has exercised considerable control in the selective, politically controlled allocation of licenses for electronic media and in the allocation of economic resources, such as loans and advertising, from the numerous sectors of the economy, including banking and numerous trading and manufacturing companies that the state has controlled. A gradual trend toward privatization of state companies since 1989 does seem to be slowly reducing governmental power in these licensing and resources controls.

Government Control via Advertising and Investment

The Brazilian government was more active in promoting and even financing TV than it had been with radio, and much more so than it had been with print media. The military governments were far more active and interventionist in media, including the financial aspects, than were their predecessors. After the 1964 Revolution, the government initiated a low-interest loan program for the purchase of TV sets, built a microwave network that enabled TV networks to reach the more remote parts of the country, and contributed a good deal of revenue through advertising by government-owned corporations and banks. The development of the telecommunications system, telephones, telegraph, telex, radio and TV was a high priority directly reacted to the military regime's perception of national security needs. The military governments saw telecommunications as vital economic infrastructure and perceived broadcasting, in particular, as a means of reinforcing a sense of national identity (particularly in the more remote regions of the country), communicating government development plans and messages to the people, and ensuring a supportive political climate (Mattos, 1984). They viewed the media, particularly TV, as a means of consolidating both a national political culture and a national consumer marketplace.

The military governments favored certain print media companies, such as the Bloch Group, and certain TV networks, particularly TV Globo, with government advertising, which was considerable, as government or state corporations, banks, trading companies, mines, steel mills, and so forth constituted nearly half the GNP for a couple of decades. As Mattos (1984) noted, the state had become the main advertiser and it could reward those media firms that carried favorable messages about it. TV Globo, in particular, used this support and momentum to build a virtually unbeatable position in TV, by hiring the best talent, reinvesting in equipment, and managing its resources very well.

Two major print media groups in São Paulo, Editora Abril and the Folha Group, probably prospered in the long run by remaining critical of the military governments. The Abril Group was denied TV licenses repeatedly, but its flagship newsmagazine, *Veja,* and its other magazines prospered. It was eventually able to enter TV via the new technologies after the military stepped out of power in 1985. Both major São Paulo newspapers *(Estado de São Paulo* and

Folha de São Paulo) were critical of the military governments. Both were penalized by prior censorship and loss of advertising. Both survived, but the Folha Group was better able to capitalize on its opposition to build a loyal reading audience (Lins da Silva, 1988).

Factors in Television Network Success and Failure

TV Globo, the first Brazilian TV network established with the capital and technical expertise from America's Time Warner, has a majority share of the audience, but TV Globo has been getting steadily more competition throughout the 1980s and 1990s. As of 1991, TV Globo drew an average share of 66 percent of the nationwide audience; SBT/TVS, 18 percent; TV Manchete, 7 percent; TV Bandeirantes, 5 percent; and all others (TV Record, public TV and independent stations), 4 percent (Straubhaar, 1991).

TV Globo has been extraordinarily successful. Roberto Marinho is now considered the second richest man in Brazil. He has branched out both vertically into all aspects of TV, including research, production, marketing and syndication, and horizontally into magazines, books, educational materials, video distribution, recording, record distribution, cellular telephony and other telecommunications (he is the Brazilian partner of NEC, of Japan), and beyond media into agriculture and other businesses. The group is also diversifying internationally. The Globo Group acquired control of Telemontecarlo in Italy for several years and in 1992 acquired one of the new private channels in Portugal.

Other networks have had difficulty competing with TV Globo. Efforts by several networks, first TV Tupi, then TV Bandeirantes and TV Manchete, to compete with TV Globo for a broad general audience have failed. So the oligopolistic, imitative competition among commercial networks for the general audience typical of the United States never took place. Instead, other broadcast TV networks found themselves pursuing smaller, more-specific audience segments largely defined by social class. SBT, owned by variety show host and entrepreneur Sílvio Santos, targeted a lower middle class, working class and poor audience. That gained it a consistent second place in ratings during most of the 1980s and early 1990s, but advertisers were not always attracted to that audience segment (Duarte, 1992).

TV Manchete targeted a more elite audience initially but found that that segment was not large enough to gain adequate advertiser support (Duarte, 1992). The large initial investment required to mount TV Manchete seems to have almost bankrupted the owner, Adolfo Bloch, who has tried to sell the network. TV Bandeirantes wavered on program lines but tended to emphasize news, public affairs and sports. All three ultimately wished to pursue a general audience with general appeal programming, such as evening serials *(telenovelas)*, but tended to find that such efforts still did not gain enough of the audience to pay for the increased programming costs.

Internationalization and New Video Technologies Change Television Industry

Brazilian TV has entered a phase characterized by its internationalization of programming and new technologies. The importation of TV programs into Brazil actually declined in the 1980s, while TV Globo and other networks began to export widely to the world (Marques de Melo, 1988; Mattos, 1990; Straubhaar, 1984; cf. Table 5-1). The advent of cable, direct broadcast satellite (DBS) and satellite master antenna TV (SMATV) has changed the landscape of Brazilian TV. In the 1980s, thousands of small towns in rural Brazil purchased satellite dishes and low-power repeaters to bring in TV. The first new consumer video technology to diffuse widely in Brazil was the videocassette recorder. Its growth was slower than in many other Latin American countries but seemed to accelerate in the late 1980s and 1990s; however, many Brazilian viewers remained loyal to TV and did not use videocassette recorders extensively.

Other new video technologies entered the Brazilian TV market in the 1990s, offering focused or segmented programming through additional advertising-supported or pay-TV systems. There are three main approaches so far: advertising-supported UHF, over-the-air pay-TV systems, and DBS systems. These main systems are competing with conventional VHF TV and with each other in terms of both programming and technological platforms.

The main UHF TV operation is a licensed Brazilian adaptation of MTV (Music TV), owned by the Editora Abril publishing group. It uses a great deal of programming from the U.S. MTV, with local announcers, local advertisements, and some Brazilian music videos (Duarte, 1992). So far only MTV has gained even a small share of the audience. Some independent UHF channels are also being started.

There are two major pay-TV operations, TVA and NET/GloboSat. TVA is a combination of earlier separate offerings by the TVA Group, Editora Abril, and the Machline industrial group. In 1996, it offered five channels (films, news [Cable News Network], sports [ESPN], a superstation-type channel, and TNT). NET/GloboSat is a DBS and SMATV satellite operation, owned by TV Globo, associated with the Multicanal cable operation. It has a programming line-up similar to TVA's, with four channels (films, news, sports, shows), although NET's channels carry a greater mixture of local and imported programming, whereas most of TVA's channels are completely imported. With a monthly cost of about $30–$40, pay-TV has been targeted at individual upper middle class households in major cities, although recent studies (Paiva, 1996) show some penetration into the lower middle class. There are probably about 1,600,000 current users, roughly 5 percent of the population (Paiva, 1996).

Increasing Concentration in Print Media

The current newspaper and magazine industries are almost completely dominated by a few large industry groups. This trend toward consolidation seems likely to continue. Multiple papers owned by the same companies, such as the Folha Group, are being consolidated. Smaller papers in the major cities are being forced out of business. In fact, despite a tradition of having multiple newspapers in each major city, the current tendency seems to be toward having a single dominant city and regional newspaper in each area, as in the United States. In São Paulo, the *Folha de São Paulo* currently dominates circulation and advertising. In Rio de Janeiro, *O Globo* of the Globo Group is emerging as dominant; in Salvador, *A Tarde*; in Porto Alegre, *Zero Hora,* and so forth. This trend seems to be driven by rising costs, declining or stagnant readership, competition for advertising by other commercial vehicles, and other factors common to newspapers in many countries.

Radio Networks Versus Localism

Major radio stations and networks tended to be associated with newspaper chains owned by a few families. The major radio network was the Diários e Emissoras Associadas: by 1938, it consisted of five radio stations grouped with 12 newspapers and one magazine in a chain, led by Assis Chateaubriand (Visão, 1978), but like the associated TV Tupi network, it declined after the 1960s. Also notable are Rádio Bandeirantes (Grupo Carvalho, linked with TV Bandeirantes) and Rádio Globo (linked with the newspaper *O Globo* and Roberto Marinho). Rádio Bandeirantes and Rádio Globo have continued to be relatively strong networks, but Brazilian radio has been increasingly localized since the 1960s.

As in the United States, radio in Brazil has moved toward fairly extensive segmentation of both formats and audiences in the 1980s and 1990s. AM and FM have developed differently. AM radio is still somewhat more widely available, in terms of both transmitters and receivers, particularly in rural areas, smaller towns and lower class suburbs of cities. Even within cities, AM remains focused on formats and musical genres that appeal primarily to lower class audiences, which include a large number of recent migrants from rural areas.

Emerging Media Economic Issues

Concentration and Cross-Ownership

One of the major issues for Brazilian media economics is the consolidation and narrowing of ownership of Brazilian media organizations. Within almost all media, except radio, ownership has been increasingly consolidated in the hands of a few family-based ownership groups. Although this is most obvious in TV, with TV Globo, it is equally true in the national magazine industry with Globo and Abril. Newspapers have not consolidated into a few national chains, as in the United States, but control of the newspaper market within each major city has increasingly settled into the hands of one or two major groups, so there is effectively oligopoly or even monopoly at the local and regional level. Even the opening up of new media or distribution channels, such as new video technologies, does not necessarily diminish the concentration of media ownership. New licenses for UHF and pay-TV channels have admitted some new companies into "broadcasting," but a number of the companies involved are familiar, such as TV Globo. The major new entrant with UHF and pay-TV is the dominant publishing house, Editora Abril, owned by Victor Civita (Duarte, 1992).

A related problem is cross-ownership across media industries. It is clear that the Globo Group is prominent in all major industries and dominant in TV. That permits them to cross-market goods, as when their radio station plays the sound-track theme of their soap opera, which is sold by their recording company and promoted by the soap opera itself. It also concentrates a great deal of political power in their hands. A number of political analysts believe that the Globo Group was very influential, almost decisive, in its role in the 1989 presidential elections and at least moderately influential in 1994 (Marques de Melo, 1994; Straubhaar et al., 1993). The Globo has started to move into computers and telecommunications, through a partnership with NEC, bidding for satellite, cellular telephone and other service contracts. This degree of cross-ownership and control worries many Brazilians. Several telecommunication analysts who preferred not to be quoted told the author that such fears helped prompt the particular form of privatization of telecommunications that seems to be emerging in Brazil: breaking up the national market for several services into a number of regional pieces and limiting any given company to involvement in only one of these areas, to limit the scope of ownership and control by any one group in the national market.

Other media groups are not as powerful but are worthy of concern in terms of oligopoly issues. For example, Editora Abril dominates magazines and is now the other major player, besides Globo, in new TV technologies.

Abril or other media groups besides Globo may well emerge as parts of consortia to bid on new telecommunications services licenses. Brazil has very little tradition of concern with monopoly regulation. One can see such regulation, however, emerging in recent efforts to depoliticize the process of radio and TV licensing, in efforts to ensure that no one company achieves a dominant position in the coming privatization of telephony and telecommunications, and in efforts to restructure the Ministry of Communications as a more neutral, effective regulator (Aufderheide, 1996).

Market Segmentation

Another issue or trend in Brazilian media seems to be toward increased segmentation. In both economic and political terms, mass media in Brazil have had strong effects in creating remarkably unified national politics and a national consumer economy. This has been particularly true for TV, whereas some of the other media, such as radio and print, have remained far more regionalized within the country. Segmentation, however, seems to be increasing not so much by region as by class and interest. A number of magazines have long targeted specific interest and class groups, as in the United States or other countries. Some of the main TV networks also are segmenting audiences by social class, and new TV systems seem to be trying to segment by interest within the upper and upper middle classes.

Import Substitution Versus New Technologies

Brazil has realized both economic and cultural benefits by substituting local content for imports in TV, music and publishing. Reversing that course would present many challenges to both economy and culture. One of the major questions about the new video technologies in Brazil, as in Europe, Asia and the Middle East, is whether they will bring in a renewed wave of imported programs. The initial lineup of new cable and satellite TV channels in Brazil seems to bear out this fear. The new channels vary considerably in how much foreign, particularly American, programming they will bring in. Duarte notes that although TVA and GloboSat have similar lineups, TVA's material is almost entirely imported in the original languages. That may well limit its appeal over time, as audience research in Brazil consistently shows a preference for local content (Straubhaar, 1984). Seemingly anticipating this factor, NET/GloboSat is drawing on TV Globo's resources to fill about 25 percent of its time with national material and to dub or subtitle 90 percent of the programming. Globo has its own correspondents and resources in journalism, a film library of 10,000 dubbed titles, and other resources to fill its channels (Duarte, 1992).

Both TVA and TV Globo's NET have recently joined Latin American region satellite TV consortia. TVA has joined with the Hughes Corporation in the Galaxy Latin America group (together with Multivisión of Mexico and Cisneros of Venezuela) to offer DirecTV to Brazil. NET/Globo has joined in the Sky Latin America consortium with Rupert Murdoch's News Corporation, Televisa of Mexico, and TCI of the United States. Both will offer DBS services to Brazil with 60–70 channels.

These multichannel offerings will largely consist of imported channels and programs, but it remains to be seen whether they will compete seriously with Brazil-based channels. Audience research over time in Brazil tends to show that the most popular programs in almost all genres except feature films are usually Brazilian produced, reflecting what Straubhaar (1991) calls a preference for programs that reflect "cultural proximity" (familiar language, scenes, faces, humor, values, music, body language, etc.) and what Hoskins and Mirus (1988) have termed a "cultural discount" against unfamiliar, foreign language and dubbed programming in favor of local programs. There are, however, indications of a potential upper and middle class audience for more diverse TV, even if it is international. It seems as though Abril is trying to break into TV via this audience, using international consortium support. Globo seems to be trying to maintain its strong existing mass audience for broadcast TV while developing options, including international partnerships, to continue to capture a more segmented upper and middle class audience, as well.

Strengthening the Brazilian competitive position in TV programming, in the 1980s and 1990s, Brazilian TV networks, particularly TV Globo, emerged as major exporters of programming to the rest of Latin America and the world, particularly of *telenovelas,* but also of music videos, variety shows, comedies and miniseries. TV Globo started in 1975, exporting the *telenovela* "Gabriela" to Portugal, followed by *telenovelas* dubbed into Spanish for the Latin American market. As of 1992, Globo had sold 65 *telenovelas* and miniseries to Venezuela, 45 to Peru and 43 to Spanish-language networks in the United States (Marques de Melo, 1994). Despite dubbing costs of around $150,000 per series, Globo already earned more than $1,000,000 in 1977 from exports and currently earns about $20,000,000 per year from exports—modest in light of roughly $700,000,000 gross yearly sales revenues (Marques de Melo, 1988).

TV Globo has exported programming to 130 countries as of 1996 and invested abroad in stations in Italy and Portugal. TV Globo's programming was sufficiently successful in Italy, Portugal and France that some European scholars examined its productions, particularly *telenovelas,* as potential models for European production (Mattelart and Mattelart, 1990). In the early 1990s, in the face of increasing competition within Brazil, Globo began to refocus on ensuring the quality and competitiveness of its productions in the national market. It also began co-productions aimed at the European market with Spanish, Swiss and Portuguese TV companies to continue to increase exports. At the same time, TV Manchete and TV Bandeirantes also began to export programs, mostly *telenovelas* and miniseries to Latin America (Marques de Melo, 1988; 1994). Overall, the growth in exports by all companies is becoming a major financial resource for Brazilian media. It also implies that TV competition has moved into the international as well as the domestic market, even though Globo remains dominant in both.

References

Aufderheide, P. (1996). Personal communication. Association for Education in Journalism and Mass Communication, August 10.

Barbero, J. M. (1987). *De los Medios a las Mediaciones: Comunicacion, Cultura y Hegemonia.* Barcelona/Mexico City: Editorial Gustavo Gili.

Bolaño, C. (1988). *Mercado Brasileiro de Televisão.* 1st ed. Aracaju: Universidade Federal de Sergipe.

Borin, J. (1991). Rádios e TVs crescem com o festival de concessões. *Comunicação e Sociedade* 10(18):19–24.

Camargo, N. and Pinto, V. (1975). *Communication Policies in Brazil.* Paris: UNESCO Press.

Caparelli, S. (1980). *Comunicacao de massa sem massa.* Sao Paulo: Cortez.

Dez anos apos Chateaubriand (1978). *Visão,* April 17.

Duarte, L. G. (1992). *Television Segmentation: Will Brazil Follow the American Model?* Unpublished M.A. thesis, Michigan State University.

Editora Abril (1995). *Almanaque Abril 1995.* São Paulo: Editora Abril.

Greenberg, B., Alman, R., Busselle, R., Straubhaar, J., Litto, F., and Gait, N. (1992). *Young People and Their Orientation to the Mass Media—an International Study—Brazil.* Unpublished Report, Department of Telecommunication, Michigan State University, East Lansing, MI.

Hoskins, C., and Mirus, R. (1988). Reasons for the U.S. Dominance of the International Trade in Television Programs. *Media, Culture and Society,* pp. 499-515.

Johnson, R., and Stamm, R. (1996). *Brazilian Cinema.* Austin: University of Texas Press.

Kottak, C. P. (1990). *Prime Time Society: An Anthropological Analysis of Television and Culture.* Belmont, CA: Wadsworth.

Kurian, G. H. (1992). Brazil. In: Kurian, G. H. (ed.). *Encylopedia of the Third World.* New York: Facts on File.

Lins da Silva, C. E. (1988). *Mil Dias.* São Paulo: Trajetória.

Macedo, C., Falcao, A., and Mendes de Almedia, C. J. (eds.). (1988). *TV ao Vivo—Depoimentos.* Sao Paulo: Editora Brasiliense.

Mais brasileiros ganham menos de um mínimo (1989). *Folha de São Paulo,* November 2, p. C-10.
Marques de Melo, J. (1988). *As Telenovelas da Globo.* Sao Paulo: Summus.
Marques de Melo, J. (1994). The cultural industries in Brazil: Television and telenovelas. *Journal of International Communication* 1(2):5–17.
Mattelart, M., Mattelart, A. (1990). *The Carnival of Images: Brazilian Television Fiction.* New York: Bergin & Garvey.
Mattos, S. (1984). Advertising and government influences on Brazilian television. *Communication Research* 11(2):203–220.
Mattos, S. A. S. (1982). *The Brazilian Military and Television.* Unpublished M.A. thesis. University of Texas, Austin.
Mattos, S. A. S. (1990). *Um Perfil da TV Brasileira (40 Anos de Histüria: 1950–1990).* 1st ed. Salvador: Associação Brasileira de Agências de Propaganda.
O "bolo" cresceu mas renda não foi distribuida (1989). *Folha de São Paulo,* October 12, p. B-6.
Oliveira, O. S. (1990). Brazilian Soaps Outshine Hollywood: Is Cultural Imperialism Fading Out? In: Nordenstreng, K., and Schiller, H. (eds.). *Beyond National Sovereignty: International Communication in the 1990s.* Norwood, NJ: Ablex.
Os números do IBGE (Census) (1990). *Mercado Global,* January, pp. 6–9.
Nordenstreng, K., and Varis, T. (1974). *Television Traffic—A One-Way Street.* Paris: UNESCO.
Paiva, A. (1996). Revolução parabólica. *Jornal do Brasil,* June 18, p. B-1.
Paoletti, R. (1996). Fall season for Globo. *Brazil,* August, pp. 8–13.
Priolli, G. (1988). Imagens que custam os tubos. *Imprensa,* March, p. 70.
Salles, M. (1975). Opiniáo Publica, Marketing e Publicidade no Processo Brasileiro de Desenvolvimento. Speech to the Escola Superior de Guerra, Rio de Janeiro.
Santoro, E. (1981). Tendencias populistas no TV brasileira ou as escassas possibilidades de acesso as antenas. In: Melo, J. M. d. (ed.). *Populismo e Comunicacao.* Sao Paulo: Cortez Editora.
Sarti, I. (1981). Communication and cultural dependency: A misconception. In: Mosco, V., and Wasco, J. (eds.). *Communication and Social Structure.* New York: Praeger.
60 anos de rádio (1983). *Propaganda,* January, pp. 10–56.
Straubhaar, J. (1981). *The Transformation of Cultural Dependency: The Decline of American Influence on the Brazilian Television Industry.* Unpublished Ph.D. dissertation. Fletcher School of Law and Diplomacy, Tufts University.
Straubhaar, J. (1982). The development of the *telenovela* as the paramount form of popular culture in Brazil. *Studies in Latin American Popular Culture* 1:138–150.
Straubhaar, J. (1984). The decline of American influence on Brazilian television. *Communication Research* 11(2):221–240.
Straubhaar, J., Olsen, O., and Nunes, M. (1993). The Brazilian case: Influencing the voter. In: Skidmore, T. (ed.). *Television, Politics and the Transition to Democracy in Latin America.* Washington, DC: Woodrow Wilson Center.
Straubhaar, J. D. (1988). The reflection of the Brazilian political opening in the *telenovela* [soap opera], 1974–1985. *Studies in Latin American Popular Culture* 7:59–76.

Straubhaar, J. D. (1990). Social class and audience responses to television and new video technologies in Brazil and the dominican republic: Toward a concept of cultural proximity. In: *International Communication Association, Mass Communication Division.* Dublin.
Straubhaar, J. D. (1991). Class, genre and the regionalization of the television market in Latin America. *Journal of Communication.*
Subervi, F., and Souki de Oliveira, O. (1989). Blacks (and Other Ethnics) in Brazilian Television Commercials: An Exploratory Inquiry. Paper given at International Communication Association, Intercultural and Development Division, 1989.
Tavola, A. D. (1985). *A Liberdade do ver: Televisao em Leitura Critica.* Rio de Janeiro: Nova Fronteira.
Troiano (1990). O consumidor nos anos 90. *Mercado Global,* January, pp. 14–17.
Valentini, R. (1978). Interview with the author. São Paulo.
Venturini, G. (1990). "Zapping." *Folha de Sao Paulo.* Data Folha relatsrio de pesquisa de opinico no. 938, May 16.
Visão (1978). *Dez anos apos Chateaubriand.* April 17.
World Bank (1995). *World Development Report, 1995.* Washington, DC: World Bank.

6

ARGENTINA

Silvio Waisbord

The Market Deluge: Privatization and Concentration in the Argentine Media Industries

Argentina was an up-and-coming, ebullient media market in the early 1970s. High literacy rates and a sizable middle class drove high levels of consumption and made Argentina a primary market in Latin America. It had the highest number of dailies and newspaper consumption per capita in the region. There were 182 newspapers per 1,000 inhabitants, significantly higher than the regional average of 80 (UNESCO, 1995). Having flourished in the years following World War II, the publishing industry serviced a growing internal market and exported to other Spanish-speaking countries. The filmmaking industry continued to churn out a sizable number of movies, although fewer than during its time of splendor in the late 1940s and 1950s, when it produced an annual average of 45 movies (Getino, 1995). A decade after its beginning, commercial television (TV) affirmed its position as the number of TV sets steadily grew.

Two decades later, that promising scenario bitterly contrasts with a situation in which media industries face severe difficulties. A long economic crisis, coupled with a brutal authoritarian regime that suffocated all forms of public life during the late 1970s and early 1980s, has devastated the once-vibrant media landscape. Chronic inflation, steady income decline, and years of negative growth have decimated the economics of media companies. The number of dailies has declined, and total readership has shrunk to only 65 newspapers per 1,000 inhabitants (UNESCO, 1995). Magazine circulation, once the highest in the region, declined and now comprises only 20 percent of the regional market. After experiencing a brief recuperation during the "democratic spring" of the mid-1980s, the filmmaking industry produced only eight films in 1994, its lowest output since the early 1930s. This is remarkable, particularly considering that domestic productions attracted more audiences than foreign productions in the previous 2 years.

Despite this bleak picture, a few vital signs suggest that the media industries are still alive. Since the early 1990s, Buenos Aires newspapers have been fiercely competing for a shrinking number of readers and a healthy advertising market (Cámara Argentina de Anunciantes, 1991-1995). Book production and exports have consistently increased during the 1990s (Reaching out, 1993). The privatization of two main TV stations in 1989 stimulated local production and competition among a handful of media conglomerates. Television producers have successfully exported *telenovelas* and variety shows and aggressively pursued foreign markets. Cable TV has boomed in the last decade, turning Argentina into the largest market in Latin America and the beachhead for foreign companies to form strategic partnerships to launch regional activities. The *Ley del Cine* ("Film Law"), sponsored by the Executive and passed by Congress in 1995, resuscitated the moribund film industry: its allocation of $30 million to support local production are responsible for the fact that more than 30 films were produced in 1996.

These developments suggest profound changes in the economics of the Argentine media. These changes are inseparable from two major transformations: economic stabilization and privatization. First, reversing the Peronist tradition and its populist electoral platform, the Menem administration espoused neoconservative policies that shaped the much-hailed "Argentine economic miracle" of the 1990s. Its policy of economic reform centered on dismantling state mechanisms through the privatization of state-owned companies and undoing much of the social welfare structure erected by Peronism in the 1940s. It applied a "shock" policy to curb inflation by pegging the peso to the dollar. From a hyperinflation of 5,000 percent in 1989, inflation decreased to 84.7 percent in 1991 and 4.5 percent in 1995. After decades of runaway inflation, economic stability was responsible for a gradual recovery of the media industries, mainly because it has stimulated advertising investments.

Second, the privatization of two main TV stations in 1989 has opened the door to private ownership concentration in the media industries. The broadcasting law of 1980, passed by the last military regime (1976–1983), decreed the privatization of the TV stations expropriated by the previous Peronist government in 1974. The process stalled, however. Initially, political disagreements among factions of the authoritarian regime delayed decisions, and only during its final months did the regime finally decide to push privatization forward when it returned the Buenos Aires–based Channel 9 to its former owner. Privatization was again suspended when the democratically elected government of Raúl Alfonsín was inaugurated in December 1983. The situation remained in a stalemate throughout the 1980s, as the Alfonsín administration only submitted its privatization proposal to Congress in 1987 (Waisbord, forthcoming). Privatization was fully implemented only when the Menem government assumed power in 1989. Without waiting for Congress to pass a new and comprehensive media legislation, the administration decided to expedite the process by circumventing the still-in-force Broadcasting Law of 1980 that banned print companies from holding broadcasting licenses. (This ban was actually ignored, as some newspaper companies owned radio licenses.) The government issued a decree that removed the limitations on cross-ownership and on the participation of foreign capital in domestic media industries. The decision favored the biggest newspaper and publishing companies that intensely lobbied to eliminate all restrictions that prevented the formation of horizontally integrated media companies.

In the context of economic stabilization and media privatization, this article reviews recent developments in the newspaper and TV industries that attest to the growing process of media concentration. The logic of this process is different from what has been observed in the recent mergers in the developed world. Argentine multiple system operators (MSOs) do not seem as concerned as the behemoth world media companies are with owning both production and distribution outlets across industries in order to use holdings synergistically. There are no big (or small) film and TV studios or publishing companies pushing to lock up the means of distribution to guarantee a smooth circulation, prolong the shelf life, and increase profitability of media products. The film industry is virtually in shambles, and TV production is dispersed among a number of small companies that have not attempted to own distribution outlets and continue to respond to the programming demands of the major TV stations (Tijman 1995).

Because of audience and advertising fragmentation, as in the U.S. market, there is no motivation to bring different media outlets and programming sources under the same corporate umbrella. Despite its high penetration, cable has not eroded audience ratings of over-the-air TV in the major Buenos Aires market, and it only shaved shares in the Interior (Rival, 1996). Having devoted minimal resources to the cable industry, advertisers still strongly support traditional mass media and virtually ignore segmentation strategies. The MSOs are certainly interested in maximizing rentability by moving media products through a horizontally and vertically integrated structure, but even after acquiring new means of distribution of TV programming, they have not emphasized the control or expansion of production capacities. Instead, their priority has been to invest in the most dynamic and profitable distribution systems, namely, over-the-air and cable TV and telephony. In light of recent technological and corporate developments elsewhere, there are strong pressures toward convergence, which so far, as discussed later in this chapter, have run against existing regulations that prohibit telephone companies (telcos) from offering audiovisual services and media firms from entering the telecommunications market. At the time of this writing, the tug-of-war between political forces, telcos, and traditional media companies has not resulted in the passing of a new communication law.

Major Media Industry Analysis

The Downturn of the Newspaper Industry

The newspaper industry had a number of worldwide prestigious dailies. Argentina still has the highest percentage per inhabitant of newsprint consumption in Spanish-speaking Latin America despite the remarkable drop since 1970. The absolute number of copies and newsprint consumption declined at the same time the Argentine population increased from 22.5 million to nearly 34 million inhabitants (UNESCO, 1995).

DOMINANCE OF MAJOR MARKET NEWSPAPERS. At the national level, newspaper ownership remains oligopolistic, and the attempts by some Buenos Aires-based newspapers to expand in the interior have been unsuccessful because they could neither attract new readers nor snatch readers away from established dailies in the major cities. The newspaper market received an average of 28 percent of total advertising revenues during the 1990s, but the trend is clearly downward: it reached 22 percent in 1995, eight points less than in 1991 and 1992. Buenos Aires dailies capture 60 percent of newspaper advertising revenues and an average of 17 percent of total advertising revenues. Newspapers in the rest of the country receive 11 percent. This is a stark contrast, especially considering that 15 dailies are from the Buenos Aires market (not all receive equal advertising monies), whereas 175 dailies are dispersed in the interior. Distributed throughout the vast Argentine territory, Buenos Aires papers are de facto national papers.

The unbalanced geographic distribution of newspaper advertising is responsible for different market structures. Whereas the city of Buenos Aires has an oligopolistic newspaper market (despite the persistent financial difficulties of several dailies), most cities and towns, especially those in regions most severely hit by the economic recession of the last decades, have shifted from oligopolies to monopolies (Getino, 1995). In a depressed market of readers and advertising investments, most newspapers face serious economic diffi-

Table 6-1. Circulation for Major Newspapers

Newspaper	Circulation
Clarín	630,897
La Nación	181,099
Diario Popular	145,000
Ambito Financiero	130,000
Olé	101,449
El Cronista Comercial	100,000
Crónica	80,000
La Voz del Interior	63,615
La Gaceta	53,523
Los Andes	52,761
Página 12	40,000

Source: From Instituto Verificador de Circulaciones (1996) and UNESCO (1995).

culties. This is particularly evident with the dailies, such as the tabloid *Crónica*, that target working-class readers: Its morning and evening daily editions decreased from 300,000 to 80,000 copies in 25 years.

SURVIVAL IN THE DECLINING NEWSPAPER MARKET. In the last decades, one of the most important developments was the consolidation of *Clarín* as the best-selling newspaper, with a circulation of 630,897 daily and more than 1.2 million copies on Sundays (see Table 6-1). Beginning in the 1970s, *Clarín* has been steadily enlarging its advertising base and readership and expanding into other media industries. In 1995, the revenues for the Grupo Clarín were $1.14 billion (Paxman, 1996). The flip side of *Clarín*'s exceptional success has been the slow demise of two traditional, reputable newspapers, *La Prensa* and *La Razón* (*La Prensa* was revamped a few years later by an industrial conglomerate, Fortabat, with mixed reviews).

In summary, most newspapers have experienced substantial economic difficulties in the last decade. No doubt, such problems are rooted in plunging sales. The lack of reliable circulation figures for all dailies makes it difficult to gauge exactly the decline, but according to informal calculations, the newspaper market has lost about one million readers since 1983 (Pasquini Durán, 1996). Neither the consolidation of press freedoms nor the rise in newspaper's share of media advertising revenues in the first half of the 1990s (Hernández, 1996) has improved the dire economic situation of most newspapers. *Clarín, Ambito Financiero* and, to a lesser degree, *La Nación* survived almost unscathed after decades of inflation and political turmoil. Most dailies, especially in the interior of the country where the prolonged crisis has decimated regional economies, have had less success in adapting to a smaller reading market.

Privatization and the Trend Toward Conglomerization in Broadcast Television

THE ABSENCE OF NETWORKS. The Argentine TV industry has historically been localized. No national networks ever developed. In addition to the state-owned Channel 7, founded in 1951, three private stations based in Buenos Aires have consistently dominated national production and attracted the largest advertising revenues. Those stations produced and nationally distributed both domestic and foreign productions. Their relation with local stations was not one of network and affiliate, but of programming sellers and buyers. Programs were distributed via mail and aired in the interior weeks after their original broadcast in Buenos Aires.

One reason for the absence of networks was poor technological development that made it impossible to broadcast shows simultaneously throughout the Argentine territory. This technological deficit could have been solved as in Brazil, where, in the 1960s, the military regime developed an extensive network with geopolitical goals that, in turn, facilitated the formation of a private national broadcasting network. The Argentine generals, however, did little in this regard and actually feared strong private media companies that might gain autonomy from government powers. The successive broadcasting laws, all passed by military regimes, banned the formation of national networks. Unlike the Brazilian military or the Mexican Partido Revolucionario Institucional, which favorably viewed the formation of quasimonopolistic and politically allied broadcasting networks, the Argentine juntas avoided allocating too much power to one company. Rhetorically, the decision was justified to protect and promote local production, but according to analysts Oscar Landi and Julio Tapia (1996, p. 4), the rationale was to "impede the development of a [network] system that could be out of governmental reach."

The TV industry experienced substantial changes after the Menem administration decided to auction off Channels 11 and 13 based in the city of Buenos Aires. (Channel 7 is the only remaining state-owned station that nationally distributes programming.) Channel 13 was allocated to Grupo Clarín, the most powerful media conglomerate in the country. Besides its flagship newspaper *Clarín,* it controls interests in radio, publishing, a news agency, cellular telephony, cable TV, and newsprint production. Channel 11 was awarded to Telefé International, a conglomerate formed by Editorial Atlántida, the main publisher of popular magazines and books that also has investments in the radio industry, Grupo Soldati (one of the largest economic conglomerates), 10 TV companies, and private investors. Telefé currently holds shares in the USA network Latin America and Sportvision, which markets soccer programming. The other two leading TV stations are Channel 2, owned by Grupo América controlled by Eduardo Eurnekián, a textile entre-

Table 6-2. Major Media Conglomerates and Holdings

	Television							
	Over-the-air	Cable	Radio	News-paper	Publishing	Cellular Telephony	News-agency	Newsprint Production
Atlántida	*	*	*		*			
Clarín	*	*	*	*		*	*	*
La Nación		*	*	*			*	*
Liberman		*						
Eurnekián	*	*	*	*				
Romay	*	*	*					
Sarmiento		*	*	*	*			

Source: Based on Terrero (1996).

preneur who in the last decades has expanded into cable TV, radio stations, and acquired a financial daily, and Channel 9, part of the Grupo Romay, which controls a handful of TV and radio stations in major cities and investments in cable (see Table 6-2).

A CHANGING ADVERTISING MARKET. The removal of the legal obstacle that prevented horizontal expansion triggered a process of economic competition. Soon after privatization, advertising expenditures surged, increasing from $1.2 billion in 1991 to $3 billion in 1995, making Argentina the second largest advertising market after Brazil in Latin America and the country with highest advertising expenditure per capita in the region (Latin statistics, 1996).

It is important to note that advertising revenues are not distributed equally among all media. From a historical share of 30 percent, TV stations now receive 40 percent of annual advertising (see Table 6-3). Nor is advertising equally distributed throughout different media markets. The recent growth seems to have intensified the traditionally lopsided geographic structure of the advertising market. Buenos Aires–based newspapers and TV stations get the lion's share as they have received an average of 40 percent of advertising revenues in the 1990s. The tendency seems to reinforce this unequal distribution as they captured 47 percent of advertising expenditures in 1995, 71 percent of which went to TV stations (Cámara Argentina de Anunciantes, 1991–1995). That is, Buenos Aires TV received 34 percent of total advertising in 1995. During 1993, the total of advertising revenues of $476 million for the five Buenos Aires stations was distributed as follows: Channel 11 received 33 percent; Channel 13, 27 percent; Channel 9, 23 percent; Channel 7, 10 percent; and Channel 2, 6 percent. These numbers indicate that the channels that were privatized in the 1980s (9, 11 and 13) command 83 percent of TV advertising. Amid an advertising market growing at a slower pace and in contrast to shrinking revenues for all

Table 6-3. Advertising Expenditures by Media and Geographic Location (in million of dollars)

	1991	1992	1993	1994	1995
Newspapers					
Buenos Aires	226	365	431	460	405
Interior	137	208	270	297	267
	363	573	701	757	672
Television					
Buenos Aires	250	419	476	578	1,016
Interior	137	189	226	270	164
	387	608	702	848	1,180
Other	386	672	1,036	1,167	1,148
Total	1,166	1,853	2,439	2,772	3,000

Source: Based on Cámara Argentina de Anunciantes (1991–1995).

other media, the private channels experienced a remarkable growth in advertising revenues and share in the first half of the 1990s.

PRODUCTION AND DISTRIBUTION OF TV PROGRAMMING. The structure of TV production has historically been oligopolistic. The three major Buenos Aires stations (Channels 9, 11 and 13) have controlled the national production of TV shows. From the early beginnings of Argentine TV, local companies formed production branches to provide programs for the parent station and for more than 20 stations (privately and state owned) scattered throughout the country. Approximately 80 percent of the shows broadcast in the interior originate in Buenos Aires. As the number of over-the-air stations grew in the 1980s and new technologies for delivering signals were introduced (cable and satellite), that pattern continued, reinforcing the one-way flow from Buenos Aires to the interior. Furthermore, privatization has intensified this dynamic as the now private stations decided to emphasize local production over foreign imports for domestic and international distribution. Although Argentina has historically produced a significant amount of TV programming, the proportion has increased from 55 percent to 65 percent of weekly schedules since privatization. For example, Telefé has decidedly emphasized production, churning out 75 percent of the 9 hours of programming daily distributed throughout the country.

The increase is related to both the high popularity of domestic productions, which consistently rank higher than foreign (mostly U.S.) shows, and the international ambitions of local producers. Although the domestic market continues to be the main target, they have aggressively expanded into the international market during the 1990s by establishing alliances with foreign distributors and programming partners. Telefé has been the most successful, exporting programming to more than 40 countries. It has negotiated distribution agreements with Solomon International for Asia and the Middle East and with the Dutch company Endemol Entertainment for Europe (Telefé aims high, 1995). It has recently agreed with the Brazilian network SBT to produce Portuguese versions of its most successful shows, which have been already sold to Latin American and European markets (Brasil hará su Perla Negra, 1997). In alliance with producer Rail Lecouna, Telefé has also participated in co-production deals with Italian mogul Silvio Berlusconi's Mediaset. Rondó Estudios, an independent production company, has also co-produced with Berlusconi for distribution in Latin America, Spain and Italy. Following in the footsteps of Brazilian, Mexican and Venezuelan companies, *telenovelas* are the staple of Argentine TV exports and, to a lesser degree, comedy and variety shows. *Telenovelas* are relatively cheap to produce (each episode ranges between $10,000 and $20,000, except for a few superproductions developed in partnership with foreign broadcasters at $50,000 each), and their selling prices oscillate between $2,000 in most Latin American countries and $40,000–$50,000 in the biggest European markets. A handful of independent companies (Cuatro Cabezas, Pol-ka, Profilm, Aries, Ideas del Sur, Estrellas Producciones, Crustel, Fernando Marin, Rondó Estudios, TM Producciones, Reytel) have also produced shows for domestic and international distribution and negotiated the distribution of advertising revenues received by their shows with local stations (Getino, 1995). Another source of programming is theatrical films, both domestic and foreign.

The Argentine TV industry rode a roller coaster in the 1990s. Few would question that it experienced a major shake-up after privatization and economic stabilization. Privatization contributed to the formation of three major private stations, which began a fierce competition for audience and advertising monies. Once hyperinflation was reduced to single-digit figures and economic growth moderately increased, advertising revenues steadily augmented. In a climate of economic bonanza, the stations invested in high-budget productions to capture larger shares of growing advertising revenues. Simultaneously, they created international divisions to export in-house productions (mostly sold to neighboring Latin American countries), in many cases by teaming up with local and foreign producers and distributors to facilitate access to overseas markets.

The situation dramatically changed in the aftermath of the financial crisis in Mexico in December 1994. The ripple effects of the crisis throughout the region led to a more cautious forecast about the prospects of the emerging Latin American economies for the remainder of the decade. Most analysts agree that the climate of uncertainty generated by the "tequila effect" was directly responsible for more modest growth in the advertising market (Tijman, 1995). As the financial situation turned sour, ambitious and expensive TV projects were shelved. To avoid risks associated with the development of new programming in a more uncertain market, stations opted to rely on independent companies (Guerriero, 1996). The optimism of the early to mid-1990s gave way to a more somber outlook. Not even the remarkable explosion of cable, which brought with it more outlets for programming and a regular cash flow, could hide the fact that the future of the TV industry looked less promising than a few years earlier.

The Phenomenon of Cable

A recent article on the state of the Argentine cable industry observes that:

> Most of the 27,000 residents of the town of 25 de Mayo, deep in Argentina's agricultural heartland, still have to walk to a downtown office if they want to place [a] phone call. But if they want to watch television, they can stay at home and tune in to no fewer than 20 channels of top local and international programming, up from one lone state broadcast less than a decade ago. While some types of communications lag in this prosperous community, cable television has found its way into 6,000 of its 7,000 homes (Helft, 1996).

This extract accurately portrays the situation of cable TV in the country at large. During the last decade, cable TV has experienced a remarkable development. Argentina's cable population is almost half the total number of cable subscribers in Latin America. A penetration rate of 60.79 percent places Argentina behind only the United States and Canada in the Americas (Asociación Argentina de Televisión por Cable, 1996). There are more cable subscribers (approximately 5 million) than telephone users (3 million), a reflection not only of the widespread development of cable but also of the low penetration of telephony, even after a 77 percent increase between 1990 and 1996 (Stiff opposition, 1996).

The dispersion of TV ownership and the absence of national networks explain the remarkable growth of cable TV in Argentina. As in the United States, cable TV in Argentina development began in small towns with community antenna TV and gradually moved into large cities (Howard and Carroll, 1993). In the early 1980s, cable made inroads in the Greater Buenos Aires, starting operations in the wealthiest neighborhoods. Two family-owned companies, Video Cable Comunicación and Cablevisión, decided to initiate activities and equally divided in two zones the biggest TV market in the country. A few years later, new companies emerged, especially in the big urban centers once the Alfonsín government authorized companies to downlink satellite signals. In turn, and fueled by the lack of government intervention, the number of cable services and subscribers mushroomed nationally.

Table 6-4. Cable Television Ownership

Company	Subscribers	Percentage of Total
Multicanal	820,000	17.40
Video Cable Comunicación	650,000	13.80
Cablevisión	530,000	11.30
Other companies	2,706,000	57.51

Source: Based on Asociación Argentina de Televisión por Cable (1996).

CONSOLIDATIONS IN THE CABLE TELEVISION INDUSTRY. The trend of cable ownership consolidations resulted in a total of 1,183 companies that own cable systems throughout the Argentine territory, down from more than 1,600 operators in the early 1990s (Asociación Argentina de Televisión por Cable, 1996). As Table 6-4 illustrates, three conglomerates control more than 42 percent of a total of more than 4.7 million subscribers. The remaining 57 percent is controlled by almost 1,200 companies disseminated throughout the Argentine territory.

The mergers in the cable industry are inseparable from two recent developments. First, once the cable market reached maturity in the early 1990s, profit margins decreased and competition increased when regulations demarcating areas for different cable companies were lifted in the largest markets. The introduction of satellite TV made it indispensable to upgrade the network technologically to offer premium channels and diversify the programming menu. This required great capital investments that only the bigger and more consolidated media groups could offer. This squeezed out small companies and, in turn, strengthened the position of the majors (Rossi, 1996).

Second, the trade agreement signed in 1991 between Argentina and the United States was fundamental. It accelerated concentration because it allowed U.S. companies to invest in the local communications industry. Soon after the treaty became effective in 1994, U.S. investors became partners in the major cable companies. Continental acquired 50 percent of Video Cable Comunicación in 1994 for $150 million. Tele-Communications, Inc. invested $750 million to purchase 51 percent of Cablevisión in 1995, acquiring an additional 39 percent in 1997 (TINTA beefs up in Argentina, 1997; Ricciardi, 1995). Citicorp bought 22.5 percent of Multicanal, whose major owner is Grupo Clarín, and the other partner is Telefónica International, the Spanish company that controls 50 percent of the telephone duopoly and has already invested in cable operations in Chile and Perú. Multicanal substantially increased its operations after purchasing 200,000 subscribers in February 1996 from Telefé, which, mired in high debts after years of explosive growth, decided to sell its cable operations and concentrate on production. Its profits were $57 million on revenues of $161 million (Argentine biz shakes up some more, 1997). A major shake-up took place in August 1997, when Citicorp sold its stake to Clarín and purchased 64.5 percent in Cablevision/TCI. The strong interest of U.S. investors to form alliances with Argentine partners follows a strategy to consolidate a subscriber base in the largest Latin American market at a time when the region has been experiencing a solid economic growth and a steady increase in the number of cable households.

Despite its remarkable growth and reach, cable TV receives only 3 percent of annual advertising expenditures. Its explosive growth in the last decade has not captured the soaring numbers of advertising expenditures. Subscribers' fees, which range between $30 and $40 per month, continue to be the main source of revenues. The lack of accurate rating measurements holds back cable's potential as an advertising medium (Landi and Tapia, 1996).

The State of Argentine Media Industries and Emerging Economic Issues

The Argentine case indicates that the contemporary worldwide trend toward media concentration may obey different processes and business strategies. Synergistic goals do not seem to be the leading factor in the process of media concentration in Argentina. Although it has remarkable horizontal expansion, Grupo Clarín controls small holdings in filmed production and publishing. Telefé, which owns a major TV station, has decided to focus on production of TV shows and has relinquished control of a sizable number of cable systems. Grupo Romay, a major producer of TV programming, holds a few TV stations and has only moderately expanded into cable. Grupo Eurnekián basically produces low-budget shows for its over-the-air and cable stations and, reportedly, has problems in keeping some of its operations (namely, a newspaper and one radio station) in the black.

Diversification certainly minimizes the risks of concentrating in one industry, as profits from other business can support losses (Gomery, 1989), especially in the Argentine market where the abrupt economic slowdown in 1995 showed the dangers of betting on one industry while economic uncertainty persists. So far, however, the primary interest of media groups has been to expand horizontally, especially in highly profitable areas (cable and telephony), while only cautiously and minimally venturing into developing sources of production to feed distribution outlets. Perhaps vertical integration will become more important in a second phase of the post-privatization period, which, in turn, is likely to reinforce even further the power of Buenos Aires media groups at the expense of small and medium-sized print and broadcasting companies scattered in the interior. The latter face a bleak future given the persistent difficulties of regional economies, stagnant or falling newspaper sales, the historical lack of TV production facilities and distribution networks, and further concentration of advertising investments in Buenos Aires media.

Despite their substantial growth in the 1990s, the biggest Argentine media groups still pale in comparison not just to U.S., European and Japanese, but even to Mexican and Brazilian communication giants. In 1995, the combined earnings of Telefé and Clarín were less than $800 million, placing them 61st and 65th, respectively, in a worldwide ranking of communication corporations (The 1995 TBI 100, 1995). Argentine companies undeniably lag behind other Latin American conglomerates in terms of overall revenues, horizontal and vertical expansion, and presence in international markets. They are latecomers to the regional and global media scenes. Even though they had a long-standing presence in the domestic market, they underwent substantial growth only after acquiring the state-run TV stations and expanding operations in the booming cable industry.

The formerly mismanaged and almost bankrupt stations turned out to be the golden goose of the Argentine media business. Ownership of the most-profitable TV stations enabled media conglomerates to strengthen their domestic position and, simultaneously, to consolidate a platform to begin international ventures in the early 1990s. By then, Mexico's Televisa, Brazil's Globo and Venezuela's Venevisión already had a strong presence and well-established global distribution networks, especially in Latin American markets.

Different domestic conditions also put Argentine media groups in a disadvantageous position vis-à-vis the Latin American giants. In 1992, Argentina's advertising market was $1.9 billion, considerably smaller than Brazil's $3.8 billion. Even though advertising expenditures in Mexico reached $1.6 billion, Televisa is in a much more solid position because it reportedly captures between 70 percent and 80 percent of that total, more than any media company in Argentina (DePalma, 1994). Moreover, no Argentine company dominates the domestic media market comparable to the role of Globo in Brazil and Televisa in Mexico. The phenomenal growth and international expansion of Televisa and Globo was rooted in the quasimonopolic positions they held in their respective TV markets until new competitors emerged in the 1980s in Brazil and in the 1990s in Mexico. This was fundamental because it gave them a sizable capital basis and well-stocked TV libraries to launch international operations. With interests in mass media, telecommunications, finance, banking and agriculture business, Globo's revenues were $1.6 billion in 1995, 70 percent of which came from its media division (Robinson, 1995). The same year, Televisa received 80 percent of the $2 billion spent on TV advertising in Mexico during 1995 (Malkin, 1995). Huge production facilities, consolidated international divisions, and sizable investments in several countries place Globo and Televisa well ahead of any Argentine media conglomerate in a race to expand globally.

Additionally, the fact that Argentine companies have basically tried to conquer international TV markets by exporting *telenovelas,* the same product the Mexican and Brazilian behemoths had not only introduced two decades ago but have consistently dominated since, makes their international prospects difficult. Peddling similar products at comparable prices and without established distribution networks, global expansion has been an uphill battle for Argentine companies. Prospects are limited even in Latin America, where audiences are already reared in the idiosyncrasies and the localisms of Brazilian, Mexican and Venezuelan *telenovelas* and, reportedly, are put off by "the Italian tilt of [the] Argentine accent" (Goyoaga, 1996). Moreover, the recent emergence of a crop of media groups (Perú's Pantel, Chile's Megavisión, Colombia's Caracol and RCN) that are vying to enter Latin American and other countries (e.g., Spanish-language TV in the United States) adds even further competition to an already crowded market of *telenovelas* providers. Under these circumstances, co-productions and multinational distribution arrangements with regional and international conglomerates are likely to be the most logical solutions for Argentine groups to strengthen their global presence.

Aside from unexpected and sudden economic downturns, the future of Argentine media conglomerates hinges on pending decisions about the regulatory framework of the industry. If deregulation happens, then further conglomerization and "survival of the fittest" dynamics among telcos and big media companies will follow. In light of technological convergence and under pressure from telcos to deregulate the communications industry, the Argentine Parliament is in the midst of heated controversies about revisions to the Broadcasting Law of 1980. This debate is fundamental in the context of an industry that has reawakened after years of economic instability and political repression, the prolonged absence of an updated legal framework to organize the unruly growth of cable TV, the so-called pirate radio stations, and the uncontrolled concentration of media ownership during the last decade. One issue unquestionably dominates congressional debates, media coverage, and discussions inside and outside media industries: whether the telcos will be allowed to deliver video signals. Telefónica and France's Telecom have invested almost $9 million in the digitalization of the network since ENTEL, the former state-owned telephone company, was privatized in 1990. The legal framework that regulated the privatization process excludes telcos from providing cable services but authorizes MSOs to offer basic telephone and data services after deregulation in 1997 or, if extended, in 2000.

Media companies strongly oppose any changes that would allow telcos to enter the audiovisual market while pushing to liberalize the telecommunications market (Ricciardi, 1995). To most analysts, the huge differences between the economic might of the telecommunication giants and the MSOs is at the heart of the debate: the former's revenues of $4,703 billion dwarfs the $720 million the MSOs received in 1995 (Landi and Tapia, 1996). All major organizations representing the most powerful audiovisual companies support the project presented by the ruling Peronist party, which offers a mix of regulatory and deregulatory policies (the proposal presented by the main opposition party offers similar policies, except for stiffer measures in terms of minimum requirements for domestic production and the time length of licenses). The official proposal prohibits telcos from entering cable TV, grants broadcasting licenses for 15 years, and puts a 30 percent cap on foreign investments in media industries. It offers neither antitrust provisions nor regulations on the amount of advertising time on TV.

The economics of the Argentine media suggest that explanations for integration in media industries that are valid in some contexts may be inappropriate or insufficient in other countries. In markets that have historically lacked strong producers of filmed programming and with media companies substantially smaller than in developed countries, different reasons may account for media concentration. A number of factors need to be considered in cross-country analysis, such as the presence or absence of powerful production companies, the structure of media markets, the overall size of the media industries, the volume of advertising revenues, the rate of penetration of cable and satellite technologies, and nonmedia companies as partners. Future comparative research is needed to reach nuanced explanations that can account for seemingly concurrent processes of media concentration in different countries that may respond to different strategic calculations and market conditions.

References

Argentine biz shakes up some more (1997). *Multichannel News*, August 11.

Asociación Argentina de Televisión por Cable (1996). *Mercado del Cable en Argentina.* Buenos Aires: Asociación Argentina de Televisión por Cable.

Brasil hará su Perla Negra (1997). *Clarín*, January 22.

Cámara Argentina de Anunciantes (1991). *Inversiones en Publicidad y Promoción.* Buenos Aires: Cámara Argentina de Anunciantes.

Cámara Argentina de Anunciantes (1992). *Inversiones en Publicidad y Promoción.* Buenos Aires: Cámara Argentina de Anunciantes.

Cámara Argentina de Anunciantes (1993). *Inversiones en Publicidad y Promoción.* Buenos Aires: Cámara Argentina de Anunciantes.

Cámara Argentina de Anunciantes (1994). *Inversiones en Publicidad y Promoción.* Buenos Aires: Cámara Argentina de Anunciantes.

Cámara Argentina de Anunciantes (1995). *Inversiones en Publicidad y Promoción.* Buenos Aires: Cámara Argentina de Anunciantes.

DePalma, A. (1994). Advertising south of the border. *New York Times,* November 23, p. D1.

Getino, O. (1995). *Las Industrias Culturales en la Argentina.* Buenos Aires: Colihue.

Gomery, D. (1989). Media economics: Terms of analysis. *Critical Studies in Mass Communication* 6:43–60.

Goyoaga, B. (1996). Big fish in a small pond. *Variety,* October 7, p. 62.

Guerriero, L. (1996). Television: La máquina de repetir. *La Nación.* Available on-line: url:www.lanacion.com (access date: May 22, 1997).

Helft, D. (1996). Argentina leads the way in cable TV. *Reuters,* July 1.

Hernández, D. (1996). Developing nation press is growing. *Editor & Publisher* 129(2):18,62.

Howard, H., and Carroll, S. (1993). Economics of the cable industry. In: Alexander, A., Owers, J., and Carveth, R., eds. *Media Economics: Theory and Practice.* Hillsdale, NJ: Lawrence Erlbaum Associates.

Instituto Verificador de Circulaciones (1996). Boletín 688. Buenos Aires: Instituto Verificador de Circulaciones.

Landi, O., and Tapia, J. (1996). La televisión por cable en la Argentina. Unpublished manuscript.

Latin statistics (1996). *Television Business International,* p. 26. Television Business International.

Malkin, E. (1995). The Rupert Murdoch of Mexico. *Business Week,* December 11, p. 61.

The 1995 TBI 100 (1995). *Television Business International,* March, pp. 28–29.

Pasquini Durán, J. (1996). Interview with the author. Buenos Aires.

Paxman, A. (1996). A quiet Clarin making moves. *Variety,* March 25, pp. 40, 60.

Reaching out (1993). *Publishers Weekly* (Argentina), May 17.

Ricciardi, B. (1995). Los operadores de cable y las telefónicas se disputan el mercado de la teve interactiva. *La Maga,* July 19, pp. 44–45.

Rival, H. (1996). Interview with the author. Buenos Aires, July 24.

Robinson, D. (1995). Brazil's Globo ready for the international stage. June, pp. 42–43. Television Business International.

Rossi, D. (1996). Argentina: de los cableros a los grandes operadores. *Chasqui* 54:29–32.

Stiff opposition to Telefónica's cable television plan in Argentina (1996). *Reuters* (Argentina), April 16.

Telefé aims high (1995). *Video Age International,* October, p. 40.

Terrero, P. (1996). Tecnopolitica, cultura y mercado en la sociedad mediatica. *Contribuciones* 2:89–103.

Tijman, G. (1995). La TV en quiebra. *La Maga,* May 31, pp. 51–53.

TINTA beefs up in Argentina (1997). *Broadcasting & Cable,* March 17, p. 98.

UNESCO (1995). *UNESCO Statistical Yearbook* (1995). Paris: UNESCO.

Waisbord, S. (1994). Knocking on newsroom doors. *Political Communication* 11:19-34.

Waisbord, S. (in press). The paradoxes of media democratization in Argentina. In: O'Neil, P. *Media and Global Democratization.* Boulder, CO: Lynne Rynner.

Zbar, J. (1996). Latin America: Need seen for standard in TV audience. *Advertising Age,* March 11, p. 32.

Europe

A collection of unique cultures, Europe is the largest individual section in *Global Media Economics.* In writing about the United Kingdom, David Goff examines the development and growth of telecommunications and cable television amid an evolving regulatory environment. C. Ann Hollifield authors the chapter on Germany, a country still dealing with political unification and home to the second largest television market outside the United States. The chapter on Spain, written by Alfonso Nieto, analyzes the primary media industries in Spain and the trend toward privatization. Robert Picard reviews the media economic activities of the Nordic Region by centering on the countries of Norway, Sweden, Finland and Denmark. The Netherlands is one of the smallest countries in Europe, yet, as Patrick Hendricks explains, the area is home to several media conglomerates. In the final chapter, Nadine Toussaint Desmoulins discusses the role France plays in the international marketplace for media goods and services.

7

THE UNITED KINGDOM

David H. Goff

The United Kingdom and the Global Media Marketplace

The United Kingdom has influenced the development of media industries throughout the world. Principles of law and press freedom established in England shaped the development of print media in the United States and other nations. The British Broadcasting Corporation (BBC) model of a noncommercial public service broadcasting system "was archetypal for the establishment of broadcasters on all continents" (Hoffmann-Riem, 1996, p. 67). Later, the development of a pluralistic system, with commercial broadcasting operating alongside the BBC influenced national systems worldwide (Head et al., 1994). In recent years, the media industries of the United Kingdom have experienced substantial change in response to international economic trends and domestic deregulation. At present, the United Kingdom is attempting to develop both a policy approach and a modern telecommunications infrastructure that will meet domestic needs and enable effective competition in European and world markets.

The United Kingdom of Great Britain (England, Scotland and Wales) and Northern Ireland was once the dominant global political and economic power, ruling nearly one fourth of the world and its inhabitants. The influence of British law and institutions remains in most of the nations that it once controlled. Throughout the 20th century, the United Kingdom has seen its empire dissolve, the influence of its currency as a world standard erode, and its role as a global military and economic power supplanted. Adjustment to these political and economic realities has been difficult for a nation rich in history and traditions (Studlar, 1996).

Since the end of World War II, both Labour and Conservative governments have attempted to solve persistent problems of inflation, trade deficits, sluggish economic growth, and diminished investor confidence (Cairncross, 1992; Lloyd, 1986; Studlar, 1996). Labour Party efforts between 1945 and 1951 extended government economic control through the nationalization of the Bank of England and numerous industries. The United Kingdom became a welfare state with a government-operated health system, support for the unemployed, and old-age pensions for all. (Lloyd, 1986). The 1950s saw improvement in the economy, but the next decade brought the beginning of a long general decline. Since 1979, Conservative Party governments have moved to reduce direct control of the economy. In contrast to the nationalization of 1945–1949, the United Kingdom has been a leader in the worldwide trend toward the deregulation and privatization of industry. Between 1979 and 1984, government-run businesses in the oil, aerospace, transportation, shipping, automobile, and telecommunications industries were transferred to the private sector, raising more than £ 7 billion (Newman, 1986).

Political and economic conditions in post-war Europe led five nations to establish the European Economic Community (later renamed the European Community) in 1957. The United Kingdom joined in 1973 and the current European Union (EU) has grown to 15 nations (The history of the Union, 1996). This agency for political and economic cooperation pursues international deregulation that will enable products and services (including media) to flow freely and untaxed among member nations. More important, the EU recognizes the importance of information and telecommunications technology and services to further development of an information economy (Gershon, 1997).

The Media Industry Environment of the United Kingdom

A full complement of traditional and developing media competes within the United Kingdom, experiencing the problems and opportunities presented both by deregulation and by changes in technology and economics. For the purpose of this analysis, three significant industry segments will be examined: newspapers, television (TV) broadcasting and the cable industry.

Table 7-1. Major National Newspapers

Daily Morning	(circulation)	Sunday	(circulation)	Publisher
Quality Newspapers				
Daily Telegraph	1,057,017	*Sunday Telegraph*	697,119	The Telegraph P.L.C.
Financial Times	295,902			Financial Times (Pearson P.L.C.)
Guardian	393,011	*Observer*	447,248	Guardian MediaGroup
Independent	270,608	*Independent on Sunday*	295,276	Newspaper Publishing P.L.C.
Times	733,236	*Sunday Times*	1,294,622	News Group Newspapers Ltd. (News Corporation)
Middle-Market Newspapers				
Daily Express	1,220,997	*Sunday Express*	1,210,010	Express Newspapers P.L.C. (United News and Media P.L.C.)
Daily Mail	2,076,951	*Mail on Sunday*	2,087,093	Associated Newspaper Group (Daily Mail and General Trust P.L.C.)
Popular Newspapers				
Daily Mirror	2,443,049	*Sunday Mirror*	2,446,627	Mirror Group Ltd.
		The People	2,056,622	
Daily Star	673,045			
Sun	4,006,979	*News of the World*	4,541,143	News Group Newspapers, Ltd. (News Corporation)
Totals	13,170,795		15,075,760	

Source: Audit Bureau of Circulation, 1996a, 1996b.

The Newspaper Industry

Two distinct newspaper industries operate in the United Kingdom, the national press and the regional press. The London-based national press, profiled in Table 7-1, is dominated by 10 daily morning and nine Sunday titles that compete for readers in three distinct market segments: quality, middle market, and popular. Quality newspapers are published in a broadsheet format and are designed to provide substantive news coverage to an upscale readership. The popular tabloids appeal to the less sophisticated reader through extensive use of pictures, sensational headlines, features and gossip. In between are the middle-market newspapers, which balance news and feature material in a tabloid format designed to appeal to a generally middle-class readership. The national dailies achieve a circulation of more than 13 million, and the Sunday circulation is 15 million (ABC national daily newspapers data 1996; ABC national daily Sunday newspaper data, 1996).

The more diversified regional and local press is large (1,439 titles) and successful, with a weekly circulation exceeding 67 million readers. The largest publishing groups own more than 100 titles each, and 16 publishers have combined weekly circulations in excess of one million. Most regional groups publish daily and weekly paid newspapers and a large number of free weeklies. Trinity International Holdings publishes 124 titles (10 dailies, 52 paid weeklies and 62 free weeklies) and has the largest combined weekly circulation (8.6 million). The Edinburgh-based Johnston Press has acquired the largest number of titles (141) and ranks fifth in total circulation at 4.27 million per week (Regional press publishers, 1996).

Terrestrial and Satellite Television Broadcasting

After passage of the Broadcasting Act of 1990, TV broadcasting in the United Kingdom entered a period of transition, from the paternalistic philosophy of the past to the consumer-determined multichannel marketplace of the future. A dual system remains, supervised by separate broadcasting authorities. The BBC operates the public system, whereas an Independent Television Commission (ITC) oversees commercial terrestrial broadcasting as well as satellite and cable TV.

The BBC operates two complementary national services. BBC 1 broadcasts general interest programming, and BBC 2 provides alternative viewing including programs that appeal to higher cultural tastes. Commercial TV broadcasting consists of three national systems (Channels 3, 4 and 5) licensed for 10-year periods by the ITC. Channel 3 service is provided by 15 regional broadcast corporations along with one production firm licensed to provide a national "breakfast television."[1] The independent news service, ITN, was appointed to provide news programs for the same 10-year period. Channel 3 licensees are required to offer a diverse, high-quality program service including "programs made in and about the region" of the license and "aimed at different areas within regions" (Foreign and Commonwealth Office, 1991, p. 6). The newest national service, Channel 5, was scheduled to begin in 1994, but licensing and frequency allocation decisions delayed the start until early 1997. Channel 5 must meet programming requirements similar to those of Channel 3 but has no obligations to broadcast regional or local programs. Despite its national role, Channel 5 transmitters reach only about 70 percent of the U.K. population (Independent Television Commission announces, 1996).

Channel 4 has broadcast since 1982, providing a single service throughout all of the United Kingdom except Wales. There the fourth channel operates (averaging 30 hours per week in the Welsh language) as Sianel Pedwar Cymru (S4C) (About S4C, 1996). Channel 4's single licensee is charged with providing wide-ranging and innovative "information, education, and entertainment programs" and "to appeal to tastes and interests not generally catered by Channel 3" (Independent Television Commission, 1996, p. 10). Programming minimums are specified for news, current affairs and educational programs.

Satellite technology is considered a form of broadcasting and is used to distribute program services to cable operators and direct broadcast satellite (DBS) service to subscribers in the United Kingdom and the rest of Europe. The dominant firm in this market segment is British Sky Broadcasting Group (BSkyB), a subsidiary of the News Corporation. News Corporation has an international reputation as the most aggressive firm in the DBS sector and holds significant investments in Star Television in Asia (Gershon, 1997). At the beginning of 1997, BSkyB provided 33 advertiser-supported and three premium channels (Financial information 1996; BSkyB demonstrates cable, 1996).

The Cable Industry

The cable industry in the United Kingdom is attempting a transformation from an unsuccessful TV delivery system into an integrated broadband telecommunications, information and entertainment service. The Telecommunications Act of 1984 and the Cable and Broadcasting Act of 1984 opened the telecommunications (telephone) industry to competition and established a mechanism for issuing broadband cable system franchises. Cable TV franchising authority resides within the Cable Division of the ITC. Franchise holders are encouraged by policy to operate also as public telecommunication operators (PTOs) by obtaining a license to provide telecommunications services within their franchises from the Office of Telecommunications (OFTEL) of the Department of Trade and Industry (DTI). Growth in the cable industry remained slow until the 1990 Broadcasting Act removed restrictions on direct foreign investment in cable franchises by companies based outside the EU. North American cable and telephone companies, stymied at home by saturated cable markets and lingering restrictions on the domestic telephone business, seized the opportunity to enter the deregulated U.K. market. Within a short span of time, partnerships and subsidiary ventures involving Telecommunications Inc., USWest, Bell Canada, Cox Cable, NYNEX and others were formed, providing U.K. firms with financial backing and the U.S. partners with a foothold in a new market, access to Europe, and experience in building and running the "information superhighway" still being discussed in the United States. Among the largest firms in the cable industry, Telewest represents a merger of the U.K. cable interests of Telecommunications Inc. and USWest. Birmingham Cable, a joint venture of Telewest, ComcastUK, and General Cable is the largest single franchise. NYNEX Cablecomms UK (60 percent owned by the U.S.-based NYNEX, Inc.) has acquired seven large franchises. VideotronUK, involving Le Groupe Videotron of Canada and Bell Cablemedia, has the largest system in London (Birmingham Cable, 1996; BSkyB demonstrates cable dependence, 1996; Telewest, 1996; Videotron UK-London, 1996; NYNEX Cablecomms, Ltd., 1996; Residential cable telephone, 1996).

Subscriber growth has been slow, but it increased in 1996 when a number of newly built cable franchises became operational. By the end of 1996, cable passed 7.8 million homes (roughly one third of all TV households) and revenues topped £ 1 billion. Residential cable telephone customers increased 65 percent to 1.8 million (23 percent of homes passed), and business cable telephone connections increased 78 percent. In addition, the number of cable TV customers increased 42 percent to 1.65 million households (Cable industry's best year, 1996). As new franchises are completed and older franchises rebuilt with broadband capacity, the faster growing telephone component of the industry is expected to extend cable into more households as the use of online services and the Internet increases. As formerly separate media and information technologies converge, cable telephone customers will be able to acquire new services through the broadband pipeline that already provides telephone service to their homes.

Media Consumers in the United Kingdom

Newspaper reading is a well-developed habit in the United Kingdom. National dailies are read by 56 percent of the adult population, and 62 percent read a national Sunday newspaper (An introduction to British national newspapers, 1996). The regional press asserts that nine out of 10 adults read at least one of the regional newspapers each week (Regional press publishers, 1996). The average age of newspaper readers (currently age 44) is increasing (Lloyd, 1996). Television is found in 99.4 percent of U.K. households and 54 percent own two or more receivers. Residents of the United Kingdom averaged 220 minutes of TV viewing in 1993, the second highest level in Europe (following Portugal). Both daily and prime-time TV viewing is divided evenly between BBC and commercial sources. Viewing is greater, but more fragmented, in cable and DBS households (*Statistical Yearbook,* 1994). By 1993, 72 percent of all households had videocassette recorders (*Statistical Yearbook,* 1995). Recorded videocassette rentals and sales totaled 388 million units in 1993, a

60 percent increase over 1992 levels. The United Kingdom currently represents 30 percent of the European video market (*Statistical Yearbook,* 1995).

Advertisers in the United Kingdom

Total advertising revenue (excluding newspaper classified advertising proceeds) declined between 1989 and 1993 (*Statistical Yearbook,* 1995). Including classified advertising, total 1995 advertising revenue was £ 9.3 billion. Television received the largest share, 28.5 percent. Regional newspapers ranked second at 21.1 percent, and the national press received 15.4 percent. When classified advertising revenue is omitted, newspaper shares decrease and TV's share rises above the 40 percent level. Total commercial TV revenue in 1995 was £ 2.6 billion (Regional press publishers, 1996).

Media Regulators

The United Kingdom has "no written constitution and no law dealing with the role of the press" (Dunnett, 1988, p. 105). Governments have been reluctant to formulate formal policy, especially where the press is concerned. "Instead, policies were generally uncoordinated, reactive, expediential, partial and indirect; a matter of broad objectives . . . rather than of detailed programmes and plans" (Seymour-Ure, 1991, p. 206). Newspapers enjoy neither complete freedom of expression nor access to information. Laws expose the press to libel and contempt litigation and restrict coverage of legal proceedings. The Official Secrets Act of 1911 enables the government to intervene to protect the national interest and other laws restrict publication of material deemed objectionable or harmful (Dunnett, 1988). Newspapers are expected to exercise a level of social responsibility that transcends purely commercial considerations. Therefore, competition and consolidation in the industry are sources of concern. Mergers and the sale of larger newspapers must be approved by the Monopolies and Mergers Commission (Brennan, 1996).

The broadcasting system is under the authority of the Home Office and is viewed as "a public service accountable to the people through Parliament" (Foreign and Commonwealth Office, 1991, p. 1). Under current law, the BBC, ITC, and the Radio Authority are responsible for all broadcasting in the United Kingdom. The BBC operates under a renewable license granted by the Department of National Heritage. Unlike the BBC, the ITC is a regulatory agency and both licenses and regulates non-BBC TV broadcasting, cable TV, teletext, and satellite services (Foreign and Commonwealth Office, 1991).

Despite the deregulatory climate, all broadcast media continue to be treated as public trusts. Concentration of control and cross-media ownership is limited by policy. The ITC issues and enforces codes covering impartiality in news coverage, information gathering, privacy, offensive material, terrorism and crime, political broadcasting, and the portrayal of violence. No political advertising is allowed, and advertising for tobacco products and betting is also prohibited. A separate Broadcasting Complaints Commission also exists to consider charges of "unfair treatment" by broadcast media. Both BBC and ITC-licensed broadcasters must obtain a minimum of 25 percent of their programming from independent producers with an unspecified amount obtained from British and European sources (Foreign and Commonwealth Office, 1991). As noted, cable systems that provide telecommunications services also fall under the jurisdiction of the Office of Telecommunications of the Department of Trade and Industry. OFTEL is charged with responsibility for the economic regulation of telecommunications systems and services, but not the content of services (Office of Telecommunications, 1995).

Analysis of Major United Kingdom Media Industries

The Newspaper Industry

MARKET SUPPLY AND DEMAND. In the daily newspaper industry, both readers and advertisers find considerable choice. On the supply side, three distinct industry segments operate within an increasingly diverse media environment. The larger regional press is more dispersed, with the majority of newspapers serving small populations without direct competition. On the demand side, only 56 percent of the adult population reads a national daily newspaper. Total national newspaper demand, although substantial at 13 million daily, has been in a slow but steady decline from 16.7 million readers in the peak year of 1957 (Seymour-Ure, 1991). The regional press reaches 90 percent of adults in the United Kingdom. In terms of advertising demand, the national dailies have been hurt by lost circulation and the increased number of alternative advertising media and forms of promotion. National newspapers received 20 percent of all advertising revenue in the United Kingdom in 1964 (Dunnett, 1988). By 1995, the percentage had slipped to 15.4 percent (tied with magazine advertising), whereas the regional press received 21.1 percent (Regional press publishers, 1996).

MARKET STRUCTURE. The number of national daily newspapers has not changed substantially during the past half-century, but ownership changes have been common, especially during periods of weakness in the national economy (Seymour-Ure, 1991). Each of the three industry markets appears to be an oligopoly consisting of two to five firms. The very powerful News Corporation and United publish in two segments, and only seven firms publish all 10 national morning dailies. In addition, the two largest publishers, News Corporation and Mirror Group, control 54.7 percent of the combined daily and Sunday circulation (ABC national daily newspapers data 1996; ABC national daily Sunday newspaper data, 1996). Firms enter this industry for a variety of reasons that impact their performance and the operation of the market as a whole. Dunnett (1988) notes that "ownership of a national newspaper buys social prominence, political and economic power and influence, sometimes a peerage, and occasionally profits" (p. 103). Profits are hard to achieve owing to declining circulation and historically low profit margins. Most owners of national dailies are subsidiaries of diversified corporations that can subsidize the losses common to the operation of a national daily (Dunnett, 1988; Seymour-Ure, 1991). When losses become insupportable to the larger corporate entity, however, the decision to dispose of the daily newspaper is made.

Firms engaged in the regional press are more focused on profit than on prestige and the maintenance of a social institution. Chain ownership is common and is structured to maximize efficiency in production and distribution. The regional press has been quicker to adapt to such changes as modern composing and printing technologies. Many regional chains operate centralized facilities where multiple titles are printed. In adapting to societal and industry changes, the daily regional press shifted from morning to evening publication, opposite the course of the national daily press. In addition to increasing consolidation, the major trend of the past 25 years in the regional press has been the rapid growth in the number of "freesheets" or free advertising publications.

ANALYSIS OF COMPETITION. Format and content characteristics of newspapers subdivide the market. A news agent's display of the London dailies provides a graphic illustration of the use of format, headlines, color, and photography to position each newspaper in the mind of the public. Price competition has been used with some success by the dominant News Corporation, which cut the prices of the popular *Sun* and quality *Times,* resulting in a 21 percent circulation increase for the *Times* in 1995, another 16 percent gain the following year, and substantial profit loss at the *Guardian* and *Daily Telegraph* (Brennan, 1996). The overall strategy is to offset the loss of circulation income with increased advertising revenue. Because it takes time for advertisers to respond to circulation changes, only financially strong corporate owners can afford to compete by cutting price. In the regional press, direct competition is limited. Regional dailies compete only to a limited extent with the national dailies, and for many readers the two types complement each other. As advertising media, the regional newspapers compete with both the national press and commercial broadcasting for revenue.

Barriers to entry are substantial for the national press. The start-up cost of a national daily is prohibitive, and reader loyalty to existing titles is difficult to change (Dunnett, 1988). Purchasing a newspaper provides the most common form of market entry, but successful titles are generally unavailable, except at premium prices. Therefore, a buyer must have either a strategy for success or some other motivation to justify the purchase of an unprofitable daily. The government must approve purchases and mergers involving larger newspapers under the 1965 Mergers and Monopolies Act. In contrast to entry barriers, Dunnett (1988) notes that the financial loss that can result from selling an unsuccessful or heavily indebted newspaper for a low price can function as a barrier to exit from the industry.

At present, mergers and acquisitions are less frequent among the national dailies. Because of the government and public attitudes toward the role of the national press, transfer of a major title is newsworthy. Rupert Murdoch's reputation as a media mogul preceded his entry to the United Kingdom in 1969, and his acquisition of the prestigious *Times* in 1980 was cause for concern. Mergers and acquisitions in the large regional press are more common as the industry becomes more consolidated. Trinity International became the largest regional company in 1995 by purchasing large components of the Thomson Corporation (Brennan, 1996). A recent trend involves the sale of regional newspapers by the more diversified media groups to publishers with stronger ties to a geographic region (LeDuc, 1996). Johnston Press has made several such acquisitions in recent years and has become the fifth largest regional publisher in terms of circulation.

CONTENT AND DISTRIBUTION. Unlike electronic media which rely heavily on other sources for content, newspaper organizations produce much of their own, although news services and syndicated materials are widely used. National dailies require more diverse and extensive content owing to their more comprehensive nature. The content of regional newspapers is compiled largely at the local level, as these publications fill a niche described as "a bulletin board and transmitter of routine issues and events" (Dunnett, 1988). Distribution is a major expense in the newspaper industry, and distribution channels are largely traditional: subscriptions (mail or home delivery) and sales by news agents at retail establishments and from vending machines. The national press requires longer distribution channels involving more participants, significant transportation expenses and, in some cases, the use of satellite printing facilities.

The Television Industry

MARKET SUPPLY AND DEMAND. The BBC supplies programming that is available everywhere and funded by a license fee paid by every TV household. The commercial Channels 3 and 4 also reach virtually all TV households. For viewing by all households between 5:30 and 10:00 p.m. during the first half of 1994, BBC 1 averaged a 34 percent market share, and BBC 2 averaged 10 percent. Channel 3 held a 43 percent market share, and Channel 4 received 8 percent. Demand characteristics are different for cable or satellite households. Third quarter 1994 statistics for daily viewing in these households show the BBC market share at 24 percent for BBC 1 and 7 percent for BBC 2. Channel 3 received a 30 percent share, and Channel 4 averaged 7 percent. Programs of two popular DBS and cable packages received a combined 24 percent share (*Statistical Yearbook,* 1995).

Satellite services reach subscribers through two routes: direct reception (DBS) and through cable subscription. As the dominant supplier of DBS services, BSkyB reached 5.65 million subscribers (nearly 25 percent of TV households) by late 1996 with revenue above £ 1 billion (Financial information 1996; BSkyB demonstrates cable, 1996). The basic Sky Multichannel Package provides general interest programming, sports, movie channels, news service, and a large complement of demographic and lifestyle channels. Subscribers select from options that range from the basic tier of 33 channels without premium services to the maximum service including three premium (movie and sports) packages. Prices vary in four steps from £ 11.99 to £ 26.99 per month (Subscribe to Sky, 1996).

MARKET STRUCTURE. The structure of the TV industry is largely dictated by regulatory policy rather than marketplace forces. Although BBC services are not expected to maximize audiences in order to attract advertising revenue, they nonetheless must be perceived by both viewers and policymakers to merit payment of the required annual license fee. Viewer loyalty to the BBC has been demonstrated in commissioned surveys and by viewing levels comparable to those of commercial services. BBC financing has been an issue since the 1986 Peacock Committee Report studied and rejected the possibility of advertiser support for the BBC, recommending linkage of future license fees to the Retail Price Index (Home Office, 1986). Overstaffing and efficiency issues were addressed, with personnel reductions and cost controls saving $450 million between 1991 and 1996, and the BBC's charter was renewed for another 10 years in 1996 (Riding, 1996). The technological demands and competitive pressures of the next decade will keep the issue of BBC funding alive. The BBC realizes that it must keep pace with other services by providing advanced widescreen digital TV, 24-hour news, and interactive services. However, planned fee increases are expected to be too small to fund these improvements. As a result, the BBC must lobby the public and politicians for increased support while exploring such new revenue streams as the commercial release of programming from BBC archives (Riding, 1996).

In commercial TV, programming competition is limited by policy. The long-term goal has been to avoid duplicating the perceived commercial excesses of broadcasting in the United States (Hoffmann-Riem, 1996). Under the present system, each Channel 3 licensee serves a specific geographic region. As a national service, Channel 4 operates throughout all of the Channel 3 franchise areas but provides programming that is different by mandate and appeals to a smaller audience. With a national identity, the new Channel 5 is very likely to compete with Channel 3 and has the potential to undermine the policy of regional and local service that Channel 3 has represented since commercial broadcasting began in 1954.

Satellite TV services operate with much greater marketplace freedom than land-based competitors. British Sky Broadcasting Group enjoys a virtual monopoly in the DBS industry. Such services pose serious potential challenges to the market structure of TV in the United Kingdom by further fragmenting the viewing audience, reducing viewing of both BBC and commercial terrestrial services. Fragmentation may challenge the public's evaluation of the BBC license fee while increasing the marketplace pressure on commercial broadcasters to offer more mass-appeal programming than envisioned by ITC policies.

Commercial services such as BSkyB, supported by the economic resources of global media conglomerates, will have far greater ability than either the BBC or ITC-regulated stations to fund the transition to advanced digital TV and interactive services. British Sky Broadcasting Group already plans to subsidize partially the cost to customers of the set-top decoders that are necessary to access planned pay-per-view, sports and interactive digital TV services (BSkyB demonstrates cable, 1996).

ANALYSIS OF COMPETITION. All five terrestrial channels appeal to different tastes and needs. However, BBC 1 and 2 are programmed to complement each other, not to compete directly for viewers. Despite the programming requirements and protected revenue status of Channel 4, commercial services in the United Kingdom do compete with each other and with other commercial alternatives for advertising revenue. Commercial broadcasters are increasingly likely to schedule mass-appeal programs in order to maximize revenue as their satellite and nonbroadcast competitors operate without policy constraints (Hoffmann-Riem, 1996). Alternative commercial electronic media services are expected to grow significantly. By the BBC's own estimates, its audience share will erode to about 33 percent by 2005 and half of the households in the United Kingdom will have multichannel digital services by then (Riding, 1996). If this estimate is accurate and commercial terrestrial service audiences continue to match those of the BBC channels, then the market-driven alternative TV services will equal the audience share of the ITC-regulated services.

Barriers to entry to the TV industry in the United Kingdom are powerful. The BBC variant affords no entry. Commercial licenses are limited in number and available through a competitive bidding process every 10 years. At the most recent licensing period, the first under the Broadcasting Act of 1990, the ITC received 40 applications for 16 licenses, 12 of which were granted to incumbent franchisees (Hoffmann-Riem, 1996). Four applicants sought the single Channel 5 franchise in 1995 (Independent Television Commission announces, 1996). Although the ITC does not automatically award licenses to the highest bidder, the amount of the bid is an important factor for applicants who meet program service quality minimums. The market value of ITC licenses varies, but the cost of licensed entry is substantial. The successful Channel 5 applicant bid £ 22 million (Independent Television Commission announces, 1996). Purchasing a franchise is another option but requires ITC approval. The MAI Group purchased Anglia Television, the Channel 3 franchisee for East England, in 1994 and later merged with United News and Media (Radio and Television, 1996).

The entry stakes are high in the commercial terrestrial market, but they pale in comparison to the cost of starting a DBS service. After a merger with an early competitor, News Corporation invested vast sums in BSkyB and operated at a significant loss for 4 years before turning a profit in 1994 (Gershon, 1997). The availability of satellite transponders and access to them are another expensive consideration. The start-up costs are so enormous and the established dominance of BSkyB so great that it is unlikely that this firm will see its monopoly status challenged.

CONTENT AND DISTRIBUTION. The content market is an important component of the U.K. TV industry and is likely to experience significant growth as new demand for programs stimulates competition. The TV production capacity of the United Kingdom is substantial, with 23 of the top 100 audiovisual companies in Europe in 1993, including the BBC, BSkyB, and the majority of the commercial licensees (*Statistical Yearbook,* 1995). The BBC and most of the commercial franchises have usually produced most of their own programming and only a handful of these firms has pursued secondary markets for their programs. Lensen (1992) finds this to be characteristic European market behavior, which has had a negative impact on the film industries of Europe. The current licensing philosophy of the ITC encourages diversity in the production market through promotion of a "publisher-broadcaster" model, whereby licensees purchase or commission the production of more content from outside sources. Direct broadcast satellite and the growing number of cable channels based in the United Kingdom will further expand the program market. Even the historically self-sufficient BBC is expected to obtain more content produced outside of its facilities as it expands into subscription services and further cost control alternatives are needed. In an increasingly competitive content market, the resources of BSkyB and other powerful media firms will be difficult to outbid, leaving the BBC at a great disadvantage. The BBC surrendered rights to the coverage of several professional sports including Formula One auto racing, lost in 1995 when the commercial companies offered 10 times the amount the BBC had been paying (Time to adjust, 1995).

The Cable Industry

Within the cable industry, government has since 1981 largely pursued a course marked by deregulation, private industry initiative, marketplace competition, and a global outlook. In 1981, the telephone service was separated from the Post Office, creating the national British Telecommunications Corporation (BT). In the same year the private sector Mercury Communications firm, a subsidiary of Cable and Wireless, P.L.C., was authorized to compete with BT in local and long distance service, and the BT monopolies in network and equipment markets and in the use of telephone lines for value-added services were ended (Newman, 1986). British Telecommunications was privatized in 1984, shortly after the divestiture of AT&T in the United States. Other legislation in 1984 and the 1990 Broadcasting Act enabled the virtual relaunching of the struggling U.K. cable TV industry as a broadband service provider, enabling cable to expand into the telecommunication arena.

MARKET SUPPLY AND DEMAND. The overlap between the cable and telecommunication industries complicates discussion of market supply. British Telecommunications dominates the telecommunication sector of the U.K. economy, with 90 percent of the telephone market (Landler, 1996). The remaining 10 percent is shared by Mercury Corporation and the cable industry PTOs. By late 1996, the cable industry provided telephone services to only 1.8 of the nearly 27 million telephone households in the United Kingdom. In terms of TV services, the cable industry has the capacity to serve slightly more than one third of the TV households in the United Kingdom but lags behind the DBS sector in the multichannel marketplace. Cable TV channels overlap substantially with those provided by BSkyB and usually include the BBC and independent channels. A few of the larger and more aggressive cable companies, however, are beginning to offer services that are unique to their franchises. Both telecommunication and cable competitors are also developing the means to supply on-line service and Internet access.

The demand for residential telephone services is virtually universal. Business sector demand continues to grow as businesses adopt new information technologies. Demand for cable TV service remains low, although optimism for this sector remains high. The longstanding public service philosophy has structured a very different TV culture in the United Kingdom. For most Britons, the services provided by terrestrial broadcasters have been adequate and alternative viewing has been enabled by the use of videocassette recorders and both rented and purchased videocassettes. Subscription service growth has also been slowed by a consistently sluggish economy.

MARKET STRUCTURE. The market structures of the cable and telecommunication industries have been shaped by consistent deregulatory policies. British Telecommunications lost its monopoly status, but it still dominates the telecommunication industry. The cable industry, with aspirations to be a significant factor in the telecommunications industry of the next decade, is developing slowly. The potential of this industry has attracted investment by domestic and international telecommunications and media conglomerates, and the larger firms have acquired multiple franchises. For telephone service, calls within a cable franchise are handled end to end by the cable company usually at a lower rate than that charged by BT. Still, most calls placed outside the cable franchise are routed through the BT system, incurring an access charge. This element of market structure must change if cable PTOs are to become truly competitive.

COMPETITION. While cable firms have moved into telecommunication, BT has shown little interest in cable. It holds one franchise (Westminster) but has sold other previously acquired cable interests (Creating the superhighways, 1994). Direct involvement in the cable industry would require the diversion of BT resources at a time when its attention is directed toward European and international business telecommunications. In late 1996, BT announced plans to acquire the U.S. long distance firm, MCI (Lander, 1996). This development follows BT's formation of partnerships in Europe and Asia in anticipation of the mandated opening of state-controlled telephone monopolies to competition in most EU countries in 1998. The purchase of MCI would provide BT and its European partners with high capacity connections to the United States (Andrews, 1996). Meanwhile, the U.K. cable industry is focused on building its infrastructure and expanding its provision of broadband services to homes and businesses. Given BT's dominance of U.K. telephony, the company can probably afford to ignore cable competition while it seeks to build a major stake in the global arena.

The cable industry touts convenience and cost savings in its promotions. Customers who switch to a cable PTO usually retain their present telephone numbers and anticipate an average 10 to 15 percent savings on calls and £ 1 on the monthly line rental (Residential cable telephone, 1996). As noted, though, only certain types of calls are actually cheaper due to market structure. In an effort to overcome this obstacle, Cable and Wireless announced plans to create a merger involving its subsidiary, Mercury Communications, along with the cable holdings of NYNEX Cablecomms Group, Bell Cablemedia, and Videotron Holdings. The new company has the potential of serving six million homes, including the London market, and would be able to offer competitive long distance rates using Mercury's long distance resources and avoiding BT access charges. Successful growth would give the new entity substantial market power in negotiating for equipment purchases and TV programming (The front line, 1996). Whether this merger takes place or not, the cable industry will have to find ways to offer real price competition in both local and long distance telephony in order to attract more customers. In the short term, only marketplace remedies are available to deal with the competitive advantage of BT. Most elements of existing market structure in the cable and telecommunication industry will not be reviewed by the government until shortly after the turn of the century (Creating the superhighways, 1994).

Barriers to entry are largely economic in the cable industry. The telecommunication and cable markets are open to competition and foreign investment, and mergers and acquisitions have been commonplace in the cable industry. The free operation of marketplace forces often leads to consolidation in new industries in which there is an imbalance in the relative strength of firms. The proposed multifirm deal involving Cable and Wireless is an example, and other mergers are expected.

CONTENT AND DISTRIBUTION. The primary focus of the cable industry is on building a distribution system. In many ways the cable industry is still in a start-up phase since its relaunch after 1990 as a broadband service. New cable franchises and the rebuilding of older cable TV-only systems are expensive but necessary first steps. The content market for the cable industry is essentially the same as that used by the DBS industry, but it also includes specific program services developed by BSkyB. All providers of TV programming will be affected by increased demand in the production marketplace.

Emerging Media Economic Issues in the United Kingdom

Several issues will affect the media industries of the United Kingdom as they seek to survive and prosper in the global economy. The TV marketplace in the United Kingdom is a product of sustained public broadcasting policy and revised commercial broadcast policy. The Broadcasting Act of 1990 was created in a policy environment that espoused deregulation and increased marketplace competition. The Act, however, "is marked by an inherent contradiction between deregulation from an economic–institutional standpoint and overregulation with regard to certain programming issues" (Hoffmann-Riem, 1996, p. 108.) This inconsistent regulatory philosophy appears to hinder the ITC-licensed services and the BBC. The commercial services, while limited in their ability to compete for audiences (and consequently, for advertising revenue) do enjoy the marketplace freedom to seek new revenue streams. A number of ITC licensees are connected to other media and nonmedia corporations and do not depend exclusively on franchise advertising revenue for survival. The BBC, on the other hand, faces the difficult task of building for the expensive future with an inadequate source of funding. Worse, successful pursuit of new sources of revenue from subscription services or the licensing of program archives to commercial services could work against efforts to increase the viewer license fee. If the less-regulated commercial services are able to restructure the viewership patterns of U.K. households, public support for the BBC may wane. These issues must be addressed in the interest of the integrity of the domestic TV system.

While the TV industry grapples with the economic impact of policy constraints, segments of the cable industry struggle to grow in a very competitive environment in which other firms control the majority of the market share. Direct broadcast satellite leads cable in supplying subscription TV service, although British Telecommunications dominates telephony. The short-term key to cable industry growth seems to exist in the telephone sector. Because most cable systems are relatively new and revenues are low, owners are awash in the red ink of start-up expenses, whereas BT and BSkyB are well established and profitable. In the case of the cable industry, the free exercise of competition places cable firms at a disadvantage. If the industry survives and grows, policy will be vindicated and the vitality of marketplace forces confirmed. If the industry fails to thrive, however, government efforts to increase competition in the telecommunication sector will have been thwarted and a policy adjustment to "level the playing field" for the cable firms will be likely. The vitality of the U.K. economy in the coming years will be an important factor.

The media industries of the United Kingdom vary in terms of their apparent willingness and ability to adapt to the digital future. Both the BBC and DBS industries are actively promoting their vision of the future, and the cable industry is building an infrastructure that will have the capacity to handle virtually any advanced technology. The statuses of the newspaper industries in the digital future are less clear. Continuing loss of readership and the accompanying loss of revenue are expected as readers age and turn to other sources. Lloyd (1996) chastises the industry for doing too little in adapting thus far, although his critique may be self-serving. Lloyd writes for the News Corporation *Times* newspapers, which operate a sophisticated on-line version on the World Wide Web. The *Financial Times* is also on-line, but many of the competitors in the national press have not yet embraced the Internet.

The global role of U.K. media will be tested soon in the EU. The United Kingdom has advantages in the size of its production capacity and in the concentration of cable and DBS program production companies based in England. The early deregulation of the telecommunications industry and the aggressive action of BT in the European and international marketplaces are sources of strength. In terms of programming, differences in languages and cultures will impede the growth of an international content market to some degree. Content from the United States has not, however, suffered from this hindrance, and it is likely that the United Kingdom and other nations can surmount this problem. Content markets should be more open in the future as more "deregulated" markets are structured to give preferences to domestic and regional productions, usually at the expense of U.S. content suppliers.

Despite limited success, the United Kingdom has been a leader and is generally ahead of other EU nations in promoting private sector development of its telecommunications infrastructure. As a result of the openness of its markets to foreign investment, U.K. firms have been well received in the United States and other markets. The proposed BT-MCI merger would be less likely to receive approval if U.S. telecommunications firms were denied opportunities to invest in the United Kingdom. Media industries require enormous investments to develop the economies of scale necessary to control costs and offer competitive prices. Therefore, foreign investment remains necessary for firms based in the slow-growing economy of the United Kingdom to pursue their objectives.

References

About S4C (1996). British Broadcasting Corporation. Available on-line: http:// www.s4c.co.uk.about/eintro.html.

Andrews, E. L. (1996). Behind a giant deal, a strategy to attract customers in Europe. *The New York Times,* November 4, pp. C1, C7.

Audit Bureau of Circulation (1996a). ABC national daily newspapers data, October 14. Available on-line: http://www.abc.org.uk/nday0996.html.

Audit Bureau of Circulation (1996b). ABC national daily Sunday newspaper data, October 14. Available on-line: http://www.abc.org.uk/nsun0996.html.

Birmingham Cable (1996). Inside Cable. On-line: http://www.inside-cable.org.uk/.

Brennan, J. (1996). The British press: 1996. In: *Editor and Publisher International Yearbook,* part 1. New York: Editor and Publisher, p. IV-1.

BSkyB demonstrates cable dependence...and its digital plans (1996). Inside Cable, November. On-line: http://www.inside-cable.co.uk/users/ek80/96_11sky.htm.

Cable industry's best year (1996). Cable Communications Association, November 25. Available on-line: http://www.cable.co.uk/new/latest/index.htm#story1.

Cairncross, A. (1992). *The British Economy Since 1945: Economic Policy and Performance, 1945–1990.* Oxford: Blackwell.

Creating the superhighways of the future: Developing broadband communications in the UK (1994). Department of Trade and Industry. Available on-line: http://www.open.gov.uk/dti/broadband comms.htm.

Dunnett, P. J. S. (1988). *The World Newspaper Industry.* London: Croom Helm.

Financial information (1996). British Sky Broadcasting Group, P.L.C., June 30. Available on-line: http://www.sky.co.uk/about/finance.htm.

Foreign and Commonwealth Office (1991). *Broadcasting in Britain: Recent developments.* London: Foreign and Commonwealth Office.

The front line (1996). *The Economist,* October 26, 341:84–85.

Gershon, R. A. (1997). *The Transnational Media Corporation: Global messages and free market competition.* Mahwah, NJ: Erlbaum.

Head, S. W., Sterling, C. H., and Schofield, L. B. (1994). *Broadcasting in America: A Survey of Electronic Media.* 7th ed. Boston: Houghton Mifflin

The history of the Union (1996). European Union. Available on-line: http://www.europa.eu.int/en/ev/euhist.html.

Hoffmann-Riem, W. (1996). *Regulating Media: The Licensing and Supervision of Broadcasting in Six Countries.* New York: Guilford.

Home Office (1986). *Report of the Committee of Financing the BBC.* London: Her Majesty's Stationary Office.

Independent Television Commission announces its decision to award Channel 5 licence (1996). Independent Television Commission, October 27. Available on-line: http://www.itc.co.uk/file:///BI/PRESSCH5.HTM.

Independent Television Commission factfile (1996). Independent Television Commission. Available on-line: http://www.itc.co.uk/factfile/index.htm.

An introduction to British national newspapers (1996). Express Newspapers Research Department. Available on-line: http://www.expressnewspapers.co.uk/intronn.html.

Landler, M. (1996). MCI deal reverberates on both sides of the Atlantic. *The New York Times,* November 4, pp. C1, C7.

LeDuc, F. (1996). Regional press consolidating around true-to-type publishers. *The Times,* June 6. Available on-line: http://www.the-times.co.uk:8080D.

Lensen, A. (1992). *Concentration in the Media Industry: The European Community and Mass Media Regulation.* Washington, DC: Annenberg Washington Program.

Lloyd, C. (1996). Newspapers see writing on the wall. *The Sunday Times,* January 7.

Lloyd, T. O. (1986). *Empire to Welfare State: English History 1906–1985.* Oxford: Oxford University Press.

Newman, K. (1986). *The Selling of British Telecom.* New York: St. Martin's.

NYNEX in the United Kingdom (1996). NYNEX Cablecomms, Ltd. Available on-line: http://www.nynex.co.uk/about8.html.

Office of Telecommunication (1995). Beyond the telephone, the television, and the PC. Available on-line: http://www.oftel.gov.uk/superhwy/multi.htm.

Radio and Television (1996). In: *The Europa World Yearbook 1996.* London: Europa Publications Limited, p. 3296.

Regional press publishers (1996). Newspaper Society, December 1. Available on-line: http://www.newspapersoc.org.uk/facts&figs/images/Publ.htm.

Residential cable telephone: Pay less for your phone (1996). Telewest Communication, P.L.C., August 27. Available on-line: http://www.telewest.co.uk/residential/phone_savings.

Riding, A. (1996, November 4). The new BBC: Business as usual or just a business? *The New York Times,* pp. C1, C10.

Seymour-Ure, C. (1991). *The British Press and Broadcasting Since 1945.* Oxford: Basil Blackwell.

Statistical Yearbook 1994-1995: Cinema, television, video, and new media in Europe. (1995). Strasbourg: European Audiovisual Observatory.

Studlar, D. T. (1996). *Great Britain: Decline or Renewal?* Boulder, CO: Westview.

Subscribe to Sky (1996). British Sky Broadcasting Group, P.L.C., November 12. Available on-line: http://www.sky.co.uk/shop/subs.htm.

Telewest (1996). Inside Cable. Available on-line: http://www.inside-cable.org.uk/.

Time to adjust your set (1995). *The Economist* 341(December 23, 1996–January 5):69–71.

Videotron UK-London (1996). Inside Cable. Available on-line: http://www.inside-cable.org.uk/.

Note

1. Sixteen licenses were awarded by the ITC for Channel 3 service to begin on January 1, 1993. *Anglia Television Ltd.* serves the east of England (owned by MAI Group and United News and Media). *Border Television, P.L.C.* serves the border region between England and Scotland and the adjacent Isle of Man. Carlton UK Television, part of Carlton Communications, operates two franchises, including the lucrative London area (*Carlton Television, Ltd.*), and the Midlands region, which includes Birmingham (*Central Broadcasting*). *Channel Television* holds the small franchise for the Channel Islands. Northern Scotland, the geographically largest franchise area, is served by *Grampian Television,* P.L.C. *Granada Television Ltd.,* is the Channel 3 licensee in northwestern England, including the Manchester market. Granada is part of a multinational conglomerate with interests in broadcasting, media production, hotels, restaurants and other areas. Granada also packages programming for BSkyB service and cable interests. *HTV Group, Ltd.* serves western England and Wales. South and southeastern England is served by *Meridian Broadcasting, Ltd.,* based in Southampton. The franchise holder for central Scotland is *Scottish Television, P.L.C.* Northern Ireland is served by *Ulster Television, P.L.C.* Southwestern England, including Plymouth, is served by *Westcountry Television, Ltd.* The Yorkshire area near Leeds and the franchise for northeast England, including Newcastle, are served by a merged entity, *Yorkshire–Tyne Tees Television, Ltd.* A second London service is also licensed to operate from Friday evening through sign-off on Sunday night. *London Weekend Television, Ltd.* holds this franchise. *Good Morning TV (GMTV)* is licensed to provide a national breakfast time carried by all Channel 3 broadcasters (Radio and Television, 1996).

8

GERMANY

C. Ann Hollifield

The German Media Market in an Era of Change

The Federal Republic of Germany sits at the heart of Europe geographically, politically and economically. As Western Europe's most populous country and strongest economy, Germany has ranked as one of the Continent's largest and most powerful media markets for much of the post-War period. Consumer demand, language barriers, and cooperation within the media industry have helped German media corporations build a strong foundation in their home market. As a result, a number of German media concerns have grown to rank among the world's largest, with operations stretching around the world and plans under way for steady expansion into new geographic and product markets.

Market power notwithstanding, however, the last two decades of the 20th century have been a challenging and, at times, difficult period for Germany and Germany's media economy. No other Western European country has been so directly involved or so deeply affected by the whirlwind of political and economic changes that have swept Europe in 1980s and '90s. And although German media industries were initially enthusiastic about the potential for

The author gratefully acknowledges the assistance of Dr. Christina Holtz-Bacha, Dr. Lee B. Becker and Shari Sweeney.

expansion as a result of the reunification of East and West Germany and plans for a European economic union, much of that promise was still unrealized as the millennium approached its close. Instead, increased European and global competition and the costs of reunification threw Germany into an extended recession—a recession that many economists read as a sign that Germany needs to rethink some key aspects of its industrial and social structures. At the same time, the effort to liberalize, privatize and standardize European economic regulations in preparation for the European Union (EU) began to change significantly the competitive environment in which Germany's media industries have operated.

As the end of the 1990s approached, Germany remained one of the world's strongest media markets, and German media corporations continued to build their global market positions. Nevertheless, within Germany, media industries were undergoing major restructuring—restructuring that promised to alter fundamentally the shape of the German media landscape in the 21st century.

The German Media Economy

The modern German media system was established by the Allies at the end of World War II. Although the press had been largely privately owned in Germany prior to 1945, government censorship of content had been the rule more often than not through German history, according to the whim of the local or national government in power (Deutsches Zeitungsmuseum, 1988). After the war, however, Article 5 of the new federal Constitution forbade censorship and guaranteed freedom of the press, "reporting through radio and film," and the right of individual citizens to freely express their opinion in "word, print and image" (Artikel 5). The press was reestablished under private ownership, whereas broadcasting was organized under a public ownership monopoly because of the limited number of broadcast frequencies available in each European nation (Meyn, 1994).

By the 1990s, Germany's media industries had grown to be among the most powerful in the global media economy, and Germany itself had become one of the most desirable media markets in Europe. The country had the Continent's second largest population behind Russia, with approximately 81 million people in 1993, and boasted Europe's strongest economy. In 1994, western Germany alone had a gross domestic product (GDP) of U.S.$1.8 trillion, Europe's largest (Organization for Economic Cooperation and Development, 1996).[1] The western half of the country ranked third on the Continent for GDP per capita at U.S.$27,826. That put Germany behind Switzerland and Denmark but ahead of the United States, which had a 1994 GDP per capita of $25,512.

Moreover, as measured by the Organization for Economic Cooperation and Development (OECD), Germany's standard of living was among the Continent's highest. Western Germany ranked first in Europe in terms of passenger cars per 1,000 inhabitants in 1990 and first in terms of televisions (TVs) per 1,000 inhabitants in 1991, although—strikingly—it ranked only 12th for the number of telephones per 1,000 inhabitants in 1991. Germans also were among the most highly educated European citizens, with 85 percent of the population holding at least a high school diploma in 1994, a percentage second only to the United States among industrialized nations (Desruisseaux, 1996). Germans also enjoyed significant leisure time. In 1994, German unions negotiated a 35-hour work week for employees in many of the nation's largest industries, including the newspaper industry. Education, income and leisure time are, of course, all strongly associated with media use among consumers.

Not surprisingly, German consumers' media expenditures have been growing faster than income. In 1994, the average four-person middle-income household spent DM 147 (U.S.$91)[2] on mass media per month. That was up 8 percent from 1991, although monthly income for middle-income households increased only 6 percent during the same period. Similarly, high-income households spent an average of DM 238 (U.S.$147) per month on media products in 1994, up 11 percent from 1991, or 4 percent more than the average increase in monthly income for high-income households during that period (Media Perspektiven Basisdaten, 1995).

On a comparative basis, Germany sells more daily newspapers than any other European nation, although it ranks only 10th for the number of daily newspapers published per 1,000 inhabitants (United Nations, 1995). Similarly, Germany is second only to Russia for the number of magazines sold and diffusion of that circulation in the population (United Nations, 1995).[3] The country ranks sixth in Europe in terms of videocassette recorder penetration (European Audiovisual Observatory, 1996), and seventh both for the percentage of TV households passed by cable and the percentage of households passed by cable that subscribe to cable (United Nations, 1995).

But if Germany's media economy ranks as one of the world's strongest and most stable, in the last decade of the 20th century it was also one of the most unquiet. The reunification of East and West Germany and the collapse of the Eastern Bloc created a land rush among West German media companies as they sprinted eastward to establish footholds in both the new eastern German states and the former communist countries of Eastern Europe. It quickly became apparent, however, that neither East Germany nor Eastern Europe would be easy markets. By the mid-1990s, the shakeout among western investors was still ongoing and the long-term outlook for some West German investments was still in doubt (Keller, 1996). Moreover, both the economics and psychology of the east and west German audiences remained different enough that German media industries and statisticians continued to report operational results in the eastern states separately (Keller, 1996; Organization for Economic Cooperation and Development, 1996; Statistisches Bundesamt, 1996).

By the mid-1990s, it had also become apparent that the coming EU held less promise for German media industries than originally had been hoped (Pasquay, 1996). Although new European telecommunications regulations promised to open cross-border investment opportunities in broadcasting, telephone and on-line markets, economic union offered little by way of new opportunities in newspaper and magazine publishing because of language barriers and mature Western European market conditions.

But the key factor shaping the German media economy during the first half of the 1990s, one that promised to continue to be a major influence, was the condition of the German economy as a whole. Throughout the first half of the decade, Germany suffered an extended recession brought on by the high cost of reunification—$600 billion between 1990 and 1996—and the soaring cost structures of German industry (Cowell, 1996; Organization for Economic Cooperation and Development, 1996).

Since the end of World War II, the German economy has functioned on a "market socialism" model, with the idea of the "social state" codified in the German Constitution (Organization for Economic Cooperation and Development, 1996, p. 52). Under the market socialism model, industry is privately owned but heavily regulated to ensure a high level of social responsibility and social stability, whereas the government is expected to provide a decent standard of living for those unable to provide for themselves. Generous health care, retirement, vacation and maternity benefits are guaranteed either through the employer or the state, and labor laws give employees wide ranging rights over corporate decisions, including a voice in company decisions to hire, fire, reassign and even reschedule workers. Moreover, wages for most major German industries are negotiated at the national level between unions and the employer associations that represent the industries for which the employees in the union work.

As a result of these national labor and industrial structures, German industry finds it difficult to adjust quickly to changing market conditions. For example, despite the ongoing recession, between 1990 and 1994 wages as a percentage of GDP rose at an average annual rate of 5.2 percent in western Germany. That was the fourth highest rate of increase in Europe during the period and more than twice the U.S. level of 2.8 percent. Moreover, it considerably outpaced the average annual increase in German consumer prices of

3.3 percent for the period (Organization for Economic Cooperation and Development, 1996). At the same time, unemployment also rose steadily, reaching 9 percent in May 1996 in the west and 15.5 percent in the eastern states (Organization for Economic Cooperation and Development, 1996).

These economic conditions did not go unfelt within German media industries. Newspapers downsized their work forces through the 1990s, and circulation figures were hit by the combination of rising unemployment and rising prices for media products. Even in those media industries experiencing growth, such as the audiovisual and multimedia industries, companies noted the increased competition from countries with lower wage and more flexible industrial structures (Bertelsmann, 1996a). And, because the roots of the recession lay in structural factors within German society such as reunification and the nation's socioeconomic system, economists predicted that Germany's economy—and therefore, its media economy—would continue to be vulnerable in the increasingly competitive global markets of the future (Organization for Economic Cooperation and Development, 1996).

The nation's economic situation was not the only challenge faced by Germany's media industries. The regulatory framework governing German broadcast and telecommunications-based industries is complex, comprehensive and, in the face of rapidly changing markets and technologies, evolving. Since 1984 Germany has undertaken major reforms of its broadcast and telecommunications regulations at least three times and, as late as the end of 1996, final decisions on some questions remained to be made. In Germany, broadcast regulations fall under the authority of the individual states, or *Länder*. Changes in broadcast regulations are negotiated through interstate treaties and are subject to approval by the federal Constitutional Court.

Germany's broadcast and telecommunications industries also are subject to EU rules. Those regulations govern such things as national broadcast licensing rules, programming quotas, advertising regulations, and media concentration and competition. For example, in 1994 plans for a German pay-TV consortium between the state-owned Deutsche Telekom, Bertelsmann—the world's third largest media company—and KirchGruppe, Europe's largest film distributer, were disallowed by the European Commission as being anticompetitive (Bus, 1994). And although the foundation of broadcast regulation was laid by the EU in 1989 in the "Television Without Frontiers" directive, the rapidly changing economic and technological environments for broadcast and telecommunications meant those rules have been constantly reexamined and amended. Moreover, as the 1990s moved toward their close, several different governing bodies in the EU structure still held various degrees of authority over media regulation, leading to policy conflicts between government bodies and muddying the waters of the European media economy even further.

Major Media Industries

Within the German economy as a whole, media continued to grow in importance as an industry. In 1995, advertising contributed an estimated 1.05 percent to Germany's GDP, up from just under 1 percent in 1989 and was continuing to grow (Keller, 1996). Despite the downturn in the overall economy, advertising sales were up 7.1 percent in 1996 and 6.4 percent in 1995. That growth was spread across almost all media segments in the country, with particularly strong growth in advertising on TV and through direct mail.

In the meantime, by the mid-1990s a number of German companies ranked among the world's largest and most powerful media conglomerates within their media segments. Bertelsmann ranked as the third largest media corporation overall in the world (Bertelsmann, 1996b) and as the world's second largest multimedia conglomerate, behind only Time Warner (European Audiovisual Observatory, 1996). Among global audiovisual companies, the German public broadcasting corporation ARD ranked fifth, the private KirchGruppe ranked 10th, and Bertelsmann ranked 15th in the audiovisual sector on the basis of turnover in the 1988–1994 period. Deutsche Telekom, the German telecommunications provider, stood as the second largest cable TV company in the world behind the United States' Tele-Communications Inc.

Within the European media economy, German dominance was even more significant. ARD, which is operated by a consortium of the German states, ranked as Europe's largest audiovisual company, with KirchGruppe third and Bertelsmann fourth. Two other German companies also ranked within the top 15 European audiovisual companies: RTL at 13th and the German national public network ZDF at 14th (European Audiovisual Observatory, 1996).

In Germany's national media market, daily newspapers still make up the largest single segment in the German media economy based on annual revenues, followed by magazines, the book publishing industry and, in fourth place, TV (Media Perspektiven Basisdaten, 1995; Statistisches Bundesamt, 1996). The major commercial German media companies are almost all conglomerates with significant holdings in more than one media segment, and concentration of ownership within each specific media sector is high. Germany has had no laws other than antitrust regulations that limit concentration of press ownership, although concentration of commercial broadcasting ownership is regulated at both the state and federal levels. Moreover, cross-ownership, cooperative and partnership agreements between the major corporations are common, creating even greater concentration of media ownership than is initially apparent.

Axel Springer Verlag AG, for example, is Germany's largest newspaper publisher, controlling about 23.3 percent of the daily newspapers distributed in 1995 (Media Perspektiven Basisdaten, 1995). Springer also is the second largest magazine publisher in the country with 15.3 percent of the magazine market, half that controlled by Heinrich Bauer Verlag KG, which had 32.5 percent of the German magazine market.

In commercial broadcasting, Bertelsmann and the KirchGruppe are clearly two of the largest players, although complex cross-investments make the exact broadcast market share of specific companies extremely difficult to determine. Springer and Bauer also both have significant radio and TV holdings, as do many of Germany's other large media companies.

In addition to their domestic markets, Germany's media corporations have a strong international presence. Because German also is spoken in Austria and Switzerland, German publications circulate far beyond Germany's borders and are even widely available in countries such as Poland, Hungary, the Czech Republic and the Netherlands, where German is a common second language. More importantly, however, many—if not most—of Germany's major media concerns have invested heavily in foreign operations. Bertelsmann—the largest single media concern in Germany—Springer, Bauer and KirchGruppe, for example, all have combinations of subsidiaries, partnerships and investments in other countries, producing publications and other products specific to those foreign markets and languages (Hollifield, 1993; Media Perspektiven, 1995).

The Newspaper Industry

The newspaper industry commands the largest segment of the German mass media market, with 1994 annual revenues of just under DM 21 billion (U.S.$13 billion) (Statistisches Bundesamt, 1996; Table 8-1). Unlike all other European countries except Great Britain, Germany does not give the newspaper industry any type of direct government subsidy (Pasquay, 1996). Newspapers control the largest share of the German advertising market at 29.5 percent in 1995 (Keller, 1996), and readership levels remain high, with 81 percent of all Germans over the age of 14 reading the newspaper daily (Bauer, 1996a). The country had 438 daily newspapers in 1996, with a total circulation of 32.5 million (Keller, 1996) and, as measured by newsprint consumption, the industry was continuing to grow (Keller, 1996). Udell (1990) argues that comparing growth in newsprint consumption to growth in the GDP is the best indicator of the health of the newspaper industry. Revenue figures can be misleading because they may indicate an increase in advertising rates rather than real growth.

As previously noted, concentration of newspaper ownership is high in Germany. Today, 42 percent of the nation's daily newspaper circulation is controlled by the five largest newspaper publishing companies (Media Perspektiven, 1995). Moreover, because of cooperative working arrangements between

Table 8-1. German Media Industry

Media Industry	Revenues[a]	Largest Companies or Channels	% Market Share
Newspapers	$13 billion	Axel Springer Verlag	23.3
		Zeitungsgruppe WAZ	5.5
		Verlagsgruppe Stuttgarter Zeitung	5.0
Magazines	10.5 billion	Heinrich Bauer Verlag	32.5[b]
		Axel Springer Verlag	15.3
		Burda Holding Co.	9.3
Book Publishing	7.3 billion	N/A	N/A
Television	3.5 billion[c]	RTL[d]	33.0[e]
		SAT.1	27.4
		PRO SIEBEN	21.4
Radio	713 million[c]	Westdeutsche Rundfunkwerbung	8.1[e]
		(ARD)	7.1
		MDR Werbung (ARD)	6.7
		radio NRW (commercial)	

Source: Data from *Media Perspektiven Basisdaten 1995.*

[a]1994, U.S. dollars

[b]Adjusted for weekly publication

[c]Net advertising income, both public and private channels/stations.

[d]Ownership of each commercial television or radio channel is divided among multiple companies. Data on the total percentage of the German television market controlled by specific corporations is unavailable.

[e]Based on percentage of total advertising revenues captured. Does not reflect income from fees charged on radios or television sets. Nor does it reflect audience share.

newspaper companies, the influence of ownership concentration on content is even more pronounced than it initially appears. Smaller daily newspapers in Germany often are owned by more than one newspaper company, with the consortium usually including the nearest big-city daily or regional newspaper. As a result of such arrangements, there were only 135 completely separate newspaper products available in Germany in 1996, despite the fact that there were 375 different publishing companies producing 1,602 separate newspaper editions in the country (Bundesverband Deutscher Zeitungsverleger e.V., 1996).

Although the newspaper industry still held a comfortable position atop the German mass media market in the mid-1990s, that position was clearly eroding. While daily newspapers still absorbed the largest share of advertising in Germany in 1995 (29.5 percent), their share grew only 3.4 percent from 1994, whereas the advertising market as a whole increased by 7.1 percent over the year. The big winners in 1995 were TV (up 12.6 percent) and direct mail (up 15.4 percent). As a result, newspapers' total share of the advertising market slipped below 30 percent for the first time in the post-war period and it was predicted that if current trends continue, TV will dominate the German advertising market by 2005 (Keller, 1996).

In addition to declining advertising share, newspapers are facing rising costs and falling readership within key age groups, particularly those under 40 (Bauer, 1996a). Production costs have risen faster than revenues throughout the 1990s (Atanassoff et al., 1994), and rising personnel costs have encouraged downsizing in the industry. Between 1991 and 1994, the number of people employed by newspapers in Germany dropped 28 percent to 126,550, a number only 2 percent higher than 1981 levels (Statistisches Bundesamt, 1996).

Similarly, although West German newspaper circulation numbers remained relatively stable in the 1980–96 period, the numbers disguised a real decline in penetration because Germany's population grew sharply during the period (Keller, 1996). Almost all of that growth was, however, the result of immigration (Organization for Economic Cooperation and Development, 1996), and because of language barriers and lack of local ties, immigrants do not generally represent a viable market for local mass media products.

Another challenge facing the industry lies in the new eastern states. More than half a decade after reunification, the newspaper market there remained unsettled. Newspaper sales declined 3 percent in the east in 1996 from the year before, with subscription sales being particularly hard hit (Keller, 1996). The decrease reflected the still-troubled economy and rising unemployment rates in the region. Moreover, fallout from the rapid expansion of Western newspaper companies into the new states continued, with at least five newspapers ceasing publication in 1996 (Keller, 1996).

In general terms, then, the German newspaper industry shares many of the same challenges that face the U.S. newspaper industry as it enters the 21st century. Germany enjoys a fully developed newspaper market, which makes it more vulnerable to emerging competition from new media. The long delay in developing commercial broadcasting, cable TV and more liberal broadcast advertising regulations have created pent-up demand among advertisers for radio and TV airtime. Unlike the U.S. market, where broadcasting and cable are mature industries and are unlikely to make dramatic inroads into newspaper revenues in the future, in Germany the competition from broadcasting is just beginning for the newspaper industry. Finally, the German newspaper industry suffers from the same high cost structures, economic downturn and fallout from reunification that have troubled German industry during the 1990s.

The Magazine Industry

With DM 17 billion (U.S.$10.5 billion) in revenue in 1994, the magazine industry is the second largest media industry in Germany. Moreover, magazine publishing is the media segment in which German companies have established the highest international profile.

More than 9,000 magazine titles were published in Germany in 1994 by some 1,951 different publishing companies (Statistisches Bundesamt, 1996). That was 240 percent more titles than were published in Germany in 1975. In 1994, total magazine circulation topped 388 million copies, and general-interest magazines controlled the fifth largest share of the German advertising market with 10 percent of the total, or DM 3.5 billion (U.S.$2.2 billion), whereas the trade press controlled another DM 2 billion (U.S.$1.23 billion) (Keller, 1996).

Trade and academic journals make up the largest genre of magazines in Germany, with roughly 39 percent of all magazine titles falling into those categories (Statistisches Bundesamt, 1996). General-interest magazines make up the second largest group at 18 percent, a category that includes men's and women's magazines, hobby, travel, and TV and radio guides, among other topics. The remainder of the German magazine market is divided between different types of specialized publications. Although comparatively few in number, general-interest magazines command a proportionately larger share of total magazine circulation and revenue than other sectors of the industry and are enjoying faster growth. In 1994, about 34 percent of all magazine circulation and 49 percent of the industry's revenues were generated from the general-interest sector.

Concentration of ownership in general-interest magazine publishing is even higher than it is in the newspaper publishing industry, although there has been some dilution as the number of general-interest titles has grown. In 1994, the four largest magazine publishing companies controlled 63 percent of the total general-interest magazine market. As with newspapers, magazine ownership concentration is even higher than is immediately apparent because of partnerships, cooperative agreements and the ways in which the degree of concentration in the industry is calculated (Media Perspektiven Basisdaten, 1995).

As in the United States, a large proportion of German magazine titles are either free circulation or circulated to members of specific organizations. In general terms, just over 55 percent of the total revenue in the German magazine industry comes from advertising, with the remainder coming from circulation (Statistisches Bundesamt 1996)—a ratio similar to that in the U.S. magazine industry (Veronis, Suhler & Associates, 1995).

Magazine publishers have been no more immune to the growth of the TV market than have newspaper publishers. The industry has suffered from a weak advertising market throughout the 1990s and a steady loss in real advertising market share against other media (Keller, 1996). Since 1991, the number of magazine publishers in Germany has declined slightly but steadily, and both the number of titles and total magazine circulation dropped off slightly between 1993 and 1994 (Statistisches Bundesamt, 1996). The long-term implications of these indicators are still somewhat unclear, however, because some of the retrenchment can be attributed to fallout from early investment in the new German states and absorption of former eastern publishing operations by western companies. Additionally, German media usage surged during reunification as audiences tried to keep up with events. Consequently, the decline in circulation may simply be a return to more normal readership patterns.

There also have been a number of positive signs for the magazine industry. Magazines enjoyed real growth of 4.1 percent in the number of advertising pages in 1995 (Keller, 1996), and the number of people employed by the industry rose steadily through the early 1990s to reach 111,000 in 1994 (Statistisches Bundesamt, 1996). Moreover, research indicates that about 48 percent of all Germans read magazines—a figure that has been holding steady and perhaps even increasing slightly (Media Perspektiven Basisdaten, 1993, 1994, 1995).

A striking feature of the German magazine industry is its strong international presence. German magazine publishing companies have been actively investing abroad, and the largest publishers have substantial foreign holdings. Heinrich Bauer Verlag, Germany's largest magazine publishing firm, for example, has publications in the United States, Great Britain, France, Spain, Hungary, Poland, the Czech and Slovak Republics, and Russia. Burda, another large German media concern, and Bertelsmann have similarly widespread magazine holdings (Media Perspektiven Basisdaten, 1995; Hollifield, 1993). The German presence is particularly strong in Eastern European markets, where German publishers invested quickly and heavily after the 1989 collapse of the Eastern Bloc (Hollifield, 1993).

The German magazine industry, then, is experiencing many of the same pressures felt by the newspaper industry, particularly in terms of competition for advertising. Readership remains fairly stable in the German home market, however, and the industry has aggressively expanded into foreign markets.

Moreover, employment and revenues continue to grow. Finally, there are signs that concentration of ownership in the sector may be becoming slightly more diluted.

The Television Industry

German TV was initially established as a public monopoly after World War II. The German states were given authority over the system, but the broadcast corporations themselves had independent control of content. To ensure that broadcast content offered diversity of opinion and a balanced reflection of the differing elements of society, advisory boards made up of socially diverse and important organizations and individuals were established to counsel the broadcast corporations (Drost, 1991; Kleinsteuber and Wilke, 1992; Meyn, 1994).

Under the broadcast treaties that established the German system, two separate TV channels were established, Arbeitsgemeinschaft der Öffentlich-Rechtlichen Rundfunkanstalten der Bundesrepublik Deutschland (ARD) and the Zweites Deutsches Fernsehen (ZDF). The systems were financed primarily through a fee charged on radio and TV sets, although advertising became an increasingly important source of revenue in the 1980s. Advertising, however, was carefully regulated, with strict limits on the number of minutes, time of day, and timing during a program when commercials could be shown. In the ARD system, programming comes from both the individual member broadcasting corporations in the individual states and through joint productions that air nationally, whereas ZDF is a more centralized national system that operates under authority from the different states.

In 1984, commercial broadcasting was introduced into Germany and expanded rapidly. By 1996, there were 10 commercial TV channels operating in Germany (Holtz-Bacha, 1996) and competition for market share was fierce (Der Spiegel, 1996). The commercial channel RTL led the way with the largest share of advertising revenue (Media Perspektiven Basisdaten, 1995). Sat.1 was in second place for advertising share among the commercial stations, with PRO SIEBEN ranked third. Moreover, competition between the commercial channels and the long-established public services also was bitter. In 1993 and 1994, RTL edged the public station ZDF slightly in terms of viewership overall in Germany, with the other public service system, ARD, ranking fourth for viewership. Perhaps more importantly, however, competition from commercial stations, which operated under fewer restrictions on advertising, slashed into the public systems' advertising share. Between 1990 and 1994, net TV advertising sales for the ARD system dropped 65 percent without correction for inflation, and sales for ZDF dropped 53 percent during the same period.

German public TV is not facing this problem alone. Across Europe, competition from commercial TV has been undermining European public TV systems, cutting public service broadcasters' audience share from 82 percent in 1984 to 46 percent in 1994. In autumn 1996, the European Parliament became sufficiently alarmed to call for changes in European broadcast rules to help the Continent's public service systems be more competitive (Buckley, 1996).

Within the German media system as a whole, TV had by the mid-1990s clearly established itself as the coming commercial medium. In 1995, TV captured the second largest share of the German advertising market at 17.4 percent, which represented an increase of 12.6 percent over the previous year and a doubling of TV's advertising share over 1985 levels (Keller, 1996). Moreover, 94 percent of all Germans reported using TV in 1995, with more than 90 percent of each age group tuning in (Media Perspektiven Basisdaten, 1995). Germans were also spending a steadily increasing amount of time in front of the TV. The average time spent watching each day jumped 28 percent between 1987 and 1994 to an average of just under 3 hours.

But for all the rapid growth of German TV, a number of issues of significant concern have been facing the industry. As with other forms of German media, concentration of ownership in Germany's commercial TV stations is high. The largest investors in German TV stations are the media corporations that also hold the largest market shares of the newspaper, magazine publishing and film distribution industries, raising questions about the diversity of outlook and opinion available in the German media system. And, as with other media segments, cross-ownership between investors and joint ownership of smaller subsidiaries helps disguise the real level of concentration (Holtz-Bacha, 1996). For example, in 1994 KirchGruppe held 43 percent of German TV station Sat.1, and Aktuell Presse-Fernsehen held 20 percent and Axel Springer Verlag held another 20 percent. But Axel Springer also held 42 percent of Aktuell Presse-Fernsehen and KirchGruppe held 35 percent of Axel Springer (Media Perspektiven Basisdaten, 1995). As a result of such opaque ownership relationships, both Germany and the EU have been seeking to limit the total TV audience share that any one media corporation can reach through stations or networks it owns either in Germany or in Europe as a whole. The initial proposed limit in both Germany and in the European Commission was 30 percent of the total audience share (Holtz-Bacha, 1996; McEvoy, 1996).

Other challenges also face the German TV industry. Profits among the commercial stations were meager if they existed at all, and investors were projecting that it would be the end of the decade before they could hope for financial returns from the industry (Der Spiegel, 1996). The German cable system, which was owned by Deutsche Telekom, also was not profitable as of the mid-1990s (Grant, 1995). And although TV has clearly established itself as a major media industry in Germany, the rules by which it will be governed both within Germany and throughout Europe remained very unclear as the century moved toward its close.

New Electronic Media

New media and on-line services have been developing rapidly in Germany in the 1990s, although—as elsewhere in the industrialized world—the long-term commercial prospects for these enterprises remain uncertain. As a potential market for new media services, Germany clearly is one of the standouts in Europe because of its large, highly educated, technologically literate population. Personal computer penetration remains fairly low in Germany, with estimates of the number of households with a PC ranging from 14 percent to 30 percent in 1995 (Bauer, 1996b). Moreover, only 5 percent of German households were believed to have the equipment necessary to make an on-line connection (Bauer, 1996b; Riefler, 1996). Germany's low telephone-penetration level and high telephone rates—which include steep per-minute charges for local phone calls—discourage development of a consumer market for on-line services. The privatization of the German telephone monopoly Deutsche Telekom and opening of the German telephone market to competition are expected to sharply reduce rates and improve service by the end of the century.

Despite the slow rate at which the on-line market is developing, German media companies have been rushing onto the net. By mid-1996, just under 50 German newspapers and around a dozen German magazines had launched Web pages, and TV and radio stations and Germany's major media corporations also were busy establishing an on-line presence (Bauer, 1996b; Riefler, 1996). Moreover, Germany's major media companies were setting up partnerships to offer on-line services. Bertelsmann, Axel Springer Verlag, Deutsche Telekom and America Online, for example, set up a joint venture in Germany (Bertelsmann, 1996c). The unanswered question about these efforts was how to make them profitable.

Publicly, at least, Germany's major media corporations were optimistic about the commercial prospects for new media. Bertelsmann predicted a DM 1.5 billion (U.S.$900 million) German on-line market by 2000, while Axel Springer Verlag's projections were similarly optimistic (Bauer, 1996b). A survey of German advertisers, however, showed them to be more skeptical about the prospects of the net as a successful advertising medium (Bauer, 1996b).

Perhaps more promising in the short term is the market for multimedia in Germany. In 1994, Germany had a higher percentage of households that had

PCs with CD-ROM drives than any other country in Europe (European Audio-visual Observatory, 1996). German media companies also were investing in multimedia products. Bertelsmann, for example, which already has major international holdings in book publishing and music recording as well as TV, radio, magazines and newspapers, projected sales from multimedia products of DM 300 million (U.S.$185 million) in 1996, and rapidly increasing revenues in subsequent years (Bertelsmann, 1996d).

Future Directions and Trends

Germany's media industries continue to enjoy the strongest home market conditions of any country in Europe. In the short term, the country's major media corporations can be expected to use that revenue base as a foundation to consolidate their European market position and expand internationally. Long term, however, the competitive picture is somewhat less clear. Both the German and the European media industries have been undergoing major restructuring, and it is difficult to predict how the European media landscape will look when the dust settles.

For German media companies, the last two decades have been a period of particularly rapid change. The late entrance of commercial broadcasting into the German media market and the fact that the licensing of commercial broadcasting coincided both with the explosion of new media technologies onto the market and the opening of European markets to cross-border investment and regulation have significantly changed operating conditions within the national media economy. Additionally, within the larger German economy, the reunification of East and West Germany and increased global competition for German products are pressuring Germany to rethink some elements of its national social and economic framework.

As the German media economy evolves, several issues of paramount importance are emerging. The effects of media concentration is an issue of long-standing concern in Germany, but is gaining even greater urgency as commercial broadcasting and the development of new media technologies spur more consolidation. Additionally, the EU is opening the doors to transnational media ownership and investment. That process raises questions about both the impact of such ownership and the impact and effectiveness of multinational media regulation such as is being undertaken by the European Commission. Finally, unlike in the United States where both the broadcasting and cable industries were largely mature before the new media technologies explosion of the late 1980s and '90s took place, Germany's media market experienced an onslaught of wholly new competitors ranging from commercial broadcasting to on-line services in a very short time span. Whether, to what degree, and in what ways that will affect the German media economy over the next few years is a question worth examining in comparison with the media economies of other nations where the evolution has been more gradual.

References

Artikel 5, Grundgesetz flr die Bundesrepublik Deutschland [Article 5, Basic Law for the Federal /Republic of Germany]. Available on-line: http://www.jura-uni.sb.de/BIJUS/grundgesetz.

Atanassoff, D., Gietz, R. and von Kuk, A. (1994). Zur wirtschaftlichen Lage der deutschen Zeitungen [The economic situation of German newspapers]. In: Furhmann, H-J., Pasquay, A., and Resing, C. (eds.). *Zeitungen '94* [Newspapers '94]. Bonn: Bundesverband Deutscher Zeitungsverleger e.V., pp. 120–178.

Bauer, I. (1996a). Zur Entwicklung der Reichweiten der Tageszeitungen [The development of the reach of daily newspapers]. In: Fuhrmann, H-J., Pasquay, A., and Resing, C. (Eds.). *Zeitungen '96* [Newspapers '96]. Bonn: Bundesverband Deutscher Zeitungsverleger e.V., pp. 332–340.

Bauer, I. (1996b). Prognosen zur Entwicklung der Online-Märkt—Nutzer-Studien im Vergleich [Prognosis for the development of the online market—user studies in comparison]. In: Fuhrmann, H-J., Pasquay, A., and Resing, C. (eds.). *Zeitungen '96* [Newspapers '96]. Bonn: Bundesverband Deutscher Zeitungsverleger e.V., pp. 204–225.

Bertelsmann. (1996a). Markets still difficult: Bertelsmann Industrial Group: Stable returns, growing turnover. Press release, May 26. Available on-line at http://www. bertelsmanndo.de

Bertelsmann. (1996b). Portrait: Bertelsmann AG. Annual report, May 26. Available on-line at http://www. bertelsmanndo.de

Bertelsmann (1996c). Bertelsmann AG and America Online form international alliance with Deutsche Telekom. Press release. Available on-line at http://www. bertelsmanndo.de

Bertelsmann (1996d). Multimedia as a Growth Market. Annual report. Available on-line at http://www. bertelsmanndo.de

Buckley, N. (1996, September 18). EU MPs to demand state TV protection. *Financial Times* (USA edition) 1:2.

Bundesverband Deutscher Zeitungsverleger e.V. (1996). Zahlen-Daten-Fakten [Numbers, data, facts]. In: Fuhrmann, H-J., Pasquay, A., and Resing, C. (eds.). *Zeitungen '96* [Newspapers '96]. Bonn: Bundesverband Deutscher Zeitungsverleger e.V., pp. 481–496.

Bus, A. (1994). EU rejects German pay TV plan. *Multichannel News* 15(46):48.

Cowell, A. (1996). Kohl is an iron man, but the price is high. *New York Times*, October 30, pp. A1, A6.

Der Spiegel (1996). Bauchig rüberkommen [Going for the gut]. January 8, p. 68.
Desruisseaux, P. (1996). Government aid for colleges lags behind enrollment surge in industrialized nations. *Chronicle of Higher Education*, December 13, p. A45.
Deutsches Zeitungsmuseum (1988). *Der Weg zur freien Presse in Deutschland* [The road to a free press in Germany]. Bonn: Bundesverband Deutscher Zeitungsverleger e.V.
Drost, H. (ed.). (1991). *The World's News Media: A Comprehensive Reference Guide*. London: Longman Group, pp. 174–186.
European Audiovisual Observatory. (1996). *Statistical Yearbook '96: Cinema, Television, Video and New Media in Europe*. Council of Europe. Strasbourg, France: Council of Europe.
Grant, J. (1995, January 2). Euro cable rules eased: EC lifts restrictions for telecom. *Multichannel News* 16(2):17.
Hollifield, A. (1993). The globalization of Eastern Europe's print media: German investment during the post-revolution era. Paper presented to the Newspaper Division, Association for Education in Journalism and Mass Communication, Kansas City, MO, August.
Holtz-Bacha, C. (1996). Media concentration in Germany: On the way to new regulations. Paper presented to the Communication Law and Policy Interest Group, International Communication Association, Chicago, IL, May.
Keller, D. (1996). Zur wirtschaftlichen Lage der deutschen Zeitungen [The economic situation of German newspapers]. In: Fuhrmann, H-J., Pasquay, A., and Resing, C. (eds.). *Zeitungen '96* [Newspapers '96]. Bonn: Bundesverband Deutscher Zeitungsverleger e.V., pp. 17–95.
Kleinsteuber, H. J., and Wilke, P. (1992). Germany. In: Østergaard, B. S. (ed.). *The Media in Western Europe: The Euromedia Handbook*. London: Sage, pp. 75–94.
McEvoy, J. (1996). Media concentration plan hits delay. The Reuters European Community Report. Available on-line at Nexis News Database, July 25.
Media Perspektiven Basisdaten. (1993). Daten zur Mediensituation in Deutschland 1993 [Data on the media situation in Germany 1993)] *Media Perspektiven* (Suppl.).
Media Perspektiven Basisdaten. (1994). Daten zur Mediensituation in Deutschland 1994 [Data on the media situation in Germany 1994]. *Media Perspektiven* (Suppl.).
Media Perspektiven Basisdaten. (1995). Daten zur Mediensituation in Deutschland 1995 [Data on the media situation in Germany 1995]. *Media Perspektiven* (Suppl.).
Meyn, H. (1994). *Mass Media in the Federal Republic of Germany*. Berlin: Colloquium im Wissenschaftsverlag Volker Spiess GmbH.
Organization for Economic Cooperation and Development (OECD). (1996). *OECD Economic Surveys 1995–1996: Germany*. Paris: OECD.
Pasquay, A. (1996). Der Zeitungsmarkt in der Europäischen Union [The newspaper market in the European Union]. In: Fuhrmann, H-J., Pasquay, A., and Resing, C. (eds.). *Zeitungen '96* [Newspapers '96]. Bonn: Bundesverband Deutscher Zeitungsverleger e.V., pp. 141–156.

Riefler, K. (1996). Tanz auf dem Vulkan—Sollen sich Zeitungen online engagieren? [Dance on the Volcano: Should newspapers get involved online?] In: Fuhrmann, H-J., Pasquay, A., and Resing, C. (eds.). *Zeitungen '96* [Newspapers '96]. Bonn: Bundesverband Deutscher Zeitungsverleger e.V., pp. 158–201.

Statistisches Bundesamt. (1996). *Wirtschaft und Statistik 7* [Economy and statistics). Stuttgart: Metzler-Poeschel, July.

Udell, Jon G. (1990). Recent and future economic status of U.S. newspapers. *Journalism and Mass Communication Quarterly* 67(2):331–339.

United Nations Department for Economic and Social Information and Policy Analysis Statistical Division (1995). *Statistical Yearbook, Annuaire Statistique 1993.* 40th ed. New York: United Nations Department of Economic and Social Information.

Veronis, Suhler & Associates. (1995). *The Veronis, Suhler & Associates Communications Industry Forecast.* 9th ed. New York: Veronis, Suhler & Associates.

Wright, J. W. (ed.). (1996). *Universal Almanac.* Kansas City, MO: Universal Press Syndicate.

Notes

1. Comparisons of national media and economic data for European countries are difficult in the wake of the changes in Eastern Europe. Some sources of comparative data include Eastern European countries, whereas others do not. In the case of Germany, the dominance of the western German economy means that most economic data—including that from the 1996 OECD reports—reflect West German figures only or report figures for the new eastern states separately. In the case of the media economy, there is no significantly independent eastern German media industry. As a result of these difficulties, in this chapter comparative data are for Western European countries or West German media only, unless otherwise specified.
2. At an average 1994 exchange rate of 1.62 DM for each U.S. dollar.
3. Data on magazine sales and circulation diffusion for the United Kingdom were unavailable.

9

SPAIN

Alfonso Nieto

Geographic, Political and Economic Aspects

The Kingdom of Spain, located in southwestern Europe, together with Portugal forms the Iberian Peninsula. The country further comprises the Balearic Islands in the Mediterranean Sea, the Canary Islands in the Atlantic Ocean, and the enclaves of Ceuta and Melilla in Morocco. Spain has a surface area of 504,782 km^2 (194,894 mi^2). The principal language is Castilian Spanish. Catalan is widely spoken in the northeast, Basque in the north, and Galician in the northwest. The capital is Madrid.

According to the Instituto Nacional de Estadística (1995), the population in 1995 stood at 39,125,000: 48.7 percent men and 51.3 percent women. The distribution according to social classes is as follows: high class, 5.6 percent; middle high class, 13.9 percent; middle middle class, 41.0 percent; middle lower class, 26.1 percent; and lower class, 13.4 percent. Seventy-six percent of the population is urban dwelling; 3 percent of the population is illiterate; and 56.2 percent of the population is younger than 45 years old.

The state is organized into municipalities, provinces and 17 Autonomous Communities. The population of people age 14 years and older in the Autonomous Communities is as follows: Andalucia (17.4 percent), Aragón (3.2 percent), Asturias (2.8 percent), Baleares (1.9 percent), Canarias (4.1 percent), Cantabria (1.4 percent), Cataluña (15.9 percent), Extremadura (2.6 percent), Galicia (7.0 percent), León (6.5 percent), La Mancha (4.1 percent),

Madrid (13.1 percent), Murcia (2.6 percent), Navarra (1.4 percent), Basque country (5.4 percent), Rioja (0.7 percent), and Valenciana (10.0 percent). The Constitution clearly specifies that there should not be any differences between the Autonomous Communities that could provoke some of them to gain social or economic privileges (Constitución Española, 1978). Each Community is self-governed; the Constitution states, however, that in no case will the federation of the Autonomous Communities be permitted.

Under the Constitution approved in 1978, Spain is a hereditary monarchy, with the King as Head of State. Freedom of thought, belief and expression are guaranteed, as is the right to receive and disseminate true information, provided that in the exercise of these rights, the laws regulating professional secrecy are observed and that personal privacy and honor are respected. The Constitution also states that these rights may not be restricted by pre-censorship.

Spain became a member of the European Union (EU) in 1986 and joined the exchange rate mechanism of the European Monetary System in June 1989. Spain is a member of the Organization for Economic Cooperation and Development. In 1995, Spain's gross national product (GNP) was U.S.$533,986 million, and the GNP per capita was estimated at U.S.$13,650.

In 1993, after a long period of economic growth, Spain experienced one of the deepest recessions of the past 20 years. Since 1995, however, the economy has recovered. To meet the EU convergence criteria, Spain's budget deficit was reduced to the equivalent of 3.0 percent of gross domestic product (GDP) in 1997.

Media Usage in Spain

In 1995, the total number of homes in Spain was estimated at 11,807,000. Television (TV) is found in 99.3 percent of all households; color TV saturation is very high at 98.1 percent; and some 58.3 percent of all households have more than one TV receiver. By contrast, radio receivers are found in 96.4 percent of all households. As for other electronic equipment, videocassette recorder penetration is at 61.9 percent; the remote control is found in 73.9 percent of all households; and a personal computer, in 17.2 percent of all homes. The percentage of the population reached during a given week in 1995 by the various media forms is listed in Table 9-1 as follows: TV, 91.15 percent; dailies, 38.0 percent; supplements, 33.8 percent; weekly magazines: 38.9 percent; monthly magazines, 33.5 percent; conventional radio, 38.7 percent; radio formula, 23.7 percent; and cinema, 8.3 percent (Asociación para la Investigación de Medios de Comunicación, 1996).

Table 9-1. Population Reached by Diffrent Types of Spanish Media, 1995

Media	Percentage
TV	91.15
Radio	56.5
Magazines	54.7
Dailies	38.0
Supplements	33.8
Cinema	8.3

Source: Asociación para la Investigación de Medios de Comunicación (1996).

Press

There are approximately 126 daily newspapers published in Spain, complemented by 14 Sunday editions. A large number (173) of "free papers" are also published. In 1995, the total circulation reached 4,285,000 copies sold on the average every day, representing a 4.49 percent increase from the previous year. Unlike in many other developed nations, in Spain the ratio of circulation to population has increased each year since 1991. The number of copies sold by dailies per 1,000 inhabitants was 83 in 1991; by 1995 the number had grown to 109 (International Federation of Newspaper Publishers, 1996).

The three newspapers with the largest daily circulation are: *Marca* (sports), published by Grupo Recoletos Editorial, S.A. (421,294 copies); *El Pais* (Prisa) (408,267 copies); and *ABC,* owned by Prensa Española, S.A. (321,571 copies). The local press dominates in the various Spanish provinces. The circulation of the national daily press is greater than the local press in only eight of the 50 Spanish provinces (Oficina de Justificación de la Difusión, 1996). The consumption of newsprint paper reached 484.2 thousand tons in 1995.

Magazines

It is estimated that some 4,500 magazines are published in Spain at different intervals (Oficina de Justificación de la Difusión, 1996). These include consumer, business, professional and specialty titles. A large number of magazines consist primarily of advertising and are available to readers free of charge, similar to the "greensheets" published throughout the United States.

The "feminine" magazines claimed the largest circulation rates in 1995. The top three women's magazines ranked by readership include *Hola* (3,285,000,000), *Pronto* (3,101,000,000), and *Lecturas* (2,198,000,000).

Of the registered Oficina de Justificación de la Difusión consumer magazines in 1995, about one-half experienced circulation declines. These figures demonstrate the difficulties that this sector suffers. General-knowledge magazines are facing a crisis. Specialized magazines dealing with science, interior design and automobiles have been gaining audiences. Circulation of advertising magazines and magazines available free of charge started off with a rapid diffusion but is presently leveling off.

Television magazines and TV guides have accused the Sunday magazine competitors of including many sections dealing with TV and radio programs. This is similar to the counterprogramming technique adopted by most TV channels that eventually causes a variation between the programs finally screened and the programming initially foreseen. Magazines in this category include *Tele Indiscreta* (estimated readership, 241,889), *Super Tele* (385,891) and *Tele Programa* (283,884).

Television

There are 13 Spanish TV channels, which operate in different parts of the country. There are two national stations, TVE-1 and TVE-2, which are state owned. Private channels include Tele 5, Canal Plus and Antena 3. Several TV channels are owned by the governments of the various Autonomous Communities. These include Canal 9 (Valencian Community), Telemadrid (Madrid), Canal Sur (Andalucia), ETB1/ETB2 (Basque Country), TV3/C33 (Cataluña) and TVG (Galicia). Some statistics on the largest channels in Spain are presented in Table 9-2.

Radio

The general trend within the radio sector is the consolidation of highly fragmented stations into larger radio groups. Radio in Spain consists of two

Table 9-2. Characteristics of Key Spanish Channels

Channel	% Household Penetration	Daily Broadcasting Hours	Minutes of Advertising per Week
TVE-1	100	23.1	580
TVE-2	100	23.5	387
Antena 3	98.4	24.0	1020
Tele 5	98.4	23.5	1063
Canal Plus	96.8	23.3	73

Source: SOFRES (1996).

main groups: conventional stations, which carry a variety of programs, and "formula" radio stations, which specialize in particular formats. The three main private channels are SER (Sociedad Española de Radiodifusión), COPE (Cadena de Ondas Populares) and OCR (Onda Cero Radio). In 1995 the market share of conventional radio was split among SER (23.7 percent), COPE (22.0 percent), OCR (17.7 percent), Radio Nacional de España 1, or RN1 (12.0 percent), and others (24.6 percent). The shares among the top three formula radios are 27.1 percent for C40, 21.0 percent for DIAL, and 8.6 percent for Cadena.

In 1995 there were approximately 1,138 public radio stations (Faus, 1995). These stations were divided among Radio Nacional de España (103 AM, or medium wave, and 304 FM), the Autonomous Communities (145 FM), and various municipalities (586 FM). Private stations in 1995 totaled 742 (Faus, 1995), distributed among SER conventional (121), SER formula (246), COPE (45 AM, 138 FM), Cadena Iberica (19), Radio Top (14), and independent radio stations (159). Overall, there are some 2,064 radio stations in Spain, although not all are in operation. There are around 1,450 commercial stations that carry advertisements (Carat, 1996).

Cinema

Important information about the cinema can be summarized according to the following statistics. There are 1,188 cinemas (theaters) and 2,180 cinema screens in Spain. Research indicates that among the population visiting a screen in the past month, 30.5 percent of all patrons are between the ages of 18 and 29, along with 14 percent of all adults (Estudio General de Medios, 1996).

Advertising

Advertising investments in 1995 rose to U.S.$8.6 billion. The breakdown of this figure is as follows: U.S.$4.4 billion are spent on conventional media (press, radio, cinema, TV, external advertising), and U.S.$4.2 billion are allocated to unconventional media in the form of direct marketing, telemarketing, sponsorships and other venues (The Advertising Association and European Advertising Tripartite, 1996).

The market share of conventional media is as follows: newspapers, 31.6 percent; magazines, 15.9 percent; TV, 37.4 percent; radio, 9.8 percent; cinema, 0.8 percent; and outdoor/transport, 4.5 percent. The conventional media capture 48.40 percent of the total advertising revenues, and the unconventional media claim the remaining 51.60 percent. The supremacy of the unconventional media began in 1991 (The Advertising Association and European Advertising Tripartite, 1996).

Major Media Industries in Spain

Several media conglomerates are based in Spain. Promotora de Informaciones, S.A. (Prisa) has holdings in daily newspapers (*El Pais, Cinco Dias, As*), magazines (*Claves, El Pais Semanal*), radio (Ser, Sinfo Radio, RadioOle, M-80, C-40, Dial) and TV (interest in Canal Plus, Canalsatelite and Cablevision).

Grupo Zeta, S.A., is primarily involved in print media, with ownership of the following dailies: *El Periodico de Catalunya, La Voz de Asturias, El Periodico de Aragon, El Periodico de Extremadura,* and *Mediterráneo.* The company also owns several magazines (*Interviu, Tiempo, Conocer, Viajar, Man, Woman, Penthouse,* and *El Dominical del Periódico* [Sunday paper]). Grupo Zeta has TV interests in Antena 3 TV and Cable Antena.

Bilbao Editorial, S.A., also publishes numerous dailies, including *El Correo Español, El Diario Vasco, La Verdad, Sur, Ideal, El Diario Montañes, Hoy, La Rioja, El Norte de Castilla, El Comercio, Huelva Informacion,* and *La Voz de Aviles.* Total circulation reached 499,102 in 1995. Bilbao Editorial also is involved in magazines (*Suplemento Semanal,* a Sunday magazine), radio (participation in Emisoras Cope) and TV (participation in Tele 5).

The state owns TV1 and TV2 and has rights to the specialized information emitted by satellite. The Autonomous Communities own the TV3 channels. Shortwave and long wave radio (National Radio of Spain) are the exclusive property of the State. The presence of state-owned stations broadcasting on medium wave and FM is doubled; there are also some private stations. The state is also the owner of the news agency EFE.

The regulation of foreign investment in the press follows the general rules set for foreign capital investment. If foreign participation does not exceed 50 percent of the capital investment, then the participation is free and unencumbered by any administration peerage. If, however, it does exceed 50 percent, then the foreign participation, although still free, is subject to the rules of administrative verification. One of the consequences of Spain's incorporation into the EU is that juridical or physical persons of other countries within the Union will be treated equally as the Spaniards. This implies that there is no obstacle to the existence of a periodic publication that belongs to other countries within the EU, excluding Spain.

A law was passed in May 1988 regulating private TV stations. This law specifies that no entity, private or public, Spanish or foreign, is allowed to possess more than 25 percent of the capital owned by any given TV station.

Media Industry Analysis

Press

The circulation leaders in this field include *Marca* (sports) 475,002; *El Pais,* 420,934; *ABC,* 321,573; and *El Mundo,* 307,618. These dailies are published in Madrid. Two newspapers, *El Periodico,* 215,581, and *La Vanguardia,* 203,026, are published in Barcelona. Besides *Marca,* other leading sports newspapers include *As,* 113,559; *El Mundo Deportivo,* 78,376; and *Sport,* 101,193.

The local press occupies a top position in the circulation ranking of the majority of Spanish provinces. *Diario de Navarra,* 63,955; *El Correo Español,* 135,840; *El Diario Vasco,* 94,088; *Heraldo de Aragon,* 62,266; *La Nueva España,* 51,957; *La Voz de Galicia,* 108,753; and *Las Provincias,* 56,383, are examples of newspapers that are significant for their geographic distribution and that sell more than 50,000 copies daily. The Sunday editions of these newspapers obtain an increased diffusion of between 20 and 30 percent (Oficina de Justificación de la Difusión, 1996).

The dailies are relatively high priced ($1.03), and the advertising market is very competitive. Approximately 50 to 60 percent of their income comes from sales and subscriptions; advertising contributes 40 to 50 percent. Types of newspaper sales can be broken down as follows: single-copy (91 percent), home delivery (4.5 percent), and postal delivery (4.5 percent) (International Federation of Newspaper Publishers, 1996).

The gross profit margins (profits before taxes) for the top three Spanish dailies in 1995 were 11.36 percent for *El Pais,* 3.61 percent for *ABC,* and 7.22 percent for *El Mundo.* The revenue structure of the three main general information dailies in 1995 is presented in Table 9-3.

Table 9-3. Revenue Structure of the Top Spanish Dailies

Newspaper	Sales (%)	Advertising (%)	Others(%)
El Pais	49.1	49.9	1.0
ABC	55.5	43.0	1.5
El Mundo	63.4	34.5	2.1

Source: Noticias de la Comunicación (1996b).

There is no major dominating group in terms of the concentration of the circulation of newspapers in Spain. The Bilbao Editorial Group controls 11.6 percent of the market, followed by *El Pais,* 9.8 percent; *ABC,* 7.5 percent; and *El Mundo,* 7.2 percent. The four companies have a combined daily circulation of 36.1 percent.

Magazines

Today there is a great deal of competition in the magazine industry as a result of the new electronic media. Magazines also are facing other problems such as low investment in advertising, fragmentation of audiences, and content specialization in the traditional media, especially TV (Cabello, 1995).

The main publishers and their corresponding rates of diffusion in the magazine market are Axel Springer, with 5.66 percent; Edipresse, with 9.90 percent; G+J España, with 10.64 percent; Grupo Heres, with 11.35 percent; Grupo Zeta, with 5.97 percent; Hachette Filipacchi, with 17.01 percent; and Hola, with 7.22 percent. The Spanish magazine market is limited in that only 54.7 percent of the population reads magazines. One of the leaders in this market is the Group Hola, which publishes *Hola!* and the weekly magazine *Hello!* in the United Kingdom. In 1994, Hola's total revenues amounted to U.S.$111.5 million, with net income of U.S.$18.9 million (*Noticias de la Comunicación,* 1996a). None of the general knowledge magazines sell more than 200,000 copies.

Television

Private stations (Antena 3, Tele 5, Canal Plus) capture the largest audience share at 46.8 percent. The national public stations (Television Española: TVE-1 and TVE-2) account for 36.8 percent of the audience, and the regional channels hold a share of 15.5 percent (Asociación para la Investigación de Medios de Comunicación, 1996).

The public TV station, Televisión Española, began broadcasting on October 28, 1956, and monopolized the TV market until 1982. Because of the introduction of private channels in 1991, Televisión Española has fallen into debt. A plan to reestablish the company's economic equilibrium was launched in 1997.

In 1995, the market for TV advertising was split among the following: TVE (32.6 percent), Antena 3 (30.8 percent), Tele 5 (18.7 percent), Canal Plus (1.18 percent) and local stations (16.6 percent). Private TV stations earned a net amount of 146,031 million pesetas (approximately U.S.$ 1.0 billion) in 1995, a 16.5 percent rise from 1994. Except for Canal Plus, private stations are in great debt (more than 30 percent of their total). In Tele 5, the debt ratio of foreign resources to national resources is 6.22; in Antenna 3, the ratio stands at 2.96; and in Canal Plus, 0.63. This ratio is at an optimum when it is less than 1.

Radio

About 55 percent of its population regularly tune into various forms of Spanish radio. Profit margins tend to be low. In 1995, profit margins for the top three stations were as follows: SER, 5.6 percent, COPE 5.4 percent, and OCR, 0.9 percent. These three groups control 81 percent of the advertising on radio.

Cinema

The number of cinema spectators has grown from 89.9 million in 1975 to 403.1 million in 1996. The 10 most popular films in 1995 were all produced in America (Ministerio de Cultura, 1996). Cinema advertising expenditure rises during the months of May to June and October to December. The beverages sector does the most advertising, accounting for 20 percent of the total amount spent in cinema advertising.

Emerging Media Economic Issues

Statistics show that by the year 2000, 46.1 percent of the Spanish population will be between the ages of 15 and 44 years old; 22 percent, between 45 and 64; and 16.2 percent aged 64 and older.

It is foreseen that within the next couple of years there will be very few changes in the structure of the audience of conventional media. On the other hand, foreign investment in the media industries is expected to grow, primarily from other countries within the EU. This will contribute to the formation of a common European communications market.

As in others countries within the EU, in Spain the regulation of how the content of TV programs is designed to serve the public interest remains to be determined. This is critical in order to establish equilibrium in the TV market between public TV and commercial TV.

The tension in the Spanish information market can probably be attributed to two causes. First, as a consequence of the growing cable networks and digitalization, as well as the increased investment in unconventional media, the advertising market of conventional media has become more complex. Second, there is an increased number of multinational TV stations that offer news.

As of the end of 1996, the definitive structure of digital TV in Spain had not been specified. There are two platforms in which diverse companies of communication are integrated. One is promoted by Telefonica Nacional, and the other by Sogecable (Canal Plus) (Fundesco, 1996). The government tendency is that only one platform should exist, which would include all companies actually interested in digital TV. In the case of two digital TV platforms, the systems must be compatible.

In sum, these unconventional media are not here to replace the conventional media, but rather to complement them. Citizens are free to choose the means of media that they like best; the content offered is increasingly similar to that offered in other countries. The local redoubt tends to be more pluralistic and to offer more diversity. In 1997 the total of Spanish communication media—newspapers, magazines, radio and TV—available via the Internet increased significantly.

Major Issues Affecting Key Media Industries in Spain

Press

In the next 20 years, the concentration of local and regional dailies will likely continue, but there will not be any single company with a circulation of more than 20 percent. The market of local dailies is already saturated. In general, it is possible that there will be a growth of about 3 percent annually, most of which will be attributable to prices, which are probably among the highest in the EU. The economy of dailies is more or less equilibrated, with revenues split 50 percent from sales and 50 percent from advertising. Although this stagnates possibilities of increasing circulation, it avoids the risk of being dependent on the ever fluctuating advertising market.

Attempts during the last 5 years to launch sensationalist papers have failed. This has been partially compensated for by the presence of sports dailies, which account for a 17.9 percent of the total circulation of Spanish dailies.

There is a tendency toward advertising by sponsors in conjunction with advertising firms and even collaboration in the promotion of the sale of products and services. Sunday newspapers and weekend supplements were introduced in the early 1990s and have been very successful; their numbers are expected to increase.

Many national circulation dailies have started digitalizing their information, and even though it is thought that this will soon take place in regional newspapers, these will not really have a big impact on the economy for the time being. Among the editors of daily newspapers, it is foreseen that in 1997 some 50 dailies will be available on the Internet (Fundesco, 1996).

Television

The Spanish TV market is stabilizing insofar as national coverage channels. The deregulation process is expected to culminate in 1998 with the liberalization of telephone services and the introduction of digital TV in both private and public TV sectors. The telephone company, Telefónica, will be privatized in 1998 and will begin its own digital TV service. The second telecommunications company in Spain, Retevisión (Red Técnica Española de Television), will also be privatized in due course. After the privatization, the state will still control the license for transmission of TV signals. Retevisión will continue providing its services by subcontract.

In years to come, private TV will have to rely primarily on advertising for its revenues. The private subscriber channel, Canal Plus, will soon face competition from other subscriber channels, which will be started as a consequence of the liberalization of telecommunications in 1998.

The public TV station is in the process of restructuring to reduce losses that in 1997 are calculated to total 120,000 million pesetas. A solution could be to introduce a subsidy or quota as is done in many European countries; however, this will mean that the income earned from advertising will likely decline. The goal in programming is to provide more cultural and public interest materials. The accumulated debt of Radio Television Española (RTVE) increased in 1996 to 264 billion pesetas. The losses foreseen may total 148 billion pesetas, of which 120 billion correspond to Television Española (TVE). The total of incomes from advertising is estimated at 64 billion pesetas, and personnel costs at TVE are 68 billion pesetas (*Noticias de la Comunicación,* 1996c). The private TV companies will continue to participate in the investment of press, radio, cable and telecommunication companies.

Radio

As with TV, the radio industry also depends on the state to issue temporal concessions of an administrative character. Besides this dependence, the stability of the industry is also at a risk owing to the configuration of its advertising incomes. Advertising is directly linked to a small group of professionals who are responsible for attracting the audiences. The market is already quite saturated from the point of view of the number of stations and the volume of advertising material. Although the national radio stations such as Radio Nacional do not broadcast commercials, the competition keeps rising with the increasing number of private regional and local stations.

Retevisión is in charge of the telecommunications network and lends its services to the broadcasting of TV and radio signals in Spain. Retevisión collaborates with public and private channels and has more than 300 geographically dispersed service centers in Spain.

The distribution of audiences in 1996, ranked according to the waveband heard, is as follows: 14.5 million listen to FM and 5.8 million listen to AM. Conventional radio has an audience of 12.8 million listeners, as compared with formula radio, which has 8.1 million listeners (Estudio General de Medios, 1996). Since 1991, the audience has been steadily increasing. In 1996, 57.2 percent of the population older than 14 years of age listened to the radio. It is possible that the radio could break a record again, as it did in 1982, when it had a coverage of 62 percent. Radio is particularly affected by the increasing rate of promotional marketing now taking place throughout the country in the nonconventional means.

Advertising

Spain falls in fifth place in the ranking of investment in advertising within the European Community. The nonconventional media, especially direct marketing, telemarketing, and point-of-sale advertising, are expected to increase in the years ahead. The top 10 advertising agencies in Spain are all part of international agencies. As a result of the upward trend of inversion in unconventional media, specialized agencies dealing in direct marketing, company image, and sponsorships are being encouraged. The 1993 recession had negative effects and provoked a tightening of the budget, which consequently led to the laying off of many personnel. Presently the advertising industry is in a recovery stage and is becoming more and more demanding. Many multinational companies today prefer to make the majority of their sales promotions decisions in their central offices outside Spain (United States, Japan, Germany, etc.).

In the years to come, the content of advertising is going to have a great repercussion in the advertising market; in particular, it will affect the activities of advertising agencies and their adaptation to the local and regional market necessities. The identity of trademark (brand), company image and client annotation are three factors that are going to affect the content of advertising and the supports used to carry this out to a more specific, although not necessarily a more reduced, public. Central media buying is of key importance in Spain, and companies and are continually modernizing the services (e.g., market analysis, direct marketing, and international markets) that they offer (Pérez-Latre, 1995). It is possible that the remuneration criteria will be modified to allow advertisers to see the commission relations or relations between the media and the agency with more precision. Efforts are also being made to clarify the position of discounts, compensations and other cost-reduction measures in advertising management, especially in the field of TV.

References

The Advertising Association and European Advertising Tripartite (1996). *The European Advertising & Media Forecast. End of Year Advertising Expenditure Statistics,* vol. 11, no. 5, November. London: NTC Publications Ltd.

Asociación para la Investigación de Medios de Comunicación (1996). *Marco General de los Medios en España.* Madrid: Asociación para la Investigación de Medios de Comunicación.

Cabello, F. (1995). *El mercado de revistas en España.* La Industria de la Comunicación. “Situación.” Bilbao: BBV.

Carat (1996). *European Campaign Planner.* Issue 12, Autumn, p. 122.

Constitucion Espagola, de 27 Diciembre de 1978. Publicada en el Boleti Oficial Del Estado del 29 de Diciembre de 1978.

Estudio General de Medios (1996). Estudio General de Medios. April 1995, March 1996. Madrid: Asociación para la Investigación de Medios de Comunicación.

Faus, A. (1995). *La Radio Española.* La Industria de la Comunicación. “Situación.” Bilbao: BBV.

Fundesco (1996). *Comunicación Social 1996: Tendencias.* Informes Anuales de Fundesco. Madrid: FUNDESCO.

Instituto Nacional de Estadística. (1995). Madrid.

International Federation of Newspaper Publishers (1996). *World Press Trends.* Paris.

Ministerio de Cultura. (1996). Madrid: Ministerio.

Noticias de la Comunicación. (1996a). March.

Noticias de la Comunicación. (1996b). September

Noticias de la Comunicación. (1996c). October.

Oficina de Justificación de la Difusión (1996). *Boletín.* No. 56, September. Madrid: Oficina de Justificatión de la Difusión

Perez-Latre, F. (1995). *Centrales de Compra de Medios.* Pamplona: Eunsa.

SOFRES (1996). Sofres AM2. Madrid.

10

THE NORDIC REGION

Robert G. Picard

Although relatively small in geography and population, the Nordic region is a vibrant media market, accounting for an estimated U.S. $10 billion annually, or expenditures of $435 per capita, on media products. Most Nordic media products are intended primarily for domestic and regional consumption, so most of them are unfamiliar to persons outside the region, with the exception of film and audio, areas in which some directors and artists have enjoyed European and worldwide success.

The Nordic nations include Denmark, Finland, Iceland, Norway and Sweden and the dependencies of the Åland Islands, the Faröe Islands and Greenland. The region has a total population of approximately 24 million people, with 5.2 million in Denmark, 5.1 million in Finland, 4.3 million in Norway, and 8.8 million in Sweden. Iceland has a population of approximately 265,000. The Åland Islands, the Faröe Islands and Greenland have populations of less than 100,000 each.

The Nordic nations are highly developed economically and are technologically advanced, democratic nations, with histories of international trade and strong social welfare systems. In terms of GNP per capita, Denmark and Norway rank fourth and fifth worldwide. Norway ranks ninth, and Finland ranks sixteenth. By comparison, the United Arab Emirates ranks first; Switzerland, second; Japan, third; and the United States, sixth (International Bank for Reconstruction and Development, 1996).

Because of the histories of the countries, there are linguistic similarities between Danish, Norwegian and Swedish, and Swedish is officially the second language of Finland. When persons from different nations across the region interact, they typically use Swedish. The population has high educational levels and high literacy levels by both European and world standards.

Because of their influence in the region and the small size of the dependencies and Iceland, this review concentrates on media in the countries of Denmark, Finland, Norway and Sweden.

The region can be characterized as having high demand for all types of media, and that demand is met by domestic and regional supplies. Approximately 275 consumer magazines, 2,550 trade magazines, and 1,350 newspapers are published in the region; 750 radio stations and 35 television (TV) channels are available to serve audiences. Producers in the four nations produce an average of 58 feature films each year, and more than 40,000 book titles are published annually. Because of the size of its population, Sweden tends to dominate the region in media revenues, followed by Denmark, Norway and Finland (see Table 10-1).

Overall, the media market is increasingly competitive. Public service broadcasting monopolies in radio and TV have disappeared, augmented by an

Table 10-1. Selected Media Revenues in the Four Major Nordic Nations (in millions U.S.$)

	Denmark	Finland	Norway	Sweden
Audio recordings[a]	181	112	115	216
Cinema[a] (gross box office)	51	39	63	117
Magazine Advertising[a]	104	79	90	139
Newspaper Advertising and Sales[b]	1,107	1,024	1,389	2284
Radio Advertising[c]	16	28	28	4
TV and cable ads[c]	180	127	100	203
Video sales[a]	77	27	39	65
Total	U.S. $1,716	U.S. $1,436	U.S. $1,824	U.S. $3,028

Note: No single full data set of media expenditures is available for the region. This summary was produced using multiple sources of data from government, and industry sources.

[a]1994 data.

[b]1995 data.

[c]1993 data.

increasing number of commercial channels. Domestic and transnational satellite TV and pay cable services are becoming new programming choices.

The one problematic area for competition has occurred in newspapers. The region had a tradition of multiple newspapers, associated with political parties, located in towns and regions. During the last half of the 20th century, the number of newspapers in each town diminished because of economic forces, leading to a variety of types of state intervention in an effort to save those papers (Gustafsson, 1995; Picard, 1985, 1988). That intervention has not been very successful (Picard, 1994), but the continued strength of regional and national newspapers has kept local papers from gaining a monopoly on news production and distribution.

By far the largest media firm operating in the Nordic nations, Sweden's AB Bonnier produces half again as much revenue (approximately U.S. $1.5 billion in 1994) as its nearest competitor Egmont International Holdings of Denmark. Other major players in the region include Finland's Sanoma Corp./Helsinki Media, Norway's Schibsted A/S, three Swedish firms—Aller holding company, AB Kinnevik, and the Wallenberg group—Norway's Orkla Media A/S, and the Dutch firm Wolters Kluwer International. All of these firms had revenues in excess of U.S. $100 million in 1994 (*Nordic Media Trends*).

All the firms are diversified media companies, but Kinnevik concentrates primarily on electronic media, and Orkla and Wolters Kluwer focus mainly on print media. Bonnier and Egmont are the most internationalized of the firms, with operations and subsidiaries not only throughout the Nordic nations but in countries including Germany, Austria, Poland, Czech Republic, Ukraine, France, Russia, Estonia, Italy, and the United Kingdom.

The pattern of advertising shares for various media differs among the nations (see Table 10-2). Newspapers are still the primary recipient of advertising expenditures across the nations, but their shares are being eroded by other advertising vehicles and TV.

All major media types are available in the region, and domestic production of content for all the media is well developed.

Table 10-2. Advertising Shares for Various Media, 1995

	Newspapers (%)	Magazines (%)	Television (%)	Radio (%)	Other (%)
Denmark	34.0	15.0	15.0	2.0	34.0
Finland	58.7	13.5	21.0	3.6	3.2
Norway	37.0	8.0	35.0	6.0	14.0
Sweden	63.5	11.7	18.0	1.8	4.9

Source: Compiled by the author from various sources.

Magazines

The magazine industry is highly active and competitive in the region and the source of the greatest internationalization. This has been possible because of linguistic commonalities between Denmark, Norway and Sweden and because Swedish is an official language in Finland. Initially, many magazines were exported for trade among the Nordic nations, but it is now increasingly common for separate operations to be established in the other Nordic countries to produce separate domestic editions or new titles intended primarily for that market.

When Nordic magazine publishers have internationalized, they have focused the bulk of their activities on expansion in other Nordic nations. The magazine industries in Denmark, Norway and Sweden are now dominated by the Egmont, Aller and Bonnier groups, all of which operate in all three countries (Hafstrand, 1995).

In 1993, nearly half of all the consumer magazines (600) were produced in Denmark; 258 were produced in Finland; 347 in Norway; and 134 in Sweden (*World Magazine Trends,* 1995). Nordic consumer magazines account for about 3 percent of consumer magazines produced in Europe. Of approximately 2,550 trade, professional and business magazines in the region, almost three-fourths are produced in Finland, where linguistic issues promote domestic publication of such magazines. These Nordic publications account for about 9 percent of the total number of such titles produced in Europe.

Nordic audiences are among the highest readership of magazines in Europe. The average issue readership for any consumer magazine is 99 percent of adults in Denmark, 97 percent in Finland, 89 percent in Norway, and 90 percent in Sweden (*World Magazine Trends,* 1995).

The largest consumer magazines all have circulations of fewer than 500,000, with most in the 200,000–300,000 range. The largest circulations are held by magazines such as *ICA-Kuriren* and *Land* in Sweden, *Se og Hor* in Denmark and Norway, and *Valutut Palat* in Finland (*Nordic Media Trends*).

The magazine industry has experienced difficult times in the past decade because of volatile advertising expenditures (see Fig. 10-1) fueled by a recession in the early 1990s and by the continued development of commercial TV and radio, which reduced the overall advertising share going to magazines.

Newspapers

The region has a newspaper circulation of approximately 10.6 million daily (see Table 10-3), with an average (mean) circulation of about 40,000, except in Norway, where it is about 30,000.

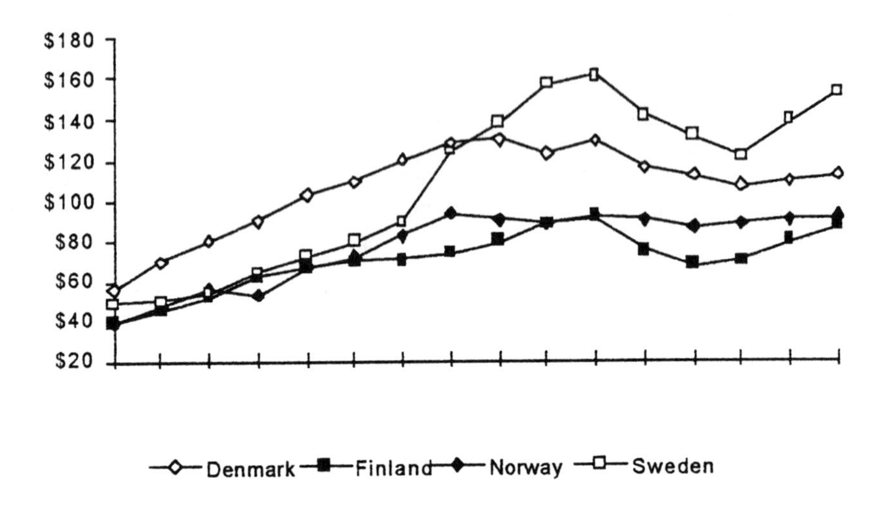

Source: Compiled by the author from various sources.

FIGURE 10-1. *Advertising expenditures for magazines (in millions of $US).*

Table 10-3. Daily Newspaper Circulation, 1995

Country	Circulation
Denmark	1,612,000
Finland	2,368,000
Norway	2,582,000
Sweden	4,041,000

Source: *World Press Trends,* 1996 (1996).

The sources of newspaper revenue in the region are nearly equally divided, with half coming from readers and half from advertisers. Sweden's newspaper industry is the largest, producing U.S. $2.3 billion in 1995, followed by Norway at U.S. $1.4 billion, and Denmark and Finland at approximately U.S. $1 billion each.

Newspaper readers in the Nordic nations are among the most avid readers in the world. Norway ranks number 1 in the world, with 600 copies sold per 1,000 inhabitants. Sweden and Finland rank third, with 464 copies. Of the nations, Denmark ranks lowest, at 310 per 1,000 inhabitants. The difference between the Nordic nations and other European nations is explained by political and sociocultural factors, including strong ties to political parties and a

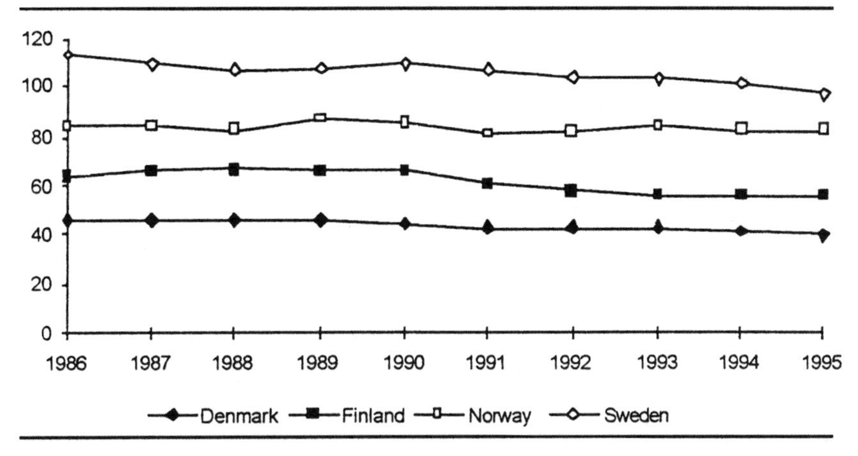

FIGURE 10-2. *Number of daily newspapers in Nordic nations.*

strong local press, according to Karl Erik Gustafsson and Lennart Weibull (European Newspaper Publishers Association, 1996).

The Nordic region produces a number of newspapers that are recognized worldwide for the quality of their journalism, including *Berlinske Tidende* in Denmark, *Helsingin Sanomat* in Finland, *Aftenposten* in Norway, and *Svenska Dagbladet* in Sweden.

Despite the high readership, newspapers continue to fall victim to economic pressures. Between the mid-1980s and mid-1990s, the region lost approximately 10 percent of its papers, with the greatest losses occurring in Sweden and Denmark, which had mortality rates of 15 percent during the period (see Fig. 10-2).

Because of their historical political press tradition, newspapers have been highly national industries and the major newspaper firms have tended to stay within domestic borders. In recent years, however, a few have begun venturing outside their traditional markets. Two of the most recent examples occurred when the Swedish concern, Bonnier, bought a significant share of the large regional paper *Ammulehti* in central Finland, and the Norwegian firm Schibsted purchased 49 percent of the tabloid, *Aftonbladet,* in Stockholm, Sweden.

Radio

Radio is well established in the region (see Table 10-4), but the structure of radio was fundamentally changed in Nordic nations during the 1980s and 1990s, as it was elsewhere in Europe, with Norway and Denmark leading with

Table 10-4. Number of Radio Stations, 1994

Country	No. of Radio Stations
Denmark	246
Finland	90
Norway	305
Sweden	112

the largest number of stations because both have had policies to encourage local radio and have permitted commercial funding as well as not-for-profit operations. The introduction of commercial radio in Finland was permitted under a different regulatory approach that did not promote noncommercial broadcasting to the extent found in other nations.

Growth in the number of stations is being fueled by the increasing number of commercial radio stations, with Sweden being the last to introduce commercial radio in 1993 and taking a far more conservative approach to its introduction (Jauert and Prehn, 1994).

Although it began with national public service channels, radio in the region has now become dominated in number by local operations, with local stations accounting for more than two thirds of all stations in each of the countries (see Fig. 10-3). Nevertheless, the strong national public service channels continue to dominate their markets by accounting for 60 to 80 percent of all listening time.

Not-for-profit community radio stations are being squeezed heavily by the lack of listenership and financial support in Denmark and Norway and are having a difficult time surviving. The Swedish regulatory system is structured to try to maintain these community radio operations, as well as state radio and commercial operations. Overall, radio developments in the region are paralleling those found in the European nations and are creating systems roughly equivalent to the more commercialized systems found throughout Europe.

Television, Cable and Satellite

During the last half of the 20th century, the Nordic nations have had some of the most technologically advanced and productive state broadcasting systems in the world. Based in the public service broadcasting model, the systems provided high-quality entertainment programming produced by the systems and purchased from abroad but were especially noteworthy for their news, public affairs, and cultural programming.

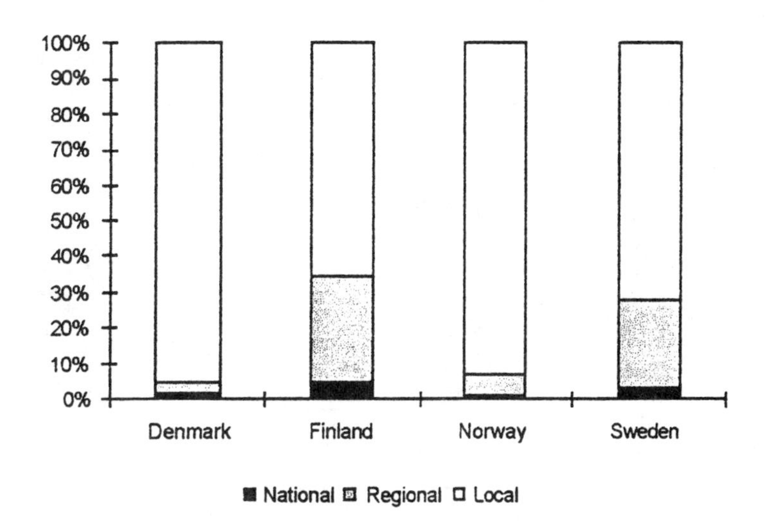

FIGURE 10-3. *National distribution of radio stations.*

Beginning in the 1980s, nations in the region began authorizing the development of domestic commercial TV operations. These moves broke the monopolies of public service broadcasting and increased the number of channels available; however, the growth potential for new domestic channels is somewhat limited by market size, and investors are seeking to regionalize some existing channels and considering new regional channels.

Today, the average viewing time in the region is about 2.5 hours per day. Viewers in each nation can choose from among six to 12 domestic channels of free and pay TV channels in some parts of the countries (see Fig. 10-4).

These figures are somewhat misleading, however, because only public service channels provide 100 percent household coverage in all four nations. Of the commercial channels, only one in Denmark, Finland and Norway and two in Sweden exceed 50 percent household coverage. As a result, the public service channels maintain average market shares of about half, except in Denmark, where it is much higher (see Fig. 10-5).

Of the 9.8 million households in the four major countries of the region, 6.8 million now have access to cable services (see Fig. 10-6) (Contamine and Dusseldrop, 1996), which are primary distribution channels for many of the new commercial TV channels. An average of 78 percent of the households passed (those that have access to cable) subscribe to cable services in the region (see Table 10-5), an unusually high number for Europe.

In addition to domestic free and pay channels, cable systems offer access to a wide variety of nondomestic channels. Among the most popular are services

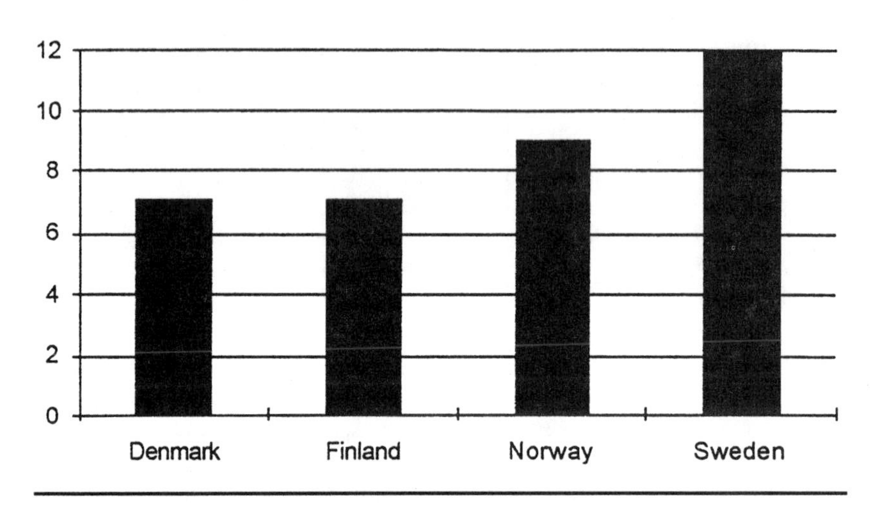

FIGURE 10-4. *Domestic free and pay television channels, 1995.*

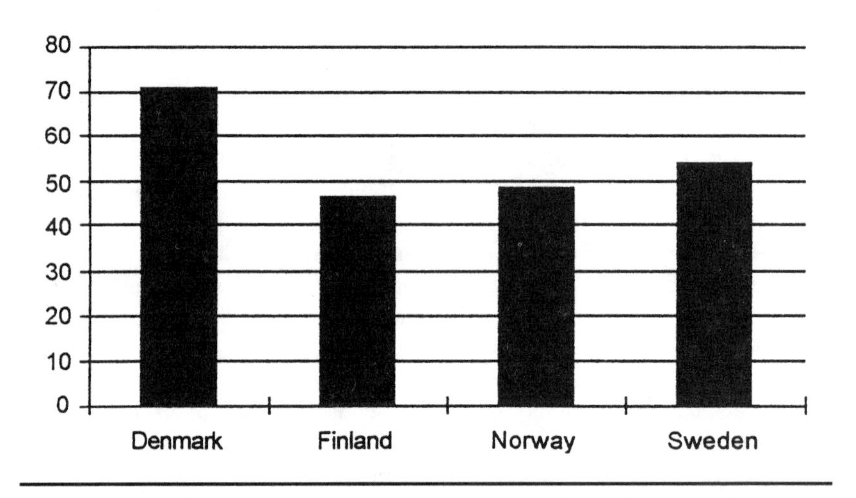

FIGURE 10-5. *Market shares of public television channels, 1994.*

such as Eurosport, MTV Europe, TV5 (France), RTL (Luxembourg and Germany), RAI 1 (Italy), Deutsches Welle, BBC World Service, CNN International, Disney Channel, Superchannel, Discovery Channel, and domestic and regional movie channels.

Satellite TV has made inroads in the region by providing an alternative to cable subscription in areas served by cable and giving rural residents signifi-

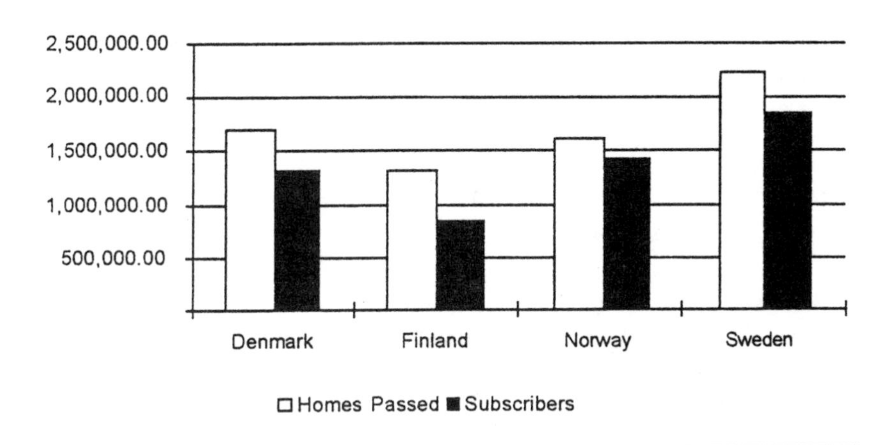

FIGURE 10-6. *Market penetration by cable television.*

Table 10-5. Percentage of Households Passed Subscribing to Cable Services

Country	Percentage
Denmark	76.5
Finland	65.4
Norway	87.5
Sweden	84.1
Average	78.4

Table 10-6. Satellite Television Penetration, 1994

Country	Percentage
Denmark	8.2
Finland	5.6
Norway	10.3
Sweden	12.5

cant reception options. Subscription is highest in Sweden and lowest in Finland (see Table 10-6).

With satellite receivers, viewers have access to all the popular channels provided by cable, as well as scores of other pan-European channels not carried by local cable systems. The increasing number of TV, cable and satellite TV channels are significantly changing the content available to residents of the

Nordic countries. Because of new internal commercial channels and new channels available from abroad, residents now receive programming in many languages and from many European and North American sources.

Film Production

The region has an active motion picture industry, especially Sweden, which has enjoyed success worldwide as an exporter of films. Denmark has also achieved success in the exportation of films, although primarily in Europe.

During the decade comprising the last half of the 1980s and the first half of the 1990s, the region produced 576 feature films, averaging 58 films annually (see Fig. 10-7).

Sweden was the largest producer, accounting for 40 percent of the total production (see Table 10-7). Finland was the second largest producer, accounting for 22 percent of the region's production during that period, but its films are rarely exported because of linguistic issues.

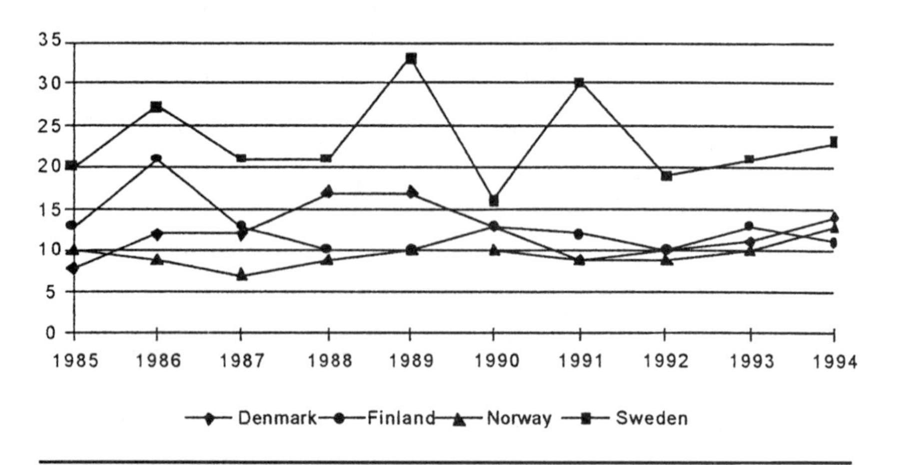

FIGURE 10-7. *Feature film production, 1985–1994.*

Table 10-7. Feature Film Production by Nation, 1985–1994

	Number	Percent of Total
Denmark	123	21.4
Finland	126	21.9
Norway	96	16.7
Sweden	231	40.1

Ticket prices average about U.S. $6.50 across the nations, and 43 million admission tickets were sold in 1994.

Audio Industries

Audio recording sales topped U.S. $624 million in 1994 on sales of 67.7 million copies of compact disc, cassette, and LP recordings. The majority of these sales were recordings of foreign artists, but the region has highly active domestic recording industries that have produced such world-renowned artists as ABBA, Ace of Base, and the Leningrad Cowboys. Audio playback equipment is well distributed among households, as evidenced by the use of compact disc players, the newest widely available technology (see Table 10-8).

Compact discs are by far the most popular recording media, now accounting for an average of 84 percent of all recordings sold in the nations.

Book Publishing

The book publishing sector is experiencing an increasing number of titles but smaller press runs, resulting in declining returns per title and the need to produce titles more inexpensively. These problems have been compounded by declining purchases by libraries and other institutions in the nations, which had provided the economic foundation on which book publishing traditionally has been based.

Figures on book publishing in Nordic nations show steadily increasing production, with a slightly higher increase in fiction than nonfiction production. Among Nordic nations, Sweden is the largest producer of book titles (see Fig. 10-8), accounting for an annual average of 31.2 percent of total titles produced in the nations from 1985 to 1994. Denmark contributed an annual average of 29 percent of the total number of titles published; Finland contributed an annual average of 26.9 percent; and Norway accounted for an annual average of 12.8 percent.

Table 10-8. Household Penetration of Compact Disc Players

Country	Percentage
Denmark	44
Finland	42
Norway	61
Sweden	58

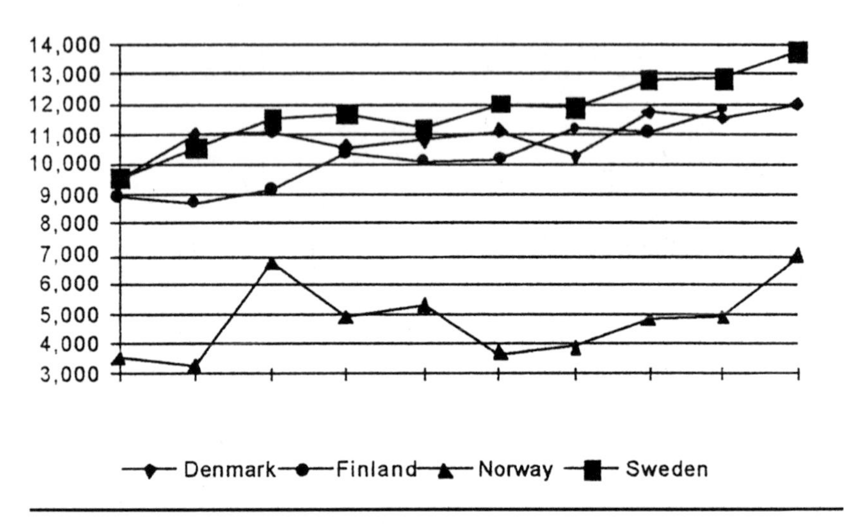

FIGURE 10-8. *Number of book titles produced, 1985–1994.*

An average of about 20 percent of the titles are translations of books published originally in other languages. About 60 percent are translated from English and 11 percent from other Nordic languages.

Summary

The Nordic region is characterized by high levels of media availability, resulting from a great deal of regional production as well as importation and from high levels of media consumption. Existing media are technologically advanced, and good telecommunications infrastructures help serve both electronic and print media.

Media are well distributed throughout the nations, and consumers have access to local, domestic, regional, European and global media. Media are well supported by advertising, and the nations rank among the top in advertising spending per capita in Europe.

The region's media offerings are expanding rapidly, particularly in electronic media, and this is creating uncertainty about how advertising shares ultimately will be divided among the media. In addition, the growth of print advertising materials such as total market coverage advertising sheets is placing additional pressures on newspapers, which have traditionally held the highest share of advertising in the region.

Changes in regulation are increasing broadcast, cable and satellite opportunities, but the ability of the market to maintain significantly more electronic video media is uncertain.

The most important media in the region are in the hands of about a dozen regional media firms that have had strong domestic presences and have turned their attentions regionally. The potential for acquisitions and future mergers among these firms raises significant concerns about concentration in the area.

References

Contamine, C., and Dusseldrop, M. (1996). *Proceedings of the 7th European television and film forum.* Dusseldorf, Germany: European Institute for the Media.

European Newspaper Publishers Association (1996). *Europeans Read Newspapers.* Brussels: European Newspaper Publishers Association.

Gustafsson, K. E. (1995). *Media Structure and the State: Concepts, Issues, Measures.* Göteborg, Sweden: Mass Media Research Unit, School of Economics and Commercial Law, Göteborg University.

Hafstrand, H. (1995). Consumer magazines in transition: A study of approaches to internationalization. *The Journal of Media Economics* 8(1):1–12.

International Bank for Reconstruction and Development/The World Bank (1996). *World Development Report 1996.* New York: Oxford University Press.

Jauert, P., and Ole Prehn, O. (1994). Local radio policy in Europe and Scandinavia. *The NORDICOM Review* 1:137–162.

Nordic Media Trends. (1995). Göteborg, Sweden: Nordic Documentation Center for Mass Communication Research (NORDICOM).

Picard, R. G. (1985). *The Press and the Decline of Democracy: The Democratic Socialist Response in Public Policy.* Westport, CT: Greenwood Press.

Picard, R. G. (1988). *The Ravens of Odin: The Press in the Nordic Nations.* Ames, IA: Iowa State University Press.

Picard, R. G. (1994). Why State Support Fails to Preserve Newspapers. A paper presented to the Biannual Conference of the Austrian Society of Communications, Salzburg, Austria, March 5.

World Magazine Trends 1995. (1995). London: Carat.

World Press Trends, 1996. (1996). Paris: International Association of Newspaper Publishers.

11

THE NETHERLANDS

PATRICK HENDRIKS

The Media Landscape in the Netherlands

The Netherlands can be characterized as small but relatively prosperous. It is densely populated: 15.4 million people inhabit an area of slightly over 41,000 km^2. Roughly the size of the state of New Hampshire, with the same number of inhabitants as New York City, the Netherlands is a relatively small country with a rather rich history with respect to media. Every day, seven national dailies and 30 regional dailies, with a circulation of between 40,000 and 750,000, are published. Some 1,200 consumer magazines and more than 1,800 trade and professional magazines are published, and since 1995, nationwide about 10 public and commercial television (TV) stations are broadcasting their programs or transferring their signal through cable TV networks. Approximately 85 percent of the household population in the Netherlands is connected to one of the local or regional cable systems. The Netherlands is the home turf of multinational publishing and media conglomerates such as Verenigde Nederlandse Uitgeverijen (VNU; professional and consumer magazines, TV and newspapers), Wolters Kluwer (professional and scientific publishing), Reed Elsevier (professional and scientific publishing) and Philips Media (CATV-system, music [Polygram] and multimedia software). The recent history of media in the Netherlands can briefly be summarized by the following statements:

- A previously state-owned telecom infrastructure (both cable and telecom/telephony) that recently has started to privatize, liberalize and deregulate;
- A (newspaper) press, 50 percent financed by advertising, that finds its roots in World War II and is strongly linked with political parties and has been guided by a strong press policy of subsidies but nevertheless has shown a high degree of concentration during the past decades. Government regulation, however, remained limited to a policy of subsidizing individual loss-making newspapers;
- A public service broadcast system finding its origin in the 1920s, which was strongly "pillarized." Since the end of the 1980s, when commercial TV emerged, the public broadcasters have had to compete for advertising money and viewers with a growing number of national commercial broadcasters. They are primarily financed by indirect taxes from people owning a TV set; only 35 percent of their income is generated by advertising.

One would expect the media industry of a small country, with its own language spoken by only 15 million inhabitants and some six million Flemish Belgians, to be focused inwardly. Instead, the industry has always been very open, not in the least because of its small geographic size, which allowed foreign broadcasters from neighboring countries to reach large parts of the Dutch audience. Dutch media companies, especially the folio publishers, have been internationalizing their business. Despite cultural and language barriers, cross-border exchange of media products and services has always been there, emphasizing the openness of the nation's economy.

An economy with a positive trade balance, a low rate of inflation (3 percent), and a relative high per capita income (Fl 42,000),[1] the Netherlands appears to be economically healthy. But the expensive social security system is a burden on the economy. A fairly large portion of the working population is unemployed, and an even larger number of people are on disability rolls. Currently, however, the social security system is being reformed to reduce the number of people using the system. At the same time, looser labor laws give companies the ability to hire temporary workers more freely and to pay lower payroll taxes for low-wage workers. Moreover, markets are being deregulated at a rapid pace, making it easier to do business (e.g., expanding the number of hours stores may be open, lessening of the number of licenses needed to operate a business). Reforming the welfare state in an evolutionary way seems to recover some of the ground the Netherlands economy lost as a consequence of the very generous, but also very expensive, social security system.

Table 11-1. Media Expenditures, 1995 (Fl million)

	1995	Market Share (%)	10-Year Growth (%)
Daily newspapers	1,631	21.6	24
Weekly newspapers	1,099	14.6	52
Consumer magazines	655	8.7	48
Professional/trade magazines	747	9.9	121
Television	1,070	14.2	237
Radio	264	3.5	266
Cable	61	0.8	771
Cinema	25	0.3	127
Outdoor	235	3.1	273
Direct Advertising	1,106	14.7	131
Directories	384	5.1	NA
Trade shows	269	3.6	NA
Total	7,546		101

Source: Vereniging van Erkende Reclame - advies Bureaus (1996).

Media Industry Analysis

The Netherlands can be characterized as a country of printed media. Traditionally, folio media have been the most important conveyors of commercial messages. Of the total of Fl 7.1 billion that was expended in 1994 on media, more than 55 percent was generated by the press (Table 11-1).

Although spending in folio media has grown, printed media has lost market share, mostly to audio-visual media. For years, spending on advertising on TV was relatively low owing to a maximum quota of advertising that was allowed for by regulation. After the introduction of commercial TV, the market for TV advertising exploded, producing double digit growth figures.

Newspaper and Magazine Publishing

With its seven national dailies and 30 regional dailies, the average reader in the Netherlands still can choose from a relatively large selection of newspapers each day, despite the decline in the number of independent newspapers during the post-war years. With a total daily circulation of almost 4.7 million, household penetration remains high at some 75 percent household coverage in 1995, down from 87 percent in 1983 (Brants and McQuail, 1997). Although circulation growth is nearly zero and relative circulation is actually declining, the newspaper industry is still an attractive market, with average margins of some 10 percent of total sales (Nederlandse Dagblad Pers, 1996).

Table 11-2. National Newspapers

Title	Circulation	Publisher
De Telegraaf	756,400	De Telegraaf
Algemeen Dagblad	400,425	PCM Uitgevers
de Volkskrant	361,200	PCM Uitgevers
NRC Handelsblad	270,950	PCM Uitgevers
Trouw	121,600	PCM Uitgevers
Het Parool	101,600	PCM Uitgevers
Reformatorisch Dagblad	56,564	Reformatorisch Dagblad
Nederlands Dagblad	29,774	Nederlands Dagblad
Total	2,098,513	

Source: CEBUCO (1995).

Table 11-3. Top Eight Regional Newspapers

Title	Circulation	Publisher
Dagblad de Limburger	199,981	VNU Dagbladengroep
de Gelderlander	176,814	VNU Dagbladengroep
Brabants Dagblad	164,559	VNU Dagbladengroep
Noordhollands Dagblad	155,468	de Telegraaf
Dagblad Tubantia/TC	152,697	Wegener
Haagsche Courant	148,078	Wegener
Utrechts Nieuwsblad/Amersfoortse Courant	147,076	Wegener
Nieuwsblad v/h Noorden	14,563	NDC

Source: CEBUCO (1995).

Despite increased competition with other media during the past decade, newspaper publishers have been able to sustain profits at acceptable levels. Increasing the scale of operations has been the most widely used method to reduce cost levels, decrease competition in local markets, and improve the competitive position on the advertising market. A strong concentration of ownership has resulted. Today some 14 independent newspaper companies control 39 independent titles (Nederlandse Dagblad Pers, 1996). Of the total circulation, more than 88 percent is controlled by the four largest publishers (Tables 11-2 and 11-3).

Currently, only two publishers are competing in the national newspaper market. Since PCM Uitgevers acquired Dagbladunie in 1995, only De Telegraaf, publisher of the largest-popular-daily in the Netherlands, is left to compete with the newly formed newspaper giant. Entry barriers are high: the economies of scale are substantial, the industry is highly concentrated, and the market has reached late maturity. The four remaining newspaper firms more or less control the market and limit competition. PCM Uitgevers controls the national market for "quality" dailies with *de Volkskrant, Trouw, NRC Handelsblad* and *het Parool.* Although PCM holds another daily, the popular *Algemeen Dagblad,* competitor *de Telegraaf* controls the market for popular mass newspapers. The market for regional dailies is divided between Wegener and VNU, both parties owning regional (near-) monopoly newspapers that control the local advertising franchise but still compete with national newspapers for readership.

As the growth in this narrow oligopolistic market decreases, the publishers are anxiously looking for new growth opportunities. For that reason most already own local weekly freesheets, but increasingly electronic media have come into sight. Regional commercial TV is an embryonic but promising market, and most newspapers are looking at ways to participate in these TV ventures. But they are also experimenting with local interactive news ventures through the Internet (e.g., Digital Cities) and interactive cable. For all of the publishers, it is clear that future growth will not come from their newspaper franchises, although they will remain attractive business ventures for a long time.

Although they are in essence different businesses, consumer magazines and professional magazines are often published by the same media companies. The dominant firm in consumer magazine publishing, VNU, actually controls several market segments, and with a market share of almost 50 percent (Table 11-4). It also plays a vital role in the market for professional and trade magazines, both of which are highly concentrated markets. Verenigde Nederlandse Uitgeverijen is setting the scene in the market for consumer, especially mass-audience,

Table 11-4. Market Shares Based on Circulation in Consumer and Professional Markets

Consumer Magazines (1,200 titles)		Professional Magazines (1,809 titles)	
Company	Percentage	Company	Percentage
Verenigde Nederlandse Uitgeverijen	50	Reed Elsevier	12
Reed Elsevier	6	Wolters Kluwer	11
Telegraaf	5	VNU	9
Wolters Kluwer	2	Wegener	2
Wegener	1	SDU	2
Others	37	Others	64

Sources: NBLC (1996), van Ankeren et al. (1996).

magazines, and a few others are following in its steps. In the market for professional magazines the imbalance is striking, more than 50 percent of the total of 1,805 titles are published by firms with only one magazine (van Ankeren et al., 1996). The entry barrier to niches in professional magazine markets is fairly low. In specific niches, the circulation that is needed to serve an audience who is willing to pay is relatively low. Still, some niches are extremely difficult to penetrate because of the presence of dominant firms such as VNU. Remarkable is the almost complete absence of medium-sized publishing firms; they are either multimedia giants or companies with as few as 10–15 employees.

Television Broadcasting and Audio-Visual Production

The public broadcasting system consists of three national TV channels. Seven main broadcasting organizations and several small organizations share these three channels. The TV airtime is allocated through a three-tier system.

> To become a member a person either takes a subscription to a program guide of the respective organization or pays an annual membership fee of Fl 10. . . . Airtime is apportioned on a 5:3:1 ratio, respectively for so-called class A-broadcasters with over 450,000 members, class B-broadcasters with between 300,000 and 450,000 members, and class C-members with between 150,000 and 300,000 members. . . . By law, all member corporations are obliged to present in their programming 30 percent information and education and 20 percent culture, 10 percent of which should be devoted to the arts. . . . For national public broadcasting there are three revenue sources: licence fees (64 percent), advertising (36 percent) and membership dues and magazine subscription (Brants and McQuail, 1997).

The Dutch TV industry is in a state of flux. For decades the public service system, with three channels, remained unchallenged. Commercial broadcasting was simply not allowed, and consequently true competition did not exist. In 1989, however, the first fully commercial TV station, RTL-4, started broadcasting. Currently, competition between the more than 10 national TV stations is fierce. The wild proliferation of networks meant a sharp increase of the level of competition for viewers, advertisers and resources. As a consequence, most new entrants are having a hard time trying to produce a positive margin. At the same time, the old public system is under strong political and economic pressure. Advertising rates are low because of competition; viewership is scattered; and resources such as successful programming are becoming scarcer every day. At present, nearly all broadcast organizations are struggling to make a profit. The slow advertising market growth and fierce price competition makes the oligopolistic industry not very attractive; hence, entry barriers are high. For a market the size of the Netherlands, with slightly over six million households, 10 TV stations seems to be the maximum. Even experienced broadcasters, such as Veronica (a former, very popular, public broadcaster that went commercial in 1995), have difficulties surviving in the turbulent TV market. One of the few exceptions seems to be SBS6, an initially low-cost TV station associated with Disney/Capital Cities.

The TV industry in the Netherlands is considered to be an industry in its early growth stage, although many experts believe the number of TV stations that can be supported by the advertising market has reached its maximum. Where the broadcast organizations all are confronted with a strong competition, the audio-visual producers (TV productions) are confronted with growth opportunities as never before. The fast growth of the number of TV stations has led to a strong increase in demand for programming. Although programming budgets of broadcast organizations are under pressure, the significant increase in the sheer number of hours of programming needed has provided firms such as Endemol and ID-TV (recently acquired by VNU) with tremendous growth opportunities. These producers have invested in program development and aimed their sights at content ownership and copyright exploitation. It seems that Dutch producers have relative strengths in developing, adapting and producing certain program categories such as game shows (see McKinsey, 1993). The growing importance of local programs in Europe provides the producers the opportunity to diversify their exports and exploit their relative strong abilities to localize TV productions.

Telecom/Cable

The telecommunications industry in the Netherlands is being liberalized in the wake of revision of the Dutch Telecommunication Act in 1988, partly initiated by the European Community regulation. Commercialization and competition are the key words: the awakening giant KPN is protecting its future cash businesses by participating in nearly every new telecommunications venture in the Netherlands. Its corporate strategy is to transform the organization into a profitable private company through internationalization and to protect its traditional home turf by aggressively launching new services.

Although competition is introduced in most telecommunications markets, and most recently in cellular telephony, potential entrants will have a hard time establishing a competitive market position. In a relative small country such as the Netherlands, the telecommunications industry is rather transparent in the sense that all parties know each other and in many instances are, through alliances, joint ventures or in some way related to each other. Potential entrants are disadvantaged because the Dutch telecommunications operator is a "spider in the web" and is involved in many business ventures, ranging from Internet-access services to cable TV networks and mobile network operations. Competition (and potential competition), however, is increasing, and the Dutch public telecommunication operators (PTOs) have to compete on more and more playing fields simultaneously. Where competition is introduced with regard to mobile communications, the market for voice telephony will be available from 1998 forward. In addition to competition in telecommunication services, the incumbent operator will also face competition with regard to its physical infrastructure.

As the number of domestic as well as foreign TV stations to be carried is increasing, and the development of new information services based on fiberglass technology is starting to take off, cable is becoming more and more important as an intermediating company. The cable TV networks have just begun to find out that their infrastructure can be worth gold, not in the least because of their high penetration. The networks who used to be controlled by local governments are being sold to private companies at a rapid pace. Although they are now funded by market capital and regulation is weakened, cable companies are still not very competitive. After years of public regulation and funding, it will take some time for them to become truly customer and market focused and efficient network operators. Next to commercialization, a concentration tendency can be observed. In 1993 the total number of network operators was 244, whereas this number was 125 in 1995 (Ouwersloot et al., 1995). This group is dominated by some large companies; more than 50 percent of the total subscriptions are controlled by the five largest operators, some of them partly owned by giant's such as PTT Telecom or Philips. The most important reason for the increasing scale is the investments needed in the CATV systems to make them ready for new digital services and the huge costs of introducing these new services.

Major Media Industries in the Netherlands

As in almost every other Western country, the beginning of the 1990s presented major changes in the information and communication industry of the Netherlands, leaving the sector in a state of turbulence. A long period of stability, in which few public or private actors dominated the three domains of communications politically and the vertical value chain economically (the state-owned and controlled PTO in telecommunications, large-scale folio publishers in the press sector, and public broadcasters in broadcasting), came to an end. Rapid technological change, the rise of neoliberalist political ideologies, globalization, convergence of communication technologies and businesses, and changing business strategies, interacted to challenge the "old order." New communication business ventures arise weekly, in most cases with a variety of participants in the respective consortia.

Among these companies are three spiders in the web: the publishing conglomerate VNU, the formerly state-owned PTO KPN, and the entertainment giant Endemol. It seems that one of these three parties is involved in almost every new business initiative in the Dutch media industry: from commercial TV stations such as RTL-4 and RTL-5, the ambitious new sports channel Sport7 (launched and failed in 1996), to new Internet start-ups such as access provider Planet Internet, and projects such as Digital Cities. It is not surprising that these companies are such active players in the field given that they have a strong reputation and track record in their core markets. Verenigde Nederlandse Uitgeverijen has been a strong multinational folio publisher that has dominated the consumer market for magazines in the Netherlands for decades and depends on advertising income for a large part of its revenue. The privatized Dutch PTO, KPN, owns and controls the Dutch telephone system and participates in a number of large cable systems, giving them the number one position in the telecommunications infrastructure. The third party, Endemol, is the fourth largest audio-visual entertainment company in Europe, whose TV productions, theater productions, and program formats have strongly influenced the character of Dutch TV in the past 10 years. As the main supplier of programming for both public and commercial broadcasters, Endemol has produced large growth figures. From its strong home base it is currently fighting the battle for the European market.

Core Media Clusters

Together, these prominent firms represent three important communication clusters in the Netherlands: folio publishing; audio-visual programming, bundling and broadcasting; and telecommunications infrastructure. The folio publishing cluster in the Netherlands has a long tradition. The Netherlands is home to relatively large multinational publishers such as VNU, Wolters Kluwer and Elsevier. Especially with respect to professional and scientific (database) publishing, this triad holds a strong international competitive position. Whereas professional information is the core business outside the home base, a strong proliferation of magazine titles and newspapers in combination with a high degree of concentration in the home market gives these publishers a fairly strong home advantage (see, e.g., Jagersma, 1994).

The second cluster consists of audio-visual-related industries and is dominated by TV production. The economic value of domestic and export production is relatively high, and the industry has produced one of the largest independent producers in Europe: Endemol. Dutch independent producers have greatly benefited from the recent growth in TV channels, although future growth is not likely to be as strong. Although TV production in the Netherlands is fairly strong, the motion picture industry is greatly underdeveloped. Of the total revenues generated in 1993 in the audio-visual industry (Fl 1,974 million), less than 25 million was generated by motion pictures, whereas more than Fl 1,650 million were attributed to TV productions (McKinsey, 1993).

The third cluster involves providers of fixed and mobile telecommunications infrastructures, including cable TV networks, copper-wire networks for telephony, mobile cellular communications systems and broadcast satellite systems. Until recently, telecommunications services in the Netherlands were strongly regulated and were predominantly provided by state-owned or -controlled organizations. Telephony-based services were the monopoly of the state-owned PTT. In 1989, however, PTT Telecom (as part of KPN) became a corporate holding company, which, in combination with deregulation, has provided the company with the challenge of market competition and the opportunities for international alliances and joint ventures. The monopolistic nature of the telecommunication market has led the PTO to make huge profits while operating inefficiently for decades.

A rather unregulated part of the telecommunications infrastructure was and still is cable TV, which until recently has functioned as a local utility. In July 1994 there were approximately 240 point-to-point cable TV broadcasting networks, mostly controlled by municipalities or public–private joint stockholding companies (Mansell et al., 1995).

More recently, however, the government has started to sell cable TV networks to domestic and foreign telecommunications companies such as KPN, Philips and USWest. The price per subscriber is in most instances fairly high, not in the least as a consequence of the high market penetration of the Dutch CATV networks and the technological advancement of the physical infrastructure (transformation to fiberglass networks). More than 5.7 million households are passed by, connected to, and subscribing to a cable network, a penetration of more than 88 percent, which is fairly high by international standards. Although highly rated as future potential competitors in the telephony infrastructure, cable system operators themselves are seriously challenged by new suppliers of TV-signals such as direct broadcast satellite providers. In the Netherlands, NetHold is the company that is persuading people to quit their cable subscription and opt for a package of channels distributed by satellite. Which infrastructure provider will be the market leader remains uncertain and will strongly depend on the developments in the TV industry. It is still not clear, for instance, whether pay TV, which is in its infancy in the Netherlands, will become a high growth market and, if so, who is able to provide and control the set-top boxes.

Core Media Companies

At present, the technological and economic convergence of these communication domains expresses itself in a hectic process of interfirm and intersector cooperation. This has created a mix of large- and small-scale (interdependent) firms, crossing sectoral boundaries, all playing different games, all meeting on the small marketplace in the Netherlands, but increasingly looking over the national boundaries. The majority of these companies are active outside the Netherlands. Because of the relative home advantage in, for example, the folio publishing markets, and the maturation of these markets, these firms are increasingly looking for growth abroad. This leads to a multitude of domestic media firms that are creating revenue growth by building a portfolio mainly through cross-border mergers and acquisitions. The following three firms are characteristic for the media industry in the Netherlands. Their growth thrust is focused on foreign expansion, and their positions on their home turf is, without exception, relatively strong.

KONINKLIJKE PTT NEDERLAND (KPN)/PTT TELECOM. The formerly state-owned agency has shifted to a corporate holding company in the past 8 years. It currently consists of a holding company, KPN, with four major subsidiaries: PTT Post (the nation's postal service); PTT Telecom (the telephone company); KPN Kabel, which owns and controls several cable TV systems; and KPN Multimedia, the newest division that is occupied with developing new telecommunications and media services. Of the three divisions, PTT Telecom is the largest, generating about 65 percent of total revenue of Fl 19.855 million. Although the strategy of PTT Telecom in the 1980s was characterized by the exploitation of economies of scale in the carriage of large volumes of traffic using a modern trunk network, the strategy of the 1990s can be characterized by statements such as network diversification and network intelligence (Mansell et al., 1995).

Although its productivity, with 250 lines per employee, is relatively high compared with European standards, it is still overstaffed when productivity figures of U.S. regional Bell companies are taken into account (275 lines per employee on average). It has a history of something like a civil service department, but the company is being reformed by management that is aware of the future threats. On January 1, 1998, telecommunication companies in the European Union became fully liberalized. This means that the telecommunication industry will be confronted by competition in its largest and most profitable business of providing telephone services to households and businesses.

PTT Telecom is faced with more and more competition in its home market. It is, however, consigning a lot of investment capital to their strategy of achieving international growth. Still, it has qualified its market leadership position in the Netherlands as crucial. Maintaining strong growth in the mobile communications market, where PTT Telecom was confronted with competition for the first time, is one of the key objectives. Continuing growth of new services and existing services is the second growth objective in the home market. PTT Telecom is well aware that it still monopolizes the domestic fixed-link businesses. Through introducing new services, for example, Internet access, calling line identification, call waiting and voice mail, for which customers will have to use the "old" telephone system, PTT Telecom hopes to tie the customer closer to it, making the switch to a competitor less easy. Without a doubt PTT Telecom will make life difficult for would-be rivals. It benefits from a familiar brand name, controls the numbering system, and has a large installed base and a stable cash flow from its public service businesses to finance new growth businesses.

Although it is strengthening its position as the national provider of the "network of networks," KPN has strong ambitions to grow as a provider of pan-European services in international markets. It believes the strong domestic position in combination with an international strategy of strategic alliances will sustain future revenue and margin growth. Besides having international ambitions, KPN is also involved in the cable TV market and is increasingly associated with multimedia content and services. Through KPN Multimedia, KPN is developing and exploiting businesses ranging from pay TV and home shopping to Internet services and video dial-tone. With the development of these new services, a pattern of cooperation and competition is emerging, wherein publishers such as VNU, content creators such as Endemol, and the electronics giant Philips are involved in numerous projects.

ENDEMOL. With double-digit growth figures, Endemol is a relatively young Dutch media company. As the result of the merger in 1994 between Joop Van den Ende Productions and John De Mol Productions (both Dutch veterans in audio-visual production), Endemol became the largest audio-visual company in the Netherlands. This public traded company, with an estimated turnover in 1996 of approximately Fl 800 million, produced a gross margin of almost 10 percent (het Financieel Dagblad, 1996a). Endemol develops and produces TV programs and several different forms of live entertainment, such as theater productions on Broadway, in London and in the Netherlands *(Phantom of the Opera, Miss Saigon, Victoria Victoria)* and ice shows *(Holiday on Ice)*. The company is widely known to the public as the home of famous and popular Dutch celebrities who host in numerous TV series (talk shows, game shows, etc.), all produced by Endemol. Its TV activities are the most important and profitable businesses (margin of more than

10 percent), as they account for more than 80 percent of total revenue. The live entertainment division on the other side is much smaller (Fl 135 million) and, at the same time, less profitable (margin almost 5 percent) (het Financieel Dagblad, 1996b).

Although Endemol has subsidiaries in eight European countries, most of the revenue of its TV production activities is generated in the Netherlands. The Dutch market for TV productions, however, is under strong pressure. As a consequence of a very rapid growth of the number of TV stations and of the stagnation of advertising budgets, programming budgets are restrained. Although 80 percent of total revenue in the TV division currently is generated in the Netherlands, most of its future revenue growth will be generated abroad.

Through internationalization, Endemol hopes to improve its international competitive position in the audio–visual industry. Currently, it ranks sixth, competing with firms such as Kirch Gruppe, Fininvest of Berlusconi, Polygram and the European subsidiaries of UIP and Time Warner. If the market definition is limited to companies active in the TV industry, Endemol takes third place.

The strategy of Endemol is strongly focused on content ownership, low-cost production and internationalization. Entrepreneurship is centered around taking risk by creating content and managing it. In that sense, its performance is strongly dependent on branding stars and constantly innovating new programming formats. One of the important growth tracks is through windowing program formats from one market to another. With its near monopoly on entertainment content and TV stars in the Dutch market, Endemol has been involved in a variety of (multi)media initiatives in the past years, although not all of them have succeeded. Without a doubt Endemol is the main supplier of popular media culture in the Netherlands, although media critics are not always very happy with the products from Endemols' "fun factory." Yet, with the moral and financial support of the stock exchange it is invading the rest of audio-visual Europe at a rapid pace.

VERENIGDE NEDERLANDSE UITGEVERIJEN. Without a doubt, VNU is the most widely known publisher of the Netherlands. With its broad and strongly internationalized and diversified portfolio in both consumer and business information markets, it is one of the largest Dutch publishers, increasingly active in foreign markets. In 1995 total revenue was slightly more than Fl 3 billion and profit, approximately Fl 430 million (margin, 14 percent). With its roots in folio publishing, VNU has transformed itself in the past decades into a true multimedia publisher with stakes in newspapers, magazines, books, TV, database publishing and Internet-based services. Among the most important business areas of VNU as a true multimedia conglomerate incorporates are the following:

- A newspaper division that owns several regional newspapers in the Netherlands, which together generate about 20 percent of total revenues of VNU, continuously increasing profitability in a mature market;
- A consumer magazine publishing division that dominates the market with women's magazines, glossies and general-interest magazines such as *Libelle, Margriet, Viva, Panorama* and *Nieuwe Revu,* accounting for more than 36 percent of total revenues;
- A business information division with subsidiaries throughout Europe, mostly publishing business-to-business magazines and in the United States, exploiting electronic business-to-business information databases. As such, it is producing strong growth and rapidly becoming the most important strategic business area in the VNU portfolio;
- A commercial TV division that should be a spearhead in VNU's expansion plans both in terms of revenue growth and margin improvement but which, in reality, is still a troublesome activity.

After being in the forefront of new media experiments in the beginning of the 1980s, and remaining a vertically integrated folio publishing company, VNU has long sought to redefine its strategy. After the divestiture of the commercial printing divisions at the beginning of the 1990s, VNU aggressively tried to build a position in commercial TV in the Netherlands and Belgium. The company formed an alliance, called the Holland Media Group, with the Endemol production company, CLT, and with Veronica, a former public service broadcaster, that has started to operate a commercial TV network. Although VNU has succeeded in building the position through participation in this alliance, financial success has remained elusive, especially with the recent divestiture of the TV businesses. Instead, VNU is aiming at establishing a position in audio-visual content creation and ownership and has acquired audio-visual production companies. Although the broadcast activities may have underperformed, VNU has been more successful with other expansion plans, especially in business information. A restructuring of the business publications divisions in Europe and a continuous acquisition of business data publishers in the United States have boosted the sales of VNU.

Emerging Media Economic Issues in the Netherlands

The Dutch communications industry is in a state of flux, illustrated by a long list of alliances, mergers, takeovers, strategic partnerships and new initiatives in almost every media market. When the communications industry is observed from some distance, it is striking to see how concentrated the different markets are. This is strongly related to the sheer size of the Netherlands, where only a national market exists for most media. Because the minimum efficient scale of operations of newspapers and telecommunications networks is fairly large when related to the total market size, concentration is likely to be high. From the perspective of competitiveness, a high degree of concentration is negative, but from the perspective of the internationalizing media company, a strong home base can be an advantage. Firms such as VNU, Wolters Kluwer and Endemol have greatly benefited from their strong (sometimes monopolistic) positions in their home markets, from which internationalization could take place effectively.

The Netherlands has a rather large and strongly developed media industry when its geographic and economic limited size is taken into account. For the most part, this seems to be the result of the strong and conservative media policy. For years the government has interfered in media economics. From press policy to telecommunications policy, they were all characterized by issues such as preservation of the status quo, noncommercialization, and public domain functions. The industries in turn were strictly separated from each other. In recent years, nearly every media market has been liberalized. As legislation became more loose and competition policy seemed to replace media policy, rapid commercialization took place. The telecommunications industry and the TV industry are the most obvious examples, although relaxation of cross-ownership regulation also affected the newspaper publishers.

As artificial barriers between different communication businesses were removed and technology convergence allowed for new forms of communication services, the industry became turbulent. After years of restriction, media firms could finally benefit from economies of scope and scale, resulting in a rush toward cooperation and acquisition. After an initial boom in both the advertising and consumer markets, growth in the TV industry slowed. At the same time, media companies became aware of the reluctance of consumers to pay for TV or other new media services. A history of nearly free TV, attributable to a public service broadcast system and local cable TV utilities, has spoiled the consumer. Illustrative in this respect is the failure of the new sports channel, Sport7, in 1996. The reason for this high-profile initiative failure directly relates to the reluctance of the consumers to pay for TV.

Whereas the demand side of the market has to mature, the supply side of the market seems well equipped to enter the new communication era. In terms of infrastructure, the Netherlands seems well prepared to build and be part of the "electronic highway." A high penetration of TV cable; an advanced telecommunications infrastructure; strong home players such as KPN, VNU, Philips and Endemol; and a rather high-educated and high-income population are only some of the assets of the Netherlands that provide it with a good starting position. In combination with a strong role of financial institutions in investing in large (new) media ventures, and a government that is transforming its direction from media and telecommunications policy to competition policy, the media industry of this small country seems to be privileged.

References

Ankeren, J. van, Bakker, P., Crombags, B., and P. Hendriks (1996). *Vakinformatie in Nederland (Professional Information in the Netherlands).* Amsterdam: Universiteit van Amsterdam/NVJ.

Brants, K. L. K., and McQuail, D. (1997). The Netherlands. In: European Research Group. (1997). *The Media in Western Europe. The Euromedia Handbook.* London: Sage, pp. 153–168.

CEBUCO [Central Bureau voor Courantenpubliciteit] (1995). *Dagbladen Oplage-specificatie 1995.* Amsterdam: CEBUCO.

het Financieel Dagblad (1996a). Endemol zoekt externe hulp voor expansie plannen. June 20, 1996.

het Financieel Dagblad (1996b). Emissie moet solvabiliteit van beursganger Endenol opkrikken. September 28, 1996.

Jagersma, P. K. (1994). Multinationalisatie van het uitgeefwezen [Multinationalisation of the publishing industry]. *Economische Statistische Berichten,* March 16, pp. 241–245.

McKinsey (1993). *Stimulating Audio-visual Production in the Netherlands.* Audiovisueel platform. Final Report, January.

Mansell, R., Davies, A., and W. Hulsink (1995). *The New Telecommunications in the Netherlands: Strategic Developments in Technologies and Markets.* Programme Information and Communication. Fatima Series. Rathenau Institute. Amsterdam: Otto Cramwinckel Uitgever.

NBLC (1996). *Gids voor de Informatiesector. Cijfers en Trends.* Den Haag: NBLC.

Nederlandse Dagblad Pers (1996). *Jaarverslag 1996 (Annual Report Dutch Association of Newspaper Publishers).* Amsterdam.

Ouwersloot, H., Fulpen, M. J. van, W.J. van Wijnen (1995). De kabeltelevisiemarkt in Nederland [The Cable Industry in the Netherlands]. *Economische Statistische Berichten,* September 27, pp. 852–856.

Vereniging van Erkende Reclame-advies Bureaus (VEA) (1996). *Reclamebestedingen in Nederland 1985-1995 (Advertising Spendings in the Netherlands 1985-1995).* Amsterdam: VEA.

Verenigde Nederlandse Uitgeverijen (1995). *Jaarverslag 1995 (Annual Report VNU 1995).* Haarlem: VEA.

Note

1. The currency in the Netherlands is the Dutch Guilder (Fl). In January of 1997, the exchange rate was Fl 100 = US$56.

12

FRANCE

Nadine Toussaint Desmoulins

France in the Global Media Marketplace

The country of France, officially known as the French Republic, comprises an area of approximately 211,000 square miles in Western Europe. The population is estimated at 57 million people. France is one of the world's major economic powers. Agriculture, as well as major industrial products such as metals, chemicals, natural gas, foods, motor vehicles, aircraft, and textiles, is important to the economy, as is tourism. The railroads, utilities, many banks, and some key industries are nationally owned by French companies.

Despite its long history, the French mass media are not a heavyweight player compared with other industries. Total mass media revenues (including press sales and advertising, broadcasting license fees and subscriptions, sales of receivers, movie box office, sales of videotapes, and compact discs and their players) was estimated around 164 billion French francs in 1995 (almost U.S.$33 billion); roughly 2.2 percent of the gross national product of France (see Table 12-1). Even though this amount is comparable to that of many other French industries, it is far from the turnover (revenues) of many big companies such as the auto manufacturer Renault, with a turnover of Fr 184 billion in 1995. But this amount does not include many losses financed by government subsidies or by various firms involved in the mass media market.

Personnel working in the mass media industries number about 500,000 (approximately 2.2 percent of the working population), with only 28,600 of

Table 12-1. Mass Media Industry Revenues (billions of francs), 1995

	Household Expenditures	Advertising Revenues	Total
Press	36.6	23.9	60.5
Broadcasting			60.3
TV		16.7	
Receivers	15.6		
Fees and subscriptions	21.8		
Radio		3.7	
Receivers	2.5		
Movies	4.5	0.3	4.8
CD and video			38.2
CD, videotapes	22.6		
Sound and video players	15.6		
Total	119.2	44.6	163.8

Source: Data compiled by the author from various agencies.

them journalists. As in the United States, many are employed part-time or on a free-lance basis across the media industries in a variety of positions (artists, journalists, sales, maintenance, etc.).

The French press and movie industries are dominated by private companies, as is the majority of the broadcast industry. The public-run broadcast activity, Radio Télévision Francaise (RTF), is still in existence. The heir to the long-lasting French public broadcasting monopoly, RTF limited diversification for newspaper groups and other industrial enterprises until privatization began under former President Francois Mitterand in 1981. Perhaps this explains why the French mass media companies appear small, with turnover between Fr 5 billion and 10 billion for the major television (TV) companies and from Fr 1 billion to 3 billion for the press and major radio companies. Two companies are exceptions: Havas and Hachette (the communication pole of the Matra Lagardére Group), with 1995 turnover of Fr 44.6 billion and 30.7 billion, respectively.

Freedom of communication is part of the French Constitution, established with the 1789 Human Rights Declaration. Liberty of the press is guaranteed by a very liberal law adopted in 1881. Broadcast stations are not provided as many freedoms. One cannot create a radio or TV station without authorization by a special regulatory agency, the Conseil Supérior de l'Audiovisuel (CSA). The CSA consists of nine members, nominated by the President of the Republic, and the Presidents of the House of Parliament.

The CSA controls many broadcasting activities, even though the general rules are voted by the Parliament or elected by governmental decrees. Indeed, the state's policies intervene in the economy of broadcasting by various and numerous means including content regulation (quotas for some programs), advertising regulations, fixed amount of the TV license fee assigned to public radio and TV and voted by the Parliament, special taxes, percentage of share holding authorized for a single owner or for non–European Union ownership, and limits on cross-media ownership (Franceschini, 1995).

To maintain diversity and promote democracy, the French government subsidizes the media providing state financial support. Newspapers are the primary beneficiaries; they receive low tax rates, special grants, and reduced postal, telephone and railroad rates. Public radio–TV losses are regularly absorbed by the state budget. The state-owned telecommunications company has also provided support for the capital-intensive cable TV and satellite industries. Further, the French government's cultural policy forces TV companies to assign part of their budget to support local TV and movie production.

For historical, political and cultural reasons, France tries to maintain its influence abroad. This so-called mission is usually carried out in a nonprofit way, often with governmental funding. Public broadcasting serves the remaining French overseas departments and territories with a special government-owned radio-TV network, Radio France Outremer (RFO). The government also maintains worldwide French state-owned broadcast companies, such as Radio France Internationale (RFI), and venture radio stations in the Middle East and Africa, whose capital is owned by both the French and foreign governments.

Television networks also receive government support, including Canal France International, TV 5 (shared with foreign French-speaking TV companies) and Arte (shared with Germany). The government provides almost half of the budget (578 million of Fr 1.2 billion) of the Agence France Presse (AFP), which is one of only three remaining worldwide news agencies, the two others being Associated Press and Reuters.

Private media companies also play a role in the international mass media market. The export potential of newspapers, TV programs and movies is restricted by the weakness of French-speaking regions when compared with the English-speaking areas and by the lack of financial resources for many of these areas (e.g., North Africa and Black Africa). Exports represent only about 5 percent of the income of the French press. In the audiovisual field (TV and movies), the trade balance shows a large gap. In 1995, imports totaled more than Fr 2 billion (coming primarily from the United States), whereas exports totaled 1.3 billion, mainly to European countries. Television programs exported to the United States in 1995 generated a mere Fr 20 million (Service Jurdique et Technique de l'Information, 1996).

Beside the exports, private companies are increasing their foreign activities. This is particularly the case of the main media conglomerates. Havas owns a share of Canal Plus and controls Havas Advertising. Hachette has numerous foreign companies in book publishing, magazines and distribution. In recent years, companies have developed many joint ventures to export successful concepts such as *Elle* or *Marie Claire* in women's magazines. The Bayard group markets children and senior citizens magazines, NRJ or Europe 2 for radio, and Canal Plus for TV. The company has also been involved with several successful movies, including *Three Men and a Baby, Sommersby, True Lies,* and *The Bird Cage.*

France has become an open market for foreign investments and acquisitions, especially from European companies that are not restrained by legal barriers to entry. This is particularly true in the magazine press, with the very successful case of Prisma Presse (the French branch of the German Bertelsmann) and, more recently, by the British EMAP; whereas Pearson, another British group, controls one of the two economic dailies *(Les Echos)* and a few other specialized titles.

Major Media Industries in France

The two largest media industries in France are the press and TV. This section centers on these two industries and the key companies that compete for audiences and advertisers.

Consumer Demand

The global turnover of the French press industry was estimated at about Fr 58.76 billion in 1995, with 59.7 percent coming from sales (two-thirds from single copy sales, one-third from subscriptions), and 40.3 percent coming from advertising. The global press circulation has been stable since 1990, which means that French consumers, although they may shift from one type of press to the other, have not increased global demand.

The French are very poor consumers of the national daily press, with only 154 copies sold per 1,000 inhabitants. Each year, the number of people who buy a daily paper only a few times a week continues to decline. French citizens instead prefer to read weekly news magazines or watch TV. This is partly due to the high price of the daily press and also to the lack of appreciation of the content of newspapers by young people and women. The average readership of daily newspapers is not only getting older, but most of the population who reads the press live in small and medium-sized cities or rural areas.

In 1996, 95.7 percent of the households in France owned a TV set and 68.2 percent a video recorder. Approximately 17.8 percent subscribed to Canal

Plus (subscription or pay TV); 7.1 percent subscribed to cable TV; and 5.3 percent subscribed to direct broadcast TV. Direct broadcast TV is quickly increasing as new digital TV networks are coming on-line. Canal Plus began in November 1996, with other competitors set to debut in 1997. The average time spent watching TV in France is around 3 hours per day.

Broadcast audience shares in 1996 were as follows. TF1, a private channel, is the leader at 38 percent, followed by public channels FR2 (26 percent) and FR3 (18 percent). Obviously, this leaves little market share for other channels and services and thus little advertising. Despite the multiplication of channels becoming available as a result of deregulation, household viewing time has not increased. Increasing fragmentation of the audience will lead to more economic difficulties for operators engaged in intense competition.

Home Companies

Two important conglomerates are far ahead of the other media groups in France. The first one is Havas, which has been in existence since 1835. Its 1995 turnover was 44.6 billion Fr, with 34 percent drawn from abroad. Havas controls more than 600 companies operating in five principal areas:

1. Regional media. Havas sells space devoted to national commercial and classified advertising for many regional newspapers and controls many local free sheets.
2. Advertising. Havas Advertising (39 percent owned by Havas) controls a great number of national and international agencies operating in all types of advertising.
3. Newspaper and book publishing. Through CEP Communication, Havas controls many very well known book publishers, such as Larousse, Nathan, Bordas, Dunod, Plon, Julliard, and les Presses de la Cité. CEP is now the largest book publisher in France. CEP also controls important news magazines such as *Le Point* and *L'Express* and an important number of specialized magazines, some of which are very profitable.
4. Broadcasting. The company owns 24 percent of the successful TV network Canal Plus and a 40 percent interest in CLT, which among others, controls RTL radio and TV networks with CLT/UFA since its recent merger with Bertelsmann.
5. Travel agencies, one linked to American Express.

Since 1987 Havas has been private; 37 percent of its capital is publicly owned; and 21 percent is controlled by Alcatel (an industrial company). The rest of the company is owned principally by banks, financial companies, and institutional investors.

The second conglomerate is Hachette (established 1826), which is part of the industrial Lagardére Groupe (formerly the Matra Hachette Groupes). Its turnover was Fr 30.7 billion in 1995. It is linked to Filipacci Médias, a smaller group that has partial control. Like Havas, Hachette is internationalized and operates principally in four fields:

1. Book publishing. Hachette controls many well-known publishers in France (Fayard, Stock, Grasset, etc.) and abroad, especially in the United States (Grolier) and Spain (Salviat).
2. Magazines. Hachette Filipacchi Press is the largest magazine publisher in France, with a huge number of titles, some of which are also published abroad as joint ventures (such as *Elle,* which is published in 28 countries). It also controls several specialized magazines in the United States, including *Première, Women's Day, Car and Driver,* and *Boating.* Linked to its publishing activities, Hachette also controls several societies in charge of selling advertising.
3. Distribution. Hachette controls a large number of societies in France, Europe and North America. Almost 40 percent of its revenues come from distribution.
4. Broadcasting. After a failure in TV, Hachette is now essentially operating in radio with Europe 1 Communication (45 percent controlled by Hachette) and in movie and TV production with Hachette Première.

Hachette is private, its capital being shared between many stockholders including the public, banks, and financial institutions. The company is managed by Groupe Lagardére, which in fact controls less than 10 percent of its capital.

The turnovers (in billions of francs) of these two groups and their main business segments in 1995 are listed in Table 12-2.

Table 12-2. Comparison of Havas and Hachette Media Segments

Segment	Turnover (billions Fr)
Havas Advertising	12.3
CEP Communication	11.3
Canal Plus	10.1
Other segments	10.9
Total Havas turnover	44.6
Hachette publishing	12.9
Distribution	12.3
Hachette Livre	2.8
Europe 1 Communication	2.7
Total Hachette turnover	30.7

Source: Groupe Lagardére, 1996; Havas, 1996.

Table 12-3. Revenue Turnovers of the Major French Media Companies

Company	Turnover (billion Fr)
Publicis (advertising)	20.5
TF1 (commercial TV)	9.4
Hersant (press)	6
France 2 (public TV)	5.2
France 3 (public TV)	5
Prisma Presse (press)	3
Radio France (public radio)	2.5
Amaury (press)	2.3
Bayard Presse (press)	2.1
M6 (commercial TV)	2

Source: Compiled by author from various sources.

Behind these two groups, the turnovers of the other major French media companies are listed in Table 12-3.

Media Industry Analysis

Press Industry

The economic situation of the French press is characterized by large discrepancies in the conditions of production and distribution, as well as in performance levels.

Even though some important press groups exist, the only significant daily newspaper chain is Hersant. Anti-concentration regulation forbids control of more than 30 percent of the circulation of national general information dailies (20 percent in case of cross- or multimedia ownership). Furthermore, the profitability of French press groups is higher with certain kinds of press (TV guide, some specialized titles) rather than dailies. National daily newspapers have experienced large operating deficits since 1970.

There are significant differences within the press between national and provincial dailies, as well as between the daily and nondaily press.

NATIONAL DAILY PRESS. There are only 10 titles (compared with 26 in 1945), with a total daily circulation of 2.5 million copies. The most important dailies reach a circulation of about 450,000 copies per day (*Le Parisien,* which is actually more of a regional paper for the large Paris suburban area). The daily press offers different political and cultural tendencies. There are also two business dailies, *Les Echos* and *La Tribune,* and two sports dailies,

Table 12-4. National Daily Circulation, 1996

Paper	Circulation
La Croix	96,814
Les Echos	128,747
L'Equipe	377,098
Le Figaro	382,021
France Soir	187,102
L'Humanité	63,342
Liberation	166,521
Le Monde	371,575
Le Parisien	459,658
Paris Turf	115,681
La Tribune	79,141

Source: *Diffusion Contrule* (1997).

L'Equipe and *Paris Turf.* None of the dailies publish Sunday editions. Circulation data for the major national dailies are listed in Table 12-4.

Entering this market is fairly difficult. Problems include high investment costs required by the printing plants, extremely favorable working conditions, and high wages negotiated by the printers' union (le Syndicat du Livre) in Paris, technological modernization, weak readership and consequently low advertising demand (Toussaint Desmoulins, 1994). These difficulties explain why all the national dailies launched after 1973 *(Liberation)* failed, including the most recent press, *Information,* in 1996.

The national French press is sold at a very high price; about Fr 7 per copy for a quality paper in 1997, Fr 5 for a popular one. Almost all newspapers dealing with general information lose money. These losses are covered by the groups to which they belong: Hersant for *France Soir et Le Figaro*, Amaury for *Le Parisien,* Bayard for *La Croix,* or by capital investments coming from industrialists (Chargeurs for *Liberation,* LVHM for *La Tribune*) and insurance companies (for *Le Monde*).

National newspapers take advantage of a cooperative paper-(newsprint) buying pool known as the Société Professionnelle des Papiers de Presse. Since 1947, a cooperative distribution organization, Les Nouvelles Messageries de la Presse Parisienne (NMPP), provides the same price conditions to each member. These efforts have eased some of the barriers to entry.

PROVINCIAL DAILY PRESS. A fairly large number of provincial (regional) newspapers still exist (about 62 compared with 153 in 1945), with a total daily circulation around 6 million copies per day. Mergers have led to regional or departmental monopolies and to the ownership of several titles by a few hands. For example, the Hersant group controls about 22 titles, most of them spread over the France metropolitan and overseas territories (with France Antilles).

The largest French daily newspaper is a provincial press. *Ouest France* has a daily circulation of 790,000 copies and also maintains control over a number of freesheets and book publishing in the region.

Production costs, circulation and distribution expenses are much lower than the national press because of less union pugnacity, which facilitated early technological modernization and thus the use of color. There are more sales by postal subscription and home deliveries, which lowers the number of unsold copies. As a result the selling price is rather low; around Fr 4.5 per copy. Nevertheless advertising and classifieds are less important (only about 37.6 percent of income) despite advertising bundling agreements between regional newspapers.

Circulation remains stable despite many efforts to attract new readers and to improve the content. The readership is aging and lives mainly in rural areas. The market is considered as being "naturally" closed in that no new launchings have been attempted for a very long time.

PERIODICAL (MAGAZINE) PRESS. There is considerable diversity in this area. Each year several new titles are launched dealing with new topics (e.g., computers, hobbies) as well as traditional areas (TV, women's magazines, sports). Competition is very harsh.

Entry into this market is much easier, facilitated by an abundance of independent printers not restrained by unions and also by the possible use of the NMPP for national distribution. Although many individuals attempt to launch new titles, only the larger groups can afford the costly market studies and advertising campaigns required for gaining significant market shares.

The periodical press collects most of the advertising investments made in the press. Most titles earn more than 50 percent of their revenues from advertising. In addition to French press groups involved in the periodical press, European press groups have operated more actively in France since 1980. These companies include Prisma Presse, Bauer, and more recently the British EMAP group. EMAP has become the third largest publisher of magazines in France behind Hachette and Prisma.

Radio Broadcasting

Radio is a very popular medium in France. More than 98 percent of the population has at least one radio receiver. Since 1982, changes in regulation induced a major upheaval in the radio industry. A new and independent authority was created, first called "Haute Autorite," then the "Conseil Superieur de l'Audiovisuel" (CSA). This body has the mission of appointing the presidents of the public service stations and assigning frequencies and authorizations to broadcast.

Moreover the 1982 law legalized private radio. Subsequently more than 1,500 stations were authorized. These stations were first financed by subsidies from listeners and grants by the state. Advertising as a source of income was authorized in 1984. From that time many commercial radio stations developed, and as a result of a 1986 law, commercial radio stations obtained the right to generate networks. Current ownership regulations forbid a single owner from serving more than 150 million people or controlling more than three national networks.

At present, one large public radio institution operates in France: Radio France with several channels: national (France Inter), regional, local and specialized (all news, classical musical, culture, etc.). There are four main private radio groups. NRJ is controlled by a single owner; RTL is partly owned by CLT and Havas; Europe 1 communication (Hachette), and RMC (still partly controlled by the government). Stations controlled by these groups are wholly financed by advertising, and public radio is financed by TV license fees, state subsidies, and very little advertising.

Despite the competition between radio stations, radio's share of total advertising has remained rather stable over the years. The French radio industry receives about 7 percent of total media advertising. Performance for commercial stations varies. Some are very profitable, although small, noncommercial, private stations endure heavy losses despite governmental subsidies.

Television Broadcasting

French TV has had a very choppy evolution since the end of the state monopoly. The primary channels that make up the French TV industry are Canal Plus, M6, TF1, ARTE, and La 5eme. Cable TV began in 1982, followed by analog satellite TV and recently digital satellite delivery. Despite this important evolution France has no TV networks with affiliated stations, and only public TV broadcasts regional programs a few hours a day (Paul, 1996).

The financing of TV is very intricate. State TV receives license fees, governmental subsidies and advertising in different proportions depending on each channel. Private TV is financed either by commercial advertisers (TF1, M6), or subscriptions and little advertising (Canal Plus), or totally by subscriptions (cable and satellite TV). Television advertising was first authorized in 1968, and TV has continued to attract more advertising investments each year, largely at the expense of the press. Table 12-5 lists the various advertising investments across the French media industries for 1995.

Table 12-5. Advertising Revenues, 1995

	Investment (in millions Fr)	Percentage
TOTAL Press[a]	23,977	47.4
National dailies	2,334	
Provincial dailies	5,053	
Magazines	7,813	
Specialized	3,710	
Free sheets	5,067	
Television	16,704	33.0
Radio	3,747	7.4
Movie	302	0.6
Outdoor	5,870	11.6
Total	50,600	100.0

Source: Data compiled by the author from various agencies.

[a]Includes display and classified.

The influence of regulation is noticeable at each level of management in the TV industry. First, the CSA must allow the creation of a private TV channel, and authorization is given for a limited period of time. Second, the amount of capital owned by a single owner is limited to less than 50 percent, as is the share owned by foreign owners outside the European Union. Third, advertising content is regulated (around 6 minutes per hour). Fourth, each TV channel devotes a certain amount (15 to 20 percent) of its budget to support production of new TV programs, and movie production financing (about 3 percent). Special taxes paid into a fund are dedicated to movies and TV production. Last, regulations force TV to devote a time, specially in prime hours, to European- and French-speaking and -produced movies and TV programs (especially fiction, documentaries and cartoons). Movies and fiction cannot be interrupted for advertising more than once on private TV, and interruptions are forbidden on public TV (Toussaint Desmoulins, 1996).

Turnovers of TV companies are fairly high compared with those of newspapers. Turnover of Canal Plus is about Fr 10.1 billion, TF1 about 9.1 billion, public France 2 and France 3 about Fr 5 billion. To date, cable TV has lost money in France.

Private TV companies are linked to industrial and financial entities. This is partly due to the high investment needed to launch a new channel and to the expensive costs of production and rights (especially for movies and sports). This explains the participation of Bouyques (public works) in TF1, of Generale des Eaux (water utility and waste treatment) in Canal Plus (in addition to Havas), and Lyonnaise des Eaux (another water utility) in M6. In cable and satellite TV, similar partnerships exist.

Television companies are diversifying into studio production and negotiating the sharing of TV and movie distribution portfolios. In France, TV production and distribution costs are also high because until recent years there has not been a viable second market or exports to allow for accelerated amortization.

Movie Production

France maintains an important movie industry despite the decline of audiences in theaters and competition from videocassette reorders. Although the theater audience fell from 180 million during the 1970s to 129 million in 1995, the number of films produced with French investments is still the same—around 140 per year. About 60 of these are entirely French financed. This places France far ahead of other European countries. Essentially, it is a consequence of the French government's cultural and economic policy.

Since 1948 the French government has set up a system meant to sustain both production and exhibition in cinema. Taxes on movie tickets (12 percent of the cost), TV budgets, and state subsidies provide a fund (Fonds de Soutien au Cinema) to support production of French-produced films. The fund also helps modernize and develop new theaters. The movie industry draws more money from the TV rights and videotape sales and rentals than from theater admissions.

To protect theater exhibition from TV competition, the government has imposed a schedule for film distribution. The first window is the theater, then 1 year later videotapes, and then TV. Quotas also limit the invasion of American films on TV, specifying the days and hours of diffusion, the number of films allowed per year, and the nationality of the film (60 percent of them having to be European, with at least 40 percent featuring French language).

Production and distribution is rather concentrated. Few groups operate in the movie industry. Gaumont is the largest, followed by Pathe and UGC.

Emerging Media Economic Issues

Technological Development

The future of the French media industries is at risk by the development of new broadcasting systems: direct digital broadcast satellite systems, radio data system (RDS), digital audio broadcasting (DAB) and, overall, by all the new multimedia systems.

For the French groups, off-line systems are still marginal, even though they are in constant growth. The spread of CD-ROM and compact disc interactive

(CDI) should not have any significant impact on their profitability, at least in the short term. Nevertheless, the target of these groups is to gain knowledge in this market so as to be in the best position at the time when penetration of the domestic computer will be higher. In early 1997 it was estimated at less than 20 percent.

In the same way, French companies have started to take great interest in on-line systems and are now investing in this field, sometimes even helped by a French governmental program that tries to accelerate the creation in France of communication superhighways. The on-line market potential, which seems each day more attractive, is doubtless. All the major media groups are entering the Internet and the World Wide Web, not only as access suppliers but also as content suppliers.

Multimedia development, like other new innovations, may be seen as a threat for the "old" media such as the printed press. Greater audience fragmentation among different audiovisual media may increase the financial difficulties of each area, especially those with limited advertising resources.

Regulatory Changes

The anticipated growth of multimedia will likely cause changes in regulation, especially in regard to concentration and cross-media ownership. The goal of helping French groups reach a size comparable to that of some other European, American and Asiatic competitors will make it necessary for the government to allow increased concentration and for a willingness to accept larger advertising revenues.

The future of the state-owned radio and TV is also a key issue. Because of its high costs and periodic losses, some lobbies want its importance to be reduced. Others suggest that it should neither be allowed to be even partly financed by advertising, nor by subsidies, but only by the license fee. Any decisions could drastically affect the performance of state-owned radio and TV in France.

Other regulatory issues must also be considered. The quota policies ardently supported by successive French governments to restrict outside TV content may be called into question as more satellite TV services emerge. Another main issue is how to adapt the very protective French copyright rules to the new communication technologies, especially with on-line systems.

Last, as far the press is concerned, the major problem at present is the necessary changes required in providing state subsidies. State budget constraints will require the government to be more restrictive in awarding subsidies and to select the recipients more accurately.

Future research should be carried out in several areas. Among the most needed are studies on the economic impacts of the new technology on media consumer practices and expenses, the impact on employment in France, and the role of professional journalists in media production.

References

Diffusion Contrule (1997).
Franceschini, L. (1995). *La Regulation Audiovisuelle en France.* Paris: Presses Universitaires de France.
Groupe Lagardére. (1996). *Document de Reference: Rapport Financier du Groupe Lagardere.* Paris: Groupe Lagardére.
Havas (1996). *Rapport Financier du Havas.* Paris: Havas.
Paul, J. (1996). *Economie de la Communication TV-Radio.* Paris: Presses Universitaires de France.
Service Jurdique et Technique de l'Information. (1996). *Indicateurs Statistique de l'Audiovisual,* 1995. Paris: La Documentation Francais.
Toussaint Desmoulins, N. (1996). *L'economie des Media.* Paris: Presses Universitaires de France.
Toussaint Desmoulins, N. (1994). Les causes economique de la crise de la presse francaise. *Quaderni* 24:47–58.

Africa and the Middle East

The continent of Africa is represented by two chapters. Osa Amienyi writes about his native country, Nigeria. One of the leading media centers in Africa, Nigeria is adapting to more privatized media ownership and less government control. On the other hand, South Africa continues to experience change due to a number of social and political reforms, which has in turn affected the key media industries in the area. Pieter Fourie and Rudolph De Jager provide insight into the transformation of South Africa after apartheid. Representing the Middle East, Menahem Blondheim examines the political climate, growing economy, and geographic isolation in shaping Israel's media environment. As in many countries in the world, the development of new telecommunications technologies is redirecting Israeli communication policy.

13

NIGERIA

Osabuohien P. Amienyi

Nigeria in the Global Marketplace

The Federal Republic of Nigeria is sometimes called "Africa's sleeping giant" because it is generally believed that it has failed since its creation in 1914 to live up fully to its economic and political potential. In spite of the socioeconomic and political difficulties that have plagued its existence in the past four decades, however, Nigeria remains preeminent among the countries in Africa and the rest of the developing world. With a quarter of Africa's population, making it the most populous country on the continent and the twelfth most populous country in the world, Nigeria has abundant physical and human resources that make it "one of the most endowed countries in the world" (Embassy of Nigeria, 1996, p. 3). Nigeria has well over 2,000 industrial establishments that operate in such sectors as agriculture, petroleum, fashion, food processing, pharmaceuticals, car assembly, and mining (iron ore, columbite, limestone, gold and coal). These provide the country's mass media system with an enormous potential source of commercial revenue.

Nigeria is the sixth largest producer of crude oil in the world and the second in Africa (Embassy of Nigeria, 1996). The gross national product (GNP) is worth more than half that of "some 45 other Black African nations combined" (Bourgault, 1995a, p. 139; see also Lamb, 1985). By almost any standard (African or the world), Nigeria is a wealthy country. Oil has been the main source of revenue for the country since it was discovered in the Niger

River basin in the 1950s. Oil accounts for more than 90 percent of export earnings and up to 80 percent of federal revenue. During the 1970s, revenues from oil propelled an unparalleled economic growth in Nigeria. Revenues soared as Nigerian oil was used to fill the void that was created by the Arab oil embargo of 1973, and the concomitant price increases implemented by the Organization of Oil Exporting Countries (OPEC) created additional incomes (Bourgault, 1995b). The economy has since slowed, and Nigeria's income per capita has fallen from $1,000 in the 1980s to $300 in 1993 (Adams, 1994).

The World Bank now classifies Nigeria as a low-income country, but this is a misleading classification. Nigeria has a surprisingly large number of millionaires (Bourgault, 1995a) and only 1 percent of the population controls more than 75 percent of its wealth. Furthermore, the World Bank initiated a series of economic reforms (known as the Structural Adjustment Programme, or SAP) that was adopted in 1986, and it has achieved success in eliminating distortions in the Nigerian economy (Emmett, 1996). Consequently, the country appears to be back on the road to economic revitalization and buoyancy. This is good news for the mass media, which must now operate almost entirely on funds derived from advertising. Nigerian advertisers have always been eager to advertise, especially on the local dramas produced in indigenous languages (Bourgault, 1995b).

Except for two intermittent trials of representative government, Nigeria has had military governments since its independence in 1960. The first attempt at a democratic government followed the British parliamentary system and was called the "First Republic." It lasted from 1960 to 1966 (Omu, 1968). The second attempt, called "The Second Republic," lasted from 1979 to 1983 and was patterned after the U.S. presidential system. The Third Republic was scheduled to begin in October 1992 but was postponed after General Ibrahim Babangida's annulment of the results of the presidential election in August of the same year. It is now scheduled to begin on October 1, 1998.

Nigeria's political restiveness has been a reflection of the absence of national integration, as the more than 250 ethnic nationalities who inhabit the country have found it difficult to coalesce into a national community devoid of parochial loyalties. This inherent social and political disintegration has been reflected in the development of the country's mass media system. Immediately after the attainment of independence, the three provinces that comprised the country pulled away from the federal structure of government and began using regional radio and television (TV) to develop their separate identities (Egbon, 1982). To forestall this separatist attitude of the regions, a multistate structure was put in place of the former tripartite regional division in 1970. This structure has created a vast media system in the country, as each new state has strived to develop its own media organizations.

It is not surprising, then, that Nigeria has the "most developed and pluralistic" (Akinfeleye, 1983) mass media system in Africa. Nigeria is Africa's largest importer of TV programs and is also the continent's biggest producer of TV programs. According to Bourgault (1995a, p. 137), "Nigeria produces more programs than any other country in Black Africa." Statistics for 1991 revealed that Nigeria produced 906 hours of TV programs per week, accounting "for nearly one-half of all television production on the continent" (Bourgault, 1995b, p. 243). Nigeria also has the most extensive media training facilities in Africa, aside from South Africa (Bourgault, 1995a). Media professionals from many countries in Africa, including Kenya, Niger, Chad, Sierra Leone, Benin and Liberia, have been trained in Nigeria.

Major Media Industries in Nigeria

Three media industries are particularly noteworthy in Nigeria: the newspaper industry, the radio industry and the TV industry. Combined, these industries wield an enormous amount of influence in Nigeria, in neighboring countries and beyond. To understand their nature and influence fully, each of these industries is discussed separately.

The Newspaper Industry

The newspaper industry is the oldest of the mass media industries in Nigeria. Its roots date back to 1859, when a British missionary, Rev. Henry Townsend, established *Iwe Irohin,* a Yoruba- and English-language religious newspaper in Abeokuta. *Iwe Irohin* became the first regularly published native language newspaper on the continent of Africa. It was also the most widely read vernacular newspaper in Nigeria and is the longest surviving native language newspaper in Africa (Akinfeleye, 1983). Copies of *Iwe Irohin* are still being sold in Nigeria today. *Iwe Irohin* was followed in 1863 by the *Anglo-African,* an English-language newspaper published in Lagos. In 1926, the first commercial newspaper, *The Daily Times,* came into existence. Seven decades later, *The Daily Times* still has the widest circulation of all newspapers and magazines in Nigeria, with an average daily circulation (ADC) of 400,000 copies (Eribo, 1995).

The Nigerian newspaper media industry is remarkably well developed. There are well over 150 consumer publications, including dailies, weeklies, periodicals, and industrial and professional journals. These circulate throughout the country, in neighboring African countries, and in other such far away countries as Britain and the United States (Embassy of Nigeria, 1996). Some of these are owned by the government, whereas others are owned by private entrepreneurs. The most established government dailies include *The Chronicle, The Daily Sketch, The Daily Star, The Daily Times, The New Nigerian, The Nigerian Standard,* and *The Observer* (Emmett, 1996). The most popular private dailies include *The Concord, The Punch, The Nigerian Tribune,* and *The Guardian* (Eribo, 1995).

The Nigerian press is exceptionally vibrant. If it is not the freest in Africa, it is indeed as free as journalism in the United States. Emmett (1996, p. 2) noted this vibrancy when he wrote that "Nigeria has a long tradition of free-speaking, searching, witty and even scurrilous journalism with deep roots." Throughout its history, the press has been subject to negative social and political forces that might have forced it to lose its independence. Journalists have been jailed and publishers have had their publications banned for presenting information that seemingly portrayed the government of the day in bad light. Four factors have, however, persisted in maintaining the relative independence of the print media industry: advertising, the historical role of newspapers, ethnic diversity, and the formation of professional regulatory organizations.

ADVERTISING. From the very beginning, the sale of space has been an avenue through which Nigerian newspapers obtained revenue. *Iwe Irohin* began carrying advertisements 5 years after its inception (Akinfeleye, 1983). Since then advertisements have been a regular feature of every newspaper in Nigeria, including those owned by the federal and state governments. The majority of the advertisements are obituaries, remembrance announcements, anniversary salutations and other forms of congratulations or expressions of gratitude or appreciation. Products and service advertisements are fewer in number and are usually smaller in size than their obituary counterparts. Obituaries, remembrance announcements, anniversary salutations, and other expressions of gratitude or appreciation are usually full-page, half-page or quarter-page advertisements; the typical product advertisement is usually not larger than a 6 x 6 column. On the whole, advertisements usually constitute between 28 percent and 35 percent of newspaper content, with the private newspapers carrying the higher percentage.

THE HISTORICAL ROLE OF NEWSPAPERS. Despite numerous assaults, the tradition of press freedom that the Nigerian press acquired from the days of anti-colonial struggle has continued to exist to date. During the colonial period, newspapers were the means by which Nigerian nationalists voiced their opposition to colonial policies. Nationalist newspapers such as the *West Africa Pilot* (owned by the man who became the first President of Nigeria, Nnamdi Azikiwe) and *The Daily Service* (owned by Obafemi Awolowo, who became the Premier of the former Western province) challenged colonial authority on a regular basis and essentially paved the way for the attainment of independence in the country. Once independence was attained, the newspapers continued with their anti-government stance. The government has tried on many occasions to eclipse this independence of newspapers to no avail.

ETHNIC DIVERSITY. As stated earlier, Nigeria is an extremely diverse country. As Eribo (1995) has described it, Nigeria is a country of approximately 100 million people and 400 languages, which conglomerates within its borders about 250 ethnic groups that have painstakingly preserved their identities. Thus, the country is so diverse that *The Economist* (After the ball, 1986) has described diversity as Nigeria's fascination. Generally, diversity has been perceived as a negative factor in many areas of national affairs, but one area where it is seen as a positive and necessary factor has been that of press freedom. The existence of press freedom in Nigeria is largely attributed to what Eribo (1995) described as the inner strength that derives from a pristine tradition of free exchange of news and information in the communal setting, such as the marketplace, village meetings, festivals and other social gatherings. This tradition has bred a plurality of voices that has translated into a plurality of media ownership. The plurality of ownership has meant, as Mytton (1983) has noted, that what one paper refuses to print, another will gladly publish; what one radio station chooses to silence, another will carry happily.

THE FORMATION OF PROFESSIONAL REGULATORY ORGANIZATIONS. A Media Council exists in Nigeria to protect the freedom of the press and to ascertain and seek to eliminate abuses in the practices of journalism in the country. The council serves as a disciplinary body that ensures that the Nigerian press achieves and maintains the highest professional standards. It prepares and enforces a code of conduct to guide both the press and journalists in the performance of their duties and inquires into complaints about the conduct of the press. The Council's work is complemented by the activities of three other professional bodies that regulate and control the activities of media professionals. These are the Newspaper Proprietors Association of Nigeria (NPAN), the Nigerian Guild of Editors (NGE), and the Nigerian Union of Journalists (NUJ). Together, these organizations maintain the necessary intransigence to ensure that the press in Nigeria operate with an enormous amount of freedom.

Newspaper readership is highest among educated Nigerians. The newspaper readership habits of Nigerians parallel those of European citizens, particularly those of Britons. Typically, the Nigeria newspaper consumer would read four to five different newspapers daily in an effort to balance government and private information. Because both types of newspapers have to subscribe to the same regulations, there is very little difference in the news presentation style of both government and private newspapers.

The Radio Industry

The Nigerian radio industry was restructured in 1978. The old Nigerian Broadcasting Corporation (NBC), which had overseen broadcasting in the country since 1957, was dissolved and a new organization, the Federal Radio Corporation of Nigeria (FRCN), was created in its place. All the radio stations that the NBC operated at the state capitals (a 19-state structure had replaced the previous three regional administrations) were handed over to the state governments. NBC stations in Lagos, Ibadan and Enugu were retained and merged with the former Broadcasting Company of Northern Nigeria (BCNN Kaduna) to form the FRCN (Federal Radio Corporation of Nigeria, 1993).

The FRCN, whose motto is "Uplift the people and unite the nation" (Secretariat of the Commonwealth Broadcasting Association, 1991/92), provides its services from four linguistic zones, with zonal headquarters located in Enugu, Kaduna, Ibadan and Lagos. The zonal centers operate autonomously, producing programs in English and in the vernacular languages of their coverage area. The FRCN broadcasts in 45 Nigerian languages about 40 percent of the time, but the emphasis is placed on the following 12 indigenous languages: Edo, Efik, Fulfulde, Hausa, Igala, Igbo, Ijaw, Kanuri, Nupe, Tiv, Urhobo, and Yoruba. By this zonal arrangement, FRCN's transmissions are received throughout the country.

With the establishment of the FRCN, the Nigerian radio industry acquired a four-tier structure: the federal national service whose network news must be carried in all the states; zonal broadcasts along broad regional lines; local grassroots services from the state stations; and as of August 24, 1992, private commercial stations. The state stations are restricted in their transmission power allocation and thus cannot broadcast beyond the confines of their state boundaries. Nigeria now has 36 states, but only about 30 of them have a broadcasting service. Altogether, there are more than 77 radio stations in Nigeria (Metz, 1992).

The FRCN's national service from Lagos operates on three channels: Radio Nigeria I, Radio Nigeria II and Radio Nigeria III. Radio Nigeria I caters to a variety of interests and tastes, combining the characteristics of public service radio with that of a viable commercial outlook and producing programs in attractive and sponsorable formats. It embodies the country's national values and aspirations. Its slogan is "We are the One; The first before the rest." Radio I broadcasts on both shortwave and medium-wave frequencies. Radio Nigeria II, the first radio station in Nigeria to broadcast in stereo, provides general entertainment services for its mainly urban listeners. Innovative and trendy in its programming, Radio Nigeria II is the highest revenue-earning radio station in Nigeria. Known as the "Sunshine Station," it broadcasts in both FM and AM stereo. Radio Nigeria III provides programming with a special grassroots appeal. Broadcasting in Hausa, Igbo, Yoruba and Pidgin English, its slogan is: "We speak to the people in the language of the people" (Amienyi, in press).

Programming on Nigerian Radio is heavily entertainment oriented, mainly music. In 1983, FM stations in Nigeria broadcast about 70 percent of foreign music, primarily from the United States, whereas only about 26 percent was Nigerian and the rest were from other African countries. A study conducted before the proliferation of FM radio in Nigeria revealed that about 54 percent of music played on Nigerian radio was of domestic origins and 46 percent was of foreign origins (Katz and Wedell, 1977; see also Bourgault, 1995b). Thus, it appears that the proliferation of FM stations has shifted music programming on Nigerian radio toward imported fare. This is not surprising in light of popularity of American country western music with the Nigerian radio audience (Bourgault, 1995b). Nigeria's only private radio station, Ray Power 100 FM, is gaining increasing popularity because its overwhelmingly foreign music content, particularly its rap and reggae music, is very popular with younger audiences.

The FRCN began accepting advertisements in 1987, almost 10 years after its inception. Since then, it has received increasingly less government subvention. Advertisements are played in blocks between music segments and news programs. An interesting advertising practice on the FRCN is the commercialization of news. Anyone who desires the coverage of an event and is not a government official must pay for the coverage. It is not clear what price the FRCN charges for this service or how much revenue it has gained from it. However, Bourgault (1995b, p. 240) has noted that "only renowned individuals outside government circles can expect to be exempt from news coverage fees."

Radio is the medium of the masses in Nigeria. Therefore, radio commands the highest percentage of audiences among the three media industries in Nigeria. Radio is popular because it parallels the very strong oral tradition of most Nigerian societies (Wigston, 1994), and its programs are not difficult to produce, as it does not require vast human, technical and financial resources (Ngarara, 1996).

The Television Industry

Despite the inception of private broadcasting in 1993, the Nigerian TV industry is dominated by the Nigerian Television Authority (NTA). which was created in 1976 to provide a coordinated TV service throughout the country. Through its own stations in each state capital, the NTA provides programming that enables it to capture the highest percentage of Nigerian viewers and a greater share of the advertising revenues. Through the years, the number of TV stations has grown under the NTA monopoly. Today, there are 24 stations, 84 transmitters, and 19 satellite earth stations linked with three INTELSAT transponders. These facilities establish NTA as Africa's largest TV network and rank it among the world's biggest TV organizations, with its annual broadcast of about 85,000 hours of different programs (Nigerian Television Authority, 1993). It is estimated that more than 40 million viewers tune to NTA each day (Embassy of Nigeria, 1996).

Like the FRCN, the NTA has also commercialized its network newscasts. In 1989, the network decided to offer anyone outside the government who desired coverage for an event the chance to have the event covered for a fee. The charge for the NTA network news coverage of an event in Lagos was about $4,000. In other parts of the country, the charge per coverage ran as high as $5,000. These charges have been extended to political advertising, as each candidate running in the 1992 Presidential primaries had to pay $500 for "recording and broadcasting interviews with the candidates" (Bourgault, 1995b, p. 240).

The Nigerian TV industry entered a new era in 1992, when the government promulgated Decree 38, which repealed the exclusive government ownership of radio, TV, cable and satellite broadcasting. The decree established the National Broadcasting Commission (NBC), an organization that is similar to the Federal Communications Commission (FCC) in the United States, and gave permission to private individuals and corporations to establish radio, TV and cable systems in Nigeria. Fourteen private TV stations and 13 cable/satellite and retransmission operators are now operating in the country (Africa South of the Sahara, 1995).

NBC guidelines stipulate that the programming standards for TV stations, other than cable or satellite systems, shall be 60 percent local and 40 percent foreign. For cable and satellite redistribution systems, the local programming content shall not be less than 20 percent on any channel (Federal Radio Corporation of Nigeria, 1993). The NTA network, however, targets the telecast of few imported programs. In 1996, 69 percent of NTA's programs were produced locally. The remaining 31 percent were imported from the United States, Western Europe, Brazil and Asian countries. The locally produced programs are telecast mostly in local languages.

The creation of NBC and the award of cable and satellite retransmission licenses to private individuals has been a positive regulatory action for the TV industry in Nigeria. The former illegal proliferation of multichannel satellite services has now been severely curtailed. This has created a conducive environment for the TV industry to blossom. Video rentals continue to challenge the TV industry for audiences, as pirated copies of film and music videos are openly sold on the streets and in stores.

The Nigerian Media Market

Nigerian media industries compete in two main markets: a consumer market for readership, listenership or viewership, and a specialized market for advertising. In the consumer market, newspapers, radio stations and TV organizations (both government and private) must compete with one another for the national audience. It can be said that the consumer market exists at the national level; however, the competition among media outlets actually occurs at the local level, where media consumption largely takes place. The situation resembles that of the *USA Today* and *The Wall Street Journal* in the United States, which are published in one metropolitan center and carry advertisements for businesses operating in that center but are sold at local newsstands throughout the country.

The number of competitors varies in each of Nigeria's local markets depending on how many media outlets are in circulation. In the largest market in the country, Lagos (with a population of about six million), consumers have access to more than 15 newspapers, 10 radio stations and eight TVs stations. In other markets, such as Benin, Enugu, Jos, Kaduna, Kano and Port Harcourt (where the population base ranges anywhere from 400,000 to more than 1,000,000), the number of available radio and TV stations and newspaper outlets are fewer than in Lagos. In Benin, for example, only two TV stations (NTA Benin, Edo Television), four radio stations (FRCN Benin, Edo Broadcasting Service, Radio O-Y-O and Ogun State Radio) and fewer than a dozen newspapers compete for the local market.

In the advertising market, the competition for advertisers is carried out mainly at the local level, particularly in the large cities in the country: Lagos, Ibadan, Benin, Enugu, Aba, Calabar, Port Harcourt, Jos, Kaduna, Kano, Sokoto, Yola and Maiduguri. These cities are home to numerous advertising agencies that act as the liaison between the local, regional, national and international marketers and various media outlets. The largest proportion of advertising is sponsored by transnational corporations, which have local subsidiaries in Nigeria. The most commonly advertised products on Nigerian radio and TV are soap, toothpaste, laundry detergent, packaged foods, beverages and nonprescription drugs. In most cases, TV programs are sponsored by a single company. Banks and breweries are the most active program sponsors.

The Nigerian Media Market Structure

There are different market structures for the newspaper and electronic media (radio and TV) industries in Nigeria. The market structure for the newspaper industry can best be described as an oligopoly: there is more than one seller of the product, and the products offered are generally differentiated by content, style and appearance (Albarran, 1996). Hatchen (1993) pointed to this product differentiation when he noted that the Nigerian press tended to stress advocacy and opinion more than information. Bourgault (1995a) agreed, noting that each newspaper tends to be wildly partisan in its account of events; consequently, as Mytton (1983) has observed, a reader must consult a range of newspapers in order to obtain the complete and accurate perspective on any given news items. All the newspapers provide news reports, features, sports and opinion, but with varying degrees of attention to each. Some newspapers provide more features than news and others provide more news than features.

The market structure for the electronic media industry is different at both the national and local levels. At the national level, the market structure can best be described as an exclusive monopoly, as the federal government owned FRCN (radio) and NTA (TV) networks are the only broadcasters. State and private broadcasters are granted a license to broadcast, but the area of coverage of their stations cannot exceed their immediate locality. This arrangement persists because the federal government wishes to "preserve the role of broadcasting as an instrument of nation-building or development" (Nwosu, 1987, p. 632). Programming on network stations falls into three general areas: news and current affairs, public enlightenment (including women's, children's, religious, public service and educational programs) and entertainment (sitcoms, comedy variety, dramatic serials and series and feature films). All stations in the country (including state and private) must connect to the NTA network nightly news at nine o'clock. All the advertising in this newscast is sold by the national headquarters of the NTA and FRCN.

At the local level, the market structure for the electronic media resembles a monopolistic competition. As Albarran (1996) explains, monopolistic competition is a market structure in which many sellers offer products that are similar, but not perfect, substitutes for one another. This is the case with Nigerian radio and TV. At the state capitals, where all of Nigeria's radio and TV stations are located, there is an autonomous NTA and FRCN station in competition with a state radio and TV station (a few cities have also had a third option in the form of private stations since 1993). These stations offer the same types of programs, but the language of delivery, proportion of program scheduled, style of on-air personalities, technical facilities, and audience appeal tend to differentiate one station from another. For example, the proportion of entertainment programs is considerably higher on the schedules of the private and state government stations than on the NTA and FRCN stations.

The stations do not make any promotional attempts to differentiate themselves, except for periodic station identification. The programs offered by the NTA and FRCN stations are more nationally oriented, whereas the state stations tend to adopt a more insular view of programming. But the format of programs delivered by both are essentially the same. The state and private government stations are also more apt to program in vernacular languages than the NTA stations, which in the interest of promoting a lingua-franca, must present the majority of their programs in English.

Emerging Media Economic Issues in Nigeria

A number of emergent forces will affect the viability of Nigerian media industries in the coming years. These forces will determine independently or collectively the extent to which Nigerian media industries can expand or contract, survive or die. They will also determine the social and political character of each industry and, by so doing, establish the nature of the relationship that will exist between the media industries and the environment in which they operate. These forces include government regulation, technological development, and corruption.

Government Regulation

Because all newspapers operations are authorized by the federal government of Nigeria, certain policies must be adhered to by all outlets. The adoption of the "development theory" of journalism means that newspapers in the country must refrain from antagonizing the government or becoming the "fourth estate" of the realm. As development theory stipulates, mass media institutions, regardless of ownership, must support the national goals, particularly those related to nation building. Adherence to this philosophy has led to the suspension of some newspapers and the jailing of some errant journalists. As a result, the journalist must exercise a certain degree of self-censorship to avert the wrath of the government.

Government and private ownership of newspapers and magazines exist side by side, with neither side enjoying a monopoly. In fact, there is a government regulation in Nigeria against print media monopolies, which was instituted to prevent the misuse of the print media by a few rich or powerful individuals or groups. This inherent "right to publish" means that Nigeria can look forward to further expansion of the newspaper industry in the coming years. But an expansion is likely to affect the economic health of each newspaper or magazine negatively, as the share of the readership for each source is bound to dwindle. Audience for the print media is small in Nigeria, as approximately 55 percent of the population still remains illiterate. This potential for loss of revenue could translate into a loss of media-related jobs.

Until 1992, ownership of the broadcast media was held exclusively by federal and state governments. The promulgation of Decree 38 that year granted authority to private stations to begin broadcasting in the country. This diversification of ownership aims at promoting healthy competition in programming and information dissemination. But because all stations (government and private) must operate under the same set of national objectives, it is doubtful whether a true oligopolistic market structure can really exist for radio and TV in Nigeria. Currently, the private broadcasting stations and satellite delivery services offer a heavy diet of entertainment programs, mainly imported materials from Europe and the United States. If the national policy objectives for the electronic media are strictly enforced, private stations may have to indigenize their programming or face the possibility of losing their license. Although this may not mean a reversion to monopolistic structure, it may mean the absence of variety in programming at the local level.

Technological Developments

Because no clear-cut telecommunications policy is in effect in Nigeria, suppliers of media technology have come to Nigeria from all over the globe. General Electric (United States), Harris (United States), RCA (United States), Philips (The Netherlands), Nippon Electric (Japan), Sony (Japan), and Thomson CFI (France) have at one time or the other supplied broadcast technologies to media installations in the country. This plurality of suppliers has created a problem of compatibility, maintenance and lack of spare parts, as local engineers have been challenged to deal with unfamiliar technology. Thus, a regular equipment turnaround has been a source of needless expenditures for stations. As the country embraces digital technology, the problem of cost overruns is bound to escalate, and purchasing and maintenance costs could exceed what stations can afford. Nigerian investors always desire quick returns on their investments. If capital investments hinder profit making, private investors may lose patience and sell off stations lacking profit potential. This would result in a loss of jobs.

With respect to programming, technological incompatibility limits the direct exchange of programs between stations. In a country like Nigeria, where all stations cannot produce their own programs, exchange of programs is a practical way for all stations to gain access to quality local programs. Nigeria has an elaborate satellite delivery system that can aid program distribution among stations, but it, too, is fraught with an incompatibility problem. Thus, the persistence of the compatibility problem will continue to present major obstacles to the adoption of new technologies and cost-saving program exchange.

Corruption

A Berlin-based independent organization, Transparency International, ranked Nigeria number one on the list of countries that business people consider the most corrupt (Survey rates Nigeria as most corrupt, 1996). Corruption is one of Nigeria's greatest social evils, and media industries must be immunized against its negative effects if they are to blossom. Corrupt practices negatively affect the economic health of media industries in Nigeria in many ways, but perhaps its most devastating consequence is the underreporting of commercial revenue and/or the diversion of revenues meant for program development or purchase to personal use. This diversion curtails the profitability of stations and may lead in some cases to the demise of the media institution.

The Economic Future of Nigerian Media Industries

Because the majority of Nigerian newspapers exist as government-owned corporations, the Nigerian newspaper industry will remain viable through the coming century. Although many of the government outlets are poorly financed, there is little indication that the industry as a whole will decline. External funding agencies that provide developmental support to the country are putting pressure on Nigerian governments to divest of their ownership in a number of sectors, including the media sector. It is not clear whether Nigerian governments will heed this pressure and privatize their newspaper holdings, although they have already done so in the electronic media sector. If privatization does occur, it will create only momentary hardships for the newly divested government newspapers. Like their already existing private counterparts, the divested government newspapers should rebound and become profitable with minimal time and institutional reorganization.

The main threat that faces the newspaper industry in the coming years will be the same one that faces it now: the forcible suspension of operation engendered by industry-unfriendly government decrees. *The Guardian* was closed for nearly 6 months in 1996. *The Concord,* owned by the jailed political leader Moshood Abiola, still remains closed. Several other newspapers, including *The Punch* and *The Daily Sketch,* have been closed at one time or the other by the action of their respective state governments. These closures have reduced the revenues of the affected papers and resulted in some loss of jobs. None of the closures have been permanent so far, and the newspapers concerned have been able to regain their vitality and lost revenue shortly after being reopened. To prevent this wanton government disruption of their operation, newspaper publishers have tempered the tone of their critical editorials and news coverage. It will take similar measures to remove this threat of government closure of newspapers permanently in the coming decades.

Although the availability of newsprint is no longer a concern for Nigerian newspaper publishers owing to the establishment of a newsprint manufacturing company in the early 1980s, the rising cost of newsprint will continue to narrow the profit margins of many newspapers. In the past, newspapers have maintained their margins by charging increases in cost of production to the customer. This option may not remain viable for long, however, if wages continue to remain stagnant in the coming years.

Nigerian radio and TV industries already have a private sector and therefore will face intense competition for audiences and advertisers well into the coming century. Competition is not expected to result in the decline of the audience base of either industry because less than 20 percent of the Nigerian population are currently using the radio and TV media. In 1995, the estimated number of radio and TV sets in the country was 17.2 and 7 million respectively (*CBA Handbook,* 1995). The electronic media industries have enormous potential to expand their audience levels, which have been steadily growing since 1960 at the small annual rate of growth of less than 3 percent. New private and government stations will enter the market in coming decades, and this entry will greatly accelerate the annual audience growth rate. Nevertheless, it will still be well into the next century before Nigeria can achieve a 100 percent radio and TV penetration.

Growth in audience levels will produce a cycle of events that will positively affect both the future economic health of the media industries and the Nigerian society as a whole. The growth in audience levels will create a concomitant expansion of the base of radio and TV advertisers. The increase in advertising will create vast markets that will mobilize disposable incomes. The mobilization of disposable incomes will stimulate the production of goods and services (including the production of radio and TV programs), which will create jobs both in the media industries and in other sectors of the national economy. The availability of jobs should increase the standard of living and broaden the distribution of wealth among the general population. These effects will create a new pool of potential advertisers, which the described cycle can again begin.

To enable this growth and its ensuing cycle of positive events, stations will need to broaden their advertiser pool beyond the multinational corporations that presently constitute the main advertisers. This will take planning and execution. At the moment, small potential advertisers (e.g., retail shop owners) are reticent about advertising because Nigeria is essentially a sellers market, where retailers see little need for advertising. Effective marketing strategies will be needed to encourage local retailers to advertise en masse. If appropriate marketing strategies are not implemented to encourage the participation of retail advertisers, the advertiser pool will remain small and insufficient to sustain a growing number of media outlets. In this setting, stations will experience low profitability, which may result in a decline of the industry.

On the whole, a brighter economic future awaits Nigerian media industries. As the literacy rates increase and the economy improves, the demand for media products should grow. This increasing demand should cause an expansion of the industries and an increase in the quality of the products offered and in the general profitability of individual outlets. Private newspapers and radio and TV stations will attract the largest of revenues through the beginning of the coming century.

Areas for Future Research

Media economics is one of the areas of inquiry that is not yet receiving significant scholarly attention in Nigeria. Because the greatest proportion of media establishments has been owned by the government, the issue of viability has never been taken seriously. Governmental subventions were never tied to performance (i.e., popularity of programs), therefore, media outlets were always provided funds to operate. Even the private newspapers are tied to other successful business enterprises, which sometimes have to support them. For this reason, many of the media economic issues that have been confronted in the United States still remain valid for Nigeria. These issues include consolidation or conglomeration, technology transfer, Nigerianization and cultural hegemony, and regulatory trends.

Consolidation or Conglomeration

The *Daily Times* group is the only true government newspaper chain in the country at the moment, in that it produces and distributes products across the local, national and international markets. The three main private newspapers, *The Concord, The Sketch* and *The Guardian,* are also chains that function as subsidiaries of vast and multifaceted conglomerates. Because of this low level of consolidation, the concentration of media resources is not an issue of serious concern in Nigeria at present. This is bound to change as more private media outlets enter the market and the pressures to increase operational capital, market share and size and to maintain quality of product force concentration to become the only viable means of survival. Such concentration would accentuate the issues of ethnic media hegemony, diversity of views, and national cohesion. For this reason, media researchers should continue to monitor the shifting patterns of ownership in Nigerian media and how these shifts affect changes in content and impact upon the process of national integration and the nature of government-media relations. It will be particularly interesting to discover how much media power and market share the federal and state governments are willing to concede to the private sector.

Technology Transfer

Since their inception, Nigerian media industries have felt compelled to use the state-of-the-art in media technology. This has meant the importation of the latest technology from Britain, Japan and the United States. Some scholars have suggested that it is not necessary for a developing country like Nigeria to attempt to keep pace with the rapid advancements being made in communications methods and technologies overseas (see, e.g., Yearwood [1985]); that such an attempt is a needless drain on the country's meager economic resources. On the other hand, it can be argued that a modern media system can have tremendous benefits for market expansion, improving products and maximizing profits. It is incumbent on media researchers to explore how a balance can be created between the utilization of advanced media technologies to improve media products and maximize profits, and the focus on the developmental needs of the Nigerian society at large. This is important especially because the emergent media technologies have the innate capacity to change existing media market structure and cultural values.

Nigerianization and Cultural Hegemony

Nigerian governments have had two main concerns regarding private media in the country. The first is that market forces would compel the private media industries to become overly preoccupied with profits to the detriment of the focus on national developmental concerns in programming. The second is that a diversified ownership structure might lead to more ethnicism and less nationalism. Over the years, advocates of the private system have argued that the government's fears lacked foundation and that private media can and would do more for national development than the government media have (Nwosu, 1987). Previously, these fears and counterarguments have been mere theoretical propositions; however, with the private media having existed for more than 2 years, there now are sufficient data to test the truism of either thesis. Scholars would need to investigate the degree to which the private media organs are catering to national development concerns. This line of inquiry is vital, as development is a national concern and the degree to which the private media organs can maintain their independence from the state would depend on evidence of and demonstration of their true commitment to national development concerns in programming.

Regulatory Trends

Over the years, Nigeria has had an unstable media regulatory environment. Since 1960, there have been 10 successive changes in the national government, and each change has brought new rules and regulations for the mass media. The latest regulation is the Nigerian electronic media privatization (Decree No. 38), which was promulgated primarily not only to curtail the broadcast of foreign programs on radio and TV but also to forestall the proliferation of foreign direct broadcast satellite (DBS) signals in the country (Onwumechili, 1996). This decree has stabilized the often chaotic electronic communication environment in Nigeria, but like its predecessors, it has lacked adequate enforcement and this has rendered it an inefficient policy guide for the media industry. For this reason, market forces have continued to bring unforeseen changes to media operation (Onwumechili, 1996). How these changes affect industry performance and future regulatory trends should be carefully examined in both cross-sectional and longitudinal studies.

There are serious policy dilemmas in regulating media industries in a pluralistic environment like Nigeria. These dilemmas emanate from the clash between the economically driven motives of stations to cater to the popular demands of a diverse audience and the general role of the media institutions as executors of government policy (Lowe, 1987). One main aim of government policy is to integrate Nigeria's multicultural/multilingual society by using the mass media as a principal instrument for imbuing the population with positive nation-building values. To achieve this socialization objective, however, media industries must first amass an audience by programming to the least common denominator (the popular audience), which they have been unable to achieve with socialization programs that are mostly thematic and audience specific. Researchers must explore how these dual goals can be balanced in the interest of the media industries. Specifically, researchers must determine what regulatory policies will be the most functional for industry growth in the coming century, as the newer communication technologies such as cable TV and satellite-delivered multichannel digital services complicated the issue of government regulation even further.

Summary

Nigerian media industries march onward toward the 21st century with hope and pride but with an eye on their past. Recent regulatory changes have moved ownership patterns away from centralized controls to more decentralized operations. The private media institutions still enjoy only as much freedom as the compliance with the requirements of the developmental theory of media has allowed. The federal government remains the exclusive operator of network stations. The private media installations are not allowed to provide signals that extend beyond the locality in which they operate.

On the whole, three media industries operate simultaneously in Nigeria. The oldest of these is the newspaper industry, which is also the freest in Africa. Nigerian newspapers circulate not only within the country but also in neighboring African countries and other far away places such as the United States and Britain. Newspapers are important elements in the daily lives of the educated Nigerian. Newspapers provide news, opinions and features and also serve as a vital liaison between the government and the people (in the sense that they interpret government policy to the people and inform government about the desires of the population) and as a commercial link between advertisers and consumers. Nigerian newspapers operate mainly from a few principal localities, but their circulation extends throughout the country.

After its restructuring in 1978, the Nigerian radio industry acquired a four-tier operational structure: a federal service, zonal services, state services and private stations. With this structure, the radio industry became the most ubiquitous in Nigeria, reaching 100 percent of the country's population with its signals. By and large, radio is the medium of the masses in Nigeria. It commands the highest percentage of the general audience for media. The FRCN is the largest and most important radio establishment in the country. The sources of revenue for the radio industry are direct government subvention, licensing fees and advertising.

The Nigerian TV industry is becoming increasingly popular among Nigerians. With the inception of private stations in 1993, diversity in programming has become part and parcel of institutional practices. But despite the advent of private stations, the industry is still dominated by the federally owned and operated network, NTA. NTA network stations coexist with state stations in many of the state capitals in the country. Fourteen private TV stations were licensed in July 1993 and are currently serving important localities. Thus, the Nigerian TV industry operates in national and local markets for consumers and advertisers. Like its radio counterpart, the sources of revenue for the TV industry are also direct government subvention, licensing fees and advertising.

References

Adams, P. (1994). Nigeria: The army calls the truce. *Africa Report* 39:47–49.

Africa South of the Sahara (1995). In: *Europa Yearbook.* 24th ed. London: Europa Publications Limited.

After the ball: A survey of Nigeria (1986). *The Economist,* May 3, p. 41.

Akinfeleye, R. (1983). Religious publications: Pioneers of Nigerian journalism. In: Nwuneli, O. E. (ed.). *Mass Communication in Nigeria: A Book of Reading.* Enugu: Fourth Dimension Publishers

Albarran, A. B. (1996). *Media Economics: Understanding Markets, Industries and Concepts.* Ames, IA: Iowa State University Press.

Amienyi, O. P. (in press). Sub-Saharan Africa: Nigeria by Gerard Igyor. In: Wells, A. (ed.). *World Broadcasting Systems: A Comparative View.* Norwood, NJ: Ablex.

Bourgault, L. M. (1995a). *Mass Media in Sub-Saharan Africa.* Bloomington, IN: Indiana University Press.

Bourgault, L. M. (1995b). Nigeria. In: Gross, L. S. (ed.). *The International World of Electronic Media.* New York: McGraw-Hill, pp. 233–252.

Commonwealth Broadcasting Association Handbook (1995). Nigeria. London: Secretariat of the Commonwealth Broadcasting Association.

Egbon, M. I. (1982). Television broadcasting in Africa. *Television Journal* [a publication of NTA, Lagos, Nigeria].

Embassy of Nigeria. (1996). The media in Nigeria. World Wide Web (http://www.intr.net/ra...eria/nigenew.htm#media), pp. 1–5.

Emmett, P. (1996). The Federal Republic of Nigeria: Communications. World Wide Web (http://www.comsec.co.u...ria.htm#communications), p. 2.

Eribo, F. (1995). Factors affecting press freedom in Nigeria. Paper presented to the Third World Studies Conference, Omaha, Nebraska, October 10–12.

Federal Radio Corporation of Nigeria (1993). *Bulletin No 3.* Lagos, Nigeria: Federal Radio Corporation of Nigeria.

Hatchen, W. (1993). *The Growth of Mass Media in the Third World: African Failures, Asian Successes.* Ames, IA: Iowa State University Press.

Katz, E., and Wedell, G. (1977). *Broadcasting in the Third World.* Cambridge, MA: Harvard University Press.

Lamb, D. (1985). *The Africans.* New York: Vintage Books.

Lowe, V. (1987). *Some policy dilemmas in coping with Malaysia's multi-ethnic audience: Their effects on the roles and status of broadcasters.* The Third Channel, 5, pp. 644–659.

Metz, H. C. (1992). *Nigeria: A Country Study.* 5th edition. Library of Congress. Federal Research Division. Washington, DC: U.S. State Department.

Momoh, T. (1987). Nigeria: The press and nation-building. *Africa Report,* 32, March/April, pp. 54–57.

Mytton, G. (1983). *Mass Communication in Africa.* London: Edward Arnold.

Ngarara, M. R. (1996). Dossier: The voice of the disabled in Chad. *The Courier,* 158, July/August, p. 51.

Nigerian Television Authority (1993). *Annual Reports & Accounts, 1993.* Lagos, Nigeria: Academy Press Plc.

Nwosu, I. E. (1987). Privatizing broadcasting for rural mobilization and national development: A qualitative and quantitative analysis of the Nigerian situation. *The Third Channel: IBA Journal of International Broadcasting,* pp. 632–643.

Omu, F. A. (1968). The dilemma of press freedom in colonial Africa. *Journal of African History* 9:2.

Onwumechili, C. (1996). Privatization of the electronic media in Nigeria. *The Howard Journal of Communications* 7(4):365–372.

Secretariat of the Commonwealth Broadcasting Association. (1991/92). Federal Radio Corporation of Nigeria/Nigerian Television Association. *Commonwealth Broadcasting Association Handbook,* pp. 115–120

Survey rates Nigeria as most corrupt nation for business (1996). *The New York Times,* June 3, p. 3.

Wigston, D. (1994). The challenge of international radio broadcasting: What's in it for Africa? Paper Read at the Intercultural/International Communications Conference, Miami, FL. Unpublished Manuscript.

Yearwood, G. (1985). Cultural values and the development of mass media. *Nigerian Television Journal*, 9, July/September, pp. 7–8.

14

SOUTH AFRICA

Pieter Fourie and Rudolph de Jager

Introduction

To write or talk about the South African media at this stage of the country's history is similar to what Siefert (1991, p. 8) said of the Russian media in the time of glasnost and perestroika:

> [I]t is like trying to rebuild a ship while in full sail. Journalists on board write a daily log, and we all take note of the troubled waters and high winds. But the future seems no more predictable than the weather and no easier to assess from shore than from the deck.

Many of the changes and developments now taking place in the South African media can be related to the political changes that have swept the country since 1990 and to the dramatic impact of these political changes on the South African society and economy. Like every aspect of South African society, the media are pressurized to transform. The emphasis is on black empowerment and an expectation to play a constructive development role in the post-apartheid society. To some in the previously white-dominated and -owned media, these changes and issues are experienced as a threat. To others, including black business, it means new opportunities.

Against this background, the following overview of the South African media, one of the most advanced and free media industries and economies in Africa, must be seen as preliminary.

South African Media in an African Context

South Africa has a total population of about 40.5 million people, of whom 31 million are black; 5.1 million, white; and 4.4 million Asian and other races. The country is divided into nine provinces. The major languages include isiXhosa (the home language of the Xhosa group), isiZulu (the home language of the Zulu group), Afrikaans (the home language of the Afrikaans [originally Dutch] population) and English. Although 11 languages are official in terms of the constitution, English is rapidly becoming the general language of communication, giving rise to tension between groups. South Africa occupies the southernmost part of the African continent.

Tables 14-1, 14-2, and 14-3 give an overview of telecommunication and media use in southern Africa and clearly point to the leading role of South Africa in this field.

Major Media Industries in South Africa

Broadcasting

Broadcasting in South Africa, which is now regulated by the Independent Broadcasting Authority, started with radio broadcasts by the South African Railways in 1923. In 1927 the Johannesburg millionaire, I.W. Schlesinger, received permission from the South African government to establish the

Table 14-1. Daily Newspapers in the Southern African Development Community, 1992

	Number	Circulation (000)	Per 1,000 Inhabitants
Angola	4	116	12
Botswana	1	40	30
Lesotho	2	14	8
Malawi	1	25	2
Mauritius	6	80	73
Mozambique	2	81	5
Namibia	4	209	136
South Africa (1996)	20	1248	31
Swaziland	3	12	15
Tanzania	3	220	8
Zambia	2	70	8
Zimbabwe	2	195	18

Source: United Nations 1995.

Table 14-2. Television and Radio Receivers in the SADC, 1992

	Television		Radio	
	Number (000)	Per 1,000 Inhabitants	Number (000)	Per 1,000 Inhabitants
Angola	62	6	282	29
Botswana	22	17	160	122
Lesotho	11	6	60	33
Malawi	—	—	2,285	221
Mauritius	239	218	395	360
Mozambique	44	3	700	47
Namibia	32	21	195	127
South Africa	3,900	98	12,100	304
Swaziland	16	20	129	163
Tanzania	45	2	640	25
Zambia	225	26	705	82
Zimbabwe	280	27	890	84

Source: United Nations 1995.

Table 14-3. Number of Telephones in the SADC, 1992

	Number (000)	Per 1,000 Inhabitants
Angola	53	0.5
Botswana	43	3.1
Lesotho	10	0.6
Malawi	33	0.4
Mauritius	107	9.6
Mozambique	62	0.4
Namibia	70	4.5
South Africa	3,660	9.0
Swaziland	16	1.8
Tanzania	85	0.3
Zambia	78	0.9
Zimbabwe	128	1.2

Source: United Nations 1995.

African Broadcasting Company. This company existed until 1936, when it was taken over by the South African Broadcasting Corporation (SABC), established by virtue of the Broadcasting Act of 1936.

The establishment of the SABC was preceded by numerous investigations and commissions. Eventually the foundation of public broadcasting in South Africa came about as a result of the recommendations by the then director-general of the British Broadcasting Corporation, the late Sir John Reith.

The introduction of television (TV) in South Africa came much later in 1976. The late introduction was mainly due to political reasons. Under the apartheid regime, it was believed by some that TV could be compared to "poison gas" and that TV images would infiltrate and corrupt the South African society. Despite the late introduction, South Africa today has one of the leading TV industries in Africa.

Radio

The SABC held a monopoly over radio until 1996, when 77 community radio stations were licensed and six of the SABC's profitable regional radio stations were sold to private owners. By far the most popular and most accessible medium in South Africa, radio reaches a daily audience of 19 million people. One of the biggest challenges for both radio and TV is to cater to the 11 official language and cultural groups in South Africa. Most of the SABC's radio stations are language and culture based.

The present SABC radio stations and their broadcast languages are Ukhozi (isiZulu), Umhlobo Wenene (Xhosa), Radio Metro (English), Lesedi (Sesotho), Thobela FM (Sepedi), Motsweding FM (Setswana), 5 FM (English), Radio Sonder Grense (Afrikaans), Munghana Lonene (Xitsonga), Good Hope FM (Afrikaans/English), Ligwalagwala (Siswati), East Coast Radio (English, to be sold by the SABC), Ikwekwezi (Sindebele), SAfm (English), Radio Lotus Stereo (English), Phalaphala (Tshivenda), and Radio 2000 (multilingual).

The private radio stations and their owners are Jakaranda 94-97 FM (Newshelf), Radio Kfm (Cresecent), Highveld Stereo (Africa on Air), Radio Oranje (New Radio), Radio 702 (Primedia), and Radio Algoa (Umoya).

The external radio station of the SABC, Channel Africa, has been repositioned and restructured to enhance trade, industry, labor, cultural and sporting ties as well as scientific and technological exchanges and cooperation with the African continent (South African Broadcasting Corporation, 1995). The channel broadcasts to African countries and islands in the Indian Ocean in nine languages. The service has a potential audience of 600 million listeners.

Television

Currently, four TV companies operate in South Africa, namely, the SABC, M-Net, BBC (Bophuthatswana Broadcasting Corporation) and Uplink Broadcasting (a satellite service operator).

THE SOUTH AFRICAN BROADCASTING CORPORATION. The SABC's TV service was relaunched by a newly constituted board on February 4, 1996. The purpose with the relaunch was to break with the apartheid-stigmatized image of the SABC.

Table 14-4. SABC Funding

	1994/1995 $m	1993/1994 $m
Advertising and Sponsorships	253.9	218.3
License fees	66.5	59.9
Other	22.9	18.2
Total	343.3	296.4

The currency used in South Africa is the Rand (R). In January 1997 the exchange rate was $1 = R4,7.

The SABC's TV service consists of three TV channels, SABC1, SABC2 and SABC3. The three channels are supposed to broadcast equally in all 11 official languages; however, the emphasis is mainly on imported English programming—a topic of much discontent and seen by many as a threat to political and cultural stability in the newfound South African democracy.

In 1996 the SABC TV channels reached a daily audience of just over 14 million viewers. Since October 1995 the SABC has also broadcast their three channels through the PAS-4 satellite. In addition to its own news services, the SABC also carries the services of the BBC World Service and CNN International.

A breakdown of the funding mix of SABC TV for the 1993/94 and 1994/95 years are shown in Table 14-4.

M-NET (ELECTRONIC MEDIA NETWORK) AND MIH (M-NET INTERNATIONAL). M-Net, which began broadcasting on October 1, 1986, and which mainly focuses on entertainment, was the first pay TV network (subscription TV network) in the southern hemisphere and only the second in the world to provide direct-to-home-satellite TV. To receive M-Net, subscribers must purchase a decoder.

M-Net had turnover (revenues) of $138.3 million during the 1996 financial year in comparison with $111.3 million in 1995 (M-Net, 1996). M-Net is owned by a conglomerate of newspaper groups and private shareholders and is listed on the Johannesburg Stock Exchange. The major shareholders in M-Net are Omni Media (24.18 percent), Perskor (8.17 percent), Nasionale Pers (19.14 percent), Natal Witness (1.26 percent), Phuthuma shareholders (9.98 percent), MultiChoice Africa (20 percent), and public shareholders (17.27 percent).

In November 1991, M-Net and Richmont bought a stake in the European pay TV company FilmNet, a company for encoded entertainment in The Netherlands, Flanders, Denmark, Norway, Sweden, and Finland. In March 1994, FilmNet reached 680,000 subscriber households.

The year 1992 marked the launch of M-Net's International Service, which was geared to the African market. On March 31, 1996, there were more than 1 million African and adjacent islands households in 36 countries that subscribed to M-Net.

MultiChoice Africa (a subsidiary of MIH) provides subscriber management services for M-Net, BBC World Service, Canal Horizons, Bop TV and the Community Service Network of M-Net. M-Net's Community Service Network (CSN) caters to specific communities broadcasting Shalom TV, Christian Network TV, TV Portuguêsa and East-Net (in Hindu and Tamil). All M-Net's signals are transmitted by Broadcast Services from M-Net in Randburg, Johannesburg.

MIH (FORMERLY KNOWN AS MULTICHOICE). On October 1, 1993, M-Net split into M-Net and MIH (previously known as MultiChoice) and from May 1995 forward, M-Net and MIH were listed separately on the Johannesburg Stock Exchange.

In December 1994, MIH and Richmont acquired a joint control over and equal shares in the TV industry Payco and bought a stake in the Italian pay TV company Telepiu. MIH and Richmont formed NetHold and became the third-largest pay TV company in Europe after Canal Plus and British Sky Broadcasting (BSkyB).

At the end of 1996, NetHold merged with Canal Plus. Canal Plus bought 100 percent of NetHold (after NetHold's interests in Greece, Cyprus, Africa and the Middle East as well as NetHold's shares in M-Net [20 percent], and Orbicom [20 percent] were transferred to MIH) in exchange for 6.1 million new Canal Plus shares (20 percent) and a payment of $45 million to MIH. As a result, Richmont owns 15 percent of Canal Plus, and MIH, 5 percent.

MIH holdings include the following:

- A 5 percent ownership in the French pay-TV Canal Plus
- A 100 percent interest in MultiChoice Africa
- A 51 percent interest in MultiChoice Greece and MultiChoice Cyprus
- A 20 percent interest in M-Net
- A 60 percent investment in Orbicom Limited—a South African signal distribution company
- A 15 percent passive investment in Information Trust Corporation Limited—a credit information company

MIH had a turnover of $265.7 million in 1995/96. MIH's major shareholders are Omni Media (35.11 percent), Perskor (11.86 percent), Nasionale Pers (25.90 percent), Natal Witness (1.58 percent) and public shareholders (22.55 percent).

MULTICHOICE'S SATELLITE TELEVISION SERVICE. The PanAmSat-4 satellite commenced service on September 5, 1995, and provides coverage to Europe, Africa, the Middle East, the Indian subcontinent and Asia. MultiChoice launched digital satellite TV (DStv) including the five thematic services of M-Net, namely M-Net, Movie Magic, SuperSport, SuperSport 2 and K-TV. MultiChoice's DStv offers 25 TV channels and 46 audio channels, including six international radio channels at a subscription fee of $37.2 per month. The number of channels increased during the first year of operation, and more channels will be offered in the future. By September 1996, MultiChoice had 52,000 subscribers.

BOPHUTHATSWANA BROADCASTING CORPORATION. The former homeland of Bophuthatswana launched Bop-TV on 31 December 1983. Although the broadcaster chiefly broadcast in the former Bophuthatswana, it was the first TV service in competition with the SABC. Over the years Bop-TV has tried to expand its service to a larger part of South Africa, but owing to opposition from the SABC, it has had little success. In 1988 Bop-TV hired transmitters and began broadcasting by satellite.

Although the Independent Broadcasting Authority's (IBA) Triple Inquiry Report (Independent Broadcasting Authority, 1995) recommended that the former TBVC state broadcasters merge with the SABC, be sold or allow the radio frequencies to be considered for community licenses, the BBC is still in operation.

UPLINK BROADCASTING. Uplink Broadcasting Limited (UBL) is the third satellite broadcaster licensed in South Africa and began broadcasting seven digital channels in 1997. Technological assistance is derived from Telkom, Scientific Atlanta and High Tech Solutions and programming support from BSkyB. Most of the SADC countries have access to UBL.

Press

The print media in South Africa began at the beginning of the 19th century with the publication of the government newspaper, the *Cape Town and African Advertiser.* Today the South African press consists of more than 5,000 registered newspapers, magazines, journals and trade publications.

The four major press groups in South Africa are Independent Newspapers (previously Argus Newspapers), Nasionale Pers, Perskor and Times Media. Together, these groups are responsible for the publication of 17 daily newspapers and 11 weeklies, with a total circulation figure of close to two million. With the exception of a few independents, these groups are also the owners of the majority of South Africa's 300 consumer magazines. In addition to consumer magazines, South Africa publishes more than 500 trade, technical and professional publications.

Although ownership of the press is mainly in the hands of these four press groups, ownership was even more concentrated before. (See the discussion of black empowerment later in this chapter.) Previously, both Argus Newspapers and Times Media were owned by Anglo American Corporation through a subsidiary. In 1994, Tony O'Reilly, owner of Independent Newspapers (INP) of Ireland, bought a 31 percent share in Argus Newspapers (now also known as Independent Newspapers). Today, INP has a 58.25 percent share in (South Africa's) Independent Newspapers. (INP owns 65 percent of the newspaper industry in Ireland; it is the fourth largest newspaper group in Australia and owns a 24.99 percent interest in the British newspaper *The Independent.* O'Reilly is also a director of the *Washington Post.*) In 1996 the National Empowerment Consortium (NEC) bought a controlling share in Johnnic, the owner of Times Media. Both these transactions saw Anglo American selling its controlling share in these two press groups.

Cinema

With more than 806,000 people attending a film on a weekly basis, cinema attendance remains a popular form of entertainment in South Africa. As far as film distribution and screening are concerned, South Africa is one of the leading countries in Africa.

Distribution of films in South Africa is dominated by UIP Warner, Ster-Kinekor (representing Columbia Tristar, Twentieth Century Fox, Disney, the independent producers Castle Rock, Rysher, UGC as well as Polygram, Miramax, Rank and Majestic) and Nu Metro (major licenses include Disney, Warner, Fox Home, as well as independent licenses such as New Line and Morgan Creek).

Screening of films in South Africa is dominated by Ster-Kinekor and Nu Metro, which have 307 (283 without Ster-Moribo) and 152 screens, respectively, in the major cities and suburbs and rural towns. According to Botha (1996), there were about 202 independent cinemas in South Africa during the 1990s, some of which were then in the process of closing down.

Ster-Kinekor International, a new venture, is Ster-Kinekor's offshore business that aims to develop about 300 screens in the next 10 years with joint venture partners in each territory, mainly in Greece, Cyprus, Poland, the Czech Republic, Hungary and the United Kingdom.

Despite its history as one of the oldest film industries in the world, the South African feature film production industry is virtually dead. Existing production houses are mainly involved with the production of documentaries, educational programs, TV programs, TV drama series and advertisements. The decline of the production of feature films can be blamed on many factors, including an insufficient government subsidy system, the U.S. dominance of the entertainment market, and the lack of a policy fostering the production of films as cultural products.

Table 14-5. Advertising Expenditures

	1995 $m	1994 $m
Print		
Newspapers	275.5	233.0
Consumer magazines	114.7	92.6
Trade and technical journals	34.9	31.9
Total print	425.1	357.5
Television	384.7	336.6
Radio	122.1	111.5
Outdoor	30.9	27.2
Cinema	7.2	7.0
Total all media	970.0	839.8
% Change from 1994 and 1993	+15.5%	+20%

Advertising

South Africa has more than 400 advertising agencies, of which 40 are so-called big agencies with international affiliations. Advertising expenditures have shown steady growth in South Africa during the past few years. The growth in advertising expenditure is partially the result of the launch and relaunch of international brands by, among others, Procter & Gamble, Pepsi, Peugeot, IBM, Daewoo, Samsung, Alfa Romeo, Saab and Virgin Airlines. Other factors are the growing number of magazine titles and launches of community radio stations in South Africa, which makes advertising more accessible with more choices to advertisers.

Table 14-5 shows the breakdown of advertising expenditures in 1994 and 1995 in South Africa (All Media and Product Survey, 1996).

South Africa's five leading advertising groups ranked by income are Ogilvy & Mather Rightford, Lindsay Smithers-FCB, Hunt Lascaris TBWA, Young & Rubicam, and Sonnenberg Murphey Leo Burnett.

Telecommunications

Telkom SA Limited, a state-owned company, is the biggest and most modern telecommunications network on the African continent, operating 39 percent of all the lines installed in Africa. Telkom supplied more than 3,919,084 telephone lines to business and households, 70,154 pay phones, and direct dialing to 216 countries and had a revenue of $2.83 billion in 1996. Through an ambitious network expansion and modernization program called Vision 2000, Telkom intends to operate a fully digital network by the year 2000, which will include adding three million new lines to the network, of which two million are earmarked for underserviced areas and one million lines, to replace obsolete equipment (Telkom, 1995 and 1996).

Telkom's monopoly over telecommunication in South Africa ended in March 1997, when the government sold a 30 percent interest in the company to a consortium of Telekom Malaysia and Southwestern Bell (South African Telkom sale, 1997).

The major cellular phone companies are Mobile Telephone Networks (MTN), which was formed under the auspices of M-Net (the pay TV service), and Vodacom, which was formed by Telkom. Vodacom had more than 400,000 subscribers by April 1996, and MTN, more than 250,000 subscribers.

Regulation of the South African Media Industry

The freedom of the South African media is protected in Section 16 of Chapter 3 of the Constitution of the Republic of South Africa as adopted by the Constitutional Assembly on May 8, 1996. It reads as follows:

> Freedom of expression
>
> (1) Everyone has the right to freedom of expression, which includes:
> (a) freedom of the press and other media;
> (b) freedom to receive and impart information and ideas;
> (c) freedom of artistic creativity; and
> (d) academic freedom and freedom of scientific research.
>
> (2) The right in subsection (1) does not extend to:
> (a) propaganda for war;
> (b) incitement of imminent violence; or
> (c) advocacy of hatred that is based on race, ethnicity, gender or religion, and that constitutes incitement to cause harm.

Other regulatory councils and agencies are described in the following section.

THE PRESS COUNCIL OF SOUTH AFRICA. The objective of The Press Council of South Africa is to "consider and adjudicate upon all alleged infringements of the code by members of the press that have voluntarily become subject to the jurisdiction of the council" (The Press Council of South Africa, 1993, p. 2).

THE ADVERTISING STANDARDS AUTHORITY. The Advertising Standards Authority (ASA) came into being in 1969 and essentially ensures that advertising is honest, legal, truthful and decent (cf. Sinclair and Barenblatt, 1993). Comparative advertising is not permitted in South Africa, although there is a growing support to legalize some form of controlled comparative advertising. The nature of politics makes it imperative for political advertising to refer to other political parties by name, and therefore political advertising is not subjected to the same restriction as commercial advertising.

THE INDEPENDENT BROADCASTING AUTHORITY. The strict legislation that hampered the media during the 1980s was seriously detrimental to the legitimacy of certain media, especially the SABC. This compelled the government to appoint a task group in 1990 to report on the future of broadcasting in South and Southern Africa. One of the task group's proposals was that an independent broadcasting authority should be established to manage and control the whole spectrum of broadcasting and monitor the technical quality of broadcasts (cf. Viljoen, 1991). The Independent Broadcasting Authority Act, 1993 (Act 153 of 1993), came into force on January 12, 1994, and the IBA was established on March 30.

The following are permanent standing committees of the IBA:

- *Broadcasting Technical Committee,* which is mainly responsible for the administration, management and planning of the broadcasting services frequency spectrum and the examination of all technical matters relevant to license applications.
- *Broadcasting Monitoring and Complaints Committee,* which is mainly responsible for monitoring compliance with license condition by license holders, monitoring compliance by license holders, specifically regarding election broadcasts and political advertisements (regarding those broadcasts licensees who are not members of the ASA or any other recognized regulatory body), and investigating complaints from the public regarding contravention of license requirements.

BROADCASTING COMPLAINTS COMMISSION OF SOUTH AFRICA. The Broadcasting Complaints Commission of South Africa (BCCSA) acts as an independent broadcasting complaints mechanism and was set up by the National Association of Broadcasters in August 1993. The BCCSA is now a formally recognized mechanism in terms of section 56(2) of the IBA Act.

THE FILM AND PUBLICATIONS ACT. The Film and Publication Act legalizes pornography but bans child pornography, bestiality, extreme violence, sex and violence, hate speech, blasphemy and the sexual degradation of women. The Act established a Film and Publication Board and a Review Board. It further provides for Classifications Committees, whose task is to examine and classify films and publications according to provisions of the Act's schedules.

Analysis

With the exception of public broadcasting (SABC), which is presently experiencing major financial problems, there is real and potential economic growth in the South African media industry. As in all other sectors of South African society, politics and economy, the emphasis is on affirmative action and black empowerment. This is evident from the changes taking place in media ownership.

Black Empowerment

In October 1996, the NEC, with New Africa Investments (Nail), Worldwide African Investments, Sipumele Investments, Nozala Investments and Vuyo Investments, bought a 35 percent controlling share (of which the business groups and the trade unions own 17.5 percent, respectively) in Johnnic (Schutte, 1996).

Johnnic is the holding company of, among others, Omni Media, which owns Times Media (91.3 percent) and which is a major shareholder in M-Net and MIH. Johnnic is also the holding company of CNA Gallo, which owns the controlling share in Nu Metro. These black business groups are members of the NEC, which is a coalition of about 40 black businesses and trade unions.

This transaction between Johnnic and the NEC is the biggest black empowerment deal struck in South Africa to date. The U.K. publisher Pearsons has shown interest in buying 50 percent of the leading financial newspaper and magazine in the Times Media stable, namely *Business Day* and *Financial Mail.*

The newspaper group Perskor (of which Nasionale Pers has a 24 percent and Rembrandt [Remgro], a 27 percent interest) and the black-controlled Kagiso publishers (an affiliate [50 percent] of Kagiso Trust Investments) merged at the end of 1996 to form a new consortium in Persbel. By so doing, Kagiso gained partnership in all the newspapers (of which the daily *The Citizen* is the biggest), magazines, printers and publishers of Perskor. Perskor gained the publishing interest of Kagiso, which publishes more than 250 titles each year.

Through the Phuthuma (Zulu for "hurry up, get going") Share Scheme, 10 percent of M-Net's shareholding was made available to members of disadvantaged communities. The major shareholders, namely Nasionale Pers, Omni Media, Times Media, Perskor and the Natal Witness reduced their stakes in M-Net, and these communities bought 28 million shares worth $14.9 million. The share offer was oversubscribed by 35 percent and resulted in 7,880 black South Africans (most of them investing in shares for the first time) becoming M-Net shareholders (M-Net, 1996).

Broadcasting, Empowerment and State Funding

With respect to broadcasting and black empowerment, the IBA ruled that the SABC had to sell six of its regional radio stations to open the market for private ownership. The selling of these stations concentrated on black empowerment. In line with the ideal of black empowerment, the SABC's board, management, staff and programming were also completely transformed. This applies to both TV and radio.

This sudden transformation, together with the opening of the airwaves to private radio and TV stations, however, signaled the beginning of the public broadcasters' financial decline and dependence on state funding. The SABC had a deficit of almost $4.5 million in 1996. Some of the reasons for this deficit follow:

- Its three TV channels and 16 radio stations were relaunched
- All the African language radio stations were upgraded
- More local programs were produced
- Three more languages were introduced on TV so that all 11 official languages of South Africa could be broadcast
- Regional TV broadcasts began on February 5, 1996
- More religions were catered to
- The viewer piracy rate escalated owing chiefly to a culture of nonpayment and the downscaling of Afrikaans
- Six profitable regional radio stations, which earned an income of R90 million (U.S.$18 million) per year for the SABC were sold to private companies. It seems likely that the profit from the selling of these radio stations will go to the central government and not to the SABC

During the first 6 months of 1996 the SABC's advertising income dropped by 2.2 percent and M-Net's grew by 23 percent. One of the reasons for the drop in advertising may be the SABC's scaling down of Afrikaans. This can be deduced from the increase in advertising in Afrikaans weekend papers by 33.4 percent, although the black, colored and Asian magazine advertising also showed healthy growth of nearly 40 percent (Klein, 1996).

Therefore, in the future, the most preferred funding option implies that the revenue mix of the SABC could change as follows: advertising, 50 percent; license fees, 25 percent; other, 10 percent; state funding, 15 percent.

The amount that the SABC wants from the government each year may rise to $92 million in 1998/1999. Payment of license fees is still a major problem for the SABC. Fifty-nine percent of its viewers did not pay their license fees in 1996 (in comparison with 29 percent in 1991), which means a loss of income of $127.7 million. Only $60 million may be secured from license fees in 1996, in comparison with $66.4 million in 1995.

Cross-Ownership

A much debated point concerns the new limits that have been imposed on cross-media ownership to prevent formation of monopolies, while encouraging a diversity of ownership. Some of the limitations are as follows:

- No person shall directly or indirectly exercise control of more than one private TV broadcasting license
- No person can own more than two FM and two medium wave radio stations
- No person who controls a newspaper may acquire or retain financial control in both a radio and a TV station
- No person who is in a position to control a newspaper may be in a position to control a radio or TV license in an area where the newspaper has an average issue readership of more than 15 percent of the total newspaper readership in that area, if the license area of the radio licensee overlaps substantially with the said circulation area of the newspaper. Substantial overlap shall be interpreted to mean an overlap by 50 percent or more. The effect of this regulation is that the newspaper will still be able to acquire or retain a financial interest in a radio or TV license but may not be in a position of control over such license, if its readership exceeds the prescribed figure

Apart from economic considerations and the accepted need to move from a mainly white-owned and -dominated media industry to a more equal, and in terms of population figures, black-dominated, media industry, the fear exists of unaccepted government interference. This fear is strengthened by periodic government criticism that the media should adapt to the needs of a developing country and, as such, play a more active role in promoting certain values and development goals, whether these might be political, social or economic.

The majority of practicing editors and journalists are skeptical of this role. To them injunctions to consciously promote anything without being allowed to be critical are tantamount to censorship. The media's responsibility is to reflect society—even to test the limits of tolerance in a changing society—not to tailor news reports to promote something. Newspapers report the news and comment thereon. Any suggestion that they could in addition, individually or collectively, deliberately embark on other projects is to make them handmaidens to a cause.

Against the background of much of Africa's depressing media history, many fear that this might happen in South Africa and that the media might have to face the same kind of political power struggles to own, control and manipulate the media as has happened in other parts of Africa. (For an overview of the media power struggles in Africa, see Ronning, 1993.)

Finally, although the freedom of the media is guaranteed in South Africa's new Constitution, the interpretation of the law must still be tested in the Constitutional Court. This is especially pertinent to section 16 of the law (see earlier discussion in this chapter), as these rights are also subjected to a number of other rights.

References

Amos, G. (ed.) (1996). Ster Kinekor. *Business Day Corporate Survey* (Supp), September.

All Media and Product Survey (1996). *Condensed Pocket Edition.* Sandton: South African Advertising Research Foundation.

Botha, M. P. (in press). South Africa. In: Cowie, P. (ed.). *International Film Guide 1997.* London: Hamlyn.

Botha, M. P. (1996). *An Introduction to South African Cinema.* Unpublished report.

Broadcasting Complaints Commission of South Africa (1996). *Annual Review.* Johannesburg: BCCSA.

CNA Gallo (1995). *Annual Report.* Johannesburg: CNA Gallo.

CNA Gallo (1996). *Annual Report.* Johannesburg: CNA Gallo

Constitutional Assembly. Republic of South Africa. Constitution of the Republic of South Africa 1996. As adopted by the Constitutional Assembly on May 8, 1996.

Cornelissen, A. (1996). AstraSat. Sport, flieks op die twee gratis SABC-kanale. *Beeld* July 5, p. 4.

Independent Broadcasting Authority (1995). *Triple Inquiry Report.* Johannesburg: IBA.

Independent Broadcasting Authority (1995). *Community Radio Stations.* Sponsored by Marketing Mix and the Independent Broadcasting Authority. Johannesburg: IBA.

Interleisure (1995). *Annual Report.* Johannesburg: Interleisure.

Interleisure (1996). *Annual Report.* Johannesburg: Interleisure.

Janse van Rensburg, H. (ed.) (1995). *South African Yearbook 1995.* Cape Town: CTP Book Printers.

Klein, M. (1996). Print eats away at TV's slice of the adspend cake. *Sunday Times, Business Times,* August 25, p. 4.

Mersham, G. M. (1993). Television. A fascinating window on an unfolding world. In: De Beer, A. S. (ed.). *Mass Media for the Nineties. The South African Handbook of Mass Communication.* Pretoria: Van Schaik.

MIH (M-Net International) (1996). *Annual Report.* Randburg: MIH.

M-Net (Electronic Media Network) (1996). *Annual Report.* Randburg: M-Net.

Omni Media (1996). *Annual Report.* Johannesburg: Omni.

Perskor (1996). *Annual Report.* Johannesburg: Perskor.

The Press Council of South Africa (1993). *Constitution, Rules of Procedure and Code of Conduct.* Johannesburg: Press Council of South Africa.

Pretorius, W. (1996). Apartheid, Censorship and the South African film. Paper delivered at the Het Zuid-Afrikaans film festival, Vrije Universitiet Brussel. October 17–24, 1996.

Ronning, H. 1993. The media and democracy in an African context. *Southern Africa Political and Economic Monthly* 6(3 & 4):3–10.

SABC whoose! into satellite (1996). *Combroad* [the magazine of the Commonwealth Broadcasting Association] 112, September/November, 5.

SARAD. (1996). *South African Rates and Data.* The guide to media selection. August, 24(4).

SA to Z. 1996. *The Decision Makers' Encyclopaedia of the South African Consumer Market.* Sandton: SA to Z Decision Maker's Encyclopaedia.

Schutte, H. (1996). 'n Warm vergadering oor Johnnic-belange. *Sake-Beeld,* October 25, p. S1.

Screen Africa. (1996). SABS set to sell 700 hours programming in 1996. 8(5), August/September, p 10.

Siefert, M. (ed.) (1991). *Mass Culture and Perestroika in the Soviet Union.* New York: Oxford.

Sinclair, R., and Barenblatt, M. (1993). *The South African Advertising Book. Make the Other Half Work Too.* 3rd ed. Halfway House: Southern.

South Africa (1995). Independent Broadcasting Authority Act No. 153 of 1993 (Statutes of the Republic of South Africa—Radio).

South Africa (1996). Constitution of the Republic of South Africa. As adopted by the Constitutional Assembly on May 8, 1996.

South African Broadcasting Corporation (1994). *Annual Report and Financial Statements.* Johannesburg: SABC.

South African Broadcasting Corporation (1995). *Annual Report and Financial Statements.* Johannesburg: SABC.

South African Telkom sale (1997). *Privatisation International,* April, p. 3.

Telkom (1995). *Annual Report.* Pretoria: Telkom.

Telkom (1996). *Annual Report.* Pretoria: Telkom.

United Nations (1995). *Statistical Yearbook.* 40th issue. Department for Economic and Social Information and Policy Analysis Statistical Division. New York: United Nations.

Van Wyk, D., Dugard, J., De Villiers, B., and Davis, D. (1994). *Rights and Constitutionalism. The New South African Legal Order.* Cape Town: Juta.

Viljoen, C. (Chairman) (1991). *Report of the Task Group on Broadcasting in South and Southern Africa.* Presented to the Minister of Home Affairs of the Republic of South Africa.

Wigston, D. (1997). Critical issues in radio studies. In: du Plooy, G. M. (series ed.) and Oosthuizen, L. M. (ed.). *Introduction to Communication: Course Book 5—Journalism, Press and Radio Studies.* Cape Town: Juta.

15

ISRAEL

Menahem Blondheim

The Israeli Media Economy: Between Openness and Closure

The Israeli media environment is Janus-faced, organized around a loose notion of openness versus closure. These contradictory overall orientations are the product of a set of intersecting forces, geopolitical, socioeconomic, ideological and cultural, played out in the course of a unique and uneasy historical experience. The peculiar evolutionary dynamic of Israeli media between the poles of openness and closure points to no less complex patterns framing the present and modeling the future structures of its media and their economics.

The "closed" look and feel of the Israeli media environment would reflect the country's nature as a small, peripheral, regionally isolated, inward-looking, relatively cohesive society, its economy centralized and stringently regulated. This image of closure would be based, above all, on the very limited dimensions of the country's home market. Hebrew, the language of most of its 5.5 million inhabitants, is one of the world's smallest grapholects. The geographic expanse of the country is small even in proportion to its modest population. Population density in Israel is second only to the Netherlands among western countries, and given the rapid rate of population growth (averaging 3.5 percent annually in the 1990s), it is expected to outstrip it early in the next century (Central Bureau of Statistics [CBS], 1996). Because of the unsurpassed density of population outside the sparsely populated, arid southern half of the country, the market is very compact for media-delivery purposes, the population is easily accessible, and there is hardly any regional diversity.

Small and dense, the Israeli media market is politically and culturally isolated from regional media flows. Although the ongoing peace process may ultimately lower the barriers between the country and its neighbors, at present it remains an island market within the Middle East, its major global trade partners being the European Community and the United States. With regard to western European and North American media flows, however, Israel is highly peripheral, linguistically, geographically, and to an extent, culturally too. Geopolitical conditions entail severe limitations on bilaterally distributed over-the-air media, and to an extent also on multilaterally distributed media, as sources of transnationalization.[1]

The newness of the state, itself the product of a relatively young national movement, coupled with the experience of physical insecurity and isolation, has stimulated active and conscious efforts at cultivating a self-sufficient national culture through public control of mass communications. This inbred, centripetal orientation was complemented, on the institutional and political economy level, by the dominant presence of government in economic as well as social arrangements. Israel has historically practiced a highly centralized media policy (Aharoni, 1991; Ben Porat, 1987; Plessner, 1994; Razin and Sadka, 1993).[2] Thus, the powerful regulatory authority has merged with geopolitical, social and cultural circumstances to forge a closed, inward-looking, self-sufficient and monolithic media environment.

At the same time, fundamental features of Israeli economy, society and culture point in entirely different directions. The Israeli population, although small, represents a kaleidoscope of second languages, ethnic traditions, and cultural orientations. As an immigrant society, a large proportion of Israelis have sensibilities that link them to foreign languages and cultures. Then, too, the high educational profile of the population (one of the highest worldwide by Unesco comparative measurements),[3] and the concentration of a relatively large part of the working force in internationally converging fields, led to a robust demand for information products and services from international media markets.

Moreover, Israel is classified by the World Bank among the world's "high income economies." Within that category it is ranked between Australia and the United Kingdom, which have slightly higher per capita incomes, and Ireland and Spain, with somewhat lower average incomes (World Bank, 1996). Present annual growth rates of gross domestic product (6.2 percent), of exports (10 percent), and of imports (12.3 percent), are among the very highest in industrialized countries (World Bank, 1996a, 1996b). Consequently, the increasing purchasing power of the population, its greater leisure time, and the rapidly swelling volume of external exchange of goods and services can be expected to increase further local consumption of information products from a variety of world markets.

This exchange, however, is highly asymmetrical. In view of its small size, language, regional isolation, unique cultural endowment and distinctive political experience, it is not surprising that Israel is a consumer of, rather than a contributor to, international media flows. In 1971, 55 percent of television (TV) programming was imported, a higher proportion than in all Western European countries (Tunstall, 1977; see Table 15-1), and in 1994, 66 percent of commercial TV (Channel 2) programs were imported (Second Television and Radio Authority [STVRA], 1995). Twenty-four percent of public TV (ITV) programming scheduled for 1997 would be imported (Israel Broadcast Authority [IBA], 1996).[4] On the other hand, only a small number of the locally produced TV programs and films were successfully exported, with the exception of some recent success in the marketing of soap operas (e.g., Turow, 1992).

Because of Israel's high visibility in international affairs, it has developed a small but vibrant industry of news-oriented production services and transmission facilities (Cohen, 1995).[5] Another field of media exports reflects Israel's centrality to the internationally dispersed Jewish community: One of Israel's staple media exports since its foundation, besides broadcast to Arab populations in neighboring countries, has been government-sponsored broadcasts to Jewish communities in the Diaspora, most notably to the former United Soviet Socialist Republic. Israel has become a significant global player in the fast-growing high-tech sector of the economy and has become increasingly involved in research and development activities focused on developing innovative communication technologies, which seem destined to take part in shaping the global media environment in the 21st century.[6]

From Scarcity to Plenty: The Evolution of the Israeli Media Market

The Israeli media environment can be characterized by the opposite poles of openness and closure, which have been accentuated over the years by the demand for improved media services and barriers to entry. Such a state is largely shaped by the significance of macro-economic vicissitudes and fundamental changes in political economy structures.

From the foundation of the state in 1948 and through 1965, the Israeli economy was characterized by one of the highest growth rates worldwide, sustained by an explosive rate of population increase.[7] It was government, however, in this phase of a centrally planned and closely controlled economy that held exclusive control over broadcast media. Because of this legislative barrier to entry, Israeli broadcast media during these decades have amounted to only two government-controlled Voice of Israel (VOI) radio channels and a popular army radio channel, civilian in its orientation.

The artificial restriction of broadcast facilities for the home market had an economic rationale. Given the smallness of the local market and the nature of broadcast as a public good, government-controlled broadcast operations seem to provide economies of scale. Such centralized arrangement was also detrimental owing to the drive for social cohesiveness in a young immigrant society, historically isolated from its neighbors. Moreover, a flourishing and variegated press appeared to take care of the demand for variety, choice and particularism. One of highest rates of per capita book publishing, originals as well as translations, supplemented the press in satisfying the demand for open, cosmopolitan and pluralistic culture consumption.[8]

The Emergence of Television

The revitalization of the economy following the Arab–Israeli war of 1967 affected significant changes in the Israeli media map. After the inauguration of public educational TV funded by the nonprofit sector, in 1968, Israel TV made its debut. Control over TV was shortly transferred to the Israel Broadcast Authority (IBA), a public entity created in 1965 by legislation for the control of Israeli radio (Caspi and Limor, 1995).

The Israeli consumer responded to the medium with a marked increase in media consumption. By 1970, adults spent an average of 54 minutes daily viewing TV of only a few hours of news, domestically produced programs, and imported programs, mostly from the United States and the United Kingdom, then available (Katz, 1993). The single TV channel also carried programming in Arabic, ostensibly for Israeli Arabs but really intended for the former Jordanian and Egyptian populations of the West Bank and the Gaza Strip, brought under Israeli control as a consequence of the war, as well as for citizens of neighboring Arab countries.

Rapid economic growth, nourished by rapid population increase, continued until 1973. The subsequent decade, however, witnessed a sharp decline in growth rates of both per capita gross national product and population. National security budgets increased sharply in consequence of the 1973 war, the energy crisis affected the balance of trade, and the rate of inflation soared, ultimately reaching an annual level of 400 percent in 1983.

Yet the performance of the economy in the 1973–1985 period was not all bleak. A budding high-tech industry began its ascendancy, with a strong emphasis on research and development in communication industries. A right-wing coalition, outwardly espousing capitalistically oriented free-market policies, came into power with the 1977 election and began liberalizing the foreign-exchange market and lifting some restrictions on foreign trade, in particular formidable customs on imports. None of the development, however, had any immediate effects on the country's media industries. The imbalance between the swelling demand for media services and the restrictions placed by government continued to grow.

The Introduction of Commercial Television

Only toward the end of this period did the Israeli policy-makers start to make significant changes. First, in the mid-1980s, the government began loosening its control over mail and telecommunication services, transferring control from the national government to state-controlled commercial corporations. The instantaneous success of these structural changes in the telecommunications sector pointed in the direction of liberalizing mass media as well.[9] In 1986, legislation authorizing the establishment of cable TV was passed, and between 1987 and 1990, most of the tenders for regional franchises were published. In March 1990, with urban centers criss-crossed by dense networks of piratical cable networks, national cable services started (Israel State Comptroller, 1994; Katz, 1996; Caspi and Limor, 1995). In the same year, after a decade of public debate and an endless parade of committees, reports, and legislative initiatives, appropriate legislation for establishing commercial TV and radio services was finally passed. The Second Channel's commercial TV broadcasts were inaugurated in September 1993. Its radio broadcasts were launched into a spectrum crowded with illegal and unlicensed radio stations in September 1995.

These structural changes on the Israeli media map coincided with decisive changes in macro-economic trends. Triggered by the mass migration of Russian Jews to Israel, then by the peace process, the economy expanded rapidly, averaging an 8.8 percent annual increase in gross national product between 1991 and 1996. With the growth in international trade and in domestic economic activities, the demand for commercial broadcast media, from both advertisers and consumers, exploded.

The Israeli Media Structure: From Shared Monopoly to Competition

Both cable and commercial TV proved an almost instantaneous commercial success (Halevi Sweck & Co., 1992). The Israeli consumer responded to the offering of cable services with a record sign-up rate. By the end of 1993, a mere 3.5 years after its inauguration, cable penetration reached 60 percent of households, ranking fourth in the world. In 1996, despite the immense popularity of over-the-air channels and the high cost of the single cable package available, the "maximum basic"—cable retained a penetration level of 61 percent of households, representing 67 percent of those passed (European Cable Communications Association, 1995; Israel Cable Television Association, 1996).[10]

By the time cable made its debut, the average Israeli had already increased his or her TV consumption. Leisure time had expanded by an average of 1 hour a day between 1970 and 1990, and Israelis in 1990 budgeted an average of 1 hour and 42 minutes for TV viewing. The figure rose to 2 hours and 5 minutes in 1991–92, with cable beginning to spread in earnest.[11] Even after the second channel had established itself in the market, cable's ratings remained high. It shared a total of 46 percent of the 1994 TV viewing share (Second Television and Radio Authority, 1995; see also, Maron, 1994; Shai, 1994) with videocassette viewing, terrestrial TV received from neighboring countries, and a minuscule number of direct to home (DTH) viewers. Business performance of the cable operators, as indicated by the publicly available balance sheet of one of the operators, is commensurate with the popularity of the service: The company made an operating profit of 22 percent in 1994 and 25 percent in 1995, on earnings of IS 207 million and IS 241 million, respectively. Extrapolating these figures to the entire industry would yield annual earnings of close to IS 1 billion.[12]

Both the popularity and the commercial success of second channel broadcasters were no less marked than those of the cable operators. Within its first full year of operation, the second channel handily overtook the veteran first channel and established a viewing share about double that of its competitor, ITV. It retained this advantage in its second year of operation, and its news company improved over the previous year by taking the lead in viewing share of the all-important evening news (Shai, 1995; Second Television and Radio Authority, 1995).[13] High ratings have their compensations, and those have been considerable for all three of the commercial franchises comprising the second channel. In 1994, the three commercial time-sharing broadcasters grossed IS 330 million, 449 million in 1995 (Second Television and Radio Authority, 1996), and an estimated IS 569 million in 1996—a 72 percent increase in 2 years.[14]

The exceptional business performance of the second channel reflected the increase in demand for mass advertising channels in a well-developed and rapidly expanding consumer society. Between 1990 and 1995, the national expenditure on advertising increased by 160 percent, from $313.5 million to $817.6 million. If in 1990 this expenditure represented 0.76 percent of gross domestic product, by 1995 it reached a respectable 0.94 percent, well within the range of expenditure for advertising in developed European economies. The second channel was to pick up much of the added resources going to advertising in 1994 and 1995. In 1994, its first full year of broadcast, the second channel's share of the advertising market reached 15.7 percent; in 1995 its share increased to 21.5 percent. The channel's gross revenues from advertising increased by 54 percent between 1994 and 1995, from $121.6 million to $187.6 million. These substantial gains did not come at the expense of the press, which remained the main public advertising medium. Although newspaper and magazine's share of the advertising market plummeted from 80.4 percent in 1993 to 63.6 percent in 1995, their advertising revenues actually increased over that period by a significant 24.5 percent.[15] The overall advertising revenue pie increased as the economy grew.

By the close of 1996, commercial TV broadcasting had securely established itself within a market formerly dominated by limited public broadcasting facilities and supplemented by a vibrant print industry. Much sooner than any of the players had anticipated, a new equilibrium appears to have been reached in the TV industry. Radio, however, is still experiencing severe turbulence, which may soon result in further structural changes. Adjacent industries, including advertising, independent program production, and outsourcing of production services and facilities, as well as the print industries and the small sector of film enterprises, are still reeling from the rapid changes in their respective market positions.

Tables 15-1 and 15-2 provide a review of the broadcast milieu in the aftermath of the structural changes of the 1990s. They identify the entities and organizations active in the field and trace their institutional arrangements and functions within the broadcast map, as it took shape by the close of 1996.

At first glance, the broadcast map of 1996 compared with that of the 1980s reflects a decisive victory for the gospel of openness. More than 40 TV channels are now available, where formerly there was only one. The commercial sector has joined the public sector in providing these multiple channels, and, within it, numerous new players, both individual and corporate, have entered the formerly monolithic mass media field. But a closer look at the map nevertheless reveals distinct indications of closure.

The new TV market is composed of three distinct patterns when it comes to revenue sources. ITV relies on license fee income and a small sum of money allocated for public broadcasting from the Prime Minister's Office and the Ministry of Education. The five cable operators all receive regional subscription fee revenues as well as pay-per-view fees. Channel 2 dominated the TV advertising revenue sources.

To some degree, there is competition between these three sectors. ITV receives some advertising revenue for the delivery of public sector campaigns and spots such as those for the national lottery and for trade and industry

Table 15-1. The Israeli Broadcast TV Environment: Inventory of Systems and Distribution of Functions Within Them

Delivery System		Terrestrial TV		Cable Television
System Function	Sector	Public Broadcasting	Commercial Broadcasting	Commercial Broadcasting
Control and management	Israel Broadcast Authority (IBA), Israel Television (ITV)	Israel Educational Television (IETV)	Second TV and radio Authority (STVRA), three time-tiered broadcast franchises and a joint News Company	Ministry of Communication Authority for CATV Broadcast, five regional franchises
Regulation	IBA (PM Office responsible)	Ministry of Education	STVRA (Ministry of Communication responsible)	Ministry of Communication
Programming (sources)	ITV Independent Producers Imports	IETV Imports	Self-production by the franchises, purchased local and foreign productions, Joint News Company, STVRA	International Satellite feeds, "must carry" channels, the five franchises, ICP, local and foreign productions
Revenue (sources)	License fee finance, public interest advertising, Government budget	Government budget nonprofit sector support STVRA royalties (from advertisements)	Advertising	Subscription fees, PPV charges, royalties from "must carry" channels
Transmission (delivery and infrastructure control)	ITV over government allocated channels	ITV and STVRA	STVRA	Self-reception from satellite feeds, supple-mented by national fiber backbone, local delivery by franchises, mainly over Telecom infrastructure

Source: Compiled from an adaptation of Cave (1989).

associations.[16] Educational TV (ETV) receives advertising income in consideration of commercials aired by STVRA in the course of broadcasting ETV programming in its allotted time slots on channel 2. Cable is also expected to benefit from advertising revenues, albeit indirectly. One sixth of its spectrum is controlled by the Ministry of Communication, which tenders broadcast licenses over cable for special interest channels to be supported by advertising. Cable

Table 15-2. The Israeli Broadcast Radio Environment: Inventory of Systems and Distribution of Functions Within Them

	Sector	Public Broadcasting		Commercial Broadcasting	Unauthorized Nonprofit	Unauthorized Commercial
System function	Network	VOI	Army radio	Local radio	Channel 7 (national), numerous others—local	All local
Control and management		IBA, Israel Radio	IDF, IDF Waves	STVRA, 11 regional franchises	Nonprofit organizations some registered	Fragmented, individual entrepreneurs
Regulation		IBA (PM Office responsible)	IDF (Ministry of Defense responsible)	STVRA (Ministry of Communication responsible)	Ministry of Communication, Israel Police	
Programming (sources)		VOI	IDF Waves	Regional franchises	Self produced, bootlegged—especially news and music	
Revenue sources		Advertising, car radio license fees, government budget	Ministry of Defense budget	Advertising	Contributions, advertising	Advertising, private investment
Transmission (delivery and infrastructure control)		IBA	IEDF	STVRA, Bezeq	Privately owned equipment, ships	

operators must carry these channels but are entitled to receive an income from the licensees for their distribution service.

The national TV market may appear to be oligopolistic, with five cable operators and three commercial broadcasters sharing power in their respective fields. Yet this multiplicity does not necessarily imply competition. In cable, the companies share power on a regional basis: only one operator provides services in any given locality; so there is no competition for subscription fees. In commercial terrestrial broadcast there is some competition for advertising budgets, but because each broadcaster's services are temporally exclusive, there is no competition for viewing share. All in all, the plurality of TV service providers may best be conceived of as "imperfect monopoly" rather than imperfect competition.[17]

It has thus been the intention of the regulators to limit the power of individual media establishments. Nevertheless, there have been practices of market power in the TV industry. In the cable industry, leaders of the regional operating companies have joined forces in programming development by establishing a purchasing and program production cartel, the ICP, which vertically integrated content provision into their joint monopoly of delivery services. After years of litigation, the ICP was ruled in restriction of trade, and it is being forced to surrender gradually much of its control over programming. This ruling spells relief to a varied sector of programming distributors, independent producers and production services providers.

More problematic, perhaps, is the drive toward oligopoly across the new mass media map. Complementing the overall trend of government disengagement from active economic activity, large, powerful conglomerates have emerged, filling the vacuum and consequently assuming considerable power in the economy. The large national banks have been prominent among these emerging economic conglomerates, as are a small number of combined industrial and financial economic titans (Plessner, 1994). Four major holders of newspaper properties, two of them units of larger economic concerns, have concentrated much power in the rapidly consolidating newspaper industry. They, too, have striven to diversify their media holdings, and the opportunity to enter into cable and commercial TV was considered a prime prospect. The consequent pattern of cross-ownership that has come to characterize the Israeli media industry is illustrated in Figure 15-1. As it appears, a small ring of bankers and industrialists, newspaper barons and affluent entrepreneurs are dominant among those replacing government in the control of the media industry. This oligopolistic control across the various media represents a potential new source of closure in Israeli media. It is positioned to retard or even counter the movement toward openness, which had been anticipated with the surrender of government control over the TV market (Lachman-Messer, 1994; Shaw-Smith, 1995; Tikochinsky, 1996).

In sharp contrast to TV, the Israeli radio scene appears to be in a state of monopolistic competition; however, the rainbow variety of broadcasts can hardly be attributed to an intentional drive toward deregulation and media pluralism. Rather, it was brought about by a powerful combination of market forces: strong demand, low barriers to entry, ineffective law enforcement, and effective sectorial political leverage.

Initially, there was little differentiation in the industry with regard to sources of revenue. IBA's VOI is financed by a combination of car-radio license fees, the national budget supporting the export of programming to Arab states and to the Jewish Diaspora, and advertising, which constitutes the main source of VOI's budgets.[18] Voice of Israel radio is locked in a fierce contest over national audience share with the Ministry of Defense-financed army radio, "IDF Waves." An unlicensed and possibly illegal third player—a right wing, religious, two-channel broadcaster—contends with both the VOI and Army Radio for national audience share and with VOI for advertising. This

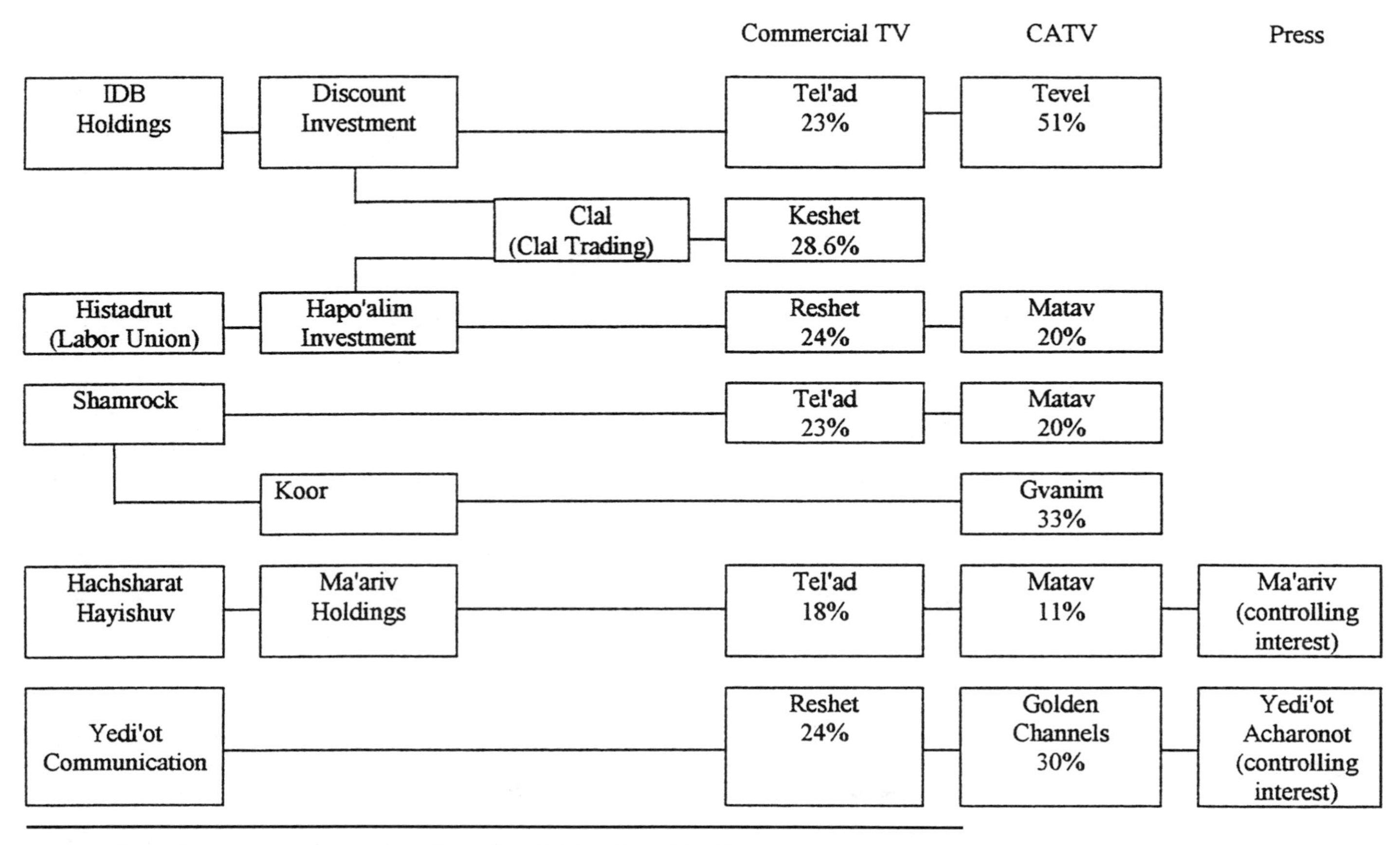

FIGURE 15-1. *Cross-ownership in Israeli media, 1996, selected holdings.*

"Channel 7," ostensibly broadcast from a ship outside Israeli territorial waters, is backed by the strong political power of the religious right wing.[19]

Dozens of illegal local broadcasters compete with the three national radio networks for audience share. Known as "the pirates," these illegal stations may be divided into two categories: one, commercially oriented enterprises supported by low-end, mainly local, advertising, their programming appealing to particular audiences through coverage of communal affairs or through special interest programming; the other category including nonprofit radio enterprises, their programming serving a variety of religious and ideological interests. In the case of some of these stations, support by contributions and nonprofit organizations is supplemented by advertising finance. Because of ineffective exercise of its monitoring and enforcement powers, complemented perhaps by political and ideological scruples, joint Ministry of Communication and police action to close down these authentic representatives of the entrepreneurial spirit and of minority opinion has proved grossly ineffective.[20]

The primary casualties of the lively free-for-all over air waves are the holders of regional broadcast licenses, painstakingly prepared and tendered by the STVRA, in the course of 1994 and 1995. The fledgling commercial local radio industry is the one media enterprise on the new media map showing distinct signs of distress. Consequently, negotiations are under way for framing a new deal for the relief of these authorized local franchises. The main proposals point in two opposing directions: a decisive regulatory crackdown, limiting VOI advertising and closely regulating its cross-media power, coupled with a head-on campaign against the pirates. The other attitude is oriented toward further liberalization. It calls for all regional STVRA stations to be licensed to broadcast nationally in competition with the VOI and IDF Waves and possibly to provide them with financial compensation from government sources. This contention between what is essentially firmer closure versus increased openness is yet to be decided in the case of radio as in the case of the media environment generally.

Openness and Closure in the Near Future and Beyond: Regulation, Technology, Convergence

To judge from recent developments in communication policy formation, a movement toward thoroughgoing liberalization of the Israeli media environment is gaining considerable momentum. Initiatives directed at opening up the communication sector through regulatory measures are under way, as are initiatives aimed at restructuring regulatory authority itself. The way in which these initiatives will crystallize into policy, as well as the extent to which such policies will be implemented, is yet to be seen. Their ultimate impact, however, will depend on a matrix of forces encompassing public demand, corporate pressures, political interests and, at least as important, economic performance and technological advances.

A committee authorized by the Ministry of Communications has recently emphatically recommended what amounts to a revolution in the current media map. This Waxe-Brodet-Leon report calls for opening up all fields of telecommunications—infrastructure control as well as service provision—to competition. In parallel, it recommended the opening up of broadcast to new enterprises. The committee suggested that the reforms be implemented by the end of 1998 (Inter-office Commission for Investigating Policy Affecting the Communications Sector and its Opening to Competition, 1996).

Government wholeheartedly endorsed these recommendations and, moreover, pronounced itself in favor of accelerating the process and having it take affect 1 year earlier.[21] This blanket endorsement and uncharacteristic haste is to be understood in the context of the recently elected right-wing government's peculiar take on the liberalization of local communications. Privatization and the disengagement of government from direct involvement in economic activity have been prominent planks of its economic platform. But economic expedience appears to be reinforced by purely political considerations. As it appears, high on the present government's agenda is an assault on the bastions of what it views as entrenched elite, prominent among them the media establishment. The latter is viewed as a closed ring of left-wingers, symbolically attached to a well-entrenched liberal academic, legal and civil service milieu. National media have been singled out for attack by the new government because of the right's notion of a distinct liberal cultural bias in the media and a left-wing political bias in its coverage of current events. The most appropriate remedy, according to this view, is an attack on the media's traditional bases of power through a combination of privatization of public broadcast and increased competition. The recommendations of the Waxe-Brodet-Leon committee may appear to government as instrumental in implementing this political and ideological agenda.

The recommendations of an earlier committee, established to consider reforms in the regulatory mechanism itself, have not been as enthusiastically embraced. The Boaz committee recommended the transfer of regulatory authority from the Ministry of Communication and other government bureaus to an independent body of professionals, modeled after the U.S. Federal Communications Commission (FCC). The committee had pointed to fragmentation, inefficiency, and lack of professional aptitude, as well as to susceptibility to pressures, as underlying the dysfunction of the existing regulatory apparatus (Public Committee for Investigating the Licensing and Regulation in the Communications Sector, 1996; cf. Report of the Professional Commission for

Investigating the Re-organization of the Communications Sector in Israel, 1993). Government did formally endorse these recommendations, but appears to be in no haste to implement them. Aside from an instinctive aversion to the surrender of powers, government's lukewarm response may reflect purely tactical considerations. It may want to hold-on to powers temporarily that will facilitate the reforms to which it is politically and ideologically committed and only then divest itself of regulatory responsibilities.

Both the Waxe-Brodet-Leon and Boaz committees have seized on recent accomplishments in deregulating telecommunications and on rapid technological change as the rationale for their recommendations (Inter-office Commission for Investigating Policy Affecting the Communications Sector and its Opening to Competition, 1996; Public Committee for Investigating the Licensing and Regulation in the Communications Sector, 1996). Indeed, just as in the case of the first wave of liberalization in the mid-1980s, the telecommunication sector appears to be leading the way toward deregulation. A series of measures taken in recent years has effectively chipped away at the power of Bezeq, the erstwhile national telecommunications monopoly. This formerly overpowering, close-knit, and cross-subsidized body is being rapidly dismembered. Moreover, significant branches of its most remunerative operations are being exposed to competition. The two most important of these have been cellular telephony and overseas calls. Once again, the benefits of open competition have been practically instantaneous, as evidenced in the cellular field. In 1994 a second cellular operator was licensed, and it began providing services in competition with the well-entrenched Bezeq-Motorola alliance, at drastically lower prices. The Israeli market responded to the now affordable novelty with its unique version of innovation diffusion: a pattern of mass contagion (Blondheim, in press). Pent-up demand was released in an outburst of consumption, setting a world record for cellular take-up rates as well as for number of calls per subscriber and their average duration. In 1995, the first year of competition, the number of cellular subscribers increased more than threefold, from 130,000 to 435,000. By the close of 1996 the number of subscribers again more than doubled, passing the 1 million mark—a number equal to fully two thirds of Israeli households (Israel Ministry of Communication, 1995;[22] Lahav, 1995). Competition in international telephony began in 1997. It is projected that tariffs would come tumbling down and that rates of use will skyrocket.

It appears that local regulatory wisdom is conditioned to consider liberalization of mass communications as an inevitable counterpart to the opening of telecommunications to competition. Although the public good nature of broadcast and its consequent overwhelming economies of scale may make this reciprocity questionable, recent technological developments have accentuated the parallelism. New communication technologies entering the market are making the differentiation of, and the borders between, telecommunications and broadcast media exceedingly hazy. Internet access services, and Internet protocol (IP)–based information services, strategically positioned between the formerly well-differentiated sectors of point to point and point to multipoint, have been opened to lively competition. The traditional distinction between kinds of content characteristic of either telecommunications or media is also rapidly fading. Indeed, four Israeli multimedia networking enterprises have received Ministry of Communications licenses for experimental services in distributing digital products and services over cable infrastructures, and as a countermeasure, Bezeq was permitted to experiment in the delivery of video products over its network of twisted-pair wires as enabled by asymmetric digital subscriber line (ADSL) technology.[23] The launch of Israel's first civilian communications satellite, the Amos, capable of providing ample facilities for both broadcast and telecommunications services, whether analog or digital, has brought the issue of the redistribution of communication functions and their regulation into focus.[24]

The challenge of the new technologies is particularly powerful in the Israeli environment. A dizzying array of some of the most advanced and imaginative new communication technologies have been born and bred in the Israeli high-tech industry. These range all the way from advanced technologies for utilizing fiber-optic infrastructures and for extending the usable limits of wireless spectrum, to improvements in XDSL, QAM, QPSK and IP technologies for data transmission over telephone, cable, satellite and Internet. They span ATM switching and MPEG compression, innovative encryption, network- and subscriber-management technologies for broadcasters, and a great variety of novel end-user multimedia applications, even digital virtual-studio and -advertising solutions for use by broadcast media.

The flourishing of this communication-enabling technology sector can be attributed to a series of unique local circumstances. Israel is endowed by the highest proportion, worldwide, of engineers and technicians in the work force, and many of them tend to demonstrate a rampant entrepreneurial spirit. Initiatives in the field are encouraged by the availability of government support and of venture capital funding. By 1996, some 2,000 high-tech companies were active in Israel, fueled by some 40 risk-capital funds specializing in high-tech, and 30 more diverse risk capital investment funds. In the course of 1996, these investment companies facilitated, and reaped large profits from, some 15 initial public offerings of Israeli high-tech companies on Wall Street, more public offerings than of any other foreign country. More general circumstances have also affected the expansion of the communications research and development sector. The general atmosphere of brisk demand for information products and services, the buoyancy of a rapidly expanding economy in the 1990s, and the lack of large, overpowering entrenched giants in the field have encouraged the spectacular growth of a variegated communication technology sector.

Convenience and, to an extent, consideration of marketing have led to pressures for first implementing the communication industries' new processes and products in the local media market. Indeed, the openness of the Israeli consumer and the peculiar dynamics of local innovation diffusion make the Israeli market an ideal playground for new communication applications and services. Pressures of the industrial and investment sector as well as the larger national interest have become a potent force for liberalizing the local communications market.

Deregulation may thus lead to a complete restructuring of the Israeli media market. It may set the stage not only for a radically transformed media environment but also for a realignment of the most fundamental forces framing it. The overall tension between openness and closure in the Israeli media environment will thus be recast in new forms. A deregulated communication environment may well breed a plethora of new technology–based "little media," which would serve the particularistic interests of closed subgroups and cohesive, nonlocal, virtual communities. Conversely, the broader horizon of "big media," formerly of a closed and exclusive national orientation, would gradually submit to pressures for greater openness. Control over mass broadcast media would become more competitive and less concentrated, with their programming more variegated and pluralistic. They would thus become powerful engines for a pluralistic, outward-looking and cosmopolitan orientation for Israeli economy and society in the 21st century.

References

Aharoni, Y. (1991). *The Political Economy of Israel* [in Hebrew]. Tel Aviv: Am Oved.

Bank of Israel (1995). *Annual Report, 1994* [in Hebrew]. Jerusalem: BoI.

Bank of Israel (1996). *Annual Report, 1995* [in Hebrew]. Jerusalem: BoI

Ben Porat, Y. (1987). The Israeli economy: The struggles of growth [in Hebrew]. In: Ben Porat, Y. (ed.). *The Economy of Israel: Maturing Through Crisis.* Tel Aviv: Am Oved, pp. 7–26.

Blondheim, M. (1997). Communication infrastructures and the knowledge sector: The Israeli anomaly [in Hebrew]. In: Caspi, D. (ed.). *Communication and Democracy in Israel.* Tel Aviv: Hakibutz Hame'uchad.

Bornstein, O. (1996). Television continues to bite off from the national advertising pie [in Hebrew]. *Otot* 193:6–7.

Boyd-Barrett, O., and Kishan Thussu, D. (1992). *Contra Flows in Global News.* London: John Libby.

Caspi, D., and Limor, Y. (1995). *The Mediators: The Mass Media in Israel, 1948–1990* [in Hebrew]. Jerusalem: Am Oved.

Cave, M. (1989). An introduction to television economics [in Hebrew]. In: G. Hughes, and Vins, D. (eds.). *Deregulation and the Future of Commercial Television.* Aberdeen: Aberdeen University Press pp. 9–37.
Central Bureau of Statistics (1995). *Time Use in Israel: Time Budget Survey, 1991/2* [in Hebrew]. Jerusalem: CBS.
Central Bureau of Statistics (1996). *Foreign Trade Statistics Quarterly* [in Hebrew], 47, July–September. Jerusalem: CBS.
Central Bureau of Statistics (1996). *Main Indicators of Economic Development, 1991–1996* [Brochure; in Hebrew], December. Jerusalem: CBS.
Cohen, J. (1995). Foreign press corps as an indicator of international news. *Gazette* 56:89–100.
Dori, Y. (1996). The advertising cake rises [in Hebrew]. *Otot* 195:14–16.
European Cable Communications Association. (1995). *Facts and Figures* [brochure], December 31. Brussels: ECCA.
Halevi Sweck & Co. (1992). *Commercial Television in Israel: A Business Plan* [in Hebrew]. September. Jerusalem.
Inter-office Commission for Investigating Policy Affecting the Communications Sector and its Opening to Competition. (1996). *Report*, December.
Israel Advertising Association (1996). *The Media Survey, 1995/6* [in Hebrew].
Israel Broadcast Authority (1996). *Budget for 1997* [in Hebrew]. Jerusalem: IBA.
Israel Cable Television Association (1996). *Report on Israel Cable TV* [Brochure; in Hebrew]. Jerusalem: ICTA.
Israel Ministry of Communication. (1995). *The Communications Revolution in Israel* [in Hebrew]. Jerusalem: IMC.
Israel State Comptroller. (1994). *44th Annual Report* [in Hebrew]. Jerusalem: ISC.
Jackson, T., and Halawi, G. (1996). *The cellular Telephone in Israel as a Social Phenomenon.* Unpublished manuscript.
Katz, E. (1993). Change in Israeli culture and Israeli media: 1970–1990 [in Hebrew]. In: Adoni, H. (ed.). *Proceedings of Conference on Change in Israeli Culture and Israeli Media.* Jerusalem: The Smart Communication Institute, pp. 31–53.
Katz, E., et al. (1992). *The Culture of Leisure in Israel: Patterns of Consuming Culture, 1970–1990* [in Hebrew]. Jerusalem: Gutman Institute for Applied Social Research.
Katz, Y. (1996). The development of cable television in Israel and its relation to the social and political system [in Hebrew]. *Patuach* 3:65–94.
Kela Committee (1994). *Report presented to the Minister of Communication* [in Hebrew].
Lachman-Messer, Y. (1994). The new media map: Structure and ownership, challenges and perils [in Hebrew]. In: Lachman-Messer, Y. (ed.). *The New Media Map in Israel.* Jerusalem: Smart Communication Institute, pp. 45–53.
Lahav, Tel Aviv University. (1995). *New times new rules: Competition and infrastructures in the telecommunications sector.* Symposium transcript [in Hebrew], *December.* Tel Aviv.

Limor, Y. (1996). *Pirate Radio in Israel.* (Smart Communication Institute Research Report [in Hebrew]), October. Jerusalem.

Limor, Y. (1996). The proliferation of pirate radio in Israel [in Hebrew]. *Qesher* 19:42–57.

Maron, U. (1994). Does cable have a message [in Hebrew]? In: Lachman-Messer, Y. (ed.). *The New Media Map in Israel* [in Hebrew]. Jerusalem: Smart Communication Institute, pp. 66–72.

1995 Annual Report of Matav (1996). Globes. Available on-line: URL:www.globes.co.il.

Nossek, H., and Adoni, H. (1996). The social implications of cable television: Restructuring connections with self and social group. *International Journal of Public Opinion Research* 8:51–69.

Plessner, Y. (1994). *The Political Economy of Israel: From Ideology to Stagnation.* New York: State University of New York Press.

Professional Commission for Investigating the Re-organization of the Communications Sector in Israel (1993) [in Hebrew]. *Report,* May 1. Jerusalem.

Public Committee for Investigating the Licensing and Regulation in the Communications Sector (1996). *Final report* [in Hebrew], February.

Razin, A., and Sadka, E. (1993). *The Economy of Modern Israel: Malaise and Promise.* Chicago: University of Chicago Press.

Second Television and Radio Authority (1995). *Annual Report, 1994* [in Hebrew]. Jerusalem: Or-Media.

Second Television and Radio Authority (1996). *Annual Report, 1995* [in Hebrew]. Jerusalem: Or-Media.

Sepstrup, P. (1990). *Transnationalization of Television in Western Europe.* London: John Libby.

Shai, N. (1994). The Second channel: Whence and whereto [in Hebrew]. In: Lal, R. (ed.). *Channel Two—Year One: Commercial television in Israel.* Jerusalem: Israel Institute of Democracy. pp. 38–51.

Shai, N. (1995). The Second channel [in Hebrew]. In: Second Television and Radio Authority (1996). *Annual Report, 1995.* Jerusalem: Or-Media, pp. 105-106.

Shaw-Smith, P. (1995). Israel earns it place among the top-flight IT nations [in Hebrew]. *Intermedia* 23:42–45.

Tikochinsky, Y. (1996). What is your business? *The Seventh Eye*, 5:4–9.

Tunstall, J. (1977). *The Media Are American.* New York: Columbia University Press.

Turow, J. (1992). *Media Systems in Society: Understanding Industries, Strategies, and Power.* New York: Longman.

United Nations. (1994). *Statistical Yearbook, 1992.* New York: United Nations.

World Bank. (1996a). *World Development Report.* New York: World Bank.

World Bank. (1996b). *The World Bank Atlas.* New York: World Bank.

Notes

1. The terminology used in this chapter follows that proposed by Sepstrup (1990).

2. The government's orientation toward a planned economy was complemented by the dominance of labor unions in shaping economic policy, even in control of a large share of the economy.

3. See a summary in Blondheim (in press). For comparative indicators of media consumption, see United Nations (1994).

4. The budget is not publicly available; its highlights, however, were reported by *Globes,* a business daily.

5. For a general discussion, see Boyd-Barrett and Kishan Thussu (1992).

6. See the later discussion in this chapter. Data on the growth of the high-tech sector are provided by the Bank of Israel (1995, 1996).

7. The country's Jewish population of 650,000 doubled between 1948 and 1951 and further increased by 4 percent annually in the 1950s and by 3 percent in the course of the 1960s. Average per capita income increase during these years was approximately 5 percent annually (Ben Porat, 1987).

8. For further information on the development of the Israeli press, see Caspi and Limor (1995); for data on book publishing, see Blondheim (1997).

9. The best summary of these developments can be found in Bank of Israel (1996).

10. These data are confirmed by the 1995 Annual Report of Matav (second largest of the five operators): It penetrated 68 percent of households passed in its region. For a discussion of social and psychological aspects of cable diffusion in Israel, see Nossek and Adoni (1996).

11. The 1970–1990 data are from Katz et al. (1992); the 1991–92 data are from CBS (1995). The increase from 1990 to 1991–92 may be due, at least in part, to methodological differences between these two studies and, in particular, to the difference in age cohorts surveyed. By September 1991, more than 10 percent of Israeli homes were connected to cable (Caspi and Limor, 1995).

12. The data are from Matav's annual reports, as summarized in *Globes* (http//www.globes.co.il).

13. More detailed breakdowns are available in Teleseker's and Gallop's conflicting monthly survey reports and in Israel Advertising Association (1996).

14. Estimates for 1996 were extrapolated from the January through September results of the three franchises.

15. The source of most data on the Israeli advertising market are the reports of the Israeli Association of Advertisers. Their data, however, reflect list prices rather than net expenditures. The figures used here are based on the slightly discrepant corrected figures provided by Dori (1996) and Bornstein (1996).

16. Projected advertising income for 1997 (NIS 23 million) was expected to yield some 3.5 percent of ITV's income in 1997 (Israel Broadcast Authority, 1996, as reported in *Globes*).

17. Considering the limited size of the local market, this lack of competition is reasonable. In fact, it is doubtful whether the advertising market could sustain two commercial channels. Given this limitation, current regulatory arrangements appear to guaranty reasonable variety of broadcasts at the same time that they minimize the costs of competition.

18. IBA (1997), as reported by *Globes.* Expected income from radio advertisements is to be NIS 82 million. However, a recent statement by VOI's GM would indicate that revenue from advertisement in 1996 is estimated at NIS 103 million; *Globes,* 23 December 1996. VOI's total budget for 1997 is NIS 192 million, NIS 28 million of which are earmarked for broadcasts in Arabic.

19. For ratings and their breakdowns, see Teleseker (1996).

20. According to a Ministry of Communication report, the number of pirate stations as of March 1996 was 51 (Limor, 1995; see also, Limor, 1996).

21. For example, see, *Globes,* 10-11 December 1996.

22. Data for 1995 as corrected by Cellcom (Jackson & Halawi, 1996).

23. These companies include Netgame, IBM (Israel), MediaNet, and Meimadim. For background, see Kela Committee (1994).

24. See, for example, *Ma'ariv,* January 9, 1996, February 18, 1996; *Globes,* May 31, 1996.

Asia and the Pacific Rim

The region of Asia and the Pacific Rim represents one of the fastest growing economies in the global marketplace. Countries in this triad region have become important trading partners, as well as attractive exporting markets for U.S. media businesses. The chapter on India, authored by Andrew Sharma, discusses the increasing strategic alliances between many Indian media companies and foreign multinational media corporations. He also addresses how two state-controlled media monopolies, All India Radio and Doordarshan, have to change their programming strategies to compete with the new multichannel media such as cable television and direct broadcast satellite. The chapter on China, written by Yiu Ming To, presents a peculiar media market that operates under a restrictive political environment but is populated by state-owned commercial media conglomerates. In the chapter on the Pacific Rim, Tuen-Yu Lau and Penghwa Ang describe a dynamic media zone that is characterized by the market structures from open competition to corporatized monopoly. The chapter on Japan, written by Kazumi Hasegawa, describes Japan's increasingly concentrated media markets and the trend toward vertical integration and international joint ventures, especially in the satellite television industry. In the chapter on Australia, Maria Williams-Hawkins details the concentrated nature of Australian media markets and the significant role the media conglomerates such as News Corporation have played in Australia and in the world.

16

INDIA

Andrew Sharma

India and Its Media: Commercialization, Liberalization and Democratization

India, with its 22 states and a population of 900 million, is a very vast and diverse country. Differences abound geographically and culturally. There are 16 major regional languages and more than 800 dialects. There is also a wide range of disparity in the country's development, wealth and education. It was said that India lives simultaneously in two centuries, with bullock carts and satellites; although new technology is quite evident and in use, many of its citizens still depend on the bullock cart for transportation (Ray and Jacka, 1996). India is committed to an official policy of socialism; however, there are a considerable number of young, highly educated capitalists who are pioneering high-tech business ventures. It has more university students than any other nation in the world today, but an estimated 45 percent of the population is still illiterate (Ninan, 1995b). In a country where there is poverty and illiteracy, film (and very recently, television) is a far more important medium for entertainment and information. Accordingly, most of India's entertainment export is made entirely of films. In spite of its huge domestic market, which comprises of more than 40 million television (TV) households and 250 million viewers (Ministry of Information and Broadcasting, 1995), India has not produced a sizable export market in made-for-TV programs. This historical limitation may be attributed to the extreme governmental control of the TV industry, which lasted until mid-1980s. Only recently has the government permitted privatization and supported TV programs that are non–film based.

Major Media Industries in India

India is undergoing a transformation in the areas of economic development and liberalization. This is giving way to new dimensions in communication media. Traditional media such as films, radio, TV and newspaper continue to play an important role in informing and entertaining the masses. But with the advent of new distribution systems such as satellites, the same media, especially TV, are making an even bigger impact on the society as the gateway to other new media technologies.

Newspapers

Newspaper is one of the largest industries in the nation. India publishes more daily newspapers than any other country in Asia and covers a range of languages and cultural diversity that is unparalleled anywhere (Singhal and Rogers, 1989). The publications in the country are in Hindi, English and all vernacular languages, and in 1992, there were a total of 31,957 newspapers and periodicals in India with a combined circulation of 63.67 million copies. Of those, 3,502 were dailies, 271 triweeklies or biweeklies (newspapers), 10,375 weeklies, 4,315 fortnightlies (periodicals), 9,555 monthlies, 2,525 quarterlies, 1,115 bimonthlies and 299 yearlies (Ministry of Information and Broadcasting, 1995). Indian newspapers are owned by individuals or by private corporations. The pattern of ownership in 1992 was individuals, 72.2 percent; societies and associations, 12.8 percent; firms or partnerships, 4.4 percent; joint stock companies, 4.4 percent; government, 2.2 percent; and others 4.0 percent (Registrar of Newspapers for India, Ministry of Information and Broadcasting, 1995). Nineteen big units published 51 dailies from the metropolitan cities, with a total circulation of 4,907,000 copies (Ministry of Information and Broadcasting, 1995). Some of the established media conglomerates are Bennet Coleman and Company, with a total circulation of 1,190,000 copies (dailies), the Goenka-owned *Express* newspapers with a circulation of 780,000 copies (dailies), and the Birla-owned *Hindustan Times,* with a circulation of 675,563 copies (dailies) (Ministry of Information and Broadcasting, 1995). The news agencies, Press Trust of India (PTI) and the United News of India (UNI) provide news in English, whereas Hindustan Samachar and Samachar Bharati provide news in Hindi and in regional languages, respectively. All four of the news agencies are privately owned.

The Indian press came under censorship during the National Emergency (1975–77) declared by then Prime Minister Indira Gandhi, and the four news agencies were merged into one, Samachar. In 1977, the Janata Party came to power, and under its rule the censorship was abolished and Samachar once again became the four different units. Also, a Press Commission was established to define the functions of the Indian Press and ensure its freedom (Mehta, 1980). In the same period, newsmagazines became more prominent and newly founded magazines like *India Today* (which today is the prominent magazine in India) capitalized on readers' unfulfilled needs for information during the Emergency Years (Singhal and Rogers, 1989). Today there is a good range of several weekly, fortnightly, and monthly magazines in India, which cover a whole range of national as well as international issues in depth.

Radio

All India Radio (AIR), popularly known as Akashwani, is the only radio network in India. The first radio program was broadcast in 1923 and was followed by the establishment of an experimental broadcasting service in 1927. When India became independent, the AIR network had only six stations and a mere 275,000 receiving sets. Now, it has grown into a network of 173 broadcasting centers, including 65 local radio stations, covering nearly 97 percent of the population spread over 89.6 percent of the country (Ministry of Information and Broadcasting, 1995). The AIR introduced commercial broadcasting in 1967. Advertisements are accepted in any language as tape-recorded spots of 10-, 15-, 20- and 30-second duration. Programming on AIR ranges from news and news-based programs to film music, plays, skits, operas and folk dramas.

All India Radio has a three-tier system of broadcasting: national, regional and local. The national channel transmits centrally originated news bulletins (in Hindi and English), music, and other topical programs, to nearly 76 percent of the country's population (Ministry of Information and Broadcasting, 1995). The regional stations transmit state specific programming. Local radio is comparable to radio broadcasting in America, where each station serves a city or a town and provides entertainment and other community-oriented programming. Besides broadcasting in India, the External Services Division of AIR broadcasts programs to various countries near the Indian region. The target areas of External Services Division span almost all the countries and include areas of West, North, East, and South Asia; North, West, and East Africa; Australia; New Zealand; the United Kingdom and Europe; and the Indian subcontinent. In addition to foreign languages, External Services Division also broadcasts in Indian languages for Indian people settled in different parts of the globe. The programs, broadcast in 24 languages, are aimed at the

Indian population staying at those countries and generally comprise news bulletins, documentaries, music and information about India's life.

Broadcast Television

Television was introduced in India in 1959, when a pilot station was established with the assistance of UNESCO as an experimental educational service. Regular daily broadcasts began in 1965 under the auspices of Doordarshan, the Indian National Television Network, as a government-owned media entity. In 1975, the U.S. National Aeronautics and Space Administration loaned India a satellite to conduct the Satellite Instructional Television Experiment (SITE) in 2,400 villages (Singhal et al., 1988) and thus began a path toward true broadcasting. The New Delhi ASIAD games of 1982 helped the growth of TV through better satellite technology when INSAT-1A was launched to broadcast the games.

Television grew rapidly through the 1980s and 1990s, adding almost one new transmitter everyday. Shifting from its strictly educational fare, the programming now started to include talk shows, quiz shows and current affairs programs. In the late 1980s, advertising (10-, 15-, 30- and 60-second spots) and sponsorship of programs by private parties (programs financed by independent producers) were permitted (Mitra, 1993). Multinational companies such as Colgate Palmolive, Hindustan Lever, Brooke Bond and Ponds occupy the top spots in advertising. From a gross revenue of Rs 80 million in 1980–81, advertising raked in Rs 1,360 million in 1987 (Thomas, 1993) and Rs 3,602.3 million in 1992–93 (Ministry of Information and Broadcasting, 1995). It was estimated that advertising would produce Rs 4,500 million in 1994–95 for Doordarshan (Indian Market Research Bureau, 1994). Doordarshan, in 1994, reached 84.5 percent of the population and 66.6 percent of the country through a network of 564 transmitters (Ministry of Information and Broadcasting, 1995). Today, the typical programming on Doordarshan ranges from information programs including news and current affairs, to educational programs, to entertainment including musicals, dance, and series and feature films.

Cable and Direct Broadcast Television

Although, Doordarshan has a historical presence in the country, TV in India has undergone a major change, which began in 1991 as a result of two significant developments: economic reform and the advent of transnational satellite broadcasting in Asia (Ninan, 1995a; Karthigesu, 1994). Monopoly broadcasters such as AIR and Doordarshan were challenged by cable TV and direct broadcast satellites. The Gulf War earlier that year sparked the Indian people's interest in cable programming. The reception of cable network programming expanded as entrepreneurs bought satellite dishes and connected them to individual households via coaxial cable to deliver war coverage news. When the war ended, these systems continued to show feature films, receiving even bigger responses (Ninan, 1995a). So, when Rupert Murdoch's Star TV, a Hong Kong–based satellite TV venture, started telecasting to several Asian countries in 1991, it found instant reception in India. This illegal network of cable systems has become the principal catalyst for the changes that have occurred in the Indian TV scene in the 1990s (Ray and Jacka, 1996; Ninan, 1995b). By early 1991 there were 3,450 operating cable systems (Ray and Jacka, 1996; Karthigesu, 1994). In 1992 the number was close to 12,000 and still growing rapidly. In 1991, a National Television Survey conducted by MRAS-Burke showed that cable penetration was the highest in the western region of India. Gujarat leads the way, with 29.6 percent houses cabled of all TV households, followed by Maharashtra with 15.9 percent, and Madhya Pradesh with 11.3 percent (Ninan, 1995b). In 1995 legislation was finally enacted to regulate cable TV. The legislation also legalized authorized reception of satellite TV programming. Now, with the availability of 13 satellite and cable TV channels, the worldwide TV networks are active in India. Cable/satellite networks such as Star, BBC, Cable News Network, Discovery, Prime Sports, ESPN, Sony, ZEE, TNT and ABN, with programming ranging from news, entertainment, music and sports, have become part of the daily media diet of many Indians.

Film

Film has a long and rich history in India. Historically it has been the dominant medium. India has developed a large film production industry, from the beginnings of cinema and for many decades; it has produced more films than any other nation. After the silent era, the advent of sound gave a further boost to the Indian film industry because of the accessibility of the languages to the population. By the mid-1930s many studios were in place, production increased and the industry grew steadily. Centers of production were developed along linguistic lines in different parts of the country: Bombay for Hindi films, Calcutta for Bengali, Madras for Tamil, Bangalore for Kannada, and Hyderabad for Malayalam (Pendakur and Subramanyam, 1996).

During World War II, investments from illegal war profits and the rise of the independent producers saw the demise of the studio system. The big studios lost their power, and independent producers started to establish themselves. Exports of films started to rise in number, and in 1958 an export promotion council (EPC) was set up by the government. Its function was to represent the film industry at international film festivals and through research and lobbying efforts, advise and provide help to film exporters. In 1963 the

Industry Motion Picture Export Corporation (IMPEC) was created to replace the EPC, and with the merger of IMPEC and the Film Finance Corporation (which was created to support serious cinema), it became the National Film Development Corporation (NFDC). Among its functions, the NFDC seeks to give direction and organize the film industry in India, promote the cause for "good" cinema, discipline the commercialism in the film business and control the film imports and exports (Da Cunha, 1984).

By the beginning of 1980, Indian films were shown in more than 100 countries (Dharap, 1983). Today, Indian films are widely viewed in parts of Africa, Asia, the Middle East, Europe and North America (Pendakur and Subramanyam, 1996). From the mid-1980s, the growth of video affected the export of films: In 1980–81, 833 films were exported, whereas in 1990–91 it had fallen to 458 titles (and 252 on video) (Ministry of Information and Broadcasting, 1995). But the overall combined revenues from theatrical and home video exports have increased. Between 1985 and 1991 the export revenues from film increased by a little less than 50 percent, whereas the revenues from film titles on video increased by about 400 percent (National Film Development Corporation, 1992).

Although the numbers of films exported are significant, the revenues from them are very small in comparison to box-office collections in India. For example, in 1987 the revenue from films was Rs 5 billion, but in contrast, the revenue from exports were only Rs 71 million (Ministry of Information and Broadcasting, 1989) which is less than 2 percent of box-office collections. In the 1980s the average number of features made in a year were well over 700 films. In the 1990s, the average number rose to over 800 films (949, 809, 836 and 812 feature films were made in 1990, 1991, 1992 and 1993, respectively) (Ministry of Information and Broadcasting, 1995). Although Indian films are sometimes regarded as a national pride historically, they are mainly used for entertainment purposes with a very limited role in social development.

Media Industry Analysis

Historical Control by State

Broadcasting in India, as in many other countries in Asia, has its origins in colonial times. The influence of the traditions of political, bureaucratic and elite cultural practices of those times is still reflected today and thus the administration, programming, centralization and decision-making processes are essentially the same as they were in colonial times (Masani, 1976). But change is the defining characteristic of Indian media today and with global changes in politics, society, economics and technology the transformations are many and varied. To understand these changes, there is a need to look at the relationship between broadcasting and the State in India.

All India Radio and Doordarshan, while modeled on the BBC, are both state monopolies. Broadcasting has always been a highly centralized operation, almost totally controlled by the Ministry of Information and Broadcasting. As mentioned by Thomas (1993), the long years of centralized control is reflected in its overly cautious approach to programming, its extreme sensitivity to criticism and its highly politicized environment. As a result, many Indians view Doordarshan as a propaganda apparatus for the ruling political party, and the credibility of the TV programs have been severely eroded (Singhal and Rogers, 1989). Although radio was the primary medium for broadcasting until the mid-1970s, the advent of TV literally led to the eclipse of radio and its downgrading as a national medium, and the vast potential for radio as a community medium has been neglected (Thomas, 1993).

After the Emergency declared in 1976–77, which imposed extreme media censorship, the Indian Parliament and the national press have often demanded that the government make broadcasting an autonomous body. The Janata government appointed a 12-member commission for policy recommendations, and the result was the Prasar Bharati Bill, which recommended a balance between commercial and public broadcasting. The Janata government delayed the issue, and by the time the bill was placed before the parliament, they had lost their majority and it was voted down. The Prasar Bharati Bill was ultimately passed in the parliament during the regime of the National Front Government, with 70 amendments. Beginning in 1980, Doordarshan started to show gradual commercialization of its airtime by accepting broadcast programs from independent producers and advertisers. Its educational and public service programming was slowly replaced by advertising-sponsored films, series, sports and other programs. The broadcasting hours increased, and more airtime was open to independent producers.

Programming Competition

In spite of all the competition from the new multichannel media, Doordarshan still dominates the Indian media industry, as satellite TV is still largely limited to an urban middle-class audience, reaching only 10 million households compared with Doordarshan's reach of 40 million households nationwide (Ninan, 1995a). Nevertheless, Doordarshan is feeling the heat from its competitors. In an attempt to block the flow of advertising revenue to other channels, Doordarshan introduced regional language services and Doordarshan Metro, an entertainment channel with some current affairs and business programs. The sponsored programs from notable independent producers, such as Nimbus and Plus Channels with high production qualities, attracted huge advertising revenues and were very successful (Ray and Jacka, 1996).

To compete for audiences' attention, Doordarshan has also become bolder, venturing into the areas of personal relationships that were considered taboo. The series genre increased in number and moved thematically from the mythological and historical to family-oriented and dealing with contemporary issues; several business programs were introduced in cadence with the liberalization of the economy; fitness, health, talk and game shows also appeared to appease the public's demand (Ray and Jacka, 1996).

Growth and Strategic Alliances

As the major Indian media companies race to stay in power, the overall media and communications industry has reached a milestone in its economic development (Da Cunha, 1995; Eve of the battle, 1996). Television entrepreneurship has developed at various levels, and salaries in Indian journalism have risen as many print journalist opt for a better future in TV (Ninan, 1995b). The local entrepreneurs and foreign investors are focusing on local TV production to serve India's expanding TV market with plans for new satellite channels and infrastructure. A few big industrial groups have formed strategic alliances with foreign partners such as Falcon Group Holding of the United States and Canal Plus of France. The Home TV channel, an English- and Hindi-language entertainment channel, was launched in April 1996 by Carlton Communication, which is a joint venture of the Hindustan Times group, Pearson of the United Kingdom, and TVB of Hong Kong. Pearson and TVB each has a 15 percent stake, and the rest is held by Schroder Capital Partners and Hindustan Times (Dalaya and Atkinson, 1996). Also in the horizon are joint ventures for TV production involving companies like the United States–based cable TV giant, Telecommunications Inc. (TCI), and News Corporation's Star TV to introduce a sports channel (Keenan, 1995). American telecommunications giant, AT&T, is also working on a cable TV partnership in India (Amdur, 1995).

The privatization of media properties has been high on the agenda of economic liberalization in India. Industrial giants such as Tatas, Birlas, and the Reliance group, as well as the established media firms like Goenka, have increased their hold over culture and information industries in India. Tatas, the largest industrial group in India, has substantial holdings in business publications, telecommunications equipment manufacturing, advertising and public relations, music industry, and the software and hardware market (Thomas, 1993). Multinational media corporations like News Corporation also stood to gain from the liberalization. In July 1993, News Corporation bought controlling shares in Star TV, and in December 1993 it owned 49 percent of the equity in Zee TV, one of the active media firms in India (Ninan 1995b). Star TV has already invested U.S.$12 million (Sunderesan, 1996) in purchasing real estate in Bombay to house its entire production facilities. It is spending a further $3.4 million (Sunderesan, 1996) to import digital equipment. Peripheral companies such as United Software Communications (which manages UTV and Star TV owns 40 percent of UTV) have also set up integrated studio facilities in the same area.

The Development of the Advertising Industry

The trend of economic liberalization has triggered a rapid development in the supporting segments of the advertising industry. There are now professional advertising research firms, and advertising agencies are venturing into program buying and hiring media planning consultants. The increase in the volume of advertising has increased the number of commercial films made in India to an estimated 25–30 percent of growth in 1994 (Ninan, 1995b). The average production budget for commercial films, which was around Rs 400,000–800,000, increased to about Rs 800,000–2,000,000 (Ninan, 1995b). Among all media, TV took the highest share from the overall advertising revenue pie. Between 1985 and 1992 the total media share spent on TV grew from 12 percent to 20 percent (Ninan, 1995b). The share of press advertising dropped from 75 percent to 67 percent, of radio from 4 percent to 2.5 percent, and of films from 3 percent to 0.5 percent (Ninan, 1995b). Newspapers, in response to competition from TV, introduced larger and brighter color supplements during the weekends and also added personality- and gossip-oriented coverage. Indian newspapers, once obsessed with just politics, have started publishing business news. Economic newspapers have enlarged sections on investments and other special features. Yet, as Ninan (1995a) observes, with the availability of all these new media, the literate population still reads newspapers and uses them as the source of in-depth information.

The Ripple Effect on Film

The TV revolution has also affected the film industry. The new TV and peripheral businesses have caused a significant change in Bombay's entertainment industry. The programming need created by cable and satellite TV is providing a boom to production houses and the city, once the center of India's filmmaking industry (Young, 1996). There is an increasing demand for both made-for-TV and film-based programming. Given that satellite TV beams also into neighboring countries, the film exports are improving because of the larger regional audience in the Indian subcontinent.

Emerging Media Economic Issues in India

In a country where there is poverty and illiteracy, TV is the major influential medium, and accordingly, the impact of the technology has been felt tremendously via this medium. The new market-driven multichannel TV expansion has opened the door to the world's largest middle-class population. Major multinational media corporations are eyeing this untapped population and its advertising potential (Ninan, 1995a). With increased privatization, these multinational corporations, armed with the global TV networks such as Star TV, provide advertising opportunities for Indian businesses to attract overseas investors, many of them of Indian heritage.

One concern about this rapid commercialization is the role of public broadcasting services. As pointed out by Thomas (1993), the trans-border information flows have presented India with a number of problems, including the impact of direct broadcast satellite on national sovereignty, culture and lifestyle and the legal concerns of advertising impacts and revenue. How this will affect India is an area that needs to be addressed at length in the future. The government is already taking steps to address the dangers of further segmenting the population. For example, it has banned tobacco and alcohol advertisements and worked on maintaining the public broadcasting system to avoid further marginalization of the poor in India. As Ninan (1995a) and Thomas (1993) reflect, economic liberalization does have its benefits, but market-oriented competition can skew a nation's priorities, further marginalizing segments of society that are already on the margin. The arrival of new media choices in India may result in further inequality in its society. The policy-makers will have to work on achieving a balance between the two.

References

Amdur, M. (1995). Passage to India: Full steam ahead. *Broadcasting & Cable,* January, pp. 10

Chandra, A. (1994). Appealing to the Arabs. *India Today,* July, p. 56.

Chandra, A. (1994). Music mania. *India Today,* November, p. 58.

Chatterjee, S., and Ghose, S. (1996). Star trekking ahead: Murdoch meets Dave Gowda with big plans for India. *Outlook,* July, p. 72.

Da Cunha, U. (ed.) (1984). *Indian Cinema, 83–84.* New Delhi: National Film Development Corporation.

Da Cunha, U. (1995). New faces on India TV map. *Variety,* October, p. 88.

Dalaya, A., and Atkinson, C. (1996). Carlton close to signing deal for launch in India. *Broadcast,* March, p. 11.

Dawtrey, W. (1994). Fremantle inks deal in India. *Variety,* October, p. 66.

Dharap, B. (1983). *Indian films 1983.* Pune: National Film Archive.

Eve of battle: Indian television. (1996). *The Economist,* April, p. 67.

Indian Market Research Bureau (1994). Doordarshan and industry estimates. *Business Today,* October, p. 8.

Karthigesu, R. (1994). Broadcasting deregulation in developing Asian nations: An examination of nascent tendencies using Malaysia as a case study. *Media, Culture & Society* 16(1):73–90.

Keenan, F. (1995). Anyone for doubles? Sports channels debate whether to play together. *Far Eastern Economic Review,* October, p. 90.

Masani, M. (1976). *Broadcasting and the People.* New Delhi: National Book Trust.

Mehta, D. (1980). *Mass Communication and Journalism in India.* Newbury Park: Sage.

Ministry of Information and Broadcasting (1995). *Mass Media in India 1994–95.* New Delhi: Publications Division, Government of India.

Ministry of Information and Broadcasting (1989). *Mass Media in India 1988–89.* New Delhi: Publications Division, Government of India.

Mitra, A. (1993). *Television and Popular Culture in India.* New Delhi: Sage Publications.

National Film Development Corporation (1992). *Value of shipping bills passed through NFDC—Language wise export of titles.* Bombay: NFDC.

Ninan, S. (1995a). Transforming television in India. *Media Studies Journal* 9(3):43–51.

Ninan, S. (1995b). *Through the Magic Window: Television and Change in India.* New Delhi: Penguin Books.

Pendakur, M., and Subramanyam, R. (1996). Indian cinema beyond national borders. In: Sinclair, J., Jacka, E., and Cunningham, S. (eds.). *New Patterns in Global Television: Peripheral Vision.* Oxford: Oxford University Press, pp. 67–82.

Ray, M., and Jacka, E. (1996). Indian television: An emerging regional force. In: Sinclair, J., Jacka, E., and Cunningham, S. (eds.). *New Patterns in Global Television: Peripheral Vision.* Oxford: Oxford University Press, pp. 83–100.

Sarkar, J. (1993). India reacts to cable TV: Channels increased to fight influx of "alien culture." *Far Eastern Economic Review,* July, pp. 33–34.

Singhal, A., and Rogers, E. (1989). *India's Information Revolution.* New Delhi: Sage Publications.

Singhal, A., Doshi, J., Rogers, E., and Rahman, A. (1988). The diffusion of television in India. *Media Asia* 15:222–229.

Sunderesan, S. (1996). Forget Timkur, it's Mumbai now: Star TV. *The Hindustan Times,* June 29, p. 5.

Thomas, P. (1993). Broadcasting and the state in India: Towards relevant alternatives. *Gazette* 51(1):19–33.

Vohra, P. (1996). PM says yes but puts conditions. *The Hindustan Times*, June 20, p. 4.

Young, D. (1996). In India it's Bombay-watch (introduction of cable TV in Indian city). *Variety,* February, pp. 43–44.

17

CHINA

Yiu-Ming To

The Marketization of Media in China: Economic Freewheeling in a Political Straitjacket

Given its 1.2 billion population and fast-growing economy, China is potentially one of the largest markets for trade and investment. Despite being an underdeveloped nation with per capita gross domestic product of U.S.$540, its growth momentum has been spectacular in the past 17 years (Bottom line, 1997; *Asia 1996 Yearbook*). Since economic reforms were implemented in the late 1970s, China has experienced phenomenal economic growth at an average annual rate of 9.6 percent from 1980 to 1993. The tremendous growth in exports, especially of manufactured goods, greatly enhances its financial and consumption power. China has now become the eighth largest exporter of manufactured products in the world. With domestic savings at an enviable rate of 40 percent of gross domestic product, China's capacity in both investment and consumption has not been fully utilized (China looming, 1996; Focus on China, 1996).

Though reform policies have been adopted to boost economic growth in the past two decades, mass media had long been isolated from market influence. Until recently, the media market was just a contradiction in terms in socialist China. Under Communist rule since 1949, China's media have long been dressed in economic and political straitjackets, which inhibit growth of the media market. Politically, the irresistible role of mass media as the official mouthpiece of the ruling party presumes monopolized control of the press by the government. Financially, the practice of planned economy restrains media from depending on funding sources other than government subsidy. Plus the factor of prohibitive legislation, the possibility of incorporating a private press is ruled out. In the overwhelming presence of the ruling party as the concurrent regulator, owner and operator of media (Chu, 1994; Chang, 1995), media are deprived of their political and economic lifelines for independence from government interference. A competitive marketplace for media was nonexistent.

Even with economic reforms coming of age in the 1980s, mass media reforms have been mainly concerned with noneconomic issues. Relieved from being exploited as a tool for intraparty political struggle, media are now redeployed as the state's vehicle for serving the nation's noble goal: modernization. The effectiveness of mass media in serving modernization topped the agenda of both officials and media personnel. The internal management of media, editorial skills, communication technologies, audience-orientation, and media education and training, among others, are major areas of concern. Although technical progress can be easily noted, the media system, political and economic, remains intact (Chu, 1986, 1989; Hong and Cuthbert, 1991).

Especially in the aftermath of the repression of the 1989 democratic movement, the Chinese government consciously tightened up control of the media. The overwhelming importance of the press as the party organ was reemphasized. Noncompliant editorial staff have been sacked, and reform plans shelved. To avoid suspicion by the central authority, media personnel are cautious not to initiate any change of media practice. They are under the political surveillance of the Chinese Communist Party (CCP). Media are being held back to an age of strict censorship, the reverse of moving toward liberalization and marketization (Chang, 1995; He, 1993). The turn of the political tide, however, has reinstated economic liberalization.

After 2.5 years of political tightening and economic entrenchment, the post–June 4 leadership relaunched economic reforms at an accelerated rate and with a wider scope in 1992. To mark a new start in its resuscitated push for economic growth, the CCP committed itself during the 14th Party Congress to building a "socialist market economy" (Bachman, 1994, 1995). The unconventional "marriage" between "socialism" and "market economy" is telling. It characterizes the Chinese thinking of economic development without political reform. In the course of national development, economic liberalization can be achieved without concurrently introducing political democratization. The reform is at once radical and conservative. On one hand, the party shows great tolerance to marketization, to the extent that the socialist state is prepared to accept the market as a legitimate vehicle for coordinating economic activities. On the other hand, the political status quo is kept absolutely intact. Power will continue to be retained in the hands of the CCP. Neglecting the need for concurrent changes of the political system, the new round of reform is set to be purely economic (China: A funny-looking tiger, 1996; Wong, 1994; Perry, 1993).

The urge for market reforms can be well understood by looking at the urgency to lessen the substantial financial burden of state enterprises on the government. From 1990 to 1995, the percentage of money-losing state enterprises rose from 27.6 percent to 43 percent. The amount of losses also increased from Renminbi Yuan (RMB) $18 billion to RMB$88.3 billion (Will the reform, 1996).

The media industry, being no exception, is not immune to the irresistible national policy of marketization without political reform. The nationwide call to build a socialist market economy grants media firms the legitimacy to endorse market measures to sort out economic difficulties (Chan, 1993; He, 1996; Chen, 1996). Though the political status quo is unchanged, media are allowed to acquire a new economic status as self-financing enterprises. Unlike industrial firms, which are grouped as units of enterprise and tasked with promoting socialist economic functions, media institutions are traditionally termed as units serving public purposes. They are tasked with public functions, including publicizing government and party policies, educating the public and mobilizing the masses. They are assessed by how well they produce social benefits as defined by the state, rather than by how much profits they make. The raison d'être for media is their being the ideological vehicle exclusively under state control. In return, the state fully finances their operations.

With unparalleled importance attached to politics, media economics was not an issue in the past (Chang, 1995). But the advent of market reforms since 1992 has sent shock waves to media. In addition to complying with party policies, media firms are under the new command of gearing toward a kind of financially self-reliant enterprise. They are retained as the party organ to serve public functions as directed by the government, but with the continuing huge budget deficits, the state cannot afford unlimited subsidies to a growing number of media firms. They are set free on the business side. Like other state enterprises heading toward marketization, media are responsible for establishing their own economic lifeline in the market, with the aim of phasing out state subsidies eventually. Accordingly, priority concern is given to revenue-generating business strategies and activities. Advertising becomes more important. Media contents are more audience oriented. They also carry out public relations functions to solicit new sources of sponsorship. New media ventures are launched. To create more sources of revenue, media managers are also keen to look for new business opportunities, ranging from entertainment, business consultancy and market surveys to real estate development (He, 1993; Chan, 1993; Chen and Huang, 1996). A new operating environment is in the making.

Major Media in China: Reform Initiatives and Constraints

Neither marketization in nonmedia businesses nor media reforms in noneconomic issues could claim novelty to China by the early 1990s. What is unprecedented is the autonomy authorized by the totalitarian regime to media for pursuing their own economic interests. Given free hands on the economic fronts, major media industries have achieved tremendous growth since 1992, after the second wave of economic reforms toward a socialist market economy was whistled to kick off.

The longest-serving mass media in Communist China, newspaper, has attained phenomenal growth. The number of newspapers grew 50 percent from 1,487 in 1990 to 2,108 in early 1995. By 1993, the number of daily newspapers rose to 398 with a total daily print-run of 50.5 million, representing growth of 137 percent in number and a 43.5 percent increase in circulation in 10 years. Such a huge expansion, however, cannot hide the fact that the daily-newspaper reading population stayed at as low as 42 per 1,000 residents. Newspaper remains a medium mostly restricted to political elites, business people and part of the urban population. They are state-run enterprises under the control of CCP's Propaganda Department (*China Journalism Yearbook 1994*; The News Survey and Research Group of the Propaganda Department of the Central Committee of the Chinese Communist Party, 1996). But market reforms did bring forth the ascendancy of local newspapers. With more reader-friendly contents, they reported substantial increases in both circulation and profits. Of the 10 newspapers with the highest advertising sales in 1994, for instance, seven were city newspapers. The rest consists of two provincial and one national newspaper (*The People's Daily,* a publication of CCP's Central Committee) (Chen and Huang, 1996). The relative decline of national newspapers is patent, if not inevitable.

Unlike newspapers, broadcast television (TV) is the most popular mass medium, which can reach 85 percent of the population. By mid-1995, nine of 10 urban households owned a TV set. More than 800 million people, one-third living in urban areas, watched prime-time TV programs. Innovations of TV programs aside, the fast growth in TV stations contributed to the growing popularity of TV. From 1978 to 1992, TV stations grew from 32 to 586. On the basis of such an enormous growth, nearly 400 new stations were launched in the subsequent three years (Zhang, 1996). As state-run enterprises, all TV broadcasters are classified and administered by a four-tier system of state governance, ranging from national to provincial to municipal to county level. At each level, broadcasters are under the joint supervision of both government and party departments. The Ministry of Broadcasting, Film and Television (MBFT) handles regulatory and administrative issues, and the CCP's Propaganda Department is responsible for imposing political and ideological control as dictated by the party (Yang et al., 1994).

Compared with newspapers and broadcast TV, the growth of the cable TV industry is even more amazing. Originally designed as a transmission network to enhance the signals and enlarge the footprint of broadcast TV, cable TV has now developed into business entities operated by local government authorities. It started from scratch in the mid-1980s and mushroomed swiftly to more than 1,200 systems by mid-1995 with a total of 30 million subscribers. The enormous growth can be attributed to the keen interests of local authorities created by the all-out drive toward making profits, in response to the central government's call for market reform.

The traditional role of cable TV as a transmitter of better broadcast signals gave way to the new role of program providers catering to the local audience. A cable system offers a host of signals from national as well as local stations. To cater to the special needs of the local audience, it also earmarks a few channels for special programs, either self-produced or acquired abroad, such as western films, music videos, sports and variety shows. Given the range of choices and their relatively low operating costs, cable TV systems present themselves as a viable and competent contender for the TV market in China (Liu et al., 1994; Zhang, 1996). For a country as large as China, which is composed of more than 4,000 counties, the present status of the network industry leaves much room for further expansion in the future.

In stark contrast to the past, when media were synonymous with party-controlled media working with the unanimous aim of publicizing state policies, media today perform multiple functions for their audience, ranging from politics to entertainment. The sweeping changes briefly mentioned here are seen to be driven by the revived momentum for market reforms inaugurated by the top party leadership. They provide essential political support to media in their endeavor to push aside obstacles obstructing economic reform. The new accomplishments in media commercialization, however, also hinge on the changing needs of the audience and the growing dependence of media on advertising revenues, among others.

As marketization proceeded at full speed in the 1990s, the advertising industry has also accelerated. It has grown at an unprecedented rate, much faster than the pace of the overall economic growth. From 1990 to 1994, the average annual growth rate of advertising expenses stood at as high as 70 percent. The momentum of growth continued in 1995 when media received a total advertising revenue of RMB$27.4 billion, representing a further increase of 37 percent. Of the total turnover of RMB$13 billion from the newspaper industry in 1994, RMB$5 billion, or 40 percent, came from advertising revenues. The financial reliance on advertising is even greater for commercially successful papers, whose advertising revenues take a lion's share of up to 75 percent of the total income (Wei, 1996; *China Journalism Yearbook 1994*). In broadcast TV, the substantial increase in advertising income sidelined the importance of state subsidies for the industry. The more they get from advertisers, the less they are paid by the government. Estimates have it that in 1994, the total advertising income of close to RMB$5 billion was more than double the amount of state grants earmarked for broadcasting stations.

Especially in more economically developed regions such as Shanghai, state subsidies have dropped to an insignificant level, amounting to just 5 percent of advertising revenues. In 1995, three newspapers and one TV station each earned an advertising revenue of more than RMB$300 million, accounting for 60 percent to 80 percent of their total revenue (Wei, 1996). The success of some media in going financially independent speaks to the fact that the booming advertising industry can take up the former government role of financing media. The change of funding sources, however, also implies that the CCP's monopolized power of control over media is now shared by advertisers. In their choice of media, advertising effectiveness takes precedence over the political authority of the media concerned.

The rising power of advertisers also asserts the concept of the audience as consumers, who emerge as a shaping force in media industry. As the economic environment improved in the 1990s, urban consumers, especially those living in eastern China, are empowered to become active purchasers in the consumer market (Contrasting consumers, 1996). Although China is still far from developed, its huge population with growing purchasing power represents a huge market potential to be tapped. It also breeds the ground for the growing use of mass media as the marketing channel to reach potential consumers.

The competition for advertising revenue makes China's media much more audience responsive. In recent years, audience surveys have been widely used by various media, electronic and print, central and local. Some are employed to assess the general pattern of media use and audience preferences of various media and types of contents. Other surveys serve specific media, ascertaining their audience profile and soliciting feedback to their performance (Market survey firms, 1996). One survey noted the wide diversity of preferences among audiences from different regions. Beijing residents considered current affairs top on their agenda of concern. Interest in the stock market is highest in Shanghai. Readers are found to favor newspapers published in their own regions more than those from elsewhere (*Ming Pao,* September 22, 1996). Sensational news, according to another survey on newspaper readers, is losing popularity or even perceived as repulsive. Audiences prefer more coverage on domestic accidents and disasters, government reshuffles, and state policies and laws. They aspire that the press can practice critical reporting and unveil malpractice by corrupt officials (Yu, 1995). Being politically correct is not enough. To boost audienceship, media managers realize that they should learn more about the audience and take heed of their needs.

The invincible move toward marketization, however, proceeds under the political confines set by the totalitarian regime. The CCP maintains itself as the strongest player in the emerging media market. The traditional role of the party-led government as concurrently the regulator, owner and operator of media remains unchanged (Chu, 1994). As the lawmaker, the party continues to set rules and regulations for media to comply with. Media and their journalists are constantly under threat, both physical and psychological, in the presence of strict rules such as the National Security Act and the Keeping State Secret Act. The public is banned from receiving satellite broadcasts without prior authorization by the state.

The booming cable TV industry is pulled into the orbit of surveillance under the Ministry of Broadcasting, Film and Television (Mainland Affairs Council of the Executive Yuan, 1994; Yang et al., 1994; Liu et al., 1994). Apart from the political effect of the state controlling by the flow of information, media law also entrenches the monopoly status of government in media. At present, only the government or party units can apply for a license to run a media firm. Nongovernment corporates, not to say individual persons, are barred from launching any media business on their own. The fact that the ownership of media firm is monopolized by the state and the party means that media are subject to a triple control mechanism. In addition to legal control from outside, media as state-run enterprises are under corporate control by government officials. They are in turn liable to the political control of party discipline in view of the inescapable reality that officials are party cadres. The unshakable identity of government official and party cadre as media owners strictly limits media's autonomy. Before the law reigns in, inappropriate contents could be self-censored or banned and personnel removed by corporate managers (Yang et al., 1994; Liu et al., 1994).

Such a media control system can be further strengthened by a double-check scheme of CCP's internal surveillance. The whole nation is administered by a four-tier system of government, from central, provincial, municipal to county. Below the central level of governance, media are placed at the cross-point of two lines of command. On one hand, they are supervised by the propaganda department in the upper-tier system of governance. The central authority is reassured that when need arises, they can pass on instructions to media organizations at lower tiers. On the other hand, the local party committee and its propaganda department also enjoy an authority not only to oversee the media they own but also media that operate in the territory under their jurisdiction. Concurrently, media are co-supervised by the central as well as local organs of power (Chang, 1995). By enforcing a multilayered system of horizontal and vertical controls, the ruling party permeates its decisive influence on each level of media organizations.

Media Market Analysis: Growth in a State of Flux

For the past few years, market reforms in media have been undertaken within the unshaken totalitarian framework of CCP-led government. The central government continues to lay the ground rules. Audience-friendly content can be introduced. Local media exercise greater discretion in economic affairs. Money-making moves are encouraged and management measures renovated. Competition among government-owned media abounds in their race for audience and advertising support. But it is not an open market. Competition is under the CCP's control and dominance. The party leadership should be strictly followed. Politically sensitive issues are to be avoided or banned. The supply side of media market remains monopolized by either the government or party-run media. It is amid such a strange mix of market and anti-market elements that the Chinese media turn over a new leaf.

Newspaper

From 1978 onward, the newspaper industry has grown at a spectacular rate. On average, a new newspaper is launched every three days. By early 1995, the number of newspapers totaled 2,108, representing an 11-fold increase over a period of 16 years. The strong urge for launching newspapers is unstopped after a lengthy period of continuous expansion. Nearly 500 applications for newspaper licenses are awaiting approval by the State Bureau of News and Publications, not counting the hundreds of applications to register as internal newspapers with restricted circulation (The News Survey and Research Group of the Propaganda Department of the Central Committee of the Chinese Communist Party, 1996). More importantly, newspapers become diversified in content and form, catering to different needs of various groups of readers. Newspapers published by government and party bureaus still hold the leading position in terms of both influence and circulation. But in terms of number, their share is lowered to 30.6 percent of the total, second to newspapers published by economic departments, corporations and professional bodies (40.7 percent). At present, nearly one thousand newspapers specialize in covering economic issues and providing business information. Among newcomers since 1991, newspapers covering various sectors of economic activities account for the highest share (43 percent). Lifestyle newspapers and enterprise newspapers rank in second (17.6 percent) and third place (14 percent), respectively. The increase of newspapers published by government and party bureaus (11 percent) lags behind the overall rate of growth (Wu and Liao, 1996; Chen and Guo, 1996; The News Survey and Research Group of the Propaganda Department of the Central Committee of the Chinese Communist Party, 1996; *China Journalism Yearbook 1994*).

The growth trend signals the growing concern for economic and personal interests in the era of marketization. It also reflects the belated need to renovate newspapers with reader-oriented content and outlook. In 1995, *The People's Daily* started a regional East China edition to allow more flexibility in content and advertising. They launched a South China edition on July 1, 1997. The move appears to result from intensifying competition not only among newspapers but also among various media struggling for survival in the burgeoning market.

Market reforms in newspaper also lead to the rise of press conglomerates, especially in major cities. The original objective of the government policy for financial self-reliance is being seized by newspapers as a chance for increasing commercialization and corporatization. In addition to publishing a major newspaper and a chain of newspapers for various specialized interests, they branch out to related businesses from publications, printing, consultancy to advertising. Gradually, some go further into real estate, finance and other businesses. The Guangzhou Daily Group, the first press conglomerate established in 1995, for instance, is a powerful economic agent in South China. With a circulation of 600,000, the *Guangzhou Daily* generates an advertising income of RMB$500 million in 1995. The corporation also operates six special-interest newspapers from child care to football to the aged. With the government's blessing, they move on to run newsprint companies, printing firms, advertising agency and retailing chain stores (Kau, 1996; Li, 1996; Guangzhou Daily Social Affairs Committee, 1996). They also invest in filmmaking, the tourist industry and the property market. In Shanghai, three press groups—the Liberation Daily, the Wenhui Daily, and the Xinmin Evening Post—dominate the market. The coexistence among the three, however, lends credence to the belief that competition could lead to an all-win outcome. Their financial success earns them the resources for to take over money-losing newspapers. A similar trend of conglomeration can be detected in Beijing. Some city-based newspapers are set to follow suit (Wu, 1996; Zhou and Zhu, 1995; Yao, 1996).

The existing competition is not, however, an open game. Existing players are well protected by a high entry barrier to the market. By law, no foreign company is allowed to enter China's newspaper market either as an independent publisher or a joint-venture partner. Neither can Chinese locals publish a newspaper without the backing of any government or party organization and approval by the State Bureau of News and Publications (SBNP). In marketing and management, flexibility is also limited by state regulations. Newspapers have no right to determine their target readers and scope of distribution. These are determined by their supervising bodies (i.e., propaganda department or government ministries at the respective level) before a final proposal is submitted to the SBNP for approval.

In newspaper pricing, the state sets the price for seven national newspapers. Provincial authorities are empowered to set the price or price threshold for provincial-level newspapers. Only newspapers with small circulations and professional newspapers are allowed to set the price on their own. To add new supplements or pages, publishers must seek prior consent by SBNP. They are also required to file an application for approval 30 days before ad hoc changes to pages or contents are implemented. In circulation, most newspapers rely on the Post Office not only for delivery but also for recruiting subscribers. Only six kinds of newspapers, mostly party organs, are allowed to be distributed nationwide. Newspapers below the provincial level are restricted within the localities to which they belong (Mainland Affairs Committee of the Executive Yuan, 1994). From market accessibility to operational decisions, the newspaper industry is far from free from state intervention.

Broadcast Television

The evolution of TV from an official mouthpiece to business enterprise is equally striking. At present, all TV stations, from central, provincial, municipal to county level, continue to be state owned. Except the national broadcaster, China Central Television (CCTV), which is answerable to the MBFT, others are run by local bureaus of MBFT at respective levels of the four-tier structure of government. Nongovernmental bodies, domestic or foreign, are not allowed to set up a station. Traditionally each local bureau is authorized to establish one TV station in each locality with an exclusive footprint. Although they are required to show some programs produced by stations higher up the hierarchy, they are shielded from competition by other stations on the same level. Market reforms since 1992 by no means alter the monopoly structure of operations (Yang et al., 1994).

But the money-making imperative drives TV stations toward a new identity of a diversified commercial corporation. At the center of such a corporation is a TV station that relies mainly on advertising revenues. Core businesses are mostly information or media related, ranging from electronic database, audio–visual production, business consultancy to cable TV stations. Moving from the core, some invest heavily in a wide range of businesses. China Central

Television, the national broadcaster, for instance, operates restaurant, hotel and property businesses. Television stations have become centers of business conglomerates throughout China (Yang et al., 1994; Chan, 1993, 1996). Furthermore, aspiring to be commercially successful, these TV conglomerates are experimenting with new ideas, among them: formation of a second TV station, abolishing life-tenure employment practiced in state-owned enterprises, and a greater variety of programs.

The huge increase in TV stations breeds a great demand for TV programs to fill up the newly created airtime. In 1995, about 30 percent of programs were imported from abroad (Zhang, 1996). Others were self-produced or commissioned productions. Television stations also purchase profitable programs from outside producers. For instance, the China International Television Corporation, a subsidiary of CCTV, bought an epic drama series, *Wu Zetien,* for RMB$10 million. In return, they earned more than RMB$12 million from advertising proceeds from CCTV, excluding potential income from the sale of copyright to TV and cable TV stations. Presently, only CCTV and some of the 30 provincial-level stations have adequate resources to produce most of their programs. Others could normally produce 10 to 20 hours of programs per week. Below the provincial level, local stations produce less than 20 percent of their programs. The rest are rebroadcasts from CCTV and provincial stations. To reduce the reliance on the vertical flow of TV programs from higher-level stations, interprovincial and intercity stations each formed an organization to facilitate program exchanges among member stations. The former, named as China Provincial-Level TV Stations Shareholding Co., is joined by more than 30 stations, and the latter, named as City Stations' Cooperative, has more than 200 members. In 1991, 40,000 hours of programs were exchanged. On average, each received a total of 1,341 hours of programs or 3.5 hours per day (Zhang, 1996; Yang et al., 1994).

Apart from increasing imports of TV programs, China also takes the initiative to participate in international communication. The international channel of CCTV broadcasts more than 250 programs totaling 7,000 hours to 160 countries. It has also signed exchange agreements with more than 100 places (Zhang, 1996; Chan, 1996).

Cable TV Systems

In less than a decade, cable TV has been transformed from a subsidiary industry to an independent medium. It was first launched as a system for distributing TV programs to remote areas and improving the signal quality of broadcast TV for urban households. With the advent of media commercialization, cable system operators sidelined the business of signal transmission and turned themselves into program providers for the local audience. By 1995, licensed cable systems totaled 1,200, serving 35 million households. Each operates scores of channels and profits from both subscription and advertising proceeds (Zhang, 1996; Liu et al., 1994).

Cable TV systems are mostly city based, according to the state's plan of "one city, one system." They are incorporated into the four-tier network of government supervision. The Ministry of Broadcasting, Film and Television's bureaus at various levels of the government structure are designated to oversee the operation of cable systems at the respective levels. The government, unlike its western counterparts, is fearless of the growth of monopoly in allowing broadcast TV stations to operate cable systems, as both of them are state run. Cable TV programming is controlled by the government through regulations. Broadcast programs by various levels of TV stations constitute the major programming source for the systems. Some are even set down as must-carry items. Among them are news programs produced by CCTV and local stations and education programs directed by the State Commission of Education. On the other hand, cable TV is obligated to cater to audience needs of the locality it serves. Each week they are required to produce a news program of not less than 30 minutes to inform local audiences.

Other than these obligations, cable TV can offer a wide range of programs such as film, sports, TV drama, music video, and Chinese opera. Some programs are imported from Hong Kong, Taiwan and other countries. At present, the import threshold is set at one third of the total of China-made programs. Prior clearance by MBFT or its local office is needed for all imported programs. Satellite TV broadcasts are not allowed to be circulated via the system. Neither can TV programs from Hong Kong be carried in the systems, except in various cities in Guangdong (Chan, 1994; Liu et al., 1994).

Despite these restrictions, cable TV presents itself as a viable commercial venture. They run at a much lower cost than their broadcast counterparts, offer more choices of programs to the audience, and secure more sources of revenues. Beijing Cable TV Station (BCTVS), for instance, operates with an establishment of about 80 staff, just one tenth of the manpower of Beijing TV Station (BTVS) or CCTV. They carry all CCTV channels and five provincial TV stations, with a better visual quality, in addition to a wide range of programs of their own selections. Some are new TV drama series. Others are co-productions with various social groups. Their access to cable channels reflect the diverse interests of the community and help consolidate community support for the system. In 1996, BCTVS was aiming at reaching an audience of 1.5 million, who provided them with a steady income base and enhanced its attractiveness to advertisers. In Beijing, BCTVS is recognized as a powerful rival of CCTV and BTVS in both viewership and the advertising market. A similar situation is developing in other major cities of China (Zhang, 1996).

Emerging Issues in China's Media Economic Reform

The Chinese experience in the economic reforms of mass media is peculiar. Control coexists with chaos. Market reforms are conducted within an obsolete political system of totalitarian control. Media are run by official and semi-official bodies approved by the state. The pre-condition for a publication license is total compliance with the state's policies and politics. Their operations are co-supervised by various levels of the MBFT and the CCP's propaganda department in the four-tier structure of government. For mass media, any violation of government and party policies, especially concerning political issues, invites stiff penalty to the extent that the license is canceled (Chan, 1995; Chang, 1995; W. Lee, 1996).

Equally repressive measures are also employed to control the international flow of information. Cross-border broadcasts and publications are subject to strict restrictions. Foreign companies are not allowed to engage in the media business. Even economic information supplied by foreign news agencies has to be processed and cleared by the Xinhua News Agency before feeding into China (Censorship or economic common sense, 1996). The omnipresence of government influence reassures the central leadership that commercialized party organs are still in their firm grips. Competition does not give rise to an enlarged public sphere for political free speech.

On the other hand, economic reforms in mass media have opened the floodgate for malpractice that causes confusions and undermines market principles. With the dependence on advertising proceeds growing, media are open to abuse by its advertisers negligently or intentionally. Misleading advertisements with exaggerated or even false claims are rampant. Usually they are widely published for a period in which the advertisers launch a city-wide campaign promoting the products. Some publishers, attracted by the advertising expenses, do not bother to validate the advertised contents. Consumers are set to lose. In Guangzhou during the first half of 1996, for instance, 328 advertisements were found to be giving false information (W. Lee, 1996).

The rise of paid journalism also corrupts the integrity of mass media. It is widely practiced and condemned that money in "red packets" is paid to reward journalists who interview the manager of an enterprise. Newspapers are also keen to organize special supplements or feature articles to promote a region, an enterprise, or an entrepreneur and in return solicit sponsorship from the interviewed subjects (A *People's Daily* commentator, 1996; Siu, 1996; Wang,

1996) . The frantic abuses have caused grave concern among the public. One survey reveals that as much as 78 percent of respondents believe that economic rewards in cash and in kind by subjects of reporting assignments constitute the major part of a reporter's income. The majority of the public (61 percent) regards paid journalism as a disservice to the credibility of mass media, and 47 percent think that paid journalism degrades the moral standard of journalists (The Editing and Writing Group for Contemporary Professional Ethics of Journalism, 1996a, 1996b).

The decline of reliability aside, market irregularities are observed in mass media as a result of ineffective law enforcement and lack of professional ethics. Infringement of copyrights is widespread in print and electronic media products. Some cable channels and even some broadcast stations in remote areas are seen to have shown unauthorized foreign films and video productions. Newspapers are also found to carry pirated stories and articles copied from other newspapers and publications. The book market is no exception. Numerous works by prominent Chinese writers and translations of western bestsellers are among major subjects of copyright infringement. The copyright of one Chinese writer's works, for instance, was infringed 108 times by 30 publishers in 1995 (Yang et al., 1994; Lau, 1994; *Communist China Yearbook,* 1996).

Competition is fierce but restricted and unfair. Nongovernmental bodies, corporates or individuals are barred from joining the market race. Competition occurs among state-run media. The four-tier system of mass media delineates the scope of distribution and fences off competition among media on the same level. It also prohibits mass media from launching new ventures beyond their home areas. Local monopoly is protected and strengthened. The show of power preponderates over the show of ability in market competition. In newspaper subscribers recruitment, for instance, some compete not with content but with the power of the publishing authority. The more subsidiary offices under the leadership of the government department running the newspaper, the more subscriptions are guaranteed. The economic law of supply and demand gives way to administrative intervention.

Going marketized but leaving the political system untouched is never easy. It only works on the viability of separating economics from politics. The experience of media economic reforms in China testifies well the difficulty in achieving a full-fledged market economy in a totalitarian institution. The dual role of government as regulator and market player poses a dilemma for the government to be an impartial referee of the market. It also affects its commitment to the rule of law, given government's vested interests in the media business. On the other hand, resorting to administrative means by media managers deemphasizes the importance of playing by the rule of fair competition.

Dissemination of distorted information because of advertising malpractice and paid journalism impairs media's credibility. It also unfairly places readers in an inferior position in the market. If such abuses do not stop, advertisers and mass media alike are condemned to lose audience support. Eventually, it will adversely affect their long-term interests, as well as the growth of market economy. Fair competition, the rule of law and access to accurate information, among others, are the cornerstone of market economy. There is no reason that the socialist market economy in China should be an exception.

References

Asia 1996 Yearbook (1996). Hong Kong: Far Eastern Economic Review.

Bachman, D. (1994). China in 1993—Dissolution, frenzy, and/or breakthrough? *Asian Survey* 34(1), January.

Bachman, D. (1995). China in 1994—Marking time, making money. *Asian Survey* 35(1), January.

Bottom line (1997). *Asiaweek,* February 21.

Censorship or economic common sense? (1996) *China Media* 4(2), March.

Chan, J. M. (1993). Commercialization without independence: Trends and tensions of media development in China. In: *China Review.* Hong Kong: The Chinese University Press.

Chan, J. M. (1994). Media internationalization in China: Processes and tensions. *Journal of Communication* 44(3), Summer.

Chan, J. M. (1995). Calling the tune without paying the piper: The reassertion of media controls in China. In: Lo, C. K., and Brosseau, M. (eds.). *China Review.* Hong Kong: The Chinese University Press.

Chan, J. M. (1996). Television in greater China: Structure, exports, and market formation. In: Sinclair, J., JAcka, E., and Cunningham, S. (eds.). *New Patterns in Global Television: Peripheral Vision.* New York: Oxford University Press.

Chang, T. M. (1995). An analysis of the current situation of the news businesses in mainland China. In: *The General Situation of the News Businesses in Mainland China.* Taiwan: Mainland Affairs Council of the Executive Yuan, June.

Chen, H., and Guo, Z. (1996). The double faces of China's media under reform: A media sociology perspective on the commercialization of China's media content. A paper presented at the Annual Convention of Association for Education in Journalism and Mass Communication, Anaheim, CA.

Chen, H., and Huang, Y. (1996) A study of the uneven development of mass media commercialization in mainland China. *Mass Communication Review* 53 (July):191–208.

Chen, X. (1996) A study of the distribution task in the "big market." *News Reporter,* Shanghai, May, pp. 32–34. Quoted from *Journalism Quarterly,* a reprint of newspapers and publications information compiled by the Books and Publications Information Centre of the People's University of China, Beijing.

China: A funny-looking tiger (1996). *The Economist*, August 17.

China Journalism Yearbook 1994. Beijing: The China Journalism Yearbook Publication House.

China looming (1996). *The Economist*, August 17.

Chu, L. L. (1986). Press freedom under the five-star flag: Constants and variables of press reform in Communist China. *Ming Pao Monthly,* February, pp. 32-39.

Chu, L. L. (1989). The Chinese Communist press reform and communication strategies. *Hong Kong Economic Journal Monthly,* September, pp. 60-69.

Chu, L. L. (1994). Continuity and change in China's media reform. *Journal of Communication* 44(3), Summer.

Contrasting consumers (1996). *China News Analysis*, No. 1557, April 1.

The current situation of the news publications business in mainland China and problems being faced. In: *Communist China Yearbook 1996.* Taipei: Chinese Communist Studies Publication House

The Editing and Writing Group for Contemporary News Professional Ethics (1996a). A survey of the current situation of news professional ethics. *Journalism University,* Shanghai, Summer, pp. 41–46. Quoted from *Journalism Quarterly,* a reprint of newspapers and publications information compiled by the Books and Publications Information Centre of the People's University of China, Beijing.

The Editing and Writing Group for Contemporary News Professional Ethics (1996b). A survey of the current situation of news professional ethics; report put forward by four journalism faculties and departments. *News Reporter,* Shanghai, April, pp. 9–11. Quoted from *Journalism Quarterly,* a reprint of newspapers and publications information compiled by the Books and Publications Information Centre of the People's University of China, Beijing.

Focus on China (1996). *Far Eastern Economic Review,* August 29.

Guangzhou Daily Social Affairs Committee (1996). Establishing a modern socialist press conglomerate; searching for a new path for the reform and development of the newspaper industry in China. *Journalism University,* Shanghai, Summer, pp. 12–15. Quoted from *Journalism Quarterly,* a reprint of newspapers and publications information compiled by the Books and Publications Information Centre of the People's University of China, Beijing.

He, Z. (1993). Press freedom in mainland China: Past, present and future. A paper presented at the Conference on Chinese Communication Studies and Education, Tao Yuen, Taiwan.

He, Z. (1996). Behind the big distribution battle of mainland newspapers. *Hong Kong Economic Journal,* February 23.

Hong, J., and Cuthbert, M. (1991). Media reform in China since 1978: Background factors, problems and future trends. *Gazette* 47:141–158.

Kau, C. Y. (1996). *Guangzhou Daily* pioneers conglomerated business operation. *Ming Pao Monthly,* July.

Lee, W. (1996). Loopholes everywhere in newspaper advertisements. *Hong Kong Economic Journal,* June 18.

Lee, Y. (1996). The Chinese Communist Party stresses the importance of political scrutiny. *Ming Pao,* December 23.

Li, G. (1996). The first press conglomerate earned RMB$800 million in a year. *China Youth Post,* Beijing, May 7, 1996. Quoted from *Journalism Quarterly,* a reprint of newspapers and publications information compiled by the Books and Publications Information Centre of the People's University of China, Beijing.

Liu, Y. L., Liu, Y. L., Lin, M. W., Lin, C. Y., Chen, M. H., and Choi, E. L. (1994). *The Current Situation of Cable Television in Mainland China and a Study of Regulatory Policies.* Taiwan: Mainland Affairs Council of the Executive Yuan, June.

Mainland Affairs Council of the Executive Yuan (1994). A study of the investment environment of mass communication businesses in mainland China: publications. Taiwan, August.

Market survey firms and China's media boom (1996). *China Media* 4(1), January/February.

Newspaper, television, broadcasting: the three major mass media dominate the urban cultural life (1996). *Ming Pao,* September 22.

The News Survey and Research Group of the Propaganda Department of the Central Committee of the Chinese Communist Party (1996). *A Survey of the Total Quantity, Structure and Cost-Effectiveness of the Newspaper Industry in China.* Beijing: Xinhua Publishing House.

Over 800 kinds of newspapers take up distribution on their own (1996). *Ming Pao,* December 7.

A *People's Daily* commentator (1996). Strengthen professional ethics, forbid "paid journalism" in *People's Daily,* May 8. Quoted from *Journalism Quarterly,* a reprint of newspapers and publications information compiled by the Books and Publications Information Centre of the People's University of China, Beijing.

Perry, E. J. (1993). China in 1992: An experiment in neo-authoritarianism. *Asian Survey,* 33(1), January.

Siu, B. (1996). Vividly making up false news, reputation of Guangdong newspapers damaged. *Ming Pao,* September 12.

Starck, K., and Xu, Y. (1988). Loud thunder, small raindrops: The reform movement and the press in China. *Gazette* 42:143–159.

Starr, J. B. (1996). China in 1995: Mounting problems, waning capacity. *Asian Survey* 36(1), January.

Survey of Chinese Media (1996). *China Media* 4(8), September.

To, Y. M. (1993). Information, market economy and press reforms—some preliminary theoretical explorations. A paper presented at Guangdong-Hong Kong Seminar on Culture and Economy, Guangzhou.

Wang, J. (1996). A commentary on the rise of "paid journalism" and ultimate cure. *The Academic Journal of Zhengzhou University,* February, pp. 118–120. Quoted from *Journalism Quarterly,* a reprint of newspapers and publications information compiled by the Books and Publications Information Centre of the People's University of China, Beijing.

Wei, R. (1996). A commentary on the interaction between the advertising industry and news media in China. Hong Kong: Radio Television Hong Kong. *Media Digest,* November, pp. 4–5.

Will the reform of state enterprises succeed? (1996). *China News Analysis*, No. 1569, October 1.

Wong, C. (1994). China's economy: the limits of gradualist reform. Boulder, CO: Westview Press.

Wu, G., and Liao, X. (1996). One regime, many voices: diversifying press structures in the reform China. A paper presented at Conference on Patterns of Communication in Cultural China, Hong Kong.

Wu, K. N. (1996). The newspaper industry heads towards conglomeration and opening up. *Ming Pao Monthly,* June.

Yang, C. H., Yang, C. H., Wang, Y. L., Yu, S. F., Su, H., Lin, Y. L., Yim, H. W., and Cheng, K. Y. (1994). A study of the investment environment of mass communication businesses in mainland China: broadcasting and television. Taiwan: Mainland Affairs Council of the Executive Yuan, September.

Yao, F. (1996). Thoughts relating to establishing press conglomerates. *Journalism University,* Shanghai, Spring, pp. 3–6. Quoted from *Journalism Quarterly,* a reprint of newspapers and publications information compiled by the Books and Publications Information Centre of the People's University of China, Beijing.

Yu, G. (1995). China's newspaper industry: facing a structural transformation—an overall analysis report of a nationwide newspaper readers survey. *The Monthly Journal of Newspapers and Publications in China,* Beijing, September, pp. 9–12. Quoted from *Journalism Quarterly,* a reprint of newspapers and publications information compiled by the Books and Publications Information Centre of the People's University of China, Beijing.

Yu, X. (1994) Professionalization without guarantees: Changes of the Chinese press in post-1989 years. *Gazette* 53:23–41.

Zhang, X. (1996). The current situation and problems of the television industry in China. *Journalism and Communication Studies,* January, pp. 11–17. Quoted from *Journalism Quarterly,* a reprint of newspapers and publications information compiled by the Books and Publications Information Centre of the People's University of China, Beijing.

Zhou, T., and Zhu, L. (1995). Press conglomerate: a scrutiny of the new phenomenon in the newspaper industry of China. *The Academic Journal of the Central China Polytechnic University,* Wuhan, April, pp. 61–63. Quoted from *Journalism Quarterly,* a reprint of newspapers and publications information compiled by the Books and Publications Information Centre of the People's University of China, Beijing.

18

JAPAN

KAZUMI HASEGAWA

From Domestic Print Media Conglomerates to International Joint Ventures

As an island nation located off the east coast of Asia, Japan's geographic area is 145,850 square miles (Famighetti, 1996), a little larger than the state of California. Ranges of rugged mountains run through nearly the full length of the country, and approximately 67 percent of the land is mountainous and covered by forests (Nippon Steel Corporation, 1984). Such terrain and mountainous geographic features have historically presented a challenge for national broadcasters. Owing to its geography, Japan's residential area accounts for only 3 percent of the land (Nippon Steel Corporation, 1984), which contributes to a highly crowded living environment (Famighetti, 1996). The country's congested situation can be illustrated by its population density of 860 per square mile, compared with the United States' 75 per square mile (Famighetti, 1996). In terms of ethnic diversity, 99.4 percent of the population is Japanese; other ethnic minorities (which are mostly Korean) account for only 0.6 percent (Famighetti, 1996). Therefore, all of the imported programs are dubbed with Japanese language except for imported theatrical movies.

Under its parliamentary democracy, the government of Japan is composed of three independent branches: legislative, administrative and judiciary. The Prime Minister, who is designated by the Diet (which is comparable to the Parliament in England), is the head of government. The Emperor, who is the head of the state, is declared as the symbol of Japan by the present constitution of Japan and has no governing power. The administrative power is bestowed on the Cabinet, which is comprised of the Prime Minister and 11 other ministers of state. Among them, the Ministry of Posts and Telecommunication (MPT) is responsible for the development of telecommunication (Maeno, 1993; Japan: From kabuki, 1989). The Broadcasting Bureau under the MPT is in charge of planning and implementing broadcasting policies and licensing and supervising broadcast stations (Broadcasting Bureau, 1997). The Machinery and Information Industries Bureau under the Ministry of International Trade and Industry (MITI) plays a major role in planning and implementing policies to facilitate the healthy development of the machinery and information industry (Machinery and Information, 1997).

Mass media play a significant role in the Japanese society. In 1992, the number of daily newspapers was 121, with a total circulation of 71,690,000 (UNESCO, 1995), which makes 1.7 per household. The total number of television (TV) sets in use in 1993 was 77,000,000 (UNESCO, 1995), which accounts for 1.8 sets per household. Thirty-three million five hundred forty-three thousand TV broadcasting licenses were issued in 1990 (UNESCO, 1995), which equals 0.8 per household. There were 113,500,000 radio receivers in use in 1993, making the radio diffusion rate 2.6 per household (UNESCO, 1995). There were 61,105,841 telephones in 1995 (Denki Tsushin, 1995), which accounts for 1.4 per household.

Table 18-1 shows the total revenue in various media industries (Financial affairs, 1996; Radio and television broadcasting, 1995).

During 1995, among all kinds of information-related communication industries, the greatest growth was seen in the telecommunication industry, up 47 percent from 1994, followed by terrestrial commercial broadcasting industry, up 9.8 percent, and cable TV (often called CATV in Japan) operators, up 12.3 percent (Ministry of Post and Telecommunication, 1996).

Japan is well known for its electronics, including color TV sets and videocassette recorders. Exports of color TVs reached 238,000 units in October 1996, with a 7.5 percent increase every year (Japan: VCR Imports, 1996). In addition to media appliances, Japan has become successful with exports of some media contents such as computer games and animation. Japan is not only the biggest producer but also the biggest consumer of computer games in the

Table 18-1. Total Revenue in Various Media Industries

	1994 (millions)	1995 (millions)
Newspaper	$19,388	$19,834
Broadcasting	$17,705	$19,105
Publishing	$20,618	N/A

world (Dawkins, 1996). In spite of its high popularity, however, only 12 percent of Japanese households own a personal computer (see Dawkins, 1996). Another emerging popular culture, Japanese animation (*anime*) has been gaining popularity among the world and has become the country's fastest growing cultural exports (Katayama, 1996). In the United States, the retail sales of Japanese animation reached an estimated $50 million in 1996, increased from $500,000 a year ago (Katayama, 1996).

In the last decade, the increasing popularity of U.S. films and music in Japan made the U.S. media properties attractive investment opportunities for Japanese multinational corporations. For example, Japan has become the largest video market for Hollywood film outside North America (McClure, 1996). The high profile acquisition of MCA Inc. by Matsushita Electric Industrial, manufacturer of Panasonic, Quasar, and Technics products (A Brief History, 1996; MCA/Universal, 1996) and Columbia and TriStar Pictures by Sony Picture Entertainment (Sony Corporation of America, 1997) triggered heated debates in the United States. Later in 1995, 80 percent of the controlling interest was transferred to the Seagram Company Ltd., one of the world's leading consumer beverage companies.

Major Media Industries in Japan

Two major media industries in Japan are presented here, namely, TV and newspaper.

From Broadcasting to Satellite Television

In Japan, an average household is able to receive about a dozen broadcasting signals, including two public broadcasting services (PBS), several commercial networks, and some local stations' channels. Both PBS services, the NHK General and NHK Educational Channels, are provided by Nippon Hoso Kyokai (NHK, or Japan Broadcasting Corporation). Nippon Hoso Kyokai finance relies on the monthly license fee that is collected from TV set owners, as it does not accept any advertisers in both its services. The license fee for terrestrial broadcasts is 1,305 yen (about $10.55) per month as of December 1996. Major commercial networks are Nippon Television, Fuji, Asahi, and Tokyo Hoso (TBS) in the Tokyo area and Mainichi, Asahi, TV Osaka, Yomiuri, and Kansai TV in the Osaka area (Links: Broadcasts, 1996). All commercial broadcasting stations depend on advertising for their revenue.

In 1978, NHK launched the first broadcasting satellite of Japan for experimental purposes (History: Survey and Research, 1996). It started test broadcasts using the broadcast satellite BS-2a, which was launched in 1984 (History: Survey and Research, 1996). In 1987, the satellite broadcasts expanded to 24-hour service. In the meantime, more broadcast and communication satellites were launched. As of August 1996, via broadcasts satellite, two services provided by NHK, the First and the Second Satellite Channels, and one commercial channel, WOWOW by Nihon Satellite Broadcasting Co. (or Japan Satellite Broadcasting as JSB) *(Gendai Yogo No Kiso Chishiki 1997,* 1997). There are 13 services provided via two main communication satellite broadcasters, Skyport Canter Corp. and CS Baan, both of which use analog signal (Lazarus, 1995; *Gendai Yogo No Kiso Chishiki 1997,* 1997). There are three services on CS Baan, and 13 services on Skyport. PerfecTV, the first digital satellite TV service via communications satellite, started its service in the fall of 1996 (Kim, 1996; *Gendai Yogo No Kiso Chishiki 1997,* 1997). It made available a total of 70 new channels, from which customers can select as many channels as which they want to subscribe (Kim, 1996). DirecTV, Sky D, and J Sky B were introduced after the summer of 1997 (*Gendai Yogo No Kiso Chishiki 1997,* 1997).

The monthly subscription fee for the two NHK services is 930 yen per month as of December 1996. To subscribe to WOWOW, one has to pay 2,000 yen (about U.S.$16.17) a month with the one-time installation fee of 27,000 yen (about U.S.$218.32). PerfecTV's subscribers pay 2,500 yen (about U.S.$20.22) per month for approximately 10 channels. In 1995, there were 7,374,885 people subscribing to NHK satellite broadcast services in Japan (Broadcasting: Number of NHK Subscribers, 1995; *Gendai Yogo No Kiso Chishiki 1997,* 1997). WOWOW, which also provides its service via broadcasting satellite, had 2,055,000 subscribers in that year (Broadcasting: Number of commercial pay satellite, 1995; *Gendai Yogo No Kiso Chishiki 1997,* 1997). A total of 516 people were subscribing to TV broadcasting via communications satellites (Broadcasting: Number of commercial pay satellite, 1995).

Compared with the penetration rate of cable TV in the United States, Japan's cable TV has been suffering from low growth rates. In 1993 the cable TV industry lost 20.9 billion yen ($1.69 billion) (Stewart, 1995). The Japanese public's poor response to cable TV was mainly due to the limited variety in programming (Stewart, 1995). Many Japanese still perceive cable TV service as expensive and unappealing (Kahaner, 1996). Since 1993, for fear of getting technologically behind other countries in building terrestrial media distribution systems, the MPT started deregulating the cable market. It now allows a single company to operate multiple cable systems (Weinberg, 1995) and more than one operator in each region (Patton, 1996). Table 18-2 below shows the change in the number of operators, facilities, and subscribers between 1990 and 1995 (The Ministry of Post and Telecommunication, 1996).

Table 18-2. The Number of Operators, Facilities and Subscribers

	1990	1991	1992	1993	1994	1995
Operators	96	126	141	150	163	183
Facilities	102	134	149	158	172	193
Subscribers	400,154	730,142	1,075,365	1,629,388	2,212,878	3,009,364

As indicated in Table 18-2, as of 1995, Japan had a little more than 3 million subscriber households, which accounts for only 7 percent of the country's 43 million homes (The Ministry of Post and Telecommunication, 1996). The 1993 deregulation policy permits not only multiple system operators (MSO) but also easier entry into telecommunications services (Kahaner, 1996; Weinberg, 1995). It dropped the requirement of community-based operators and relaxed foreign equity ownership, by increasing foreign ownership to 33 percent from the previous 20 percent and giving a future opportunity for cable companies to provide telephone service (Friedland, 1994a; Kahaner, 1996; Weinberg, 1995).

Newspaper: The Traditional Media Powerhouse

Unlike in the United States, where newspapers are traditionally a local medium, national newspapers in Japan dominate the print media market. Of the total circulation of 52,855,000, national newspapers have a circulation of 27,329,000 (51.7 percent of the total circulation) versus local papers with 19,183,000 (36.3 percent) (Museum: Circulation, 1996). The major national newspaper companies are Asahi Newspaper, Mainichi Newspaper, Yomiuri Newspaper, Nihon Keizai (or Nikkei) Newspaper, and Sankei Newspaper. Most of these national newspapers issue both a morning version and an evening version, with relatively high subscription rates.

Advertising and Media

Japan is one of the leading advertising markets in the world. In 1995, a total of 5,426.3 billion yen (about $43.88 billion) was spent on advertising on media in Japan, which increased by 5.0 percent from the previous year (Dentsu Inc., 1995a). Table 18-3 below shows the money spent for each medium (Dentsu Inc., 1995b).

One third (32.2 percent) of the total advertising expenditure was generated in the TV industry in 1995, with 6.8 percent increase from the previous year (Dentsu, Inc., 1995a). The advertising expenditure for newspaper and radio increased as well. While advertising money spent in 1995 for new media

Table 18-3. Advertising Expenditures Generated (by Media Type)

Media	Advertising Expenditures in billions (component ratio)			Increase Ratio	
	1993	1994	1995	1993–94	1994–95
Newspaper	$ 8.96 (21.6%)	$ 9.07 (21.7%)	$ 9.43 (21.5%)	1.1%	4.0%
Magazine	$ 2.76 (6.7%)	$ 2.81 (6.7%)	$ 3.03 (6.9%)	1.6%	7.8%
Radio	$ 1.71 (4.1%)	$ 1.64 (3.9%)	$ 1.68 (3.8%)	6.0%	2.6%
Television	$12.85 (31.0%	$13.29 (31.8%)	$14.19 (32.3%)	3.4%	6.8%
New Media	$ .10 (0.2%)	$ .10 (0.3%)	$ .13 (0.3%)	5.0%	26.4%
Other	$15.08 (36.4%)	$14.89 (35.6%)	$15.42 (35.2%)	–1.3%	3.6%
Total	$41.46 (100.0%)	$41.79 (100.0%)	$43.88 (100.0%)	0.8%	5.0%

is 15.8 billion yen (about $0.13 billion), comprising 0.3 percent of the total, it is up 26.4 percent increase from 1994 (Dentsu, Inc., 1995b), clearly showing a strong growth of new media systems especially in the area of cable TV.

Major Media Industry Analysis

The contribution and the importance of NHK in Japan's broadcasting history has been enormous since its establishment. Naturally, it has the power and influence to direct the path of Japan's broadcasting industry, including recent development of multilanguage broadcast, satellite TV, high-definition TV (HDTV, called Hi-Vision in Japan), digital broadcasting system, international satellite TV broadcasting, and so on. NHK's impact in Japan is also reflected by its programming products. Among them, documentaries are highly regarded, some of which NHK produced, some are co-produced with other countries, and some are purchased from other countries. Nevertheless, the centrality of Japan's TV environment gradually shifted as more new media arrived.

The market structure of Japan's commercial media industry is oligopolistic, which is especially prominent in the news media. Asahi Newspaper and Yomiuri Newspaper are the largest media conglomerates in Japan (Friedland, 1994a).

Table 18-4. Entry to New Media Business by Selected Major Newspaper Companies

	Data-base	CATV	Broadcasting Distribution	Videotex	Computer Communi-cation	Satellite Broad-casting	Fax Data Service	CD-ROM
Asahi	X	X	X	X	X	X		X
Mainichi	X	X	X	X	X	X	X	X
Yomiuri	X	X	X	X	X	X	X	X
Nikkei	X	X	X	X	X	X	X	X

These conglomerates usually own businesses across different media and other industries. For example, both Asahi and Yomiuri have multiplied their business activities in various areas from newspapers to radio and TV broadcasting, cable TV, satellite broadcasting, and electronic data transmission, to home video production, to publishing and printing, and even to advertising, real estate, insurance, and the travel business (Asahi Shinbun, 1997; Yomiuri Shinbun, 1997). As of May 1996, Asahi's affiliates numbered 164 in both Japan and overseas. Its combined sales of the main affiliates totaled 764.5 billion yen (about $6.18 billion) in 1993, and 786.4 billion yen (about $6.36 billion) in 1994. Especially aggressive entry of newspaper companies into the new media market has been observed in the last few years, as shown in Table 18-4.

The author has observed more competition in the multichannel TV market since MPT started deregulating the cable and satellite TV industries. The U.S. companies seem to be one of the most active international presences of growth and competition. During 1995, four United States–Japan joint venture groups announced their plans to enter Japan's cable and satellite markets (Friedland, 1994b; Weinberg, 1995). The largest is Jupiter Telecommunications Co., operating four pilot systems with 362,000 cable homes passed. It is a joint venture between a giant trading company, Sumitomo Corp., with 60 percent share and Tele-Communications International (TCI), with 40 percent (Weinberg, 1995). Jupiter plans to build cable systems in newly franchised areas and to buy existing systems, including at least some of the 21 systems covering 2.5 million home, in which Sumitomo already has invested. It is also investing in six to eight programming services, which were scheduled to air within 18 months (Weinberg, 1995). Jupiter's main competitor is Titus Communication. The joint venture was established between, from Japan, the trading company Itochu, which marked the largest sale in 1995, electronic manufacturer Toshiba, and from the United States, Time Warner (TW) and USWest (Weinberg, 1995). Their plan is to spend $400 million signing up 2 million homes by the year 2000 (Weinberg, 1995). It is also planning to invest in the programming business.

In the satellite TV industry, DirecTV is a joint venture of digital satellite broadcast, formed by Hughes Communications and three Japanese companies:

Japan's largest franchised renter of videos and music, Culture Convenience Club, Ltd. (CCC), Japan's largest printer Dai Nippon Printing (DNP), and Space Communications Corp. (SCC) (Hughes formed joint venture, 1995; Weinberg, 1995). Hughes and CCC each owns 42.5 percent of the venture; SCC, 10 percent; and DNP, 5 percent (Hughes formed joint venture, 1995; Weinberg, 1995). U.S. DirecTV is its program provider. It started its service in the summer of 1997. A challenge to DirecTV is a consortium, PerfecTV, which is formed by a number of big Japanese trading companies, and has Nihon TV, Nihon Keizai Shinbun (Nikkei Newspaper) and other leading Japanese entertainment companies as program providers (Weinberg, 1995; *Gendai Yogo No Kiso Chishiki 1997,* 1997). Sky D and J Sky B would start its service in the summer of 1997 and 1998, respectively. Sky D is backed by Asahi Newspaper, Sony, Japan Cable TV (JCTV) and others (*Gendai Yogo No Kiso Chishiki 1997,* 1997). Its program providers are Mainichi TV, Toei, Asahi TV, Toho, UIP-U.S. and some other publishers (*Gendai Yogo No Kiso Chishiki 1997,* 1997). J Sky B, which will offer approximately 100 channels, is a joint venture by Australia News Corp., Softbank and one of Japan's leading publishers Obunsha (*Gendai Yogo No Kiso Chishiki 1997,* 1997). Its programs will be offered by Asahi TV, Twentieth Fox Entertainment, Toei, Asahi Newspaper, and so on (*Gendai Yogo No Kiso Chishiki 1997,* 1997). More than the competition inside the industry itself, satellite broadcast companies are worried about possible threats from the regional cable operators, which are able to provide all the satellite channels in addition to interactive services (Lazarus, 1995).

The most competitive area of media in Japan seems to be in the wireless market. The continuous showdown is between the domestic print media–based conglomerates and international joint ventures; both are highly integrated into the programming market. The cable TV penetration in Japan is expected to increase from 7 percent to the present U.S. penetration level for both cable and digital satellite TV during the next decades (Weinberg, 1995).

Japan's current media market offers great opportunities for content providers, as there is a growing need of entertainment programs from cable and satellite TV service providers. For example, Turner International, Asia-Pacific, which is a marketer in the Asian region for Turner Broadcasting's programming such as CNN International and the Cartoon Network, has been very successful (Weinberg, 1995). The current deregulatory climate made Japan an even more attractive programming market for multinational media firms. For example, after the deregulation, Star TV and Turner Entertainment Networks Asia were able to distribute the first satellite programming via domestic cable operation (Japanese PTT, 1995).

Japan's major domestic film companies are vertically integrated. For example, Toei Group has ownership at all production, distribution, and exhibition levels. Its strong production and distribution divisions have made some children's programs such as *Power Ranger* and *Masked Rider,* both of which were very popular in Japan during 1970s, revived and became a big hit in the United States and in other Asian countries (Toei Co., 1996).

Japanese love of foreign films is well illustrated by the film industry's sales figures; it accounted for about 64 percent of the 71.8 billion yen ($580.6 million) in total distribution revenue generated in Japan in 1993 (Hollywood rides high, 1996). American films are far more popular than any other foreign movies, such that 60 percent of all imported films were from the United States in both 1992 and 1993 (UNESCO, 1995). United International Pictures Far East Inc. (UPS) obtained an 18 percent share of the foreign-film market in Japan with *Jurassic Park* alone and the top spot in box-office receipts in 1993 (Hollywood Rides High, 1996). In 1995, United International Pictures Far East Inc. (UIP) still keeps its leadership position with 17.7 percent market share, followed by Toho Co. (16.6 percent), Twentieth Century Fox Film Corp. (13.4 percent), Toho-Towa Co. (9.8 percent), and Toei Co. (9.3 percent) (Business Browser: Market, 1996). The theatrical film industry is competitive and there is no guarantee that U.S. distributors will be successful just because a film was a big hit in the U.S. For example, the performance of the *Flintstones,* which made record sales in 1994 in the United States resulted in disappointment to UIP in the Japanese market (Hollywood rides high, 1996).

The strong presence of foreign films in Japan created a ripple effect in Japan's home video market, which includes disc-type software such as laser discs and video compact discs, as well as sell-through and rental videos. The market earned a total wholesale value of 260.38 billion yen ($2.11 billion) in 1995 (McClure, 1996). With sixty-eight percent of the market, prerecorded videotapes had the largest share mainly due to the strong sales of non-Japanese blockbuster movies accounting for 29.8 percent of the share (77.7 billion yen/$628.3 million, up 14.2 percent over 1994) (McClure, 1996). The top company in prerecorded videotape shipments in value is Victor Entertainment Inc. (17.2 percent, down 3.4 points), followed by Buena Vista Japan (15.4 percent, up 8.5), Pony Canyon Inc. (12.8 percent, down 11), Time Warner Entertainment Japan Inc. (8 percent, down 0.1), and Toei Video Co. (5.8 percent, down 8.6) (Business Browser: Market, 1996).

Emerging Media Economics Issues in Japan

Under its government's leadership, Japan is in a crusade to develop a converging system of interactive multimedia, the so-called integrated services digital Broadcasting (ISDB), which plans to integrate cable TV and telecommunication networks completely. The government is now hastily trying to establish a digital broadcasting transmission standard so that cable TV and telecommunication can launch multimedia services similar to those in the United States. New service such as video-on-demand and self-selective camera angles during sports events are also in the plans (Kellar, 1994).

This trend of integration and digitalization has influenced the way MPT administers its responsibilities over media industries. When MPT started its telecommunication administration, it made a clear distinction between communication, which is defined as limited communication of small volume of data, and broadcasts, which means unlimited transmissions of large quantities of data (Maeno, 1993). The distinction led to the establishment of two different satellite distribution systems: a communications satellite for transmitting communication information and a broadcast satellite for broadcasting transmission. To deal with these two types of communication industry, MPT set up two separate organizations: the Communication Policy Bureau and the Telecommunications Bureau. The MPT has recently consolidate the two regulatory units to increase its operating efficiency (Yamazaki, 1994). This is a good example of how technology is taking the lead in shaping a country's regulatory environment.

As in many developed countries, there has been a trend toward market concentration in Japan's media industries. The integration of media companies in all levels from content production to distribution and exhibition is pervasive mainly because of the deregulation of broadcast media and the telecommunication markets. In Japan, Australia's News Corp. and Japan's Softbank formed a joint venture and purchased Obunsha Media, which was a subsidiary of Obunsha, one of Japan's leading publishing companies (*Gendai Yogo No Kiso Chishiki 1997,* 1997). Through the purchase of Obunsha Media, News Corp. and Softbank now own 21 percent of Asahi TV's stock (*Gendai Yogo No Kiso Chishiki 1997,* 1997). It is speculated that News Corp. is interested in Asahi TV's production expertise because News Corp. is planning to enter communication digital broadcasting in Japan in a few years (*Gendai Yogo No Kiso Chishiki 1997,* 1997). It is expected that the Japanese would see even more megamedia involving various industries such as movie, broadcasting, cable, telephone, computer, electronic manufacturing industries.

It is a truly exciting time to live and watch how the media industries in this country will develop and change. Interesting research areas exist in many aspects. Regulation and government policy change will be inevitable as new technologies develop. Appearance of megamedia is expected to have a strong impact on the structure of Japan's media and other related industries, as well as in pricing and distribution of programs. Switch from analog to digital technology might affect the distribution of media content and further audience consumption pattern. High cost of production in digital format would facilitate international cooperation in production. Increase in availability of services and channels would change the nature of current demand and supply. It would also promote Japanese consumer fragmentation, resulting in competition for advertising money. Increase of program outlets in addition to the development of satellite broadcasting, which has a wider footage to cover more than one country, would have an impact on the flow of programs between different countries that would further affect international trade of program content.

References

Asahi Shinbun (1997). Multimedia corporation. *Asahi.* Available on-line: http://www.asahi.com/cinfo/Japanese/corporation.html.

A brief history of Matsushita (1996). *A Brief History of Matsushita English.* Available on-line: http://media.mei.co.jp/corp/hist/hist-e.html.

Broadcasting Bureau (1997). *Outline of MPT.* Available on-line: http://www.mpt.go.jp:80/outline/borad.html#3.

Broadcasting: Number of commercial pay satellite broadcasting's subscribers (1995). Yusei gyosei data [The Ministry of Post and Telecommunication administrative data]. Available on-line: http://www.zaimu.mpt.go.jp/tokei/1995/jo95.html.

Broadcasting: Number of NHK subscribers (1995). Yusei gyosei data [The Ministry of Post and Telecommunication administrative data]. Available on-line: http://www.zaimu.mpt.go.jp/tokei/1995/so95.html.

Business browser: Market share survey (1996). *Nikkei Net.* Available on-line: http://www.nikeei.co.jp/enews/BB/ranking/share7.html#68.

Dawkins, W. (1996). Games nerds get hooked on reality. *The Financial Times,* May 6, p. 9.

Denki tsushin: Kanyu denwa-tou danyu-su [Electric communication: the number of telephone registered] (1995). Yusei gyosei data [The Ministry of Post and Telecommunication administrative data]. Available on-line: http://www.zaimu.mpt.go.jp/tokei/1995/so95.html.

Dentsu Inc. (1995a). Data: Overview of advertising expenditures in Japan for 1995. *Dentsu Web Site.* Available on-line: http: www.dentsu.co.jp/DHP/DOG/ENG/5/5_1_1.html.

Dentsu Inc. (1995b). Data: Advertising expenditure by Medium. *Dentsu Web Site.* Available on-line: http: www.dentsu.co.jp/DHP/DOG/ENG/5/5_1_3.html.

Famighetti, R. (ed.) (1996). *The World Almanac and Book of Facts 1997.* Mahwah, NJ: World Almanac Books.

Financial affairs: Revenue in various media (1996). *Press Net.* Available on-line: http://www.pressnet.or.jp/MUSEUM/handbook/finance/finance1.html.

Friedland, J. (1994a). Out of print. *Far Eastern Economic Review,* 157, March 10, p. 46.

Friedland, J. (1994b). Watch this. *Far Eastern Economic Review,* 157, August 25, pp. 34, 40.

Gendai Yogo No Kiso Chishiki 1997 [Basic Knowledge and Information for Modern Terminology 1997] (1997). Tokyo, Japan: Jiyu-kokumin Sha.

History: Survey and research that have traced the progress of broadcasting (1996). *Broadcasting Culture Research Institute*. Available on-line: http://www.nhk.or.jp/bunken/en/b6-e.html.

Hollywood rides high in Japan (1996 September). *JETRO*. Available on-line: http://www.jetro.go.jp/JETROINFO/FOCUSJAPAN/94-9.html.

Hughes formed joint venture (1995). *Television Digest,* 35, October 2, p. 8.

Japan: From kabuki to crime drama (1989). In: Browne, D. R. *Comparing broadcast systems: The experiences of six industrialized nations.* Ames, IA: Iowa State University Press.

Japan: VCR imports continue clime in Japan 12/05/96 (1996). *Newsbytes Pacifica Headline*. Available on-line: http://www.nb-pacifica.com/headline/japanvcrimpotscontin_796.shtml.

Japanese PTT. (1995). *Television Digest,* 35, April 24, p. 4.

Kahaner, D. K. (1996). ATIP96.103: Japan's emerging cable TV industry. *Asian Technology Information Program (ATIP)*, November 21. Available on-line: http://www.atip.or.jp/public/atip.reports.96/atip96.103.html.

Katayama, F. (1996). Japanese animation takes on the world. *CNNfn*, May 27. Available on-line: http://cnnfn.com/news/9605/27/japan_animation.

Kellar, D. (1994). Japan plays catch-up in multimedia revolution. *Electronic News,* 40, January 10, p. 32.

Kim, E. (1996, September 16). Digital sats target Japan. *Variety,* 364, p. 58.

Lazarus, D. (1995). Time running out for satellite broadcasters. *Tokyo Business Today,* 63, February, pp. 34–35.

Links: Broadcasts (1996). *Press Net*. Available on-line: http://www.pressnet.or.jp/LINKS/docs/osakab.html.

Machinery and Information Industries Bureau (1997). *MITI: Ministry of International Trade and Industry*. Available on-line: http: www.miti.go.jp/gsosikih.html.

Maeno, K. (1993). Plans and confusion re Japan's optical communication infrastructure. *Journal of Japanese Trade and Industry,* 4:40–42.

MCA/Universal human resource: Universal Studio Recreation Service Group (1996). *Employment Opportunities*. Available on-line: http://www.mca.com/unicity/hr/rsg.html.

McClure, S. (1996). Video still turning Japanese profits. *Billboard,* 108, July 13, pp. 72–73.

The Ministry of Posts and Telecommunication (1996). Info-communications in Japan, 1996. *Communication in Japan 1996: Summary*. Available on-line: http://www.mpt.go.jp:80/policyreports/english/papers/CommunicationsInJapan1996/contents.html.

Museum: Circulation (1996). *Press Net*. Available on-line: http://www.pressnet.or.jp/MUSEUM/handbook/circulation/circulations3.html.

Nippon Steel Corporation, Personnel Development Division (1984). *Nippon: The Land and Its People.* Tokyo, Japan: Gakuseisha Publishing Co., Ltd.

Patton, R. (1996). Japan telecom deregulation strolls along. *Electronics,* 67, September 26, p. 4.

Radio and satellite programming schedule (1996). *Asahi Shinbun* [Asahi Newspaper], December 29, p. 15.

Radio and television broadcasting: commercial broadcasters revenue/expenditure (1995). Yusei gyosei data [The Ministry of Post and Telecommunication administrative data]. Available on-line: http://www.zaimu.mpt.go.jp/tokei/1995/so95.html.

Sony Corporation of America: Outline of principal operations (1997). *Sony On Line.* Available on-line: http://www.sony.com/SCA/outline.html#NOTES.

Stewart, H. (1995). Foreign companies — vital to cable television's growth. *Journal of Japanese Trade & Industry,* 14(2), March/April, pp. 44–46.

Toei Co. (1996). Business: Production and distribution of TV programs. *Toei, Co.* Available on-line: http://www.toei.co.jp:80/annai/tv.htm.

UNESCO (1995). *UNESCO Statistical Yearbook 1995.* Lanham, MD: UNESCO Publishing & Bernan Press.

Weinberg, N. (1995). Cable come to Fuchu. *Forbes,* 156, November 6, pp. 44-45.

Yamazaki, T. (1994). Cable TV madness. *Tokyo Business Today,* 62, 6-9.

Yomiuri Shinbun. (1997). Yomiuri Shinbun general guide. *The Yomiuri Shinbun.* Available on-line: http://www.yomiuri.co.jp:80/info/info-j.html.

19

AUSTRALIA

Maria A. Williams-Hawkins

The Home of the Media Conglomerates

An analysis of Australia's economy reveals a country that has learned to make business agreements with the world. Populated by people from all parts of Europe, as well as a few Aborigines, Australia is divided into six states. The country has two mainland territories: the Australian Capital Territory and the Northern Territory. More than 85 percent of Australia's 18 million population is concentrated along the southeastern quarter of the country, primarily in New South Wales, including the cities of Melbourne and Sydney.

An examination of Australia's national and state telecommunication media owners reflects the industry's ability to work well with others of different cultures and heritages. We look first to Australia's national economy.

Australia's Economic Status

Australia's mixed-capitalist economy is comparable to other industrialized West European countries. It is an established supporter of Asian countries and has improved its relationship with the United States. Like many other Organization for Economic Cooperation and Development countries, Australia experienced slow growth and high unemployment during the early 1990s. In

1992–93, the economy recovered. It is experiencing a 5.1 percent inflation rate and has an 8.7 percent unemployment rate (*CIA Factbook,* 1995). although the country exports media products, agricultural products still account for 30 percent of its export revenues. Australia is the world's largest exporter of beef and wood. In media production as well as agriculture, its major trade partners are Japan (25 percent), the United States (11 percent), South Korea (6 percent), and New Zealand (5.7 percent) (*Europa World Yearbook,* 1996).

Australia experienced trade deficits in the mid 1990s. In 1995, Australia's trade deficit was U.S. $4,490 million. In addition, there was a deficit due to a balance of payments equal to U.S. $15.2 million. Australia's indebtedness continued to increase in 1996. By June of 1995, its principal sources of imports were Japan (17.1%) and the USA (8.1%). Japan was also a principal export partner. In 1996, Japan was the principal market for exports (24.3%), while the Republic of Korea was the second market at 7.9%. Australia's other major trading partners include the United Kingdom, New Zealand, Singapore, Taiwan, The People's Republic of China and Germany (*Europa World Yearbook*, 1997).

In this chapter, the status of Australia's media and telecommunications-based industries is examined, including the availability and profitability of telephone services, newspaper, radio, television (TV), and film and video production. The major corporations in these industries are presented as well as the individuals who have made them successful. The significant strategic alliances between Australian media firms and some foreign conglomerates are identified, and the role of Australian media in the years to come is discussed.

Major Media/Telecommunications Industries in Australia

The federal government owns and operates Australia's postal, telephone and telegraph systems. Australia's Postal Commission runs the postal system. The Telecommunications Commission operates the country's telephone and telegraph system. Like any industrialized country, Australia has reasonable success offering access to telephones, newspapers and broadcast entertainment to its citizenry.

Telephone Services

There have been steady increases in the proportion of households in Australia with telephone services. Comparisons between Australian phone access and U.S. phone access reveal similar reasons for having or not having telephones (Thornberry and Massey, 1988; Smith, 1987). The Australian Bureau of Statistics (1996a, 1996b) provides a number of statistics relative to media and technology use. Their recent figures indicated that only 5.6 percent of all

Australia's households are phoneless, yielding a 94 percent connection rate (Australian Bureau of Statistics, 1996b). Connection rates vary from state to state. The Australian Capital Territory has a 97 percent connection rate. In the Northern Territory, only 83.7 percent of the households have phones. Digital phone services such as call waiting, electronic mail via digital exchanges, and integrated digital network services are expected to be available to 85 percent of the Australian population by December 1997 (Department of Communications and Arts, 1996). As media companies diversify their services, phone use and availability will have a greater impact on media economics. American companies have already established joint ventures with Australian telephone companies. The status of ventures in the areas of phone, entertainment and satellite operations is discussed later in this chapter.

Newspapers

Newspaper circulation is very high. The Roy Morgan Readership Survey (1996) indicates a daily readership of 13,440,000, about 77 percent of the population. In the areas with lower populations, weekly newspapers are even more popular (*Europa World Yearbook,* 1996). Only two newspapers can be considered national daily papers, *The Australian* and the *Australian Financial Review.* Three national magazines are produced: (1) *Time Australia,* (2) *Business Review Weekly,* and (3) *The Bulletin.*

Newspaper ownership in Australia can be traced to five families. Books have been written on each of these families. Most of the families still remain on Australia's millionaire and billionaire rolls after a wave of mergers and acquisitions (*Best of Australia,* 1996). In 1987, there were four media giants with histories in newspaper ownership: The News Corporation (News Corp.), John Fairfax Group, Consolidated Press and the Herald Weekly and Weekly Times. Today's ownership list reveals blurred lines of ownership. Although News Corp. remains intact, John Fairfax Holdings now owns the Fairfax Group. Consolidated Press is now PBL (same owner, Kerry Packer). The Herald Weekly, once owned by many investors has been eliminated from the big list. Two other companies appear as major media groups, but neither operates newspapers or magazines as a primary business. Although the three remaining companies were established and maintained by their newspaper profits, their profits are now derived from owning broadcast or satellite operations. Diversification is a must for newspaper survival in Australia.

Radio

Australian radio broadcasting is concentrated in the heavily populated cities of New South Wales and Victoria. Operating both government-run and commercial stations, the Australian Broadcasting Corporation (ABC) operates

114 AM stations, 414 FM stations, six domestic and 14 overseas short-wave stations called Radio Australia (*Europa World Yearbook,* 1996). There are 268 radio service companies (Australian Bureau of Statistics Statsite, 1996b). Over seven thousand employees are paid in the radio industry with nearly ten thousand volunteer employees. Most radio stations are privately owned, employing fewer than 20 employees each.

Australian radio is promoted as the best vehicle for reaching women and considered "the last word" that a woman will hear before making a shopping decision. Radio advertising is inexpensive, making it easy for even the smallest businesses to advertise their product or service. Gross income for the radio industry was A$800 million in 1994. With expenses equaling A$782 million, radio broadcasting maintained a before tax profit of A$18 million (Australian Bureau of Statistics Statsite, 1996a).

Today, Australian radio broadcasting is trying to increase profitability through joint ventures with American, Irish and Asian corporations. Clear Channel Communications, one of the major radio groups in the United States, has invested $135 million in Australia and New Zealand. Clear Channel Communications has partnered with Australian Provincial Newspapers Holdings Ltd. to purchase all commercial FM licenses in Australia (Petrozzello, 1997).

Television

In the 1940s, ABC decided to award broadcast licenses in the two most metropolitan areas only. Two commercial licenses and one government license would be awarded to each city. A rumor was spread that TV ownership would be an unprofitable proposition. Some banks even refused to loan money to anyone wanting to compete for a license. The companies that did compete were those that had made their money from newspaper ownership. The original licensees were (1) Fairfax and Macquarie Broadcasting, (2) Sir Frank Packer's Australia Consolidated Press, (3) The Melbourne Herald Group, (4) Melbourne Argus, the Age and the Electronic Industries Combine. Packer was the first to begin operation and disprove the rumor about unprofitable TV. Within 3 years, his company was paying dividends (Windschuttle, 1985). The rumor was a myth. Today, 99 percent of Australia's homes have TV (CEASA, 1996). The *Australian Financial Review* (1996) indicated that 315,000 homes are connected to pay TV.

The structure of Australian TV has had a great impact on its success. Cunningham (1992) expresses the belief that Australian TV was able to balance issues of ownership and cultural inclusion by the 1980s. Australia has three types of broadcast operations: national, public and commercial. National stations in Australia are state funded. ABC and SBS are the two national stations. In 1990, the government privatized its telecommunication businesses. The Australian Bureau of Statistics (1996b) indicated that 43 private and three public broadcasters supported Australia's TV service industry. The TV industry provides jobs for more than 12,000 employees. The TV industry generates A$2.7 million in gross income. With operating expenses totaling A$2.3 million, Australian TV saw a profit of A$376 thousand in 1994. Public broadcasters generate 17 percent of the gross income through government funding.

Similar to U.S. stations, Australian stations located in the major states are most profitable. In addition to location, profitability can be attributed to the stations' programming approach. Research shows that the stations broadcasting more inexpensive American or other international programming make the greatest profits (Windschuttle, 1985).

Film and Video Production

National statistics on Australia's success in film and video production are sparse. The Australian Bureau of Statistics reported the 1994 results in 1996. Figures at that time indicated that more than 1,000 businesses were in operation in the film and video production industry, employing 6,000 employees and generating about A$468 million from the sales of goods and services. The data indicate that another A$121 million was earned from the sale of rights for completed works.

Overall, film companies are not very profitable. The 1993–94 years suggest that the industry lost just over A$98 million. When comparing the larger companies (those employing 100 or more employees) only, they earned A$1.4 million.

The industry spent A$463 million for the production of films and videos, including A$184.2 million for made-for-TV productions, A$87.3 million for feature films, and A$56 million for non-TV productions. A total of A$135.4 million was spent on the production of commercials and other forms of advertising for the film industry (Australian Bureau of Statistics Statsite, 1996a).

While Australia's success in film and video production and distribution lags behind many other countries, media moguls whose companies are based in Australia are making significant profits in this area. Given that this is a new addition to News Corp.'s holdings, it might be wise to keep an eye on Australia's film production while News Corp. continues in that direction.

Media Industry Analysis

Australia's commercial media has a highly concentrated ownership (Windschuttle, 1985). In 1985, four major players controlled eight of the 15 metropolitan commercial TV stations. The group was identified as owning nearly all the national magazines and suburban newspapers and a substantial radio interest. Today, five conglomerates control Australia's media. Each owns stock in at least one of the other conglomerates. The following section examines the major media conglomerates, highlighting the role of the controlling investor. While primary attention is paid to the top three, information on the other two and how they fit into the plans of the first three is considered.

Major Media Conglomerates

THE NEWS CORPORATION. The News Corp. is owned by Rupert Murdoch. The conglomerate's holdings are diversified, including TV, film, book publishing, magazines, multimedia and newspapers. Specific properties and ventures include the following: in television and film, Fox Broadcasting Network and 22 U.S. Fox-affiliated TV stations; British Sky Broadcasting (BSkyB) satellite delivery system at a value of A$1.3 billion; 64 percent of Star TV's satellite system for Asia, the Middle East and India, at a value of A$120 million; and Twentieth Century Fox Studios, valued at A$2.3 billion. In book publishing News Corp. owns HarperCollins at a value of A$1.2 billion dollars, and in magazine publishing, it owns TV Guide and free-standing inserts for newspapers at a value of A$1.5 billion. In multimedia, Murdoch owns Delphi Internet Services, valued at A$25 million, and he entered a joint venture with MCI in 1995 for an amorphous product/service. Although the value has not been disclosed, MCI paid U.S.$2 billion for their share of its development. News Corp is engaged in this venture as an "acquisition vehicle" (Grover and Oneal, 1995). Prognosticators suggest that the venture will bring in U.S.$2 billion. News Corp.'s original business, that of newspapers, occasionally shows profits. British holdings include *The Times, The Sunday Times, Today, The Sun* and *News of the World.* In the United States, it owns *The New York Post.* In Australia, News Corp. owns 100 papers, including *The Australian, The Daily Telegraph Mirror,* and *The Herald-Sun.* Nine of Fox's TV stations are in the Top 10 U.S. TV markets, giving Fox access to 40 percent of all American homes (Bloomberg Business News, 1996).

At the end of 1996, News Corp. reported net earnings of U.S.$222 million, resulting in an operating profit of 7 percent (Bloomberg Business News, November 12, 1996). This increase was marginalized by lower earnings from Fox TV operations, some of News Corp.'s Australian newspapers, down 6 percent, and its book publishing unit, down 69 percent (Lippman, 1996). Earnings from News Corp.'s Fox Filmed Entertainment unit rose 150 percent per unit, which produced the third highest grossing film in history, *Independence Day.* News Corp.'s British newspapers rose 18 percent, and their U.K. satellite TV service rose 30 percent. Fox attributed its losses in broadcasting to the poor performance of several of its new shows. Murdoch personally predicted 1997 would show increased profits in the range of 20 percent.

JOHN FAIRFAX HOLDINGS LIMITED. Once one of the premier Australian press conglomerates, John Fairfax Proprietary Limited lost its financial standing. Founded in the 1800s, the paper was in receivership in 1990. Employees, competitors and the government attempted to interrupt the bidding for this conglomerate, but one bidder emerged successfully. Control of the Fairfax Group was awarded to Conrad Black when he bid A$1.5 billion for it. Black, a Canadian millionaire media magnate, took 15 percent control through the Tourang Group on December 23, 1991. The group invested $365 million in equity (Scherer, 1991).

John Fairfax Holdings Limited, as it is now known, owns 35 subsidiaries, 33 wholly, in Australia, New Zealand, the United Kingdom and the United States (Moody's, 1996). Described as a holding company whose subsidiaries' principal activities are information and entertainment publishing in newspaper, magazine and electronic formats, Fairfax became Australia's second largest media group (Foltz, 1991). Fairfax owns *The Sydney Morning Herald* and *The Australian Financial Review* among other papers and magazines.

Since purchasing Fairfax, Tourang has liquidated some assets, trimmed the staff, and continued to attract venture partners from other countries. A comparison of 1994 to 1995 net assets indicates an A$65 million dollar profit; however, the company has an outstanding debt of three quarters of a billion dollars (Moody's, 1996). During 1995, the company's profits were said to sag because of increased newsprint prices and weak advertising. Fairfax projected lower profits for 1996.

PUBLISHING AND BROADCASTING LIMITED. Publishing and Broadcasting Limited (PBL), as well as Consolidated Press Holdings (CPH), is controlled by Australia's richest billionaire, Kerry Packer. Packer's corporation is valued at U.S.$2 billion (Martin, 1996) and includes newspapers, magazines, broadcast and cable operations, casinos and sports holdings. PBL's Nine Network is dominant in Australia. It dominates TV and magazine publishing in Australia.

Publishing and Broadcasting Limited is part of a third-generation newspaper-driven dynasty. No longer a newspaper business, PBL's holdings include part of a chemical company, half of a company that handles money-off coupons in newspapers, real estate, magazines including the *Bulletin,* and pay TV (5 percent in Optus Vision, 16 percent in Australis, and 14.4 percent of The John Fairfax group). Like News Corp., PBL owns rights to rugby players and gambling casinos.

SEVEN NETWORK. Although PBL and News Corp. gain the most attention in Australian media, others continue to run profitable businesses. Seven Network (Seven), owned by Kerry Stokes, has an estimated net worth of A$250 million (Karp, 1995). Seven owns Australian Capital Equity. Based in Perth, Seven bought 13.7 million shares of Murdoch's Seven Network for

A$44 million. His holdings are diversified, including Golden West Network in Western Australia, a partnership in the R.M. Williams clothing group, and a 19 percent stake in the Packer's Nine Network affiliate in Perth.

NETWORK TEN. Network Ten (Ten) was formed from the 1965 merger of Sydney, Melbourne, and Brisbane TV stations. It began operations with a short cash supply and a decision to spend more than half of its yearly budget on one variety show in its first year of operations (Timeline, 1995). The network's program fare was comprised of U.S. reruns and a few local productions. By 1972, Ten was out of its financial doldrums owing, in part, to a controversial nighttime soap opera that was a huge rating success.

News Corp. bought Ten and its Melbourne sister station in 1979. During the Murdoch years, Ten was able to increase its program budget to acquire more U.S. movies. In 1985, however, Murdoch became a U.S. citizen, forcing News Corp. to relinquish control of Ten to a shopping center magnate, Frank Lowy. Lowy bought Ten for U.S.$1 billion, but through bad management, the company was later sold to Westpac Bank.

Ten has been revived. By 1995, Network Ten was described as "a lean, mean, money-making machine" (Groves, 1995a). Network Ten was bought by Canadian-based CanWest in 1993. CanWest owns 57.5 percent of Network Ten financial stock but maintains only 15 percent of the company shares because of Australian laws on outside ownership. CanWest owner, I. H. "Izzy" Asper, whose net worth is estimated at U.S.$600 million, is said to be expanding its international holdings.

Mergers, Acquisitions, and Other Strategic Alliances

A *New York Times* headline read, "Mergers Continue Record Pace . . . " (November 2, 1996). There's no better way of saying it. With Australia's media moguls, mergers and alliances are constantly occurring. In May 1995, News Corp. formed an agreement with MCI for future products or services. By the end of 1996, they had added a new twist. MCI and British Telecommunications (BT) decided to join forces to create Concert PLC (Kind, 1996, Rose, 1996). The new company would own 13.5 percent of News Corp. MCI agreed to give BT 13.5 percent of its News Corp. stock. News Corp. and MCI were engaged in joint ventures designed to provide entertainment services to the U.S. market via satellite. The ventures are called American Sky Broadcasting (ASkyB) and SkyMCI. Ventures such as these create great concern. If allowed to form, it would create one of the largest cable TV and telephone companies in the world. British Telecommunications and MCI have advantages in their distribution systems. The addition of News Corp. would give the two companies a source for programming creation and purchase.

In July of 1996, News Corporation acquired New World Communication for $80 million (In a spin, 1996). It had attempted to buy Metro-Goldwyn-Mayer, but lost out on the bidding. Not to be left out completely, the successful bidder, Kirk Kerkorian will take a portion of his purchase price from Seven Network. Seven Network is controlled by Kevin Stokes but 15 percent of Seven Network is owned by News Corp.

Programming Development

According to de Bens et al. (1992), Australia is the leading supplier of series material into western European markets. Today, Australia makes a name for itself as a global TV program producer. Australian TV productions generate over $9 billion dollars annually (Cunningham et al., 1994). The Australian Bureau of Statistics offered a conservative estimation that Australia earned over $65 million dollars in 1991 from its combined audiovisual sector. Australian soap operas have found homes in Canada, New Zealand, the Netherlands, Ireland, and, most often in the United Kingdom. Australia has a service-based rather than a program export relationship with some countries. It sells programs to Star TV and other TV distributors. This approach ensures that Australia's programs are distributed over a wider area than if they were sold one country at a time.

Australia's Impact on the Global Media Marketplace

Personalities

People around the world may not always think about Australia's media connections, but they should. Recognition of the country often comes through recognition of the corporate controllers. In the United States, Rupert Murdoch's control of Fox Television Network resulted in acquisition of enough stations to reach 40 percent of the country. That does not include the programs produced for Fox and other broadcast and satellite operations. Outside the United States, his impact is felt in London, China and, through his music-based companies, the Middle East and India. Murdoch signed a pact with France's Canal Plus and Germany's Bertelsmann to provide satellite pay TV in Europe (Murdoch in European pact to provide satellite pay TV, 1996). Packer, whose company is totally Australian based, has operations in China as well. If he continues to invest in rugby players and U.S. casinos, U.S. citizens may hear his name more frequently. Izzy Asper is in the early stages of establishing his international conglomerate. With his Canadian base, he has moved past every obstacle to gain access to Australia and is well on his way to a United Kingdom collaboration.

International success for Australia is based on the tenacity of the media moguls who have placed it on the media map. They have chosen to look for paths to profitability that are not based on the critical acclaim of their programming but on the parsimony principle. Each major player has found success in their broadcast operations using this approach.

Regulations

Media regulation is tied heavily to the political groups in power. Many restrictions have been established by "gentlemen's agreements." When Frank Lowy decided to break the restriction on increased U.S. programming, nothing was done. When Packer wanted to increase his ownership in a company, the government increased the percentage of ownership allowable so that he would not break the law. Similarly, when Murdoch purchased more stations than the U.S. Federal Communications Commission permitted, the agency found a way to allow him to do so and encouraged other U.S. stations to follow suit if they were unhappy with their decision (Andrews, 1995).

The two areas of regulation that may continue to concern Australians are cross-media ownership and foreign ownership. Cross-media ownership laws restrict the types of media companies a conglomerate can hold. Under the old law, TV station owners were once limited to owning two TV stations or six radio stations. The numbers held, regardless of whether the stations were in major cities or small villages. There were no restrictions on ownership of newspapers, radio, and TV stations in the same market (MEAA Media Inquiry, 1996). Later the rules were relaxed to allow TV stations to build national networks. Now broadcasters are fighting cross media laws because they believe the laws force artificial boundaries.

Australia has a concentrated media ownership. Media operations range from 35 percent to 79 percent foreign ownership. Only Seven and Nine networks are limited to 19.9 percent foreign ownership. The government has recognized the problems concentrated ownership and foreign investment could cause. Participants are still arguing their cases on these issues.

Australia in the Years to Come

The last quarter of this century will be remembered as the time in which Australia left its parochial print focus and expanded geographically as well as financially. This era will be characterized by the bold steps taken by its media moguls. This may also be the decade that marks the end of success for Australia's original media barons. The men and families who established Australian media may be confined to the 1900s. As we move into 2000, who will control the Australian media?

Scholars interested in future research on Australia's media should consider keeping abreast of the media moguls in the 21st century. Who will they be and will any vestige of the 1800 media dynasties exist? The effect of regulation should become of greater interest in the next decade. Will Australia maintain the profits from its media, or will the money be spent in other countries? Finally, as Australia finds success in U.S. programming schedules, will that trend continue in Canada and other countries doing business in Australia? A test of the geolinguistic theory is in order. Why does it not help Australia's film industry? The study of Australian media economics allows numerous opportunities.

References

Andrews, E. (1995). F.C.C. set to give Murdoch waiver in ownership case. *The New York Times,* July 27, vol 144, p. C7.

Australia: Packer sets resignation from media firm (1996). *Facts on File Yearbook,* March 28, p. 209.

Australian Bureau of Statistics Statsite (1996a). Australia's film and video production and distribution industry. ABS Statsite, May 21.

Australian Bureau of Statistics (1996b). Australia's radio and television services industries, September 2. ABS Statsite 79/96, pp. 193–194.

Australian Financial Review. (1996) Homes connected to pay TV, as cited in MEAA Inquiry—Full Submission, http://www.allianc.

Best of Australia (1996). http://www.2000.fa. Fairfax

Bloomberg Business News (1996). Hit film helps News Corp. post 7% increase in operating profit. *The New York Times,* November 12, vol. 146, p. D6.

Budget Speech (1996–97). http://www.finance.gov.au/budget96/speech.html.

Central Intelligence Agency Factbook, 1995.

CEASA (1996). As cited in MEAA Media Inquiry—Full Submission, http://www.allianc.

Cunningham, S. (1992). *Framing Culture: Criticism and Policy in Australia.* Sydney: Allen & Unwin.

Cunningham, S., Miller, T., and Rowe, D. (1994). *Contemporary Australian television.* Sydney: University of New South Wales Press.

de Bens, E., Kelly, M., and Bakke, M. (1992). Television content: Dallasificiation of culture? In: Siune, K., and Truetzschler, W. (eds.) for the Euromedia Research Group. *Dynamics of Media Politics: Broadcast and Electronic Media in Western Europe.* London: Sage.

Department of Communications and Arts (1996). A new deal for rural phone users, September 26. http://www.dca.gov.au/mediarel/isdn.html.

Europa World Yearbook (1996). vol. 1. London: Europa Publications.

Europa World Yearbook (1997). vol. 1. London: Europa Publications. p. 434.
Grover, R., and Oneal, M. (1995). Man buys world. *Business Week,* May 29, pp. 26–29.
Groves, D. (1995a). Cox's plan for cable network Down Under hits roadblock. *Variety,* March 6, p. 48.
Groves, D. (1995b). Facing the challenge: resurrected Oz broadcaster makes a solid comeback. *Variety,* November 6 (Special Section), p. 57.
Groves, D. (1996). Things looking up for media stocks: Australia. *Variety,* January 1, p. 77.
Groves, D. (1996a). Aussies target U. S. for partners, growth. *Variety,* January 16, p. 50.
Groves, D. (1996b). Oz's overhead battles: Aussie cabler fighting rival Foxtel, local pols. *Variety,* January 22, p. 69.
In a spin (1996). *The Economist,* July 20, p. 53.
Karp. J. (1995). Stoking a stake. *Far Eastern Economic Review*, April.
Kind, P. (1996). Concert targets Asia-Pacific, Foxtel press release, May 6 (02) 387 1111(0419) 223 626 SYDNEY.
Lippman, J. (1996). News Corp. profit falls 2.2%, Hurt by U. S. TV unit. *The Wall Street Journal,* November 12, p. B8.
Martin, G. (1996). Rival media scions plot growth in Asia-Pacific; sons of Murdoch, O'Reilly, Packer see opportunities for newspapers. *Advertising Age,* September 16, p. 46.
Moody's Investor Service (1996). *Australia: Moody's International Manual.* New York: Moody's Investor Service, Inc.
Murdoch in European pact to provide satellite pay TV (1996). *Los Angeles Times,* March 7, vol. 115, p. D4.
Petrozzello, D. (1997). Trading market explodes. *Broadcasting & Cable,* February 3, pp. 18-19.
Rose, M. (1996). Murdoch may be important factor in BT-MCI merger. *The Wall Street Journal,* November 6, p. B8.
Roy Morgan Readership Survey, 1996. As cited in MEAA Inquiry—Full Submission, http://www.allianc.
Scherer, R. (1991). Australia's Fairfax Sold to Canada Magnate, *Christian Science Monitor,* December 17, vol. 84, p. 3.
Shares of showboat rise 12% amid speculation (1996). *New York Times,* September 18, p. D4.
Sinclair, J., Jacka, E., Cunningham, S. (1996). *New Patterns in Global Television: Peripheral Vision.* New York: Oxford University Press.
Smith, T. W. (1987). Phone home? An analysis of household telephone ownership. *International Telephone Survey Methodology.* Charlotte, NC: American Association for Public Opinion Research.
Thornberry, O. T., and Massey, J. T. (1988). Trends in U.S. telephone coverage across time and subgroups. In: Groves, R. M., et al. *Telephone Survey Methodology.* New York: Wiley, pp. 25–50.
Timeline (1995). *Variety,* November 6, p. 66.
Twentieth Century Fox (1996). *Broadcasting and Cable,* May 13, p. 55.

Windschuttle, K. (1985). *The Media: A New Analysis of the Press, Television, Radio and Advertising in Australia.* Ringwood: Penguin.
Woods, M. (1996a). Rupert rails at Packer, rugby brawl broadens *Variety,* April 1, p. 51.
Woods, M. (1996b). Galaxy to bow new channel just for laughs. *Variety,* p. 171.
Woods, M. (1996c). Galaxy merger plan. *Variety,* February 12, p. 23.
Woods, M. (1995a). Timeline (Network Ten Australia-Thirty years. *Variety,* November 6, p. 66.
Woods, M. (1995b). Feevee cabler Optus Vision rocks Oz boat. *Variety,* September, p. 38.
Woods, M. (1995c). 9 yanks 7's shows: Australian channels switch U.S. partners. *Variety,* August 14, p. 38.
Woods, M. (1995d). Kids TV summ hammers out but can't nail charter. *Variety,* March 13, p. 17.

20

THE PACIFIC RIM

TUEN-YU LAU AND PENGHWA ANG

The New Media Economic Dynamics

Asia, be it labeled as "dragons" or "flying geese" in the Western media, has drawn global attention because of its decade-long phenomenal economic growth (*Business Week* 1996). It is projected that by 2025, one quarter of the world's populations will be living in Asian cities (Sim, 1996). The deputy Prime Minister of Singapore, Mr. Lee Hsien Loong, said in London in November 1996 that Asia's total economy will surpass that of Europe in 2020 (*Lianhe Zaobao,* 1996). Academics and business people tend to believe that Asia is the new dominant center, with the global economic, political and cultural gravity slowly shifting from West to East (Sim, 1996). Although Japan and several more advanced Asian nations, such as Singapore and South Korea, have faced an economic slowdown in 1996, the huge total populations in Asia still offer opportunities for business romanticists. Parallel to its economic developments, Asia is also a plum for domestic and international television broadcasters to capture. This chapter examines the dynamics of the media developments in Asia, specifically television economics in the Pacific Rim countries.

Conceptually speaking, Asia is a huge land mass, covering more than 30 countries. The regional English-language magazine, *Asiaweek,* usually covers the following countries in its news map: Australia, Bangladesh, Brunei, Cambodia, China, The Gulf Countries, Hong Kong, India, Indonesia, Iran, Japan, Laos, Malaysia, Mongolia, Myanmar, Nepal, New Zealand, North Korea, Pakistan, Papua New Guinea, The Philippines, Russia, Singapore, South Korea, Sri Lanka, Taiwan, Thailand, Turkey and Vietnam. They include three of the world's most populous countries: China with almost 1.2 billion people; India, 900 million; and Indonesia, 200 million. The economic philosophies these countries are practicing span the perfect competition and monopoly bipolar spectrum. Culturally speaking, they represent the Confucian, Muslim, Christian and other influences. Therefore, it is inappropriate to describe the Asian nations and people as a whole, as is often grouped in the Western media.

It also is impossible to cover the media economics of all these countries in this chapter. India, China and Japan have already been covered elsewhere in this book; therefore, several countries in the Pacific Rim have been selected to illustrate the concepts as explained in the "Industrial Organization Model," a subfield in economics used frequently to examine mass communication issues. This chapter discusses mainly the market structure, with special focus on two policy issues related to the triangular relationship between the government, service suppliers and people (Lau, 1992). Before selecting the countries for analyses, the differences between the structures of the general market versus and television broadcasting market must be distinguished.

Spanning the bipolar spectrum of the general market, several Asian countries may provide a market structure close to perfect competition. When it comes to the television broadcasting (TV) market, however, almost all Asian countries exercise close governmental control. The reason is that airwave frequency allocation is a public good that the government acts on behalf of the people's best interests. Additionally, the governments are concerned about the impact of foreign cultures on their people. Therefore, TV broadcasting markets in Asia do not practice perfect competition.

Using these criteria, the TV broadcasting markets of Hong Kong, Singapore and Indonesia are examined in order to illustrate the various media economic dynamics based on the industrial organization model. These three media economies represent various market structures. Hong Kong has been billed as the world's freest economy for the third consecutive year by the U.S. Heritage Foundation and *The Wall Street Journal* (Hughes and Manuel, 1996). Singapore was also ranked among the top 10 free economies among the more than 150 countries surveyed. Hong Kong and Singapore ranked higher than the United States and Switzerland, which ranked fourth and fifth, respectively (Hughes and Gren, 1996). In terms of the TV broadcasting market definition, Hong Kong has a more "open" policy in Asia regarding regulations on the number of TV broadcasters competing for the provision of services.

Table 20-1. Advertising Expenditures in Selected Asian Countries, 1995

Country	Total Advertising Expenditure (in million $)	Growth Rate (%)	Advertising Spend by Medium					
			Television[a]		Radio		Newspapers	
			Advertising Expenditures	Growth Rate (%)	Advertising Expenditures	Growth Rate (%)	Advertising Expenditures	Growth Rate (%)
Japan	64,103	5	20,736	7	2,460	3	13,771	4
South Korea	6,525	23	1,782	25	229	17	2,824	20
Taiwan	3,570	15	1,072	–1	147	17	1,416	22
Hong Kong	1,953	7	961	19	126	20	566	–12
Thailand	1,522	16	756	12	—	—	477	9
Indonesia	1,495	46	734	54	76	22	482	45
India	1,215	25	325	34	32	11	781	22
Philippines	1,009	28	636	27	179	28	194	28
China	843	23	595	35	595	35	248	2
Malaysia	821	23	272	24	24	41	463	24
Singapore	755	8	256	4	40	11	388	11
Vietnam	62	—	29	—	1	—	13	—

Source: A regional ranking of ad spend and agency billing in 1995, April 19, 1996, pp. 12–14.

[a]Television includes terrestrial, cable and satellite TV.

[b]The "other category" in Taiwan includes cable TV.

The Singapore and Indonesia governments heavily regulate their TV broadcasting markets. Despite a monopolistic approach in regulating TV broadcasting, Singapore government claims, however, to provide a competitive environment within the monopolistic market structure to strive for efficiency and maximum customer satisfaction. Singapore also has been trying hard to attract international TV broadcasters in order to establish itself as a regional media hub. In Indonesia, the private sectors play an important role in pushing for rapid broadcasting developments. The existence of five commercial TV broadcasters makes Indonesia the most competitive terrestrial TV market in Asia. In sum, these three selections all have terrestrial TV and cable or satellite TV provisions. They will illustrate various models of interactions between the service providers, government policymakers and people. The media economic issues illustrated in the following discussions will highlight the commonalties in the Pacific Rim region.

Commonalities of the Region

Advertising supports most media in Asia. Table 20-1 shows the total advertising expenditure of 12 selected Asian countries in 1995. These markets can be classified as two types: mature and emerging, depending on the growth rate of total advertising expenditures in 1995. Japan, Hong Kong and Singapore, which all had one-digit growth in 1995, are the more mature markets.

Advertising Spend by Medium							
Magazines		Cinema		Outdoor		Other	
Advertising Expenditures	Growth Rate (%)	Advertising Expenditures	Growth Rate (%)	Advertising Expenditures	Growth Rate (%)	Advertising Expenditures	Growth Rate (%)
4,422	8	—	—	22,528	4	187	26
232	13	—	—	1,180	20	279	31
185	7	—	—	—	—	750[b]	33
232	9	6	–24	51	12	12	10
144	13	1	11	143	116	—	—
95	36	5	0	103	31	—	—
—	—	3	13	73	28	—	—
194	28	—	—	—	—	—	—
—	—	—	—	—	—	—	—
48	11	3	11	—	—	11	12
45	1	6	4	11	—	10	–12
5	—	—	—	16	—	—	—

Japan has 60 percent of the advertising spend in Asia. But it is Indonesia that led in growth rate with a year-on-year increase of 46 percent. It is the fastest emerging market in Asia. Specifically, in terms of TV broadcasting advertising growth rate, Indonesia also grew the fastest, with 54 percent in 1995. Hong Kong and Singapore registered 19 percent and 4 percent growth rates, respectively, in TV advertising.

Statistics show (Table 20-2) that TV broadcasting in Asia still has ample room for growth. In some populous countries, such as Indonesia and India, TV penetration rates in 1996 were 76 percent and 42 percent, respectively. Although cable TV penetration rates reached about 60 percent in the United States in 1996, cable TV in Asia, except for Taiwan and Philippines, is still in its infancy. In satellite TV development so far, only Hong Kong, Indonesia, Japan, Malaysia and Thailand have a significant number of satellite TV receivers and subscribers. Therefore, the overall TV broadcast markets in Asia, especially in the pay or subscription TV sectors will see more growth in the future.

Hong Kong: The Case of More Open Competition

Market Concentration

Hong Kong has terrestrial, cable and satellite TV services for its 6.2 million population. The two networks, Television Broadcasts Limited (TVB) and

Table 20-2. Television Broadcasting Statistics in Asia

Countries	No. of Terrestrial Television Stations	No. of Cable and Satellite Broadcasters	No. of Cable Operators	No. of Satellite Operators	No. of Television Homes
China	469[a]	—	14	—	280,000,000
Hong Kong	4	11	1	—	1,702,200
Indonesia	21	—	—	1	31,803,000
India	1	15	8	—	45,000,000
Japan	6	18	—	1	43,229,000
Malaysia	4	—	—	1	3,031,440
Pakistan	4	1	—	—	2,600,000
Philippines	132	5	15[a]	—	7,687,000
Singapore	4	7	13	—	771,210
Taiwan	5	—	10[a]	—	5,359,000
South Korea	50	25	—	—	14,153,000
Thailand	4	3	—	—	13,511,000
Vietnam	2	—	—	—	6,000,000
Total					454,846,850

Source: Fung, 1996.
[a]These statistics only include the major stations or operators.
MMDS = multipoint multichannel distribution services.

Asian Television (ATV), each owns and operates two channels, one Chinese and one English. They transmitted almost 585 hours of programming per week. As required by law, these two commercial networks have to carry about 10 hours of programs supplied by Radio Television Hong Kong (RTHK), a public broadcasting organization. Five hours of programs are broadcast during the prime time on both Chinese language channels during the week. The financial arrangement is that the commercial networks will get the advertising revenues while RTHK will provide the programs free of charge. The mission of RTHK is to produce programs not sufficiently provided by the commercial broadcasters (Hong Kong Annual Report, 1996).

Cable TV is provided by Wharf Cable, which began its exclusive franchise to cable 1.5 million homes in 1994. They now provide a line-up of 20 channels, with 15 in the basic package. Besides six channels devoted to local and international news (such as Cable News Network [CNN], Asian Business News), other channels include movies, sports, family entertainment, education, children, youth and women (*Hong Kong Annual Report,* 1996).

Percentage of All Homes	No. of Cable Homes	Percentage of All TV homes (%)	No. of Satellite/ MMDS Homes	Percentage of All TV Homes
78	28,000,000	10	—	0
98	260,000	15	418,000	25
76	0	0	17,000	0
42	11,800,000	26	—	0
100	3,100,000	7	9,800,000	23
93	40,000	1	18,000	1
—	20,000	1	—	0
87	450,000	6	—	0
100	18,000	2	—	0
98	3,602,000	67	—	0
99	976,418	7	—	0
91	240,000	2	26,000	0
37.5	0	0	—	0
—	48,506,418		10,279,000	

Hong Kong is also home to the first pan-Asian satellite TV service, Satellite Television for the Asian Region (STAR TV). Owned by the media tycoon Rupert Murdoch, it delivers a mix of free-to-air and encrypted channels providing sports, music, entertainment, news and Chinese- and Hindi-language programs to more than 220 million TV viewers in 53 countries, stretching from Japan to Turkey and from Indonesia to Mongolia. At the end of 1995, 447,230 Hong Kong homes could receive STAR TV and other satellite TV programs through Satellite Master Antenna Television (SMATV) programs. Additionally, seven satellite broadcasters uplink their services from Hong Kong. They are CNN/TNT & Cartoon Network, Chinese Television Network (CTN), ESPN, TVBI, NBC Asia and Chinese Entertainment Television (CETV) (*Hong Kong Annual Report*, 1996).

As Hong Kong is leading other Asian cities in adopting new communication technologies, an optical fiber cable network transmitting a near video-on-demand (VOD) service was proposed by the once-monopoly telephone provider, Hong Kong Telecom, in 1997. The hold up of introducing VOD is due to the government's drafting of a law on subscription TV to clarify whether VOD is subject to telecommunication or broadcasting or a combination of both regulations.

With a 6.2 million population, Hong Kong is a small market. The total advertising expenditures of HK$1,953 million (U.S.$250 million) ranked fourth in 1995 among all Asia Pacific countries (see Table 20-1). Therefore, the Hong Kong broadcasters have defined the concept of the market beyond geographic boundaries. They have first created the Chinese communities globally. They use the same product for a global market. For example, a Hong Kong newspaper will publish the North American edition, and TVB will package a TV channel on satellite and cable TV networks in the United States. Because of the rising economies in Taiwan and Mainland China, they have redefined in terms of the Chinese cultural and linguistic links by conceptually defining a "Greater China market." For example, TVB helped launch a TVB-S Mandarin language channel in Taiwan. Therefore, based on the needs for expansion to look for additional revenue streams, the Hong Kong media companies have used an aggressive global expansion strategy.

On the other hand, the Hong Kong broadcasters have to compromise with the coming of foreign satellite TV channels. Traditionally, foreign print media and TV programs have entered the Hong Kong market freely. Some satellite broadcasters also use Hong Kong as an Asian operational headquarters to implement their global expansion plans. Their revenues are based on the English-speaking communities in the Asia Pacific region. With the introduction of a localization strategy of dubbing and subtitling, they also try to widen their market to non-English speaking sectors in the region.

Product Differentiation

In the analysis of the broadcast services available in this market, product differentiation can be examined at two levels: the overall market level and broadcaster's internal level; that is, the strategies within a broadcaster to spin off added values of its original product. The overall broadcast market has two levels: mass and narrowcasting. The two networks provide mass entertainment for the total population. Cable TV seeks to siphon off the networks' audiences by providing specialized programming, such as 24-hour all-news channels in Cantonese and all-movie channels. The satellite TV channels provide similar programming fares to compete with the exclusive cable TV franchise in Hong Kong. Then, the VOD services have tried to provide *a la carte* customer-chosen programs based on a menu available to the customer.

The broadcasters' efforts to differentiate their programs from those of other broadcasters have given rise to the program production costs. This is in terms of local versus foreign programs, and in-house versus independent productions. The increasing number of terrestrial TV stations, and the introduction of a multichannel environment because of cable and satellite TV, means that all broadcasters are scrambling for more programs. Foreign programs, especially from the United States and Brazil, are readily available to fill the expanded broadcast hours. Some U.S. program suppliers have taken advantage of this increased demand to raise program prices. Additionally, some major U.S. program suppliers have introduced the U.S. concept of allowing pay TV to get the first window for the broadcast of movies and blockbusters. Though terrestrial TV broadcasters, such as TVB, have suggested that they have more audiences than cable TV, they find it difficult to compete. Therefore, the coming of cable and satellite TV in Hong Kong has forced the terrestrial broadcasters to seek more new sources of quality foreign movies and drama series.

Barriers to Entry

Various forms of government regulations are the main barriers to entry for new players in Hong Kong. Wharf Cable holds an exclusive franchise of providing cable TV. Its franchise will be up for discussion in 1988. The regulations also stipulate that cable TV cannot broadcast commercials in its first 3 years of franchise, thus protecting the interests of the existing terrestrial broadcasters.

New telecommunication technologies have also introduced new players, in particular, video-on-demand by Hong Kong Telecom. Its plan to introduce the service in 1997 was delayed because of the need to clarify whether VOD is considered a broadcast system and, thus, subject to the same regulations as other broadcasters. The government in 1996 decided that such a service was not broadcasting and issued two licenses, with the second going to a new company called New World Telecommunication (*Hong Kong Annual Report*, 1996).

The entrance of foreign broadcasters is also controlled. At present, no more than 10 percent of the ownership can be controlled by a foreign company or individual. Cable TV is subject to similar regulations. Satellite TV may be up to 49 percent foreign owned. There are no restrictions on foreign broadcasters using Hong Kong as an operational headquarters for uplink. At present, STAR TV, MGM Gold (Movie Channel), and NBC Asia use Hong Kong as the headquarters for uplink to the entire Asia Pacific region. In December 1995, TVB also was granted an uplink license to provide two satellite TV channels.

Vertical Integration

The success of TVB is based on a vertically integrated operation that controls the production and distribution of TV programs and, to some extent, the "ownership" of the actors. Except the import of foreign programs, all programs are made in-house because Hong Kong does not have a similar U.S. financial-syndication rule. Then, the entry of satellite TV, STAR TV, cable TV, and Wharf Cable, changed the rules of the game. Both STAR TV and Wharf Cable tried to contract out their program productions in order to break TVB's monopoly of the production forces and resources. This has resulted in a growing number of independent producers and rising product costs for the terrestrial broadcasters.

Singapore: The Case of Corporatized Monopoly

Market Concentration

The TV market in Singapore is characterized by monopoly for historical reasons. Television broadcasting began as a department in the government. It was then instituted as a statutory board, which meant that it had to reduce its dependence on funding from government. Most recently, the broadcasting functions have been spun off into several companies. Although they are all entirely owned by the Singapore government, the mechanisms are in place for the companies to be publicly listed. In short, the broadcast industry has become more market sensitive.

The main reason for such a rejuvenation is the awareness of a possible threat from other sources. For example, the radio industry has been rejuvenated because an Indonesian entrepreneur set up a radio station on an island 45 minutes away by boat from Singapore. At its high point, 70 percent of all radio listeners were tuned to it (Ang 1995). Acknowledging TV as a medium of mass entertainment and a source of revenue, in 1994, the Singapore government restructured the entire broadcast industry. All the functions that had been under one entity—the Singapore Broadcasting Corporation—were now spun off into several smaller companies and with a firm eye on allowing competition.

The umbrella company, Singapore International Media (SIM), owns most of the broadcast media. It has 10 of the 14 radio stations in Singapore, as well as a stake in the only cable TV company. The largest and most profitable of the new companies is the Television Corporation of Singapore (TCS). It operates an English and a Chinese station on a commercial, not public service, basis. The English station has a smaller audience but commands higher advertising revenues because English is still the language of those with higher demographics. The Chinese station has a larger audience, sometimes reaching more than a million in a city-state with a population of just 3 million. Its main strength lies in its local productions. Nine of the top 10 most popular shows are locally produced and are from this station (Television Corporation of Singapore, 1995).

Public service TV is broadcast from TV12. It operates two channels—one for the minority groups of the Malays and Tamils and one channel in English geared toward documentaries and fine arts. Ratings are low, and the company continues to be subsidized by the government. The company recently attempted to outsource local production through a scheme that is discussed later in this chapter.

As a transition to cable TV, Singapore Cablevision started a UHF pay TV station that broadcasts Home Box Office (HBO), CNN and a Chinese variety channel on a subscription basis in 1992. Its charges, however, are expensive (about U.S.$20 per channel and U.S.$40 for all three). Coupled with some technical problems in installing the UHF antennas on the roofs of apartment blocks that are occupied by most Singaporeans, penetration has therefore been abysmal.

Singapore's cable TV system was rolled out only in June 1995 through Singapore Cablevision. It was formed in April 1992 as a joint venture of the daily newspaper monopoly Singapore Press Holdings (20 percent), a government-linked conglomerate Singapore Technologies Ventures (24 percent), SIM (31 percent), and Continental Cablevision of the United States (25 percent) (*Business Times,* 1995).

Penetration, however, has been low at around 35 percent with a churn rate of 4 to 5 percent among subscribers. Penetration rate of 35 percent among households wired (*Business Times*, 1995). Several reasons have been given for this low penetration in a country that has one of the highest cinema attendance per capita in the world.

Singapore Cablevision is also regulated in its finances: its regulator, Singapore Broadcasting Authority, has mandated that advertising may form only 25 percent of its total income. And advertisements are limited to 14 minutes per hour (Tan, 1995). The company expects to accumulate losses totaling U.S.$25 million in its first 2 years and to break even after the third year (*Business Times,* 1995).

Satellite TV dishes are banned from use in homes. But a subsidiary of the SIM group repackages local programs and broadcasts DBS signals to the region. A video-on-demand trial is under way, conducted by Singapore Telecoms among its employees.

Despite its tentative approach to the broadcast industry locally, Singapore hopes it can develop itself to be a broadcast hub for the region. Thus far, 19 broadcast companies have established themselves in Singapore. Among them are ESPN, Asian Business News, HBO, Disney, Discovery, Music TV and U-TV of India. These companies use Singapore for post-production and as a site for uplinks and regional distribution (Toh, 1997).

Product Differentiation

Singapore is one of the few markets in Asia where TV advertising is not the market leader. Television commands about 30 percent of the advertising expenditures against a little more than 50 percent for daily newspapers. The gap is not likely to narrow soon, especially as cable TV is still struggling to gain acceptance (Newspapers lift share, 1996).

With just one buyer for the market, Singapore is a monopsony, an advantage the TV companies are not shy about exploiting. They buy foreign programs at half to a tenth of the cost of that paid by even a Hong Kong broadcaster with its small base. Nevertheless, there has been a drop in foreign imports of programming (Waterman and Rogers 1994).

The TV stations have become aware that local productions sell better. A local production, *Extraordinary People,* has an average viewership of 330,000 against 192,000 for the foreign program that used to occupy the slot (Tan, 1995). The dominant TCS has produced comedies, dramas, soap operas, variety shows and some documentaries.

TV12 has been left behind in the push to localize. In 1997, however, the Economic Development Board developed a scheme called the Local Industry Upgrading Program, whereby S$20,000 (U.S.$14,000) is given as a grant to local production houses to produce mainly documentaries and some dramas and soap operas. The programs will be telecast, but all residuals and advertisement revenues from the telecast will go to the TV station, not the producers.

Barriers to Entry

The major barrier to entry is regulatory. First, unless exempted by the government, no one may own more than 3 percent of a company broadcasting into Singapore. Foreigners may not own the majority stake in a broadcast company and cannot form more than half of the board of directors. The licensing of TV stations is also regulated. The high cost of doing business in Singapore is also a deterrent. A production worker is expected to earn around U.S.$800 a month. Various parties have explored setting up production houses in Malaysia (U.S.$400 a month for a production worker) and Indonesia (U.S.$150 a month for a production worker). Also, until this year, local TV stations broadcast only in-house productions.

As already discussed, censorship has not posed as much of a barrier as might be expected. Indeed, Asian Business News, the first TV news network to be set up in Singapore, was part owned by both Dow Jones and the Singapore government.

A second major barrier is the smallness of the market. Television is divided into the English- and Chinese-language streams. The Chinese watch more TV but have lower demographics than the English. The highest rated TV show ever had a viewership of just over 1 million. To overcome this, Singapore companies have talked about going regional, that is, producing TV programs for the region. There has been some success in producing for the Chinese market. TCS dramas are sold to TV stations in China, Taiwan, Indonesia and other Asian countries. A more likely market is that of Indonesia and Malaysia. But these are in languages that are in the minority in Singapore. There has been some talk of co-productions in Malaysia, but the venture has yet to take off.

Vertical Integration

Given the combination of history and regulation, it is understandable that the TV industry has been highly vertically integrated. The 1995 Singapore Broadcasting Authority Act established a regulatory body whose functions used to be in the Singapore Broadcasting Corporation. Then, various subsidiaries such as TV production, advertisement production, transmission and uplink, and TV guide publishing were established to position itself for the increasing competition from the private sector.

Indonesia: The Case of Unplanned Rising Competitions

Market Concentration

There were seven TV channels serving Indonesia's population of 200 million as of March 1997. Except for two government TV channels, TVRI-1 and TVRI-2 of Televisi Republik Indonesia, five commercial TV stations are competing for the about U.S.$800 million in advertising. Television broadcasting before 1988 was not competitive, with only a commercial TV network, Rajawali Citra Television Indonesia (RCTI), offering one channel via a subscriber-paid decoder box. Surya Citra Television (SCTV) began broadcasting in 1990 and Indonesian Educational Television (TPI) in 1991 (Idris and Marwah, 1993). Two more commercial TV networks, Anteve (ANTV) and Indosiar Visual Mandiri (IVM), joined the competition in 1994 and 1995, respectively. As of today, TV penetration rate nationally was about 76 percent, with the capital, Jakarta, averaging about 80 percent. The maximum TV rating points in 1996 were about 50, totaling 10 million people watching during prime time. It is therefore not surprising to find that TV advertising expenditure is growing rapidly, with a growth rate of 54 percent in 1995, topping all other Asian countries. In 1993, TV advertising expenditures exceeded the print media for the first time, making the print media owners very nervous.

The five commercial TV networks are backed by influential conglomerates in Indonesia. Both RCTI and SCTV are owned by the Bimantara Group, which is controlled by President Suharto's son. Indosiar Visual Mandiri is owned by the largest privately owned company in Indonesia, Salim Group, while ANTV is owned by the Bakrie Group. These conglomerates have the deep pockets necessary to support these networks' operations. As of today, only RCTI is turning a profit, whereas the rest of the networks are trying to find the right programming mix to attract ratings and advertising.

The government channels are supported by various sources, including direct subsidies from the government; 12.5 percent of the advertising revenues generated by each of the five commercial TV networks, and TV license fees collected from TV set owners.

As a group of many islands, cable TV is not appropriate for Indonesia. A state-of-the-art digital satellite TV service, Indovision, is run by the conglomerate consisting of the Bimantara group (owner of RCTI and SCTV), and Salim Group (owner of IVM). Indovision began with only five channels: news (CNN), movies (HBO), sports (ESPN), children (Disney) and educational (Discovery). Indovision has signed a management contract with STAR TV and the launch of an S-band satellite, Indostar, in July 1997 increased the channel line-up from 5 to 20, with new channels such as, CNBC, NBC, BBC Worldwide Service, and the MGM Gold.

In terms of the number of terrestrial TV stations, Indonesia has the largest number (five, with a sixth TV station just introduced in 1997), after Japan. Therefore, it has one of the keenest competitions in the Asia Pacific region; however, it also has the potential of reaching more audiences as the number of TV households will expand from 76 percent, provided Indonesia's economy continues to grow 7 percent annually. Then, the growth of number of TV viewers will make the cost-per-thousand rate for advertising on TV more attractive than other media, notably print. Moreover, the satellite TV service, Indovision, is going after the more affluent middle and upper classes who must spend U.S.$1,000 to $3,000 to purchase a satellite reception dish and pay the monthly subscription fees. The number of subscribers is estimated at 10 percent of the population. This represents 20 million people, about the total population of Australia.

Product Differentiation

The beginning of commercial TV station RCTI's success was due to the popularity of foreign action dramas. With the coming of more competitors, especially the amply funded IVM in 1995, the whole TV scene changed. Indosiar Visual Mandiri used the more culturally proximate Asian programs, especially Chinese Kung-fu drama series, dubbed into Bahasa Indonesia to dominate the prime time 7:30 to 8:30 drama slot for eight consecutive weeks. Using the strip programming strategies of broadcasting the serial drama, *Return of the Condor Heroes,* from Monday to Friday, it captured almost 80 percent audience share. Other commercial TV stations followed suit but with limited success. As Indonesian audiences again turn to local drama, there are only 10 active TV program production houses in the country. Therefore, there is a shortage of programs for the commercial TV broadcasters (Leung and Lau, 1996). Most TV stations are just beginning to be equipped with studios and production facilities, staffed by mostly inexperienced production crews. The new broadcasting bills passed in December require 51 percent of the TV programs to be locally produced. This will be an added demand on the terrestrial TV broadcasters.

The satellite TV channels available can be broadly classified as wholesale retransmission of foreign channels. The only localization efforts are to use subtitles in Bahasa Indonesia for these channels. Because of HBO's emphasis of using original soundtrack as its major selling point and the different sources and perspectives of the foreign news channels, other channels still have to undergo more "rigorous re-packaging efforts" to localize and add values to these foreign channels. The terrestrial and satellite TV broadcasters are hamstrung by the lack of local production abilities to create clear product differentiation. Several local terrestrial broadcasters are attempting to carve out their market niche; for example, ANTV seeks to get the younger viewers with the broadcast of 6 hours of Music TV each day.

Barriers to Entry

The Indonesian government prohibits foreign ownership of broadcast media. Foreign specialists, however, may serve as technical advisors. There is no clear indication of how many terrestrial TV broadcast licenses will be issued and how many TV licenses each company can hold. The Indonesian government has not indicated whether the existing satellite TV will be totally by subscription support or whether it can later broadcast commercials, thus competing with the terrestrial TV broadcasters for the advertising expenditures.

Vertical Integration

Vertical integration of the production and distribution of TV programs is allowed in Indonesia. Most terrestrial TV broadcasters are trying to beef up their in-house production. The independent TV producers, without their own outlet except to sell their programs to the terrestrial TV broadcasters, are trying to delay the rising market power of the broadcasters by urging the government to specify a percentage of programs that the broadcasters have to purchase from them. Because the independent producers have a longer history of producing the programs, and because of their good relationship with the actors, their programs consistently achieve high TV ratings. Several independent producers thus still have strong access to the TV stations. Some can even negotiate a profit-sharing deal, by which they can get a minimum guaranteed price of each drama series; they set up their sales teams, in addition to the TV network's sales team, to ensure that all the commercial airtime is sold. Some of the weaker networks may be willing to sell their entire time slot to the independent producers for a guaranteed income.

Emerging Issues in the Pacific Rim Region

As indicated earlier, this is a very diverse region. When attempting to analyze this part of the world, one may define the market by geographic locations, as well as by languages or cultural criteria such as the Greater China Confucian market, the Muslim market, and the Hindu market. These distinctions are important because the definition of a market goes beyond the traditional geographic boundaries, especially in the age of satellite TV. Many satellite TV providers, for example, HBO Asia and Discovery Asia, want to use the same product for various Asian countries. The linguistic and cultural links are equally important in exploring the profit potentials and cultural impact of terrestrial, cable and satellite TV. They will force the TV broadcasters, government policy-makers, and peoples to be aware of the implications of the import of foreign programs and channels in meeting their information and entertainment needs.

The Asia market, consisting of about 455 million TV households, has tremendous growth potential. Terrestrial and cable TV are confined by geographic boundaries. Satellite TV, theoretically, is boundaryless. But the experience of STAR TV and other similar satellite TV ventures in the region suggests that regionalization and globalization of the media do not work. That means the same product cannot meet various peoples' information and entertainment needs simultaneously. Now these satellite TV broadcasters have turned to the buzzword "localization." The president of NBC Asia, S. K. Fung, identified four localization approaches: (1) production of local programming, (2) use of local language, (3) rescheduling of programs to suit local viewing tastes, and (4) packaging and promotion to create the look and feel of the channel (*Television Asia,* 1997). In fact, there is a potential market that has yet to be fully explored, that is, the English-language community with strong purchasing power in the Asia Pacific region. An Asian TV broadcaster that has a plan in capturing this market is the Television Corporation of Singapore, which has a well-run 24-hour English-language channel and has been trying to establish its English drama production lines (*Television Asia,* 1997).

Additionally, markets based on linguistic and cultural relationship still have significant growth. The most notable market growth is in the "Greater

China regions," consisting mainly of China, Taiwan, Hong Kong and to some extent, Singapore, Malaysia and Thailand. The Hong Kong broadcaster, TVB, is the most successful in capturing this "Greater China market" by selling directly to these markets and establishing cable or satellite TV channels, for example, the TVBS channels in Taiwan (To and Lau, 1995).

There is an intensive competition within and across the Asian nations in terms of TV programming. For local broadcasters, local programming is the key to staying alive against other local and satellite TV broadcasters. Except perhaps Hong Kong and Singapore, where most of the local programs are produced in-house, many broadcasters rely on independent production houses to supply their programs. Most Asian local broadcasters, except Hong Kong and Singapore, are hamstrung by the lack of TV professionals in producing quality programs. Additionally, the more qualified producers and production staff are recruited by the satellite broadcasters headquartered in the region. Therefore, the key in the future success of the broadcasters, be they local or foreign, must establish a sound production management system (Berfield, 1996; Johnstone, 1996). So far, Television Corporation of Singapore (formerly Singapore Broadcasting Corporation) is the most successful in recruiting foreign expertise and then successfully building up its homegrown TV production teams.

Many local broadcasters in the region, faced with its self-imposed pressure of long broadcast hours running from 16 to 24 hours a day, take an easy way out by buying programs from the United States, Hong Kong, India or Brazil. Increasingly, these local broadcasters find that the Hollywood programs are no more the trump card to winning audiences. This has encouraged the intra-Asian program sales, as evidenced in the 3-year-old MIPASIA program market held in Hong Kong in December every year (Marich, 1996). The form of cooperation between Western and Asian broadcasters in the future may be in the technology transfer and skills transfer. Western broadcasters may devise strategies for more co-productions so that the local broadcasters will believe that they own part of the program and simultaneously learn the latest skills in TV production.

So far, the impact of the entry of foreign and mainly American satellite TV broadcasters has been limited to increasing the appreciation level of the elite and practicing TV professionals. Direct broadcast satellite is not as popular as cable TV in the region. Asian local governments prefer to develop cable systems because it allows them more control of the number of program suppliers and their content. Singapore is an example that other Asian countries may emulate. So far, cable TV is a significant force in Taiwan, India, the Philippines and Thailand.

In the development of terrestrial, cable and satellite TV systems in Asia, most Asian nations are capable to provide their funding for these projects. They may seek strategic alliances with foreign partners to gain management expertise; for example, Indovision is using STAR TV as its management consultant. MEASAT in Malaysia has two foreign experts as its chief executive officer and chief operating officer. Only recently, Singapore Cablevision's chief executive officer, an American, stepped down to become advisor to the chairperson.

With the launch of about 60 new satellites over the next 8 years in the region, including Indostar in July 1997, and the technical feasibility of digital compression, there will be a greater proliferation of satellite TV (Agence France Presse, 1996). Parallel with the new technological development, such as video on demand, Asia will not be falling behind with the American or European counterparts.

The pace of economic development in Asia is at two extremes; it seems that the recent developments are technology, rather than market, driven. The entrepreneurs and conglomerates have set their dreams to keep up with the Joneses, but they have yet to find ways to beef up their local program production capabilities so that they will add value even to the import of foreign satellite TV signals into their territories. This is only possible if the government broadcasting regulations in these Asian nations can keep up with this rapid development. Two policy issues relate to the triangular relationship between the government, service providers, and people, namely: Does the government provide a fair and equal environment for the service providers? Does the government policy serve the best interests of the people? These questions have yet to be answered. The future of TV broadcasting in Asia is full of potential, but how it will be realized remains to be seen.

References

Agence France Presse (1996). Singapore: Arianespace targets Asia growth. *South China Morning Post*, Internet Edition, December 18.

Ang, P. H. (1995). Singapore Broadcast Scene. *Media Digest.* Radio Television Hong Kong, August, pp. 10–12.

Ang, P. H., and Berlinda, N. (1996). Censorship and the Internet: a Singapore perspective. *Communications of the ACM* 39(6):72–78.

Berfield, S. (1996). Asia's no pushover: In the fight for the region's television audiences, the satellite giants are meeting tough resistance. *Asiaweek,* November 9, pp. 38–46

Business Times (1995). SCV sees losses totalling $36m for this year and next. December 28.

Business Week (1996). Internet Edition cover story, November 26.

Busterna, J. C. (1989). Concentration and the industrial organization mode. In: Picard, R. G., Winter, J. P., McCombs, M. E., and Lacy, S. (eds.). *Press Concentration and Monopoly.* Norwood, NJ: Ablex Publishing.

Fung, S. K. (1996). The industry forum for comment and opinion. *Television Asia,* December, p. 77.
Heuvel, J. V., and Everette, E. D. (1993). *The Unfolding Lotus: East Asia's Changing Media.* New York: The Freedom Forum Media Studies Center.
Hong Kong Annual Report (1996). Hong Kong Government Printers.
Hughes, D., and Gren, M. (1996) HK takes freest economy title—Again, *The South China Morning Post,* Internet Edition, December 17.
Idris, N., and Marwah, D. I. (1993). Communication scene of Indonesia. In: Goonsekera, A., and Holaday, D. (eds.). *Asian Communication Handbook.* Singapore: Asian Mass Communication Research and Information Center, pp. 59–86.
Johnstone, H. (1996). Asian television companies take lead in local content. *Asian Business,* October, pp. 26–36.
Lau, T-Y. (1992). From cable television to direct broadcast satellite: Emerging policy issues in the Asia Pacific Region. *Telecommunications Policy,* October.
Leung, W., and Lau, T. Y. (1996). The impact of competition on Indonesian television, 1994–1996. Paper presented at the Association for Education in Journalism and Mass Communication annual conference, August, Los Angeles, CA.
Lianhe Zaobao (United Daily) (1996). November 22, p. 1.
Marich, R. (1996). Asia television takes great leap from many Sat platforms. *Variety,* November 8, p. 23.
Masters, N. (1997a). UTV Opens KL Studio for RTM Soap Opera. *Television Asia,* January, p. 8.
Masters, N. (1997b). Leading the Way: Interview with TCS CEO Lee Cheok Yew. *Television Asia,* January, p. 19.
Newspapers lift share of advertising sales (1996). *Straits Times*, May 13.
A regional ranking of ad spending and agency billings in 1995 (1996). *Asian Advertising and Marketing* 10(8):12–14.
Sim, S. (1996). Overtaking the West: Asia's teeming urbanites. *The Strait Times,* December 9, p. 41.
Television Asia (1997). Indovision's programming lineup revealed. January, p. 2.
Television Corporation of Singapore (1995). *Annual Report.* Singapore: Television Corporation of Singapore.
Tan, S. Y. (1995). Viewer's choice. *Business Times,* July 29.
To, Y. M., and Lau, T-Y. (1995). Global export of Hong Kong television: Television Broadcasts Limited. *Asian Journal of Communication* 5(2):108–121.
Toh, H. S. (1997). Business spending by media industry up 51%. *Business Times,* January 23.
Waterman, D., and Rogers, E. M. (1994). The economics of television program production and trade in Far East Asia. *Journal of Communication* 44(3):89.

6

Patterns and Issues

The previous chapters in this book exhibit the diverse range of issues affecting the media industries in nations and regions around the globe. Yet, despite this diversity, there are also commonalities that exist. In the concluding chapter, co-editors Albarran and Chan-Olmsted summarize and discuss the common patterns and issues in the contemporary global media marketplace.

21

GLOBAL PATTERNS AND ISSUES

ALAN B. ALBARRAN AND SYLVIA M. CHAN-OLMSTED

This book has examined the numerous changes affecting the media industries in various countries around the globe. Clearly, we are experiencing a dramatic transition toward a dynamic, competitive marketplace. Although this evolution is far from complete, several interesting patterns are emerging that will impact the development of a global media marketplace.

In this summary chapter, we review five of the major trends that many countries and regions of the world are experiencing simultaneously. Although these trends do not necessarily apply to every region and country presented in this text, a majority are applicable. As such, these trends illustrate more commonalities than differences with regard to business practices among the nations.

1. Many Countries Are Experiencing Rapid Change and Transformation

A combination of economic, political, social and technological forces are affecting media industries around the globe (Albarran, 1996). Economic forces are observed in expanded trade policies such as the North American Free Trade Agreement (NAFTA) in North America and the move toward common currency and open trade across Europe. In terms of political forces, regulatory reforms such as the 1996 Telecommunications Act in the United States and the World Trade Organization's recent move toward open markets in telecommunications (Fleming, 1997) will lead to a redefining of the media marketplace.

Social forces, both with respect to demography and social policy, are also having an impact. Perhaps no country has experienced as much social change as South Africa, with its shift toward black empowerment and greater access to the media for all citizens. Other countries are wrestling with what we in the United States refer to as "universal service," or balancing the needs of the consumers with the needs of the marketplace, and the desire to provide information services and products at a reasonable cost. In sum, the forces of commercialization, concerns in public interest, and the national pride in developing a technologically sophisticated media infrastructure have led to policy changes in many countries.

To complicate the matter, technological convergence has erased the boundaries that previously separated the communication industries into disparate parts. For decades broadcasting, cable, computers, and telecommunications operated within their distinct markets. The shift toward a digital environment has blurred the lines between content creation, distribution, packaging, and exhibition (Tapscott, 1996). As discussed earlier in the book, it may be more appropriate in the near future to define media industries and companies by their functions rather than by the individual markets they are engaged in.

2. The Emergence of Aggressive Media Conglomerates and Expanded Concentration

A number of major media conglomerates are rapidly positioning themselves to acquire a foothold in the global media marketplace. In the United States, Disney, Time Warner and Viacom have acquired a number of well-known brands across a number of media markets. News Corporation is one of the most aggressive of all companies, with interests in a number of key segments: publishing, broadcasting, film production, television programming, and satellite distribution. Other companies likely to remain major players include Microsoft, Bertelsmann, Hachette, Sony, Reed Elsevier, and British Telecommunications. The global presence of News Corp., a non–United States-based multinational media conglomerate, illustrates the complexity of today's global media marketplace. Using mostly the direct broadcast satellite (DBS) technology, a logical cross-border communication system, and through strategic alliances with local media organizations, News Corp. has become a strong media competitor in many regions and countries.

Although no single company has yet acquired what would be considered dominance of any individual media market (Albarran and Dimmick, 1996), the growth and expansion of global media conglomerates raises concern over consolidation and its impact on competitors and ultimately the consumers. Policymakers will have to maintain a watchful eye over future mergers and acquisitions to ensure media markets remain competitive. Some analysts suggest that eventually large international consortiums will be created, combining companies from around the globe, specializing in such areas as content creation, distribution and networking, telecommunications, and wireless services. These consortia will be in the best position to utilize both economies of scope and scale in their regular business activities.

3. Liberalization of Media Industries

In many countries of the world, governments have loosened control of individual media markets and opened the marketplace to private forces. Television has been one of the primary beneficiaries of this trend, especially in the deployment of multichannel services such as cable and satellite. Telecommunication services targeted to both businesses and consumers are another area that will continue to develop with the unbundling of network architectures closed prior to deregulation.

It is apparent that governments in many countries that have traditional state-controlled media structures are trying to strike a balance between commercialization and the public interest. Not only should the needs of business and industry be considered but also the impact such decisions will have on social policy.

Many countries are also addressing the need for more private sources of funding as opposed to government supported subsidies and other costly programs. This has created a growing reliance on advertising as a major revenue source, increasing commercialization and stimulating economic growth in many regions of the world. U.S. companies have been quick to enter a number of foreign markets to take advantage of this trend.

4. Increasing Strategic Alliances Between Local Media Companies and Foreign Multinational Media Conglomerates

Expansion into new markets is challenging, and many companies are utilizing a number of strategic alliances to help expand their global presence. Strategic alliances present a commercial relationship between two or more firms that choose to integrate operational functions, share risks, and align corporate cultures to achieve a collective market advantage. Strategic alliances range from mergers and acquisitions to joint ventures, formal and informal agreements, and cooperative partnerships (Albarran, 1997). Joint ventures in which both parties are equal partners in terms of providing capital and sharing risks tend to be common among firms based in different countries.

Strategic alliances seem to offer the best opportunity for success when implementing new media or telecommunications systems or when introducing new products as companies are able to not only combine resources but also capture a developed customer base. There are other clear advantages to entering into a strategic alliance with a home country, rather than attempting to enter the market as a foreign outsider. First, the domestic-based company has a much better understanding of the culture, language, regulatory environment, marketing potential, and business climate within the home area. Second, existing governmental policy decisions may restrict or prevent the expansion of foreign nationals without some sort of strategic partnership. Third, in most cases it will be less expensive to enter into a partnership with an existing company than to try and enter alone. In other words, barriers to entry will be less formidable in cases where partnerships exist.

A few examples of joint alliances involving firms of different nationalities include British Telecommunications and MCI; USWest and TCI's alliance to offer cable services in the United Kingdom, News Corp.'s alliances with many media firms to provide cable services in the United Kingdom and the Pacific Rim, and Bertelsmann's investment in America Online. News Corp. also formed several DBS coalitions around the globe with several domestic partners but was unable to break into the U.S. market as a sole operator. Eventually the company settled for a minority interest in Primestar Partners LP, one of the leading competitors for DBS service in the United States (Lippmann and Robichaux, 1997).

5. *Digitalization*

The shift to a digital environment is happening at a slow and gradual rate in most countries. The print industries have been the first to convert to digital technology in most regions of the world as a way to reduce costs and improve production. Analog broadcasting will remain the norm into the next century, but many countries are making plans for the transition to digital broadcasting. Satellite and cable services are moving toward digitalization in several countries. In countries where multichannel service has yet to diffuse, companies are most likely to deploy systems capable of delivering digital television to homes using either direct-to-home (DTH) transmission with satellites or hybrid fiber-coaxial (HFC) systems via cable.

As in the United States, the potential of multimedia and the Internet around the world is too early to predict, although there is great anticipation that the Internet will be a major source of commerce in the next century (Stipp, 1997). As homes with personal computers and modems continue to expand, the number of users worldwide will continue to double every few months. New innovative technologies, such as Internet telephony and "web" TV receivers (capable of receiving both regular broadcast channels and the Internet) will also enhance business development.

One major obstacle to overcome is the need for expanded bandwidth for those customers with high-capacity needs. Several options are possible, among them integrated services digital networks (ISDN), fiber-to-the-curb (FTTC) and fiber-to-the-home (FTTH), HFC, two-way satellite transmission, high-speed cable modems, and wireless (Fowler, 1997). Which method or combination of methods may survive will depend on a number of factors, including cost, consumer demand, ease of operation, and efficiency.

Concluding Observations and Issues

The emerging global marketplace is filled with both opportunities and pitfalls for media companies around the world. Increasing interdependence among nations, more effective regional and global monetary policies, and the potential for new expansion into regions such as Europe, South America, Asia, and the Pacific Rim is helping to fuel expansion in the global arena. To be successful, companies must not only understand the converging technology but also the regional and local markets in which they strive to compete.

What media industries have the greatest growth potential? The contributors to this book have identified several areas with high expectations.

Telecommunications

Telecommunications services, ranging from full-service digital networks to plain old telephone service (POTS), may dominate the global communications industry for several years. Too often, local telephone service is taken for granted, yet as recently as 1996, more than 50 percent of the world population did not have access to a local phone (Sheth, 1996). Global expansion of cellular and paging services, Internet applications, and broadband networks will spur much development. The World Trade Organization has adopted the 1996 U.S. Telecommunications Act as a template for other regions; if fully implemented, global telecommunications has potential to produce significant growth margins for the next several years.

Content

Content creation is another area where strong growth is expected. Traditional content such as television programming and filmed entertainment, along with video games, interactive digital media, and various forms of publishing, will battle for consumer attention. Specialization is anticipated among content providers, content distributors, and content packagers. The creators and packagers are likely to reap the highest revenues, with distributors reaping the lowest revenues along a theorized content "value chain." The number of global households accessing content through the Internet will continue rapid growth into the 21st century.

Multichannel Video Services

Multichannel video services (DBS, cable, fiber, and wireless) represent another growth area in several regions around the globe. Which type of distribution system will emerge as dominant is speculative and may depend on the geographic characteristics of the country, but we can anticipate high-capacity digital systems will attempt to saturate the consumer market early in the next century. In some cases, these services will be bundled with other types of information services, such as telephony and cellular, to offer one-stop shopping for consumers. Because the content will likely be qualitatively similar across these distribution methods, "winners" will be those companies providing excellent customer service, good value at a competitive price, and strong marketing and brand awareness.

Although telecommunications, content, and multichannel video appear to offer the most lucrative opportunities for growth, all media companies face several challenges in finding their own competitive position in the global marketplace.

Maintaining company value in an era of rapid expansion will be a challenge for media companies across all industries. The growth of the world economy has encouraged investment in global markets, and companies must somehow meet the demands of stockholders while acquiring capital for expansion. Historically, companies have tried to provide both stock appreciation and regular dividends to shareholders. The demands of global competition may force companies to concentrate more on asset accumulation as a way to increase value for investors. This is especially true for telecommunications industries, which are historically positioned as an income rather than a growth investment option. As discussed earlier, strategic partnerships will enable companies to pursue international markets with less direct investment, but returns may be slow in developing.

Shifts in governmental regulatory policy can also cause havoc in company business plans. While deregulatory policies are introduced almost everywhere, countries with different political economies have focused on different areas of reform. For example, for those countries that have a historically state-controlled media environment such as China and Indonesia, the implementation of integrated technologies and controlled commercialization seem to be more important to the policy-makers than content creation for new media systems or privatization.

In the United States, the Telecommunications Act of 1996 significantly altered the media market structure in this country by eliminating entry barriers such as the telephone company and cable cross-ownership rules, regulation that separated long distance and local telephone companies, and broadcast station ownership limit. Such regulatory changes signaled a green light for companies to seek strategic alliances in preparing for the showdown of an integrated global information marketplace. According to the IT M&A Forecast '96 (Telecom Frenzy, 1996), one third of the telecommunications firms in the United States reported that they were more likely to pursue mergers and acquisitions in 1996 than they were in 1995. Nineteen percent of media companies reported that they were more likely to pursue mergers and acquisitions in 1996 after the deregulation. According to the report, larger firms are most likely to pursue acquisitions, with 78 percent reporting that they were likely to do an acquisition in 1996. In the United States, the total dollar spent in mergers and acquisitions in the broadcasting industry increased over 204 percent from 1995 to 1996 (Petrozzello, 1997).

In summary, competition in the global media industries represents both internal and external opportunities and challenges for media firms around the world. What then lies ahead for the study of media economics? What role will media economists play in helping understand the implications of a global media marketplace?

In terms of research, media economists have many options in building a research agenda. Certain topics are obvious. Researchers will need to keep abreast of the structural changes taking place across industries in the form of mergers and acquisitions and the effect on concentration. More research may be focused on the pattern of corporate strategies in mergers, acquisitions, and divestitures on a global scope. Albarran and Dimmick (1996) explain that traditional methods of measuring concentration (e.g., concentration ratios, HH Index) may be less useful in trying to gauge concentration across, as opposed to within, industries. More research and theory development needs to be conducted in order to understand industry concentration, especially as market boundaries become transparent.

Consumer demand is another topic where more research is warranted. With the numerous information and entertainment options available to consumers growing significantly, methods to gauge usage, satisfaction, and ultimately value will be in high demand at both a theoretical and practical level. Further, researchers need to consider many variables when assessing demand, and not just descriptive items such as market share or revenue categories. What factors influence demand? How is demand affected by changing economic conditions? How will cross-elasticities of demand be measured in blurring markets? These are just a few of the questions that deserve investigation.

Implications of policy decisions and court actions will need to be studied and interpreted at several levels of analysis, and this is another area where media economists can make important contributions. Policy actions should be analyzed not only at the consumer level, but also at the state, national, industry, and international levels as applicable. Researchers have tremendous opportunities to conduct research and studies that can be utilized by policymakers at all levels of government. Historically, media economists have not held a significant role in governmental hearings and proceedings. This must change if our research and analysis is to have any practical significance.

Finally, researchers need to expand their methodological foci and work on integrating and building more theory into their research agendas. From a methodological perspective, media economists have tended to rely on existing and limited data sources in conducting research. Too many of the studies appearing in our journals are descriptive as opposed to analytical, and singular as opposed to longitudinal. Topics such as econometrics and political economy are often overlooked for their potential value. Cross-cultural research is a natural outgrowth of the shift to a global economy and represents another area where numerous studies can be conducted in a variety of different levels.

In terms of theory, too much of our historical research is atheoretical in nature. When theory is integrated, studies tend to rely on long-standing economic models (i.e., Industrial Organization Model) or abstractions of markets (monopoly, oligopoly, monopolistic competition, etc.) that may no longer be applicable in a rapidly changing environment. Media economic researchers need to be creative and take chances in generating new theories and models of inquiry that can only enhance our understanding of industries and markets.

The emerging trends toward commercialization, concentration, and integration in today's global media marketplace present a tremendous challenge as well as an opportunity for innovative media researchers and practitioners.

References

Albarran, A. B. (1996). *Media Economics: Understanding Markets, Industries, and Concepts.* Ames, IA: Iowa State University Press.

Albarran, A. B. (1997). *Management of Electronic Media.* Belmont, CA: Wadsworth Publishing Company.

Albarran, A. B., and Dimmick, J. (1996). Concentration and economies of multiformity in the communication industries. *Journal of Media Economics,* 9(4):41–50.

Fleming, H. (1997). Will trade deal promote foreign broadcast ownership? *Broadcasting and Cable,* February 24, p. 20.

Fowler, T. B. (1997). Internet access and pricing: Sorting out the options. *Telecommunications,* February, pp. 41–44; 67–70.

Lippmann, J., and Robichaux, M. (1997). News Corp. gains entry to cable market. *The Wall Street Journal,* June 12, pp. A3, A11.

Petrozzello, D. (1997), Trading market explodes. *Broadcasting & Cable,* February 3, pp. 18-19.

Sheth, J. N. (1996). *Industry Convergence: What the Future holds.* Presentation to the International Engineering Consortium, Dallas, TX, June.

Stipp, D. (1997). The birth of digital commerce. *InDepth,* March-May, pp. 21-22.

Tapscott, D. (1996). *The Digital Economy.* New York: McGraw-Hill, Inc.

Telecom frenzy (1996). *Mergers & Acquisitions,* May-June, pp. 11-13.

INDEX

Italicized page numbers indicate entries in tables or figures.

Iowa State University Press
2121 South State Avenue
Ames, Iowa 50014

Orders: 1-800-862-6657
Office: 1-515-292-0140
Fax: 1-515-292-3348
Web site: www.isupress.edu

ISBN 0-8138-2690-X

MUHLENBERG COLLEGE LIBRARY
3 1542 00205 4264